deleted

D1173827

ECCLESIA IN VIA

STUDIES
IN MEDIEVAL AND
REFORMATION THOUGHT

EDITED BY

HEIKO A. OBERMAN, Tübingen

IN COOPERATION WITH

E. JANE DEMPSEY DOUGLASS, Claremont, California
LEIF GRANE, Copenhagen
GUILLAUME H. M. POSTHUMUS MEYJES, Leiden
ANTON G. WEILER, Nijmegen

VOLUME VIII

SCOTT H. HENDRIX
ECCLESIA IN VIA

LEIDEN
E. J. BRILL
1974

ECCLESIA IN VIA

ECCLESIOLOGICAL DEVELOPMENTS
IN THE MEDIEVAL PSALMS EXEGESIS AND THE
DICTATA SUPER PSALTERIUM (1513-1515)
OF MARTIN LUTHER

BY

SCOTT H. HENDRIX

LEIDEN
E. J. BRILL
1974

ISBN   90 04 03865 5

To my parents

TABLE OF CONTENTS

PREFACE

In its original form, this work was accepted in 1971 as a dissertation by the Fachbereich 'Evangelische Theologie' of the University of Tübingen. As it appears here, the study has been revised and slightly abridged, although no attempt has been made to disguise its original *Sitz im Leben*.

The appearance of this book is due above all to the assistance of Prof. Heiko A. Oberman. Not only did he promote its publication in this series. More importantly, he was present at every stage of the research and writing, supplying careful guidance and searching criticism. I gratefully acknowledge his steady encouragement, both personal and scholarly.

Many others in Tübingen supported my work in important, sometimes unconscious ways. Among them I would like to thank Steven E. Ozment, now Associate Professor at Yale University, for his indispensable orientation to life and study in Tübingen. Reinhard Schwarz, currently Professor at the University of Munich, graciously shared with me the results of his work on the new edition of the *Dictata* and provided many helpful insights. Prof. Ulrich Wickert kindly consented to read and evaluate the original dissertation. I also owe collective appreciation to my former colleagues at the Institut für Spätmittelalter und Reformation for the personal and professional associations I enjoyed there. Finally, a grant from the Lutheran World Federation helped make it possible for me to remain in Tübingen and complete my work on the spot.

Thanks are also due to two of my colleagues and former teachers at Lutheran Theological Southern Seminary for assistance in the last pre-publication stages: H. George Anderson, now president of the seminary, and W. Richard Fritz, librarian.

Prefaces and obituaries have at least one thing in common: they cast wives in the role of survivors. My wife was much more than that; she enthusiastically made Tübingen our home.

Columbia, S. C.   Scott H. Hendrix
March 1, 1973

ABBREVIATIONS

CChr	*Corpus Christianorum, Series Latina.* Turnholti, 1953ff.
DS	*Enchiridion Symbolorum,* ed. Henricus Denzinger and Adolfus Schönmetzer. 34th ed., Freiburg, 1967.
KuD	*Kerygma und Dogma.* Göttingen, 1955ff.
MThZ	*Münchener Theologische Zeitschrift.* München, 1950ff.
NZSTh	*Neue Zeitschrift für systematische Theologie und Religionsphilosophie.* Berlin, 1959ff.
PL	*Patrologia Latina,* ed. J. P. Migne. Paris, 1844ff.
RAM	*Revue d'ascétique et de mystique.* Toulouse, 1920ff.
REA	*Revue des Études augustiniennes.* Paris, 1955ff.
Sch	*Scholastik.* Freiburg i. Br., 1928ff.
ThR	*Theologische Revue.* Münster i. W., 1902ff.
ThS	*Theological Studies.* Woodstock (Md.), 1940ff.
ThSK	*Theologische Studien und Kritiken.* Hamburg, 1828-1941.
WA	*D. Martin Luthers Werke. Kritische Gesamtausgabe.* Weimar, 1883ff.
ZKG	*Zeitschrift für Kirchengeschichte.* Stuttgart, 1877ff.
ZKTh	*Zeitschrift für katholische Theologie.* Innsbruck, 1877ff.
ZSavRG	*Zeitschrift der Savigny-Stiftung für Rechtsgeschichte* (Kanonistische Abteilung). Weimar, 1880ff. (1911ff.)
ZThK	*Zeitschrift für Theologie und Kirche.* Tübingen, 1891ff.

N. B. References within a note to other notes refer to notes in the same chapter unless otherwise indicated.

In the notes to Chapters V-VII some texts from *WA* 3 and 4 have been corrected with permission of Dr. Reinhard Schwarz according to *WA* 55. The most important of these are identified by: [corr *WA* 55].

INTRODUCTION

In 1960 Albert Brandenburg observed that, despite much research on the subject, it is still unclear what Luther has to say about the church in his first lectures on the Psalms.[1] The present study is based on the conviction that this remark still holds true a decade after its utterance. To be sure, Luther's early ecclesiology did not hold stage center in the ongoing production of Luther studies during the ten-year period highlighted by the 450th anniversary of the Reformation. Even so, the few important works devoted to the subject, while increasing our knowledge of the *content* of Luther's statements about the church in his early exegetical work, were not able convincingly to dispel the mist of uncertainty surrounding the *significance* of these statements for the formation of his ecclesiology and its subsequent employment in the controversy with Rome.[2]

The continuing lack of clarity in this latter regard is due to the neglect of researchers up to this point to undertake a thoroughgoing comparison of Luther's ecclesiological utterances with those of the various medieval traditions to which he was heir. As the most fruitful recent Luther research has made clear, it is not enough to read Luther alone in order to rediscover Luther's own Reformation discovery, i.e. to determine that element or elements in his theology which set him apart from the preceding *doctores ecclesiae* to such an extent that it led to his break with the Roman Church. Nor can the continuity between Luther and his predecessors be established on the basis of Luther's works alone. Rather, it is necessary to begin where Luther himself began — with those medieval works which made up the curriculum of Luther's own theological studies as well as those works on which he relied in the preparation of his courses as professor in Wittenberg. The profile of Luther's early theological statements stands out distinctly only against such a background.

---

[1] Albert Brandenburg, *Gericht und Evangelium* (Paderborn, 1960), p. 97.

[2] We have in mind especially the only book to be devoted exclusively to Luther's ecclesiology in his first Psalms lectures: Joseph Vercruysse, *Fidelis Populus* (Wiesbaden, 1968). For our discussion of this work and the other literature, see Chapter IV.

1

It is not surprising, however, that this method of procedure has not so far been applied to the study of Luther's early ecclesiology. A survey of medieval ecclesiology, which would be of considerable assistance in setting up the background for such a study, does not exist up to the present time. The *locus, De ecclesia,* is the most elusive of all the theological *loci* in medieval literature. Unfortunately, Peter Lombard did not do us the favor of devoting a special distinction in his *Sentences* to an explicit discussion of the nature of the church. Consequently, it is not possible to distill the ecclesiology of the systematic tradition out of the commentaries on this medieval textbook by tracing one distinction through all of them. Investigations into the nature of the church, or rather treatments of individual ecclesiological problems, are diffused throughout the entire medieval corpus. Some of these are found in concentrated form in the later Middle Ages in various tracts which arose out of the conflict between the ecclesiastical and secular arms as well as out of the intra-church debate over the respective powers of Pope and council. For the most part though, this ecclesiological material is lodged piecemeal in all the traditions of medieval theology, most prominently in the exegetical and canonistic works.

To present a comprehensive survey of medieval ecclesiology as the launching pad for an investigation into Luther's understanding of the nature of the church is clearly impossible without having read the entire medieval corpus. Thus, it is necessary to limit the scope of the present investigation to a representative, but at the same time, the most homogeneous group of sources possible. Since we purpose to concentrate our study of Luther upon his first lectures on the Psalms, the *Dictata super Psalterium (1513-1515),* the selection of the most significant medieval Psalms commentaries as the basis for this study commends itself as the most appropriate way of doing justice to this methodological requirement. We recognize, of course, that other medieval streams besides the Psalms commentaries flowed into that reservoir of ecclesiological ideas from which Luther drew in his early exegetical works. Nevertheless, the Psalms commentaries remained the handiest tool for Luther as he began his own work on the Psalms, and the common text handled by Luther and his predecessors makes these commentaries the most suitable object for investigation and comparison.

The following medieval Psalms commentators, who carry the most weight in their own right as well as for Luther, have been selected to form the background for our study: Jerome (d. 420),[3] Augustine (d. 430), Cassiodorus (d. 583), the *Glossa interlinearis* and the *Glossa ordinaria*,[4] Peter Lombard (d. 1160), Hugo Cardinalis (d. 1263), Nicholas of Lyra (d. 1340), Paul of Burgos (d. 1435), Matthias Doering (d. 1469), Jacobus Perez of Valencia (d. 1490), Faber Stapulensis (d. 1536).[5] Because of the amount of material contained in these commentaries themselves,[6] it is necessary to put a further limitation on our research. As a working hypothesis, we have concentrated our attention on thirteen psalms whose exposition forms a central exegetical context for ecclesiological interpretations in the medieval commentaries and in Luther's *Dictata*. These psalms also represent the total compass of the Psalter and hence of the individual commentaries themselves. The psalms chosen are: 8, 15, 41, 44, 59, 68, 73, 79, 83, 88, 100, 110, 121.[7] The exposition of these psalms by the above-named medieval commentators forms the basis of Part I of our study.

[3] The *Breviarium in Psalmos* (cited: *Brev. in ps.*) attributed to Jerome and known to Luther under his name is not authentic and likely stems from seventh or eighth century Ireland. See B. Fischer, *Verzeichnis der Sigel für Kirchenschriftsteller. Vetus Latina* I/1 (2nd ed., Freiburg, 1963), p. 307. Most of this material, however, is taken from the two authentic Psalms commentaries of Jerome: *In Psalmos homiliae* and the *Commentarioli*.

[4] The *Glossa interlinearis* and *ordinaria* originated in the school of Anselm of Laon (d. 1117), and the *Glossa* on the Psalter is even attributed to Anselm himself by Beryl Smalley, *The Study of the Bible in the Middle Ages* (2nd ed., Notre Dame, 1964), pp. 60ff. The *Glossa* is to be regarded as a unity (*ibid.*, p. 56), but we shall quote them separately. From the fifteenth century on, it was usually printed together with the *Postilla* of Lyra, the *Additiones* of Paul of Burgos and the *Replicae* of Doering.

[5] Our selection of the above commentators has been influenced by the results of the work of Reinhard Schwarz, editor of the new edition of Luther's *Dictata* which is appearing in fascicles as Volume 55 of the Weimar Edition. In his preparation of the apparatus containing relevant texts from the medieval tradition, the works of the above commentators, among the Psalms exegetes, have proved to be the most valuable sources of material. Of the commentaries we have taken into consideration, we are certain that Luther knew all of them except Perez. For a discussion of the tantalizing evidence regarding this problem, see the very helpful monograph of Wilfrid Werbeck, *Jacobus Perez von Valencia: Untersuchungen zu seinem Psalmenkommentar* (Tübingen, 1959), pp. 47ff.

[6] The remark of J. S. Preus (*From Shadow to Promise* [Cambridge, Mass., 1969], p. 153) is unfortunately all too true: "Although the ideal would certainly be to examine these medieval commentaries *in toto*, it would take years."

[7] All psalm and verse numbers follow the Vulgate enumeration. Passages cited from older printed editions of the medieval commentaries are identified according to psalm and verse number only, since folio and page enumeration have little worth in light of the various editions and since passages can be readily found within the exegesis of individual verses. Passages cited from modern editions, however, are located in these editions.

A conceivable procedure—resulting in a corresponding chapter division—would be to set up a psalm by psalm comparison of the ecclesiological material in these commentaries with that of the *Dictata*. Such a procedure, however, would refract too diffusely the insights gained through such a comparison. All of the Psalms commentators, Luther included, make important ecclesiological references at varying points in their exegesis. We occasionally do make explicit comparisons at particular verses between Luther and the tradition, as well as within the tradition itself, whenever it contributes to our understanding. Nevertheless, the structure of our study is determined not by the psalms themselves, but by the ecclesiological content found in their exposition. This structure is further dictated by our desire to include the entire *Dictata* as the primary source for Part II of our investigation. Thus the comparison which we have set up between Parts I and II, between the selected medieval Psalms commentaries and the *Dictata* of Luther, is a comparison of ecclesiological themes and not primarily that of the exegesis of individual psalms. In this way, the similarities and differences regarding the understanding of the church surface most readily.

To reduce the disadvantages of the necessarily subjective selection implicit in our working hypothesis, we have not restricted our research exclusively to the exposition of the indicated thirteen psalms in the medieval commentaries or to the *Dictata* of Luther. In Part I we draw into consideration the treatment of other Psalms passages which are given to ecclesiological interpretation in the medieval commentaries. Furthermore, in order to help clarify the ecclesiological themes in these commentaries, we make use of other primary sources of medieval thought about the nature of the church, as well as significant secondary sources which throw light on our subject. To avoid overgeneralization we have confined the employment of these sources as much as possible to specific themes. The sources chosen are by no means intended as justifying the expansion of our conclusions to all medieval traditions.

As far as Luther is concerned, no wide-ranging judgments about the influence of his early ecclesiology upon his stance over against Rome can be formed solely on the basis of the *Dictata*. A tantalizing solution to this problem offers itself through the addition of a third part to our study in which the ecclesiology of the *Operationes in Psalmos (1519-1521)* would be drawn into the comparison between the medieval commentaries and the *Dictata*. In view of the events and writings which lie between the latter and the *Operationes*, however, this would be an incomplete and unsatisfying way of carrying out the present task. A thorough treatment of all the works of Luther and his opponents through 1521 lies beyond the scope of a single study and, besides, would compromise the homogeneity of our sources which we consider essential. Nevertheless, we are not only interested in looking backwards from the *Dictata*, but also ahead to the development of Luther's ecclesiology after the *Dictata* and especially to its application in the conflict with Rome. Thus we will indicate how certain aspects of Luther's ecclesiology in the *Dictata* compare with that of his subsequent works and risk some conclusions on the basis of this evidence.

The selection and limitation of sources is not the only methodological problem to be solved in preparation for a study of Luther's early ecclesiology against its medieval background. Equally important is the content given to the term "ecclesiology" itself, which all too often has suffered promiscuous handling. What exactly does the "doctrine" of the church involve? If, as stated above, we have structured our study according to ecclesiological content and not according to the exegesis of certain psalms, this "content" must be clearly delimited.

In his article, "Ecclesia ab Abel," Yves Congar maintains that the development of an ecclesiology *proprement dite*, which treats the church as an institution or an ensemble of the objective means of grace, evolves first in the milieu of the thirteenth century under the dual pressure of theological elaboration and the confrontation with developing errors and heresies. He employs the meanings of the term *congregatio fidelium* given by Moneta of Cremona (d. c. 1260) to illustrate two basic ways of treating the church: as the community defined in terms of an "unconditioned" faith (*fides simpliciter*) within the context of Christology and soteriology; or as the community defined in terms of a faith historically and ecclesiastically "conditioned," i.e. an ecclesiastical institution such as the Roman Church.[8]

---

[8] In *Abhandlungen über Theologie und Kirche: Festschrift für Karl Adam* (Düsseldorf, 1952), pp. 92-93. See also Congar's article, "L'ecclésiologie de S. Bernard," in *Saint Bernard Théologien. Analecta Sacri Ordinis Cisterciensis* 9 (1953), pp. 179ff. Moneta makes his distinction in *Adv. Catharos et Valdenses* v.2 (ed. Ricchini: Rome, 1743), pp. 408-409.

The question is, however, whether an ecclesiology developed in the context of Christology and soteriology is any less an ecclesiology "properly speaking" than one which directs itself primarily to the church as institution. Congar apparently did not intend for his remarks to be taken in this way, for he is concerned to demonstrate the primacy of the "spiritual-personal" character of the church in the view of medieval theologians from Augustine to the Scholastics. But, in so many words, he is still operating with the traditional distinction between *Heilsanstalt* and *Heilsgemeinschaft* which has often provoked oversimplified interpretations of the relationship between medieval and Reformation ecclesiology. Although these terms may have some validity in indicating various ecclesiological emphases, they are laden with too many prejudiced connotations to serve as interpretive categories for the present study.[9]

Rather than allowing the superimposed definitions of the church as community and institution to determine the structure of our study, we run less danger of forcing the material into inappropriate molds when medieval ecclesiological categories themselves are employed. What are these categories? Recognizing the equivocal use of the word *ecclesia* by his predecessors, Gabriel Biel enumerates the various definitions of the term in *Lectio* XXII of his *Canonis misse expositio*.[10] Because a

---

[9] F. Merzbacher employs this distinction in effect to characterize the ecclesiology of the late Middle Ages when he writes ("Wandlungen des Kirchenbegriffs im Spätmittelalter," *ZSavRG* 70 [kan. Abt. 39] [1953], p. 355): "Für die spätmittelalterliche Kirche erlangte das Recht höchste Bedeutung, zumal hier die 'Geistkirche' weitgehend von der starren 'Rechtskirche' überwunden wird." Cf. *ibid.*, pp. 277, 278, 281, 355. Such a generalization does not apply, however, to the medieval exegesis of the Psalms. On the other hand, in his assessment of the ecclesiology of the thirteenth and fourteenth centuries, G. de Lagarde does not find "the slightest invitation" to make such a distinction (*La naissance de l'esprit laïque au déclin du moyen âge*, Vol. V: *Guillaume d'Ockham: Critique des structures ecclésiales* [rev. ed., Paris and Louvain, 1963], p. 10).

[10] *Lect.* 22 C-G (ed. Oberman and Courtenay, Vol. I [Wiesbaden, 1963], pp. 197-202). Biel summarizes the definitions in *Lect.* 22 G (p. 202) as follows: "Possunt autem acceptiones ille diffuse breviter sic summari: Ecclesia accipitur aliquando pro rationali creatura, in bono pro ecclesia sanctorum, quandoque in malo pro ecclesia malignantium. In bono universalissime pro congregatione omnium angelorum beatorum et viatorum fidelium. Quandoque tantum pro ecclesia triumphantium. Quandoque tantum pro congregatione deo militantium. Et sic tripliciter, vel omnium a primo iusto ad ultimum in fine mundi nasciturum, et sic comprehendit synagogam et christi ecclesiam; secundo pro sola congregatione christianorum tam preteritorum quam presentium; tertio pro congregatione omnium fidelium nunc existentium. Et quelibet harum ecclesiarum dicitur ecclesia universalis vera, et ecclesia universalis representativa que est concilium generale. Accipitur etiam ecclesia non pro congregatione universali

6

number of his definitions of the church find no significant treatment in our sources, they play no role in our considerations: the church as the material temple (i.e. the church building), the spiritual temple (i.e. every rational creature) and the various kinds of geographically limited church bodies. The remaining definitions, which occupy the interest of our medieval exegetes, boil down to three major themes: (1) the church as *congregatio fidelium*; (2) *ecclesia militans* and *ecclesia triumphans*; and (3) *ecclesia* and *synagoga*. It is around these three themes that we have chosen to build our study. The special case of the universal church as represented in a general council has been intentionally excluded from consideration both because its treatment presupposes an entirely different set of sources and because the conciliar debate is an ecclesiological problem which requires independent investigation.[11]

The first heading under which we will pursue our study, the church as *congregatio fidelium*, sums up the ambiguity surrounding the question of who belongs to the church, or stated differently, what empirical reality (or non-empirical as the case may be) the word *ecclesia* is supposed to encompass. The reference point of the word *fideles*, the most frequently used word for denoting members of the church, gives us the best clue for unravelling the riddle, although it bears an ambiguity of its own which stems from the simultaneous existence of both *boni* and *mali* within the framework of the church. We will be particularly interested in pursuing the defining characteristics of the *boni*, or true *fideles*, at the core of the church, since this definition is central to an author's ecclesiology. Thus the word *fideles* will be the major focus of our attention rather than such terms as *corpus Christi, sancti,*

omnium fidelium existentium nunc, sed pro congregatione aliqua particulari tam clericorum quam laicorum unius provincie, diocesis, civitatis vel domus. Quandoque etiam pro congregatione clericorum tantum. Quandoque pro uno homine tantum. Accipitur pro domo materiali divino cultui dedicata." The definitions given here by Biel form a primary source of the material included under *Ecclesia* by Altenstaig in his *Vocabularius theologiae* (Hagenau, 1517), fol. 72ᵛ-73ʳ.

[11] This is not to say that an author's view of the role of the council is unrelated to his ecclesiology as a whole, but rather that the inclusion of this topic would stretch the present study to unmanageable proportions. C. Tecklenburg Johns has shown convincingly that Luther's own view of conciliar authority is based precisely on his ecclesiology as a whole (*Luthers Konzilsidee in ihrer historischen Bedingtheit und ihrem reformatorischen Neuansatz* [Berlin, 1966], p. 165). In order to demonstrate this in the scope of one book, however, she is forced to rely to a great extent upon secondary sources for her discussion of the latter (*ibid.*, pp. 165ff.).

praedestinati, etc., which will be handled only secondarily in this context.

The second major topic of our investigation is the relationship between the *ecclesia militans* and the *ecclesia triumphans*. The goal of every pilgrim in the militant church is to persevere and become a member of the triumphant church. The way in which the medieval exegete defines the *ecclesia triumphans* often determines the way in which he defines true membership in the *ecclesia militans*, and vice versa. In addition, the continuity which he establishes between the two is decisive for his understanding of the true *fidelis*, who is pursuing his way at the heart of the militant church toward the beatitude of the heavenly Jerusalem. Certain psalms lend themselves especially to this kind of ecclesiological interpretation.[12] As far as we can tell, the relationship between these two states of the church has simply been taken for granted and has played no significant role in the interpretation of medieval and Reformation ecclesiology. Because the understanding of this relationship is crucial for the definition of the *fideles*, however, we will be on the alert to see if key ecclesiological conceptions might crystallize around the handling of this very topic.

The theme *ecclesia* and *synagoga* has always been problematical for the church insofar as it has had to deal with the embarrassing continued existence of the Jews alongside itself. The church has attempted to set itself off in both positive and negative relief from the synagogue. On the positive side, the synagogue often functions as the best of a set of preliminary proofs for the photograph which is the church itself. Although the proof provides the essential image, it still must be touched up and given the gloss finish of the New Testament before it can really become the church. On the negative side, the synagogue is precisely the negative of the photograph which is the church, where everything that is dark in the synagogue, such as the shadow of unfulfilled promises and inadequate rites, becomes light in the fulfillment accomplished in the church and its sacraments. And at the same time, all that is the dim light of the synagogue, such as the fulfillment of earthly promises, becomes the dark side of the church if the church limits its gaze to such a shadowy, earthly fulfillment.

Aside from the many polemical writings on this subject which

---

[12] For example, the psalms in which the word *atrium* appears, such as 83 or 121, or for that matter, the whole series of Psalms 119-133, which are provided with the title *Canticum graduum*.

8

arose out of external hostilities,[13] the exegetical tradition was the most prominent scene of literary activity on the theme of church and synagogue. In particular, the interpretation of an Old Testament book such as the Psalms forces the exegete to come to terms with the problem of when the church began, i.e. to what degree the Old Testament faithful can be regarded as members of the church. The answer to this question depends in large measure upon how one defines membership in the church, and, in turn, the pondering of the question itself exerts its own influence upon this definition. As in the case of the relationship between the two states of the church, the diffuse ecclesiological references of an exegete are forced to come to a head when he handles this concrete theme. For this reason, we will be attentive especially to the interpretive categories employed in this context.

These three headings, therefore, determine the structure of our comparative study. We will devote two chapters to each of them — one each to the medieval commentators and Luther respectively. In this way the symmetry which such a study should exhibit is preserved. Since we are not primarily interested in the hierarchical structure of the church or in the criticism of this structure as it is offered by our exegetes, we shall not devote separate chapters of our study to this subject but will treat the material at those points where it is relevant. The same applies to the sacramental theology found in these commentaries. This does not mean that the role of the hierarchy and the sacraments in an author's ecclesiology is unrelated to the themes under consideration.[14] Rather, the way in which the *fideles* are defined and the conception of the relationship between the two states of the church influence the function assigned to the hierarchy as well as the significance attributed to the sacraments.

Finally, we have decided not to devote a separate chapter to the discussion of the hermeneutical principles of the authors with whom we are dealing. There is no question that the hermeneutical principles which an author employs in exegeting the Psalms determine to some extent where he will mention the church and what he will say about

---

[13] For an interesting survey of the material with particular attention to the artistic portrayal of this theme in the Middle Ages, see Wolfgang Seiferth, *Synagoge und Kirche im Mittelalter* (München, 1964). A selection of the most pertinent texts on the subject (albeit only in German translation) with an historical commentary is given in the sourcebook *Kirche und Synagoge: Handbuch zur Geschichte von Christen und Juden*, Vol. I, ed. Karl_H. Rengstorf and Siegfried von Kortzfleisch (Stuttgart, 1968).

[14] As, for example, Merzbacher (p. 356) in so many words has maintained.

9

it. In light of the key role that the hermeneutical question has played in Luther research,[15] it will be necessary to devote special attention to this subject in Part II of our study. Nevertheless, the present study is not an investigation into the hermeneutical principles of the exegetes of the Psalms from Augustine to Luther, but rather an examination of the ecclesiology found in their commentaries.

There is one fundamental question which we will constantly be asking ourselves in the course of this study: in the application of the ecclesiological categories under consideration by the medieval exegetes of the Psalms, does there exist a consensus to a sufficient degree that we can determine where Luther in the *Dictata* retains this consensus and where he begins to apply these categories in a unique way? It has been maintained that there was no unified medieval ecclesiology to confront Luther in the early years before the break with Rome.[16] We do not deny the complexity of medieval theology; nor do we view medieval ecclesiology as a monolithic structure against which Luther was banging his head from the very beginning. Nevertheless, the complexity of medieval ecclesiology is not sufficient reason to neglect the search for common themes with which Luther's early ecclesiology can profitably be compared. The existence of such common themes is not essential in order for the results of our study to be labeled positive. Even if the ecclesiological comments of the medieval exegetes are so diffuse as to render a composite comparison with Luther almost impossible, this would be a yield well worth the effort. On the other hand, the existence of consistent answers by the medieval commentators to the ecclesiological questions we will be asking would create a backdrop against which the degree of deviation, if any, in the *Dictata* would show up most distinctly.

[15] We think here of the fundamental work done in this area by Gerhard Ebeling. See especially his essay: "Die Anfänge von Luthers Hermeneutik," *ZThK* 48 (1951), pp. 172-230. Particularly intriguing is the recent study of J.S. Preus, *From Shadow to Promise,* which also sees in Luther's hermeneutic the key to his unfolding Reformation theology — though quite differently from Ebeling. Since Preus' interpretation touches on important ecclesiological categories, we will often have occasion to enter into discussion with him.

[16] For example, by Hubert Jedin, "Ekklesiologie um Luther," in *Fuldaer Hefte*, Heft 18 (Berlin and Hamburg, 1968), p. 28. This presupposition should be seen together with Jedin's thesis that Luther had no distinctive ecclesiology until he was forced to develop one after the Roman Church refused to accept his new doctrine of justification. Jedin formulated this earlier in his *Geschichte des Konzils von Trient,* Vol. I: *Der Kampf um das Konzil* (2nd ed., Freiburg, 1951), pp. 137f. See further our discussion of the literature in Ch. IV.

We recognize that both the method of procedure and the selection of sources outlined above can easily be made the object of criticism. In a comparative study of this nature it is impossible to cover all one's flanks. As we have said, we do not claim that whatever conclusions we reach are valid for the whole of medieval ecclesiology. Our hope is that this study will provide the impetus for extending the limits of our investigation to include other medieval sources and thus lead to a more comprehensive unfolding of the ecclesiology of the young Luther.

PART ONE

THE MEDIEVAL PSALMS COMMENTARIES

CHAPTER I

CONGREGATIO FIDELIUM

1. The Problem

The question of different degrees of membership in the church, and particularly the problem of determining the sense in which sinners belong to the church, were well-known to both Jerome and Augustine. In his Galatians commentary Jerome maintains that the word *ecclesia* can be taken in a twofold manner: as referring to the church which has neither spot nor wrinkle, that is, to those members who are characterized by fully developed and perfect virtues and who truly make up the body of Christ; and secondly, as referring to those who lack these virtues and are only in the beginning or progressing stage.[1] The problem to which Jerome offers this solution arises through St. Paul's calling the very communities of Christians in Galatia "churches" which afterwards in his epistle he describes as being "perverted with error."[2] Is it not inconsistent to bestow the title "church" upon a group of Christians who are tainted by such a severe accusation?

This was apparently no problem for Paul, but Jerome and the rest of the tradition[3] were compelled to reconcile this loose usage of the word *ecclesia* with the more elevated descriptions of the church found in the New Testament—namely, as the body of Christ and the church

---

[1] *Comm. in ep. ad Galatas* i.1 (*PL* 26, 313): "Ex quo noscendum dupliciter Ecclesiam posse dici, et eam quae non habeat maculam aut rugam, et vere corpus Christi sit, et eam quae in Christi nomine absque plenis perfectisque virtutibus congregetur. Quomodo sapientes bifariam nuncupantur, tam hi qui sunt plenae perfectaeque virtutis, quam illi qui incipiunt, et in profectu positi sunt."

[2] *Ibid.*: "Quod autem ait: 'Ecclesiis Galatiae;' et hoc notandum quia hic tantum generaliter non ad unam Ecclesiam unius urbis, sed ad totius provinciae scribat Ecclesias, et Ecclesias vocet, quas postea errore arguat depravatas."

[3] Luther himself quotes Jerome to Gal. 1 : 2 in the following form: *WA* 57/II, 54. 17-24: "Beatus Ieronimus: 'In ceteris epistolis ad unius urbis scribit ecclesiam, hic ad multarum et tocius provincie scribit ecclesias; et "ecclesias" vocat, quas tamen arguit errore depravatas. Ex quo noscendum est dupliciter posse "ecclesiam" dici, et eam, que "non habet maculam neque rugam," et eam, que in Christi nomine absque plenis perfectisque virtutibus congregetur. Quomodo "sapientes" bifariam nuncupantur, tam hi, qui sunt plene perfecteque virtutis, quam illi, qui incipiunt et in profectu positi sunt.' " One of the main aims of our investigation can be summed up under the question: How did the intervening tradition, and its last representative in Luther, understand this distinction?

15

"without spot or wrinkle" (Eph. 5 : 27). The answer suggested by Jerome exemplifies both the problem with the ambiguity of the word *ecclesia* and the direction which the solution will take in the subsequent tradition, albeit under many different forms and with many refinements. Basically, it is a question of the existence of a "mini-church" inside the broader community of the baptized, both of which are called "church." The tradition will devote itself to the difficult task of working out a clear definition of this mini-church and its relationship to the wider ecclesiastical community.

Jerome himself does not help us very much with the actual definition. When compared with other remarks he makes about the church, the solution proposed above is not as lucid as it first appears. Jerome works with two categories—those of "saint" and "sinner." At first he appears to define that mini-church with full and perfect virtue as the collection of the saints since he speaks of a *congregatio sanctorum* in the church.[4] This terminology is also consistent with his description of the city of God as the *ecclesia sanctorum* and the *congregatio iustorum* from which sinners must be dispersed in the sense that they be led to repentance.[5] When Jerome actually juxtaposes the two categories, however, he pictures the *sancti* as those who daily progress and increase in virtue, in contrast to the sinner who daily decreases.[6] This would mean that the definition of the saint does not correspond to that of the mini-church, but rather to that of the church in the broader sense of the word above, i.e. as encompassing those who do not have fully developed and perfect virtue but who are in a state of beginning and progressing.[7] Although we are tempted to think that the two meanings of "church" can be embodied in the two categories of *sancti* and *peccatores*, the failure of the various statements to coincide fully is typical of the ambiguity surrounding the whole subject.[8]

---

[4] *Brev. in ps.* (88 : 30; *PL* 26, 1089): "Congregatio enim sanctorum quae in Ecclesia est, in qua Deus tamquam in throno residet, sicut sol fulgebit in regno Patris."

[5] *Ibid.* (100 : 8; *PL* 26, 1126): "Utinam et nos disperdamus de civitate Domini operantes iniquitatem. Civitas Domini est Ecclesia sanctorum, congregatio iustorum. Disperdam, hoc est, arguam, increpem eum qui peccat, ut poenitentiam agat, et disperdat iniquitatem de corde suo."

[6] *Ibid.* (83 : 6; *PL* 26, 1072): "Quicumque sanctus est, quotidie in priora extenditur, et praeteritorum obliviscitur .... Quomodo qui sanctus est, quotidie proficit: ita qui peccator est, quotidie decrescit."

[7] Cf. *supra*, n. 1.

[8] Landgraf gives a nice example of this ambiguity in his *Dogmengeschichte der Frühscholastik*, IV/2 (Regensburg, 1956), p. 48. He compares two passages from

2. The Augustinian Foundation

The anti-Donatist works.—That definition of the mini-church which was to become basic for the medieval tradition received its stamp through Augustine. This clarification of the issue was not primarily the result of lofty theological speculation, but rather the outcome of a very concrete and even bitter controversy, in which the church in Africa had to fight for its very life against the assault of the Donastists.[9] Aside from the historical dimension of the dispute over the guilt of *traditio* and the validity of the competing episcopal successions, the primary reproach of the Donatists against the catholics in the time of Augustine was that the catholics allowed obvious sinners to remain in the communion of the church and yet, simultaneously, considered themselves to be the true church. The Donatists could see only a contradiction in this simultaneity because they insisted that members of the true church must exhibit a high degree of personal holiness and that sinners could exist in the church only, so to speak, by mistake. The reply of Augustine to this charge was a twofold reply which would echo in various forms throughout the rest of the medieval tradition. Before we turn to the *Enarrationes in psalmos*, it is important for us to understand this reply to the Donatists, which forms the basis of Augustine's ecclesiology.

Augustine realistically admits that there is sin in the church and that there are openly sinful members of the church, but he insists that they must exist there together with the righteous until the day when the Lord will come to judge his church. Thus the first element of his reply to the Donatists is an appeal to what we might call the

Jerome's Commentary on Ephesians. The first clearly makes *sancti* and *peccatores* members of the church (= *corpus Christi*): *Comm. in ep. ad Eph.* i.1 (*PL* 26, 463): "Quomodo enim caput plurima sibi habet membra subiecta, e quibus sunt nonnulla vitiosa et debilia; ita et Dominus noster Iesus Christus, cum sit caput Ecclesiae, habet membra eos omnes qui in Ecclesia congregantur, tam sanctos videlicet quam peccatores, sed sanctos volunate, peccatores vero sibi necessitate subiectos." The second passage explicitly denies such a membership to sinners until they have been "cured": *ibid.* iii.5 (*PL* 26, 531): "Ecclesia Christi gloriosa est, non habens maculam neque rugam, aut quid istiusmodi. Qui ergo peccator est, et aliqua sorde maculatus, de Ecclesia Christi non potest appellari nec Christo subiectus dici. Possible autem est, ut quomodo ecclesia quae prius rugam habuerat et maculam in iuventutem et munditiam postea restituta est, ita et peccator currat ad medicum (quia non habent opus sani medico, sed male habentes) et curentur vulnera ipsius, et fiat de Ecclesia, quae corpus est Christi."

[9] For the historical background of the controversy, consult W. H. C. Frend, *The Donatist Church: A Movement of Protest in Roman North Africa* (Oxford, 1952; reprinted 1971). For a fresh look at the place of Donatist ecclesiology in the North African tradition, see W. Simonis, *Ecclesia visibilis et invisibilis*, Frankfurt/Main, 1970.

eschatological argument—the necessity for good and bad Christians to remain in the church until the last judgment because of the inadequacy of human judgment to make an accurate distinction in the present age. To illustrate this argument, Augustine often makes use of the parable of the wheat and the tares in Matthew 13 : 24-30. In this story the owner of the field in which the enemy had sown tares commands that they be allowed to grow together with the wheat until the harvest, when it will be possible to separate them properly. With unmistakable clarity, Augustine applies this parable to the premature judgment of the Donatists by asking: "Was Donatus then the chief reaper, or had harvest time already come when they cut themselves off from the whole world?" The answer, of course, is negative, since the Lord himself said that the harvest is the end of the world and the reapers are the angels.[10] Or, as Augustine unequivocally expresses it elsewhere: "For the field is the world, not Africa; the harvest is the end of this age, not the era of Donatus."[11]

In appealing to the eschatological argument, Augustine is obviously trying to justify the presence of evil men in the church, the presence of tares among the wheat. In opposing the "over-realized" eschatology of the Donatists, he appeals to a very "futuristic" eschatology. But although he maintains that the sins of the tares in the church are not able to contaminate the wheat unless the wheat consent to them,[12] Augustine has still not met the challenge of the Donatists head-on. He still must answer the question: how can the tares, i.e. evil men and sinners, be said to be *in* the church at all?

This question is not unlike the one which Jerome asks himself when confronted with Paul's application of the word "church" to those Galatians whom he thereupon reproaches for being perverted with error.[13] Augustine sets up the problem in the following way:

> Now, therefore, the question is how men of the party of the devil can belong to the church which has neither spot nor wrinkle nor anything

---

[10] *Contra epist. Parm.* i.14.21 (*PL* 43, 49): "Numquid aut Donatus fuit maior messor, aut eo tempore quo se isti a terrarum orbe separarunt, tempus messis advenerat: cum idem Dominus ne alicui liceret interpretari quod vellet, apertissime dixerit: 'Messis autem est finis saeculi; messores autem angeli sunt ....'"

[11] *Contra litt. Pet.* iii.2.3 (*PL* 43, 349): "Ager est enim mundus, non Africa; messis, finis saeculi, non tempus Donati."

[12] *De bapt.* vii.5.9 (*PL* 43, 228): "Si autem, sicut se habet firmissima veritas, Ecclesia permansit et permanet; non nisi in consensione intelligenda est communio peccatorum, ..." Cf. *Enarr. in ps.* 129.4 (*CChr* 40, 1892): "Consensio enim ad peccatum alterius, tuum fit peccatum."

[13] Cf. *supra*, n. 2.

else of the kind [Eph. 5 : 27], and about which it is said: "My dove is one" [Song of Songs 6 : 8]. As a result, if they cannot, then it is clear that she groans among strangers, who are both lying in wait treacherously from within and barking at her from without.[14]

The formation of the question and the tentative answer which follows show that Augustine is forced, as was Jerome, to speak of a mini-church which does not include evil men or tares, even though they be "within" the community of the baptized. This mini-church has its locus only among the wheat, which he fondly describes in the terminology of the Song of Songs as that "garden enclosed" and "fountain sealed."[15] Merely to posit the existence of such a mini-church does not solve the problem, however. The most difficult task still remains: to set up a criterion according to which membership in this church "without spot or wrinkle" can be determined, even if the tares remain inseparable from the wheat until the last judgment. The establishment of such a criterion forms the all-important second part of Augustine's reply to the Donatists.

According to Augustine, this church is set apart by the *caritas* of her members, who are described as the "good," the *boni*. The invisible unction of *caritas* is the peculiar property of the good, in opposition to the visible sacrament which is shared—though with quite different results—by good and bad alike.[16] The invisible bond of *caritas* unites true Christians to one another and causes the enemies of *caritas*, even if they appear to be "inside," to be designated as "pseudo-Christians" and "antichrists."[17] The true Christians are the *sancti* and *iusti*, with whom evil men and open sinners do not have *caritas* in common,

---

[14] *De bapt.* iv.10.16 (*PL* 43, 163): "Nunc ergo quaeritur, quomodo poterant homines ex parte diaboli, pertinere ad Ecclesiam, non habentem maculam aut rugam, aut aliquid eiusmodi, de qua etiam dictum est, 'Una est columba mea'. Quod si non possunt, manifestum est eam inter alienos gemere, et intrinsecus insidiantes, et extrinsecus oblatrantes."

[15] *Ibid.* vi.29.56 (*PL* 43, 216): "... in illam petram, in illam columbam, in illum hortum conclusum et fontem signatum, qui non nisi in tritico, non autem in paleis agnoscitur, sive longe a vento separentur, sive usque ad ultimam ventilationem commixti videantur."

[16] *Contra litt. Pet.* ii.104.239 (*PL* 43, 342-343): "Discerne ergo visibile sanctum Sacramentum, quod esse et in bonis et in malis potest, illis ad praemium, illis ad iudicium, ab invisibili unctione caritatis, quae propria bonorum est."

[17] *De bapt.* iii.19.26 (*PL* 43, 152): "Huius autem fraternae caritatis inimici, sive aperte foris sint, sive intus esse videantur, pseudochristiani sunt et antichristi. Inventis enim occasionibus foras exeunt, sicut scriptum est: 'Occasiones quaerit qui vult discedere ab amicis' [Prv. 18 : 1]. Sed etiamsi occasiones desint, cum intus videntur, ab illa invisibili caritatis compage separati sunt. Unde Ioannes dicit: 'Ex nobis exierunt, sed non erant ex nobis: nam si fuissent ex nobis, mansissent utique nobiscum' [I Io. 2 : 19]."

although they may share baptism with them.[18] Augustine gives positive content to this mark of *caritas* by explaining that true Christians are those who follow the word of the Lord to love him and keep his commandments.[19] It is this concrete aspect of *caritas* as love to Christ which leads Augustine to exclude the *mali* from the body of Christ, although they are mixed with the good in the church of the sacraments.[20]

Even this clearly formulated definition of the mini-church as the communion of the *boni* in the bond of *caritas* is rendered ambivalent from two sides. In the first place, Augustine appears to speak of *caritas* on two levels. One is the deeper or inner level, of which we have just spoken, where *caritas* functions as the identifying brand of the *boni* or the church of the saints. But Augustine also speaks of *caritas* on a more external level as the mark of unity of the *ecclesia catholica* over against schismatics and heretics, and in particular, the Donatists. When the Donatists quite naturally ask how they would profit from a reunion with the catholics, since they themselves already have faith and a valid baptism, Augustine's answer is that they lack *caritas*.[21] It

[18] *Ibid.* v.27.28 (*PL* 43, 195): "Et quod in Cantico canticorum Ecclesia sic describitur, 'Hortus conclusus, soror mea sponsa, fons signatus, puteus aquae vivae, paradisus cum fructu pomorum' [Ct. 4 : 12-13, 15]: hoc intelligere non audeo nisi in sanctis et iustis, non in avaris et fraudatoribus, et raptoribus, et feneratoribus, et ebriosis, et invidis, quos tamen cum iustis Baptismum habuisse communem, cum quibus communem non habebant utique caritatem. . . ."
[19] *Ibid.* iii.19.26 (*PL* 43, 151): "Qui sunt autem veri Christiani, nisi de quibus idem Dominus dicit: 'Qui diligit me, mandata mea custodit' [Io. 14 : 21]? Quid est autem custodire mandata eius, nisi in dilectione persistere?" For Augustine *dilectio* and *caritas* are essentially synonymous. Cf. S. Grabowski, "The Role of Charity in the Mystical Body of Christ according to Saint Augustine," *REA* 3 (1957), p. 39.
[20] Cf. Grabowski, *ibid.*, p. 57. Also his article, "Sinners and the Mystical Body of Christ according to St. Augustine," *ThS* 8 (1947), pp. 648-649. The restriction of the category *corpus Christi* to the *boni* or the *ecclesia sancta* is a modification by Augustine of the *corpus domini bipertitum* of the Donatist Tyconius. Hofmann (*Der Kirchenbegriff des heiligen Augustinus* [München, 1933], p. 236, n. 114) maintains that the term *corpus permixtum* for Augustine does not mean that he conceived of the body of Christ itself as composed of good and evil in this age, but rather it refers to the *corpus Christi* composed only of the *boni*, which is found mixed with the *mali* in the communion of the sacraments. Augustine prefers to speak of an *ecclesia permixta* in place of the *corpus bipertitum*. Cf. *De doct. chr.* iii.32.45 (*CChr* 32, 104-105). J. Ratzinger (*Volk und Haus Gottes in Augustins Lehre von der Kirche* [München, 1954], p. 147, n. 43) maintains that *corpus Christi* never refers to the *mali*. This means that where Augustine employs his hermeneutical schema of the *corpus Christi* in the *Enarrationes*—where Christ speaks for himself or in the person of his members—his members can include only the *boni*.
[21] *Contra litt. Pet.* ii.77.172 (*PL* 43, 311-312): "His enim nos apostolicis verbis, commendantibus eminentiam caritatis, vobis solemus ostendere quomodo non prosit

is *caritas* which those do not have who are cut off from the communion of the catholic church, and it is *caritas* through which they are reinserted into this communion.[22] At this level *caritas* is tied to the *ecclesia catholica,* while at the more inward level *caritas* is the property of the *boni* alone. At the first level *caritas* is synonymous with unity, at the second with sanctity and righteousness. At the first level it is heretics and schismatics who are guilty of lacking and even violating *caritas*; at the second level it is the *mali,* the pseudo-Christians, who are marked by the absence of *caritas.* This means that heretics (together with schismatics) and pseudo-Christians are on the same plane insofar as they are both removed from the inner communion of the *boni,* but they are removed, so to speak, at different distances. The former have *caritas* neither at the first nor at the second level; the latter appear to have *caritas* at the first level, but not at the second.[23]

If we were to denote the *caritas* of unity as *caritas* I and the *caritas* of the *boni* as *caritas* II, then the relationship could be tentatively represented as follows:

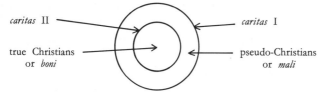

caritas II   *caritas* I

true Christians   pseudo-Christians
or *boni*   or *mali*

hominibus, quamvis in eis sint vel Sacramenta vel fides, ubi caritas non est; ut cum ad unitatem catholicam venitis; intelligatis quid vobis conferatur, et quantum sit quod minus habebatis: caritas enim christiana nisi in unitate Ecclesiae non potest custodiri: atque ita videatis sine illa nihil vos esse, etsi Baptismum et fidem teneatis, et per illam etiam montes transferre possitis. . . . Tenemus autem caritatem si amplectimur unitatem. . . ." Cf. *De bapt.* i.8.11 (*PL* 43, 116): "Quid ergo prodest homini vel sana fides, vel sanum fortasse solum fidei sacramentum, ubi letali vulnere schismatis perempta est sanitas caritatis, per cuius solius peremptionem etiam illa integra trahuntur ad mortem?"

[22] *De bapt.* iii.16.21 (*PL* 43, 148): "Ipsa est enim caritas, quam non habent qui ab Ecclesiae catholicae communione praecisi sunt. . . . Non autem habent Dei caritatem, qui Ecclesiae non diligunt unitatem: ac per hoc recte intelligitur dici non accipi nisi in Catholica Spiritus sanctus." Cf. *ibid.* vii.53.102 (*PL* 43, 243): "Nequaquam dubitarem habere eos Baptismum, qui ubicumque, et a quibuscumque, illud verbis evangelicis consecratum, sine sua simulatione, et cum aliqua fide accepissent: quanquam eis ad salutem spiritualem non prodesset, si caritate caruissent, qua *catholicae insererentur Ecclesiae*" (Italics mine).

[23] Ratzinger (p. 137) also admits a "Doppelstruktur" of *caritas* here. He regards *caritas* at the inner level as parallel to the Donatist rebaptism, that is, as effected in the laying on of hands, which was the sign of the sinner's reconciliation to the church. This *caritas,* as he puts it, is "das innere Gut der Heilsgnade, das zwar durch den äußeren Kirchenrahmen angezeigt wird, aber doch grundlegend von ihm verschieden ist."

Such a diagram presupposes, however, that the *mali* in the communion of the sacraments possess *caritas* in its external form, i.e. the *caritas* of unity. But as J. Ratzinger correctly notes, there is no passage which states positively that this is the case.[24] Augustine always stops short of such an affirmation and contents himself with the identification of *caritas* and unity. If, as we admit, it is highly unlikely that Augustine would attribute *caritas* in any form to the *mali*, how can the perplexing parallelism of *caritas* and unity be understood?[25]

In our opinion, the key to the solution lies in the fundamental issue which is at stake in the Donatist controversy—the validity and efficacy of baptism. The Donatists have a valid baptism, which does not have to be overhauled by rebaptism if they reunite with the catholics. Their baptism, however, is not sufficient in order for them to be saved, but must be rendered efficacious through *caritas*. Where is this *caritas* to be found? Only in the unity of the catholic church.[26]

It does not necessarily follow, however, that all those who are safely in the fold of the catholic church have this *caritas*. Augustine, as far as we can see, never makes this assertion. Rather, only the *boni* in the catholic communion have a baptism made efficacious by *caritas*. In this respect, the *mali* are no better off than the schismatics; both have a valid baptism but neither is able to be saved through this baptism alone. Augustine makes this clear in *Tractatus* VI of his running commentary on John, which he directs specifically against the Donatists.[27] There he admonishes the Donatists not to boast of their baptism because the whole catholic church acknowledges that it is the same as its own. Even the "dove," the church of the *boni*, recognizes this fact. But that is not enough. The dove says:

[24] *Volk und Haus Gottes* . . ., p. 138.

[25] Ratzinger's own solution is unsatisfying. Because he is anxious to avoid a "doppelter Kirchenbegriff" in Augustine, he pushes the two-pronged reference of *caritas* into the background and attempts to establish unity between the church of the saints and the church of the sacraments by means of a Neoplatonically-based relationship between *sensus* and *intellectus* (pp. 145-148). Grabowski is less perceptive when he allows the identification of *caritas* and *unitas* to lead him to the conclusion that the church as *corpus Christi mysticum* is identical with the visible Catholic Church and to the untenable statement ("The Role of Charity in the Mystical Body . . .," p. 57): "Those who are members of the visible and sacramental Church are members of Christ's Mystical Body." Even he is forced to admit a double reference of *caritas*, however, when he immediately adds: "Moreover, charity is the mark distinguishing between those who inwardly, truly and really are members of Christ's Body and those who apparently are members of it but who, devoid of charity, in truth do not inwardly constitute it."

[26] Cf. *supra*, notes 21 and 22.

[27] Cf. *infra*, n. 37.

Even the *mali*, among whom I am constantly groaning, and who do not belong to my members (but it is imperative that I suffer in their midst), even these *mali*, do they not have the same thing of which you boast? Do not many drunkards have baptism? Many greedy men? ... Even these have baptism, but the dove groans surrounded by ravens. Why are you so happy because you have it? For you have the same thing which the *malus* has. Better to have humility, *caritas*, peace. Have something good which you do not yet have so that what you have might do you some good.[28]

The identification of *caritas* and unity must therefore be understood in the following way: *caritas* is only present within the unity of the catholic church; but the boundary of *caritas* is not coextensive with the boundary of the catholic communion of the sacraments. The *mali* are better off than the schismatics to the extent that they are already in unity and are able immediately to become *boni* through the attainment of *caritas*. The schismatics, however, must take a preliminary step. They must first reunite with the catholic communion before they even have the chance to become *boni* and cash in their baptism for salvation through *caritas*. There is only one *caritas* functioning for Augustine—that which we have shown above as *caritas* II, the *caritas* of the *boni*. It is the *caritas* of unity because it is only found within the catholic fold.

Or is that always the case? Before we revise our diagram, we must take account of the second complication in Augustine's ecclesiology—the relation of the predestined to the overall structure. It appears that the *boni*, the *iusti* or the *sancti* who make up the mini-church are also the *praedestinati*, for these *iusti* constitute the "certain number of the saints predestined before the foundation of the world."[29] But Augustine makes three distinctions even within this inner group:

> Some of these live spiritually and embark upon the excellent way of *caritas*. ... Others, though still hampered by their own natural desires,

[28] *In Ioh. ev.* 6.17 (*CChr* 36, 62): "Ait tibi columba: Et mali inter quos gemo, qui non pertinent ad membra mea, et necesse est ut inter illos gemam, nonne habent quod te habere gloriaris? nonne multi ebriosi habent baptismum? nonne multi avari? ... Et isti habent baptismum, sed columba gemit inter corvos. Quid ergo gaudes, quia habes? Hoc habes quod habet et malus. Habeto humilitatem, caritatem, pacem; habeto bonum quod nondum habes, ut prosit tibi bonum quod habes." Cf. *ibid.* 6.14 (*CChr* 36, 60-61).
[29] Referring to the same *iusti* as in note 18 above: *De bapt.* v.27.38 (*PL* 43, 195): "In illis videlicet iustis ... in quibus est numerus certus sanctorum praedestinatus ante mundi constitutionem. Illa vero multitudo spinarum, sive occultis, sive apertis separationibus, forinsecus adiacet super numerum."

press forward vigorously, and are nursed along with the milk of the sacred mysteries until they become capable of digesting the solid food of spiritual matters. .... And there are even some out of this number who for the time being lead despicable lives, or who lie dormant in heresies or in pagan superstitions; and yet even there "the Lord knows his own" [II Tim. 2:19]. For in that ineffable foreknowledge of God, many who seem to be outside are really within, and many who appear to be inside are really standing outside. Thus all those who, if I might put it this way, are inside secretly and inwardly, make up that "garden enclosed, fountain sealed, well of living water, orchard full of pomegranates" [Song of Songs 4 : 12-13].[30]

First it is important to note the distinction between the perfect and the imperfect, or between the beginners and advanced, within the predestined *iusti*—a distinction which will find its own place in the medieval tradition. But more problematically, it appears that a part of those who belong to the number of the predestined can exist not only outside the inward communion of the *boni,* who express their *caritas* outwardly, but also outside the communion of the sacraments insofar as they "lie dormant in heresies or in pagan superstitions." According to Augustine, even these partake of that *caritas* which is the peculiar property of the *boni,* although they share the sacraments (as many as may be baptized we must assume) with the *mali.*[31]

What are we to do with these predestined outsiders who are part of the mini-church of the *boni* and *iusti*? There is some justification for the assertion that Augustine always holds the predestined in the closest connection with the baptized community.[32] After all, Augustine appears to assume that they will have been baptized in some form or other.[33] In the following section of *De baptismo,*

---

[30] *Ibid.* (*PL* 43, 195-196): "Ex hoc numero quidam spiritualiter vivunt, et supereminentem viam caritatis ingrediuntur; ... Quidam vero adhuc carnales et animales provectus suos instanter exercent, et ut cibo spiritualium fiant idonei, sanctorum mysteriorum lacte nutriuntur. ... Sunt etiam quidam ex eo numero qui adhuc nequiter vivant, aut etiam in haeresibus vel in Gentilium superstitionibus iaceant: et tamen illic 'novit Dominus qui sunt eius'. Namque in illa ineffabili praescientia Dei, multi qui foris videntur, intus sunt; et multi, qui intus videntur, foris sunt. Ex illis ergo omnibus, qui, ut ita dicam, intrinsecus et in occulto intus sunt, constat ille 'hortus conclusus, fons signatus, puteus aquae vivae, paradisus cum fructu pomorum.'"

[31] *Ibid.*: "Horum munera concessa divinitus, partim sunt propria, sicut in hoc tempore infatigabilis caritas, et in futuro saeculo vita aeterna; partim vero cum malis perversisque communia, sicut omnia caetera, in quibus sunt et sacrosancta mysteria."

[32] So Ratzinger, p. 145, n. 37 and Hofmann, pp. 242-243.

[33] Cf. *supra,* n. 31.

Augustine emphasizes the indispensability of baptism for being saved aboard the ark of the church.[34] In this case, the ark, the church of the *boni*, extends beyond the catholic communion of the sacraments since its members belong according to the heart and not according to the body. And yet, it does not cross the boundary of baptism *per se*, since the members in question are those who have been baptized "outside" in schism but who nevertheless belong to the ark through the foreknowledge of God.

It is impossible to affirm with certainty, however, that all of the predestined *iusti* who belong to the mini-church of the *boni* marked by *caritas* have at one time been baptized.[35] In his confrontation with the Donatists, it is not baptism *per se* (which they also have) that Augustine is concerned to stress, but rather that which is required in addition to (or perhaps apart from) baptism in order to assure membership in the true church of the *boni: caritas* and the foreknowledge of God. What we can assert on the basis of the above texts is that the mini-church of the predestined *boni* and *iusti* is defined by the *caritas* of her members. Nevertheless, in view of his repeated assertions that *caritas* is found only in the catholic communion, there does not appear to be sufficient evidence to extend the boundary of *caritas* beyond this communion. It is on this basis, therefore, that we revise the above diagram to reflect more accurately Augustine's concept of the structure of the church:

---

[34] *De bapt.* v.28.39 (*PL* 43, 196-197): "Si autem in Ecclesia, utique in arca: et si in arca, utique per aquam. Potest ergo fieri ut et quidam foris baptizati, per Dei praescientiam verius intus baptizati deputentur; quia illic eis aqua incipit prodesse ad salutem; neque enim aliter dici possunt salvi facti in arca nisi per aquam: ... Certe manifestum est, id quod dicitur, in Ecclesia intus et foris, in corde, non in corpore cogitandum; quandoquidem omnes qui corde sunt intus, in arcae unitate per eamdem aquam salvi fiunt, per quam omnes qui corde sunt foris, sive etiam corpore foris sint, sive non sint, tanquam unitatis adversarii moriuntur." According to the last lines of this text, the unity in question is not that of the catholic sacramental community, but that of the ark, the church of the *boni*. Insofar as Augustine means this kind of *unitas* in identifying *caritas* with *unitas*, no problem arises in regard to a twofold reference of *caritas*.

[35] Especially in view of Augustine's concept of the two cities. E.g., in *De civitate* i.35 (*CChr* 47, 33-34) Augustine admonishes the citizens of the city of God that some of her enemies are destined to become fellow-citizens, and she should therefore bear what they inflict "until they become confessors of the faith." In the same breath, however, he maintains that the two cities remain intertwined up to the last judgment. In addition, there are the Old Testament *iusti* who certainly have not undergone baptism, but who were able to have *caritas*, as Augustine says of Abel: *In epist. Ioh.* 5.8 (*PL* 35, 2017): "Non fuit caritas in Cain: et nisi esset caritas in Abel, non acciperet Deus sacrificium eius."

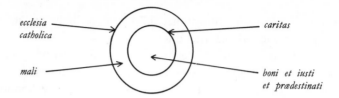

Possibly all the complex dimensions of space and time involved in Augustine's ecclesiology can be expressed in terms of modern set theory.[36] However, this is not the goal of our investigation. Rather our concern is to clarify the status of the *boni* in Augustine's ecclesiology as it was forged out in the crucible of the Donatist controversy. The function of *caritas* as the definitive mark of the *boni* and *iusti* in the mini-church is the feature element in Augustine's view of the church which will be taken over by his medieval successors.

The Enarrationes in psalmos.—After this brief, but necessary, treatment of the foundation of Augustine's ecclesiology, we turn now to that work which will have the most direct influence upon the medieval Psalms commentators—the *Enarrationes in psalmos*. These extensive sermons on the Psalms, delivered over a period of some twenty years, yield the same picture of the church as that which

[36] We admit with R. Seeberg (*Lehrbuch der Dogmengeschichte*, Vol. II [Darmstadt, 1965], p. 472) that the invisible bond of *caritas* is "an sich" not identical with the number of the predestined, since some who have *caritas* at one particular moment may not be predestined to retain it forever. For this reason Hofmann (p. 242) represents Augustine's picture of the church through three concentric circles where the predestined who persevere to the end form a smaller circle within the *boni* and *iusti*. We will show futher on in this chapter, however, that perseverance for Augustine means perseverance in *caritas* (*infra*, pp. 35f.). Therefore, the coextension of the boundary of *caritas* with the number of the predestined signifies the *boni* who will persevere to the end in *caritas*. We do not exclude the possibility that *caritas* can exist outside the catholic communion or that some predestined will never be baptized, as indicated in n. 35 above. But these possibilities must be considered as the exception rather than the rule, especially in the anti-Donatist writings. For example, in n. 30 above, the phrase "for the time being" (*adhuc*) implies that those predestined still living outside will become part of the baptized community and there partake of *caritas*. An overdose of emphasis upon the predestined character of the *boni* leads to a view such as Karl Holl expresses in his study, "Die Entstehung von Luthers Kirchenbegriff," *Gesammelte Aufsätze*, Vol. I: *Luther* (7th ed., Tübingen, 1948), p. 299. For Holl, Augustine conceives of the inner church of the predestined saints as a purely timeless entity, called into being only by God's "other-worldly will," and in which there exists no connection among the individual members. Seen over against Augustine's stress upon the mark of *caritas*, however, any such interpretation of Augustine's ecclesiology shows up as clearly one-sided. This is not the direction in which a fruitful comparison with Luther can be made.

evolved in the Donatist controversy. This is hardly surprising since the span of their production overlaps almost all of the major anti-Donatist works and since some of the sermons themselves were directed specifically to the schism.[37]

The necessary presence of both *boni* and *mali* in the church is a prominent theme in these sermons. Augustine maintains that the word *torcularia*, "wine presses," in the title of Psalm 8 can be taken for the churches; for just as wheat must be separated from the chaff on the threshing floor and grapes from their seeds in the wine press, so the *boni* are separated from the "multitude of secular men" who are gathered together simultaneously with them in the churches.[38] True, in the present they are separated not spatially, but only *affectu*. But the time will come when the grain will be put away in the barn and the wine in the cellar, for the Lord says: "He will store the grain in the barns, but the chaff he will burn with inextinguishable fire (Luke 3 : 17)."[39] Augustine comments further on verses 7-8 of the psalm:

> Think of wine presses having both grapes and seeds, and the threshing floor containing the chaff and the wheat, and the nets in which good and evil fish are entangled, and the ark of Noah in which there were both clean and unclean animals; and you will see that the churches, in the

---

[37] The dates of composition of the *Enarrationes* are uncertain, but according to the chronological table of Zarb given in *CChr* (38, xv-xviii), the sermons were delivered between 392 and 418. Fischer (p. 114) gives 396 and "after 415" as the termini. According to H. Rondet ("Saint Augustin et les psaumes des montées," *RAM* 41 [1965], p. 4), the *Enarrationes* on Psalms 119-133 were preached alternately with the first twelve tracts on the Gospel of John at Hippo in the winter of 414-415. His dating is based on the chronology worked out by M. Le Landais in "Deux années de prédication de Saint Augustin," in *Études Augustiniennes = Théologie* 28 (1953), pp. 7-95. According to Le Landais, the interval extends from December 414 to Easter 415 (*ibid.*, pp. 35, 60) and includes the *In epistolam Iohannis ad Parthos tractatus X* dated in the Easter season of 415. The Donatist controversy, which was still hot at this time, shows through especially in these sermons (*ibid.*, p. 73). For this reason we take these Johannine works into consideration along with the *Enarrationes*.

[38] *Enarr. in ps.* 8.1 (*CChr* 38, 49): "Torcularia ergo possumus accipere ecclesias. ... His ergo vel integumentis vel sustentaculis, id est paleis in area frumenta, et vinaciis in torcularibus vina exuuntur; sicut in ecclesiis a multitudine saecularium hominum, quae simul cum bonis congregatur, quibus ut nascerentur et apti fierent verbo divino, necessaria erat illa multitudo, id agitur, ut spiritali amore per operationem ministrorum Dei separentur."

[39] *Ibid.*: "Agitur enim nunc, ut non loco, sed affectu interim separentur boni a malis, quamvis simul in ecclesiis, quantum adtinet ad corporalem praesentiam, conversentur. Aliud autem erit tempus, quo vel frumenta in horrea vel vina in cellas segregentur. 'Frumenta,' inquit, 'recondet in horreis, paleas autem comburet igni inexstinguibili' [Lc. 3 : 17]."

present and even up to the final judgment, contain not only sheep and
cattle, i.e. holy lay people and holy ministers, but "beyond that also the
beasts of the field, the birds of the air, the fish of the sea which travel
the paths of the sea." The "beasts of the field" are best taken for men
reveling in the desire of the flesh. . . . See now the "birds of the air," the
proud. . . . And understand the "fish of the sea," that is, curious men. . . .
Moreover, these three kinds of vices—lust, pride and curiosity—cover all
sins.[40]

In the exposition of this one psalm we have already the essential distinction between the *boni* and the *mali* within the outward community of the sacraments, the identification of the *boni*
with the *sancti* (the holy lay people and clergy), and the explicit
characterization of the *mali* through the sins of lust, pride and
curiosity.[41] Simultaneously, however, the necessity of their remaining
mixed together in the churches until the last judgment is clearly
enunciated.

The same distinction between the *boni* and the *mali* in the church
is made at many places in the *Enarrationes*. There are many who adore
Christ but will not reign with him.[42] There are many in the city of
God who work iniquity, but that is only because the present age is a
"time of mercy." The time of judgment will come when the chaff will
be cut away and thrown on the fire while the grain will be stored in
the barn. Only the *boni* adhere to the Lord, not the *mali*, who will be
expelled from the city of God, the "society of Jerusalem, the society
of the saints, the society of the church."[43] They are not part of the

---

[40] *Enarr. in ps.* 8.13 (*CChr* 38, 56): "Veniant in mentem torcularia habentia vinacia
et vinum, et area continens paleas et frumentum, et retia quibus inclusi sunt pisces boni
et mali, et arca Noe in qua et immunda et munda erant animalia; et videbis ecclesias
interim hoc tempore usque ad ultimum iudicii tempus, non solum oves et boves
continere, id est sanctos laicos et sanctos ministros, sed 'insuper et pecora campi,
volucres caeli, et pisces maris, qui perambulant semitas maris.' Pecora enim campi
congruentissime accipiuntur homines in carnis voluptate gaudentes. . . . Vide nunc
etiam volucres caeli, superbos. . . . Intuere etiam pisces maris, hoc est curiosos. . . . Haec
autem tria genera vitiorum, id est voluptas carnis, et superbia, et curiositas, omnia
peccata concludunt."

[41] The evil Christians are also depicted as *praevaricatores*, and in this sense are
equivalent to those outside the church of the baptized: *Enarr. in ps.* 100.5 (*CChr* 39,
1410): ". . . vel in ipsa ecclesia bonum iter capitis in via immaculata; non eos tantum
qui foris sunt odisse debetis praevaricatores, sed et quoscumque intus inveneritis. Qui
sunt praevaricatores? Qui oderunt legem Dei; qui audiunt illam, et non faciunt,
praevaricatores dicuntur."

[42] *Enarr. in ps.* 59.11 (*CChr* 39, 763): "Alienigenae, non pertinentes ad genus meum.
'Subditi sunt', quia multi adorant Christum, et non sunt regnaturi cum Christo."

[43] *Enarr. in ps.* 100.12 (*CChr* 39, 1415-1417): "Sunt ergo in civitate Domini
operantes iniquitatem, et quasi parcitur eis modo. Quare? Quia misericordiae tempus

council of the upright who will sit upon the twelve thrones judging the twelve tribes of Israel. When the *iusti* are gathered together, no false brethren such as Judas, Simon Magus or any wolf in sheep's clothing will be tolerated in this elite number, although it is necessary for the church to groan in their midst for now.[44] The vestments of the king Christ are his saints, his elect. They alone constitute that church which is displayed before him without spot or wrinkle, whose blemish he washed out with his blood, and whose wrinkle he ironed out on the cross.[45]

So far Augustine uses categories with which we are already familiar to set off the members of the mini-church from the *mali*; they are *sancti, iusti, boni, electi,* the "grain," and the church "without spot or wrinkle." But what about the term which will interest us the most: the *fideles.* How does this all-important category fit into Augustine's ecclesiological structure? In his exposition of Psalm 8 : 8-9, where he designates the sheep and cattle as holy laymen and ministers parallel to the *boni,* Augustine also refers to them as the "holy souls of the faithful either in the people or in the ministers."[46] To these he again opposes all the types of sin represented by the *mali*—the beasts of the

---

est; sed veniet et iudicii, quia sic coepit psalmus: 'Misericordiam et iudicium cantabo tibi, Domine.' Iam enumeravit superius quia non illi adhaeserunt nisi boni. Malis non adhaesit, ... Non conciditur nisi palea; triticum spoliatur superfluis, et veniet ventilatio, et inveniet puram massam, quem invenit granum mittit in horreum suum, et acervum paleae comburet igni inexstinguibili." *Ibid.* 100.13 (*CChr* 39, 1417): "Et quare interficientur? Ut dispergantur de civitate Domini, de societate Ierusalem, de societate sanctorum, de societate ecclesiae. ... Frates, nemo sibi blandiatur: interficientur omnes operantes iniquitatem; interficiet eos Christus in matutinis, et disperdet eos de civitate sua. Sed modo cum tempus misericordiae est, audiant eum."

[44] *Enarr. in ps.* 110.2 (*CChr* 40, 1622): " 'In consilio', inquit, 'rectorum et congregatione': credo, qui sedebunt super duodecim thronos, iudicantes duodecim tribus Israel [Mt. 19 : 28]. Nullus enim iam inter eos iniquus, nullius Iudae furta tolerantur, nullus Simon magus baptizatur, Spiritum volens emere [Act. 9 : 18], dum cogitat vendere, nullus Alexander aerarius [II Tim. 4 : 14] multa mala ostendit, nullus ovina pelle tectus falsa fraternitate subrepit; inter quales nunc necesse est ecclesia gemat, et quales tunc oportet, cum omnes iusti congregabuntur, excludat." The struggle in the womb of Rebecca signifies the necessity for the church to groan amid the presence of the *mali: Enarr. in ps.* 123.8 (*CChr* 40, 1863). Cf. also *Enarr. in ps.* 128.8-10 (*CChr* 40, 1885-1887).

[45] *Enarr. in ps.* 44.22 (*CChr* 38, 509): "Vestimenta eius sunt sancti eius, electi eius, tota ecclesia eius, quam sibi sicut vestem exhibet, sine macula et ruga; propter maculam, abluens in sanguine; propter rugam, extendens in cruce."

[46] Cf. *supra,* n. 40. *Enarr. in ps.* 8.13 (*CChr* 38, 57): "Propter torculariorum itaque significationem, subiecta sunt pedibus eius non solum vina, sed etiam vinacia; non solum scilicet oves et boves, id est sanctae animae fidelium, vel in plebe, vel in ministris; sed insuper et pecora voluptatis, et volucres superbiae, et pisces curiositatis. Quae omnia genera peccatorum nunc bonis et sanctis mixta esse in ecclesiis videmus."

field, the birds of the air, and the fish of the sea—which are found mixed with the *boni* and *sancti* in the churches.

The designation of the *boni* and *sancti* as *fideles* is indicative of the way in which Augustine employs this important term: it is another name for the members of the mini-church. This is clear from a number of contexts in which the *fideles* appear. Most striking is the synonymity which obtains between the temple of God, the body of Christ and the *congregatio fidelium*.[47] As we know, for Augustine only the *boni* come into consideration as members of the body of Christ.[48] Thus, when Augustine coins the groundbreaking definition of the church as the congregation of the faithful in the same breath with the body of Christ, he is filling this phrase with specific content. It covers only the *boni* and *sancti* in the mini-church. As we shall see, however, neither this phrase nor the definition of the church as the body of Christ will maintain this limited reference in the commentaries of Augustine's successors. Precisely in these two definitions of the church can best be seen how phrases remain superficially the same while their content radically changes.

Part of the responsibility for this change in content is found in one peculiar property of the term *fideles*, which already in Augustine points to a broader reference of the word. This property involves the formation of the antonym. Whereas the *boni* are contrasted to the *mali*, and the opposite of *sancti* is best taken as *peccatores*, the antonym of *fideles* is not properly *infideles*, who are the pagans with no relation to the church, but rather the *falsi* or *mali fideles* who correspond to those simply denoted as *mali*, the chaff in the community of the sacraments.[49] The fact that the antonym of the word *fideles* must be formed with the word itself plus a negating adjective opens up the possibility that the term itself, *fideles*, can apply to all members of the sacramental community. As a result, those *fideles* who are *boni* must be explicitly designated as such in contrast to the *mali*

---

[47] *Enarr. in ps.* 130.3 (*CChr* 40, 1899): "Hoc autem templum Dei, hoc corpus Christi, haec congregatio fidelium unam vocem habet, et tamquam unus homo cantat in psalmo."

[48] Cf. *supra*, n. 20. The *fideles* are equated with the members of Christ elsewhere. Cf. *Enarr. in ps.* 68, s. 1, 10 (*CChr* 39, 911): "Utique in corpore, in membris; in illis fidelibus, unde illi haerabat iam membrum illud quod confitebatur peccata sua." When Augustine takes over in modified form the rule of Tyconius in regard to the body of Christ, he refers explicitly to the *fideles*: *De doct. chr.* iii.31.44 (*CChr* 32, 104).

[49] *Enarr. in ps.* 132.4 (*CChr* 40, 1928): "Tam sunt enim monachi falsi, quam et clerici falsi, et fideles falsi." The phrase *boni fideles* does occur at least once in Augustine's writings; cf. *De civ.* xx.15 (*CChr* 48, 726).

fideles or *falsi fideles.* This problem of the antonym lies at the root of the ambiguity involved with the category *fideles* which will manifest itself after Augustine.

But back to Augustine himself. A further clue to the fact that the *fideles* in his mind only refer to the *boni* is the use of the term as a synonym for the predestined. This usage not only comprehends the *boni* who are at any one time present within the boundaries of the catholic communion, but also those who have existed prior to us as *sancti* and who will be *fideles sancti* in the future. Many familiar descriptions of the mini-church of the *boni* turn up in this context—the temple of God, the city of God, the *sancti*, the grain—as well as Augustine's proof text for God's predestination: "The Lord knows his own" (II Tim. 2 : 19).[50] The equivalence which prevails between the *fideles* and the predestined is one reason why it was necessary to include the latter in our diagram of the structure of the church, where we can now add the *fideles* to the area occupied by the *boni* and the predestined.

If the *fideles* also belong to this territory, then like their counterparts, they must be explicitly defined in terms of the *caritas* which marks off this area. This is in fact the case. The living stones from which the church as the temple of God is constructed are the *fideles*, who are joined together by the mortar of *caritas*.[51] Augustine's

---

[50] *Enarr. in ps.* 126.3 (*CChr* 40, 1858): "Quae autem domus Dei, et ipsa civitas. Domus enim Dei, populus Dei; quia domus Dei, templum Dei. Et quid dicit apostolus? 'Templum enim Dei sanctum est, quod estis vos' [I Cor. 3 : 17]. Omnes autem fideles, quae est domus Dei, non solum qui modo sunt, sed et qui ante nos fuerunt et iam dormierunt, et qui post nos futuri sunt, adhuc qui nasci habent in rebus humanis usque in finem saeculi, congregati in unum fideles innumerabiles, sed Domino numerati, de quibus dicit apostolus: 'Novit Dominus qui sunt eius' [II Tim. 2 : 19]; grana illa quae modo gemunt inter paleas, quae massam unam factura sunt, quando area in fine fuerit ventilata; omnis ergo numerus fidelium sanctorum, ex hominibus commutandorum ut fiant aequales angelis Dei, adiuncti etiam ipsi angelis, qui modo non peregrinantur, sed exspectant nos quando a peregrinatione redeamus; omnes simul unam domum Dei faciunt, et unam civitatem." Cf. the clear parallel drawn in *In Ioh. ev.* 26.15 (*CChr* 36, 267): ". . . sancta ecclesia in praedestinatis et vocatis, et iustificatis, et glorificatis sanctis, et fidelibus eius." (Cited by H. Riedlinger, *Die Makellosigkeit der Kirche in den lateinischen Hoheliedkommentaren des Mittelalters* [Münster, 1958], p. 56, n. 33).

[51] *Enarr. in ps.* 44.31 (*CChr* 38, 515-516): "Templum regis ipsa ecclesia, intrat in templum ipsa ecclesia. Unde construitur templum? De hominibus qui intrant in templum. Lapidi vivi qui sunt, nisi fideles Dei? . . . Iunctura lapidum viventium caritas est." Cf. the same imagery in reference to the *sancti* and the ark: *In Ioh. ev.* 6.19 (*CChr* 36, 63). Also the same function of *caritas* in the body of Christ: *Enarr. in ps.* 125.13 (*CChr* 40, 1854): "Sic se ergo tenet corpus Christi, membra socia sic compinguntur et adunantur in caritate et in vinculo pacis, cum quisque id quod habet praestat ei qui non habet; . . ." E. Mersch (*Le Corps mystique du Christ*, Vol. II [3rd ed., Paris

interpretation of the *ora vestimenti* of Psalm 132 : 2 also helps to establish this mark of the *fideles*. According to one of his earlier anti-Donatist works, this border around the top of the robe signifies the *perfecti fideles* in the church.[52] When he reaches this psalm in the *Enarrationes*, he defines these *perfecti* more precisely. They are those in whom the perfect *caritas Christi* is found, "for those who do not have the perfect *caritas Christi*, though they be in unity, nevertheless are odious, irksome and troublemakers, always bothering others. . . ."[53] The *fideles* take up their position along with the *boni* and *iusti* in the mini-church distinguished from the *mali* by *caritas*.

What is this *caritas* which Augustine has set up as the criterion for membership in the true church of the saints and the faithful? Content-wise it is love of God and love of neighbor—a definition which Augustine never tires of repeating.[54] Thus *caritas* has both a vertical and a horizontal reference. It describes the relationship of the *fideles* to God and to one another; it forms the bond between the *fideles* and God as well as among the *fideles* themselves.[55]

This twofold dimension of *caritas* comes to expression in Augustine's attempt to find a way around the contradiction posed by two statements in I John: "If we say we have no sin, we deceive ourselves and the truth is not in us" (I John 1 : 8) and "No one who is born of God commits sin" (I John 3 : 9). Augustine extricates himself from the dilemma by setting up one sin, the commission of which makes all other sins stick, but whose avoidance causes other sins to be forgiven. This sin is the sin against *caritas*, against the commandment of Christ to love one another. Whoever sins against *caritas*, against the command to love the brother, cannot boast that he

and Brussels, 1951], pp. 130ff.) emphasizes the essential nature of *caritas* to the mystical body for Augustine.

[52] *Contra litt. Pet.* ii.104.239 (*PL* 43, 341): "Ora vestimenti haec datur intelligi, quae in capite vestimenti est, qua vestientis caput ingreditur: per hanc significantur perfecti fideles in Ecclesia."

[53] *Enarr. in ps.* 132.12 (*CChr* 40, 1934): "Quos significant montes, hos significant barba, hos significant ora vestimenti. Barba non intelligitur nisi in perfectis. Non ergo habitant in unum, nisi in quibus perfecta fuerit caritas Christi. Nam in quibus non est perfecta caritas Christi, et cum in uno sint, odiosi sunt, molesti sunt, turbulenti sunt, anxietate sua turbant ceteros, . . ."

[54] E.g., *Enarr. in ps.* 31.ii.5 (*CChr* 38, 228): "Amor Dei, amor proximi, caritas dicitur; . . ." Cf. also Augustine's interpretation of the parable of the Good Samaritan where the two denarii through which we are healed in the *stabulum* (the church) are the *caritas dei* and *caritas proximi*: *Enarr. in ps.* 125.15 (*CChr* 40, 1856).

[55] Cf. *supra*, n. 51 and the entire discussion of the unitive power of *caritas* by Grabowski, "The Role of Charity in the Mystical Body, . . ." pp. 42ff.

is born of God, whereas he who guards this *caritas* can rest assured in the fact that *"caritas* covers a multitude of sins" (I Peter 4 : 8).[56]

Although the definition of *caritas* itself in this context only deals with love of the brother,[57] Augustine binds this horizontally-directed *caritas* inseparably with the love of God and the vertical relationship between the Christian and God. The status of sonship, "being born of God," depends completely upon the possession and the actualization of *caritas*. In other words, *caritas* is the decisive factor soteriologically as well as ecclesiologically. Augustine makes this clear by taking a lead from I John 3 : 10 ("By this can be seen who are the sons of God and the sons of the devil; he who is not righteous is not of God, nor he who does not love his brother"):

> Thus *dilectio* alone distinguishes between sons of God and sons of the devil. They can all cross themselves; they can shout "Amen"; they can all sing "Alleluia"; they can join the church and build churches. But the sons of God are not set apart from the sons of the devil by anything but *caritas*. Those who have *caritas* are born of God; those who do not have it are not born of God. It alone decides the verdict and makes the cutoff. ... This is the pearl of great price, *caritas*. Without it nothing you have does you any good; but if you have it alone, you need nothing else at all.[58]

Augustine is here making the same claim for *caritas* in the soteriological sphere as he did in the ecclesiological sphere, when he set up *caritas* as the prerequisite for belonging to the mini-church of

---

[56] *In epist. Ioh.* 5.3 (*PL* 35, 2013-2014): "Est quoddam peccatum quod non potest admittere ille qui natus est ex Deo; et quo non admisso solvuntur caetera, quo admisso confirmantur caetera. Quod est hoc peccatum? Facere contra mandatum Christi, contra testamentum novum. Quod est mandatum novum? 'Mandatum novum do vobis, ut vos invicem diligatis' [Io. 13 : 34]. Qui facit contra caritatem et contra dilectionem fraternam, non audeat gloriari, et dicere natum se esse ex Deo: qui autem in dilectione fraterna constitutus est, certa sunt peccata quae non potest admittere, et hoc maxime ne oderit fratrem. Et quid de caeteris peccatis facit, unde dictum est: 'Si dixerimus quia peccatum non habemus, nos ipsos seducimus, et veritas in nobis non est?' Audiat securitatem de alio loco Scripturae: 'Caritas cooperit multitudinem peccatorum' [I Pt. 4 : 8]."

[57] *Ibid.* 5.4. (*PL* 35, 2014): "Perfecta ista caritas est, ut paratus sis mori pro fratre. Hanc ipse Dominus in se exhibuit. ... Perfecta ergo caritas haec est. Si quis tantam habuerit caritatem, ut paratus sit pro fratribus etiam mori, perfecta est in illo caritas."

[58] *Ibid.* 5.7 (*PL* 35, 2016): "Dilectio ergo sola discernit inter filios Dei et filios diaboli. Signent se omnes signo crucis Christi; respondeant omnes, Amen; cantent omnes, Alleluia; baptizentur omnes, intrent Ecclesias, faciant parietes basilicarum: non discernuntur filii Dei a filiis diaboli, nisi caritate. Qui habent caritatem, nati sunt ex Deo: qui non habent, non sunt nati ex Deo. Magnum indicium, magna discretio. ... Haec est margarita pretiosa, caritas, sine qua nihil tibi prodest quodcumque habueris: quam si solam habeas, sufficit tibi."

the *boni* and *fideles.* The sons of God in the above text are none other than the *boni* and *fideles.* And the supremacy and self-sufficiency of *caritas* expressed in this text recall the more explicitly ecclesiological thrust against the Donatists where Augustine extolled *caritas* above faith and the sacraments.[59]

Two themes are interlaced here, both of which will exert decisive influence upon Augustine's successors in the exegesis of the Psalms. First and most important is the dominance of *caritas* over *fides* (and the sacraments) as the definitive mark of the mini-church of the *boni* and *fideles.*[60] Faith, however, is not only relegated to secondary importance in the ecclesiological sphere, but also in the soteriological realm,[61] because—and this is the second influential theme—soteriology and ecclesiology are intimately related for Augustine. This arises out of the nature of *caritas* itself—as love for God and the neighbor—and its salutary function of covering enough sins so that the *fideles* can be set apart as sons of God from the sons of the devil.[62] Augustine does not claim that the *fideles* are without sin, and yet it is clear that they exist in the mini-church without deadly sins because their *caritas* does not allow them to harm their brother to such an extent that it nullifies their adoption by God.[63] To exist in the

[59] Cf. *supra,* notes 18, 21, 22.

[60] Cf. also *In Ioh. ev.* 6.21 (*CChr* 36, 64-65): "Sed quid dicit Iacobus? "Et daemones credunt, et contremiscunt' [Iac. 2 : 19]. Magna est fides, sed nihil prodest si non habeat caritatem. Confitebantur et daemones Christum. Ergo credendo, sed non diligendo dicebant: 'Quid nobis et tibi?' [Mc 1 : 24]. Fidem habebant, caritatem non habebant: ideo daemones erant." Augustine expands on this theme in *Enarr. in ps.* 130.1 (*CChr* 40, 1898) using some of the same imagery as in n. 51 *supra.*

[61] See Ratzinger, pp. 150-151.

[62] It does not serve our purpose here to trace in detail how Augustine's concept of *caritas* is reworked into the anthropological framework of medieval theology and its *ordo salutis.* Augustine certainly regards *caritas* as the greatest gift of the Holy Spirit and as a *virtus* (see Grabowski, "The Role of Charity in the Mystical Body ..," pp. 34f. and 39ff.). Suffice it to point out that Lombard leans heavily on Augustine's *De Trinitate* to support his identification of *caritas* and the Holy Spirit (I *Sent.* d. 17). Lombard quotes a passage from *De Trinitate* (xv.18.32; *CChr* 50A, 507) in this context which makes the same fundamental distinction as in n. 58 above (I *Sent.* d.17 c.4). Whether *caritas* is conceived of primarily as *caritas increata* or *creata,* however, its possession remains the deciding factor in the salvation of the *viator,* and as we shall see, in the determination of one's membership in the church of the *boni.*

[63] Riedlinger (pp. 58ff.) notes that Augustine in the *Retractationes* takes back any reference in his anti-Donatist writings which would imply that the members of the mini-church of the *boni* are sinless, and says that he meant this only in an eschatological sense. This is clear from our discussion of the nature of *caritas.* And yet the medieval distinction between deadly and harmless sins is already present in Augustine, as well as the conception of existing in a particular status through the possession of *caritas* where no deadly sin, i.e. against *caritas,* is committed.

mini-church of the *boni* through *caritas* implies that one also exists in a saving relationship to God as *filius Dei* through *caritas*, and vice versa.

Another aspect of the function of *caritas* will have its effect upon Augustine's successors. This aspect grows out of the soteriological function of *caritas* as establishing the saving relation of sonship. It is the role that *caritas* plays in perseverance. The overarching factor which determines which *boni* and *fideles* will "make it all the way" is God's predestination.[64] The perseverance which holds on under the protective covering of predestination, however, is a perseverance in *caritas*. Only those whose *caritas* does not grow cold truly make up the church and belong to that tabernacle where the feet of the Lord stand (Ps. 131 : 7).[65] Here again the soteriological function of *caritas* meshes with the ecclesiological function. We have already illustrated the latter in the diagram of Augustine's ecclesiology, and here we see further justification for including the predestined inside the boundary of *caritas*. *Caritas* is not only the mark of the *boni* and *fideles* in the mini-church as seen in a still shot when the reel of the church's ongoing history is stopped. Accompanied by God's predestination, the continued possession of *caritas* is the guarantee that the *fideles* will remain faithful to the end.

The theme of perseverance in *caritas* will manifest itself most concretely in the relationship between the militant and triumphant

---

[64] This is what ensures that the *boni* (the "grain" and the "good fish"), when they sin, will respond to disciplinary treatment and attain salvation: *Enarr. in ps.* 88, s.2.4 (*CChr* 39, 1235): "... multi christiani tolerabiliter peccant, multi flagello a peccato corriguntur, et emendantur, et sanantur; multi omnino aversi, dura cervice obnitentes adversus disciplinam Patris, et ipsam omnino Dei paternitatem recusantes, habentes tamen signum Christi, eunt in tales iniquitates, ut non possit nisi recitari contra eos: 'Quoniam qui talia agunt, regnum Dei non possidebunt' [Gal. 5 : 21]. Non tamen propter hos remanebit Christus sine hereditate; non propter paleam etiam frumenta interibunt, non propter pisces malos nihil ex illa sagena mittetur in vascula. Novit Dominus qui sunt eius [II Tim. 2 : 19]. Securus enim promisit, qui nos antequam essemus praedestinavit: ..."

[65] *Enarr. in ps.* 131.13 (*CChr.* 40, 1918): "Bonum est enim illi ut coaedificetur, et habeat caritatem. Nam si ipse ruerit, stabit domus. Itaque, fratres, in his est domus Dei, quos praedestinavit et praescivit perseveraturos. De illis dictum est: "Ubi steterunt pedes eius.' Sunt enim qui non perseverant, nec stant pedes eius in eis. Non sunt ergo ipsi ecclesia; non ipsi pertinent ad illud modo tabernaculum, tunc domum. Sed ubi steterunt pedes eius? 'Quoniam abundavit iniquitas, refrigescet caritas multorum' [Mt. 24 : 12]. In his in quibus caritas refrigescit, non stant pedes eius." Cf. *ibid.* 59.10 (*CChr* 39, 762): "Inde tribulatio ecclesiae, inde olla ebulliens. ... Olla bulliente caritas refrigescit ... Persevera ergo usque in finem contra ollam scandalorum. Ardet olla iniquitatis, sed maior est flamma caritatis. Noli vinci; persevera usque in finem."

35

churches which we will take up in Chapter II. The characterization of the *fideles* through the possession of *caritas* and the intimate relationship this presupposes between ecclesiology and soteriology, however, set the stage for the continuation of our investigation into the definition of the *fideles* in the works of Augustine's successors.

3. Cassiodorus

The *Expositio psalmorum* of Cassiodorus[66] forms, so to speak, the transition between Augustine and the later commentators. As is evident from the numerous citations from his work in the *Glossa* and the commentary of Peter Lombard, his exposition has at least equal influence in its practical effect, even if his name does not carry the weight of Augustinian authority.

Cassiodorus is familiar with the basic ecclesiological categories of Augustine and employs them throughout his work. The church in the present is filled with a mixture of *boni* and *mali*; thus, it is difficult to detect the *electi* who compose the "council of the righteous and the congregation."[67] The analogy of the vine is appropriate to the church, for just as a vine produces fruit in the midst of dying leaves, so the church is decorated by the fruit of the saints among the shady crowds of sinners.[68] In explicit dependence upon Augustine, Cassiodorus denotes the *allophylos* (strangers) of Psalm 59 : 10 as *ficti Christiani*, who, although they are always present among the faithful, nevertheless will not reign with Christ because they live with a "perverse spirit."[69]

As these statements indicate, Cassiodorus is working within the

[66] The *Expositio* was written between c. 540-548 and revised between 560 and 570 (Fischer, p. 197).

[67] *Expositio psalmorum* (cited: *Expos.*) 110.1 (*CChr* 98, 1015); "Si 'consilium iustorum et congregationem' hic velis exquirere, omnino videtur difficile ut in hoc saeculo electos omnes invenias, ubi Ecclesia permixtione bonorum malorumque completa est."

[68] *Expos.* 79.9 (*CChr* 98, 743): "'Vinea' siquidem Ecclesiae et hic pulcherrime comparatur: quoniam sicut illa inter folia caduca necessarios infert fructus, sic et ista inter turbas umbratiles peccantium ornatur fruge sanctorum, qui saeculi huius afflictione tamquam torcularibus pressi, saporem norunt emanare dulcissimum."

[69] *Expos.* 59.10 (*CChr* 97, 535) "Hoc idem dicit populus christianus 'allophylos', id est alienigenas sibi 'subditos', quos iam quidem constat esse confessos. Sed istos 'allophylos' fictos vult intellegi Christianos, qui inter fideles assidua quidem frequentatione conveniunt; sed quoniam vivunt animo perverso, non sunt regnaturi cum Domino." For Augustine on the same passage, cf. *supra*, n. 42. Cf. *Expos.* 59.11 (*CChr* 97, 535).

Augustinian ecclesiological structure. He knows that, although the church in the broader sense of the word as the communion of the sacraments encompasses the mixed society of good and evil Christians, the proper locus of the word "church" is the *sancti*, the congregation of the saints in the mini-church.[70] Nevertheless, there is a tendency for Cassiodorus, perhaps more so than for Augustine, to refer to the inner circle of the church—the *sancti* and the *iusti*—as the *electi* or the predestined.[71] The "sheep" of Psalm 8 are not interpreted with Augustine merely as the *sancti*, but as the "elect Christian people" who lead an "unobjectionable way of life" by the help of the Lord.[72] The heredity of Christ is described by Cassiodorus as the "predestined multitude of the saints."[73] The flock for which God provided in his goodness are the predestined, who are prepared from the foundation of the world.[74] And in the exposition of a passage which will become the *locus classicus* for the doctrine: "Let them be deleted from the book of the living" (68 : 29), Cassiodorus affirms that the predestined number is certain and no temporal eventuality of any kind will be able to alter it.[75]

The emphasis upon the predestined nature of the church of the

---

[70] *Expos.* 44.1 (*CChr* 97, 403): "Secunda simili numero quator partibus mysticis virtutibus Sponsa praedicatur Ecclesia; scilicet quae in sanctorum hominum adunatione consistit." Cf. *Expos.* 100.1 (*CChr* 98, 891): "Congregatio illa sanctorum quam per universum mundum catholica parit et multiplicat semper Ecclesia."

[71] This emphasis is not entirely out of accord with ecclesiological thought in another part of the exegetical tradition of this period. Riedlinger (p. 76) points to the emphasis upon the *ecclesia electorum* in the commentary on the Song of Songs of Bede (d. 735) and his followers. This concentration is the result of accounting for the spotless character of the church as it is described in the Song of Songs—a source which, as we remember, is also important for Augustine's concentration upon the *iusti* in the inner bond of *caritas*. Cf. *supra*, notes 15 and 18.

[72] *Expos.* 8.8 (*CChr* 97, 93): " 'Oves' electum populum significant christianum, sicut in evangelio Dominus Petri dicit apostolo: 'Pasce oves meas' [Io. 21 : 17]. Qui ideo comparantur ovibus, quoniam se, praestante Domino, innoxia conversatione moderantur; deinde quia mundi exuvias sine aliquo sensu doloris amittunt." For Augustine, cf. *supra*, n. 40.

[73] *Expos.* 15.6 (*CChr* 97, 139-140): " 'Hereditas' autem Christi est praedestinata multitudo sanctorum."

[74] *Expos.* 67.11 (*CChr* 97, 590): "Iterumque quae sint ista 'animalia' consequenter exponitur; dicit enim: 'parasti in dulcedine tua pauperis, Deus.' 'Parasti' significat praedestinatos, qui ab origine mundi, ipso miserante, praeparati sunt."

[75] *Expos.* 68.29 (*CChr* 97, 619): "Ibi enim quod scribitur deleri non potest, quia totum in praedestinatione solidatum est; et nullus eventus mutare poterit quod illa providentia superna decrevit." Holl could have argued more convincingly that Cassiodorus, and not Augustine, presents a picture of the church of the saints as a petrified mass of the predestined (cf. *supra*, n. 36).

37

saints is coupled with another favorite theme of Cassiodorus: he constantly stresses the good moral life of the saints. This can be seen as the flip-side of their predestined character—the side which they show to the world. We have already seen an indication of this above where the elect Christian people are fittingly called "sheep" because of their harmless way of life.[76] This twofold character of the *sancti* is also evident in his exposition of Psalm 15, where those who are predestined to the kingdom of heaven are described as the "innocent" and the "righteous," who are obedient to the Lord and exhibit righteous deeds.[77]

The concern for the exemplary moral conduct of the members of the mini-church is even more apparent where Cassiodorus employs the category *fideles*. Although this term appears more frequently than in Augustine's works, the essential Augustinian parallelism of *fideles* with *iusti* and *sancti* is preserved. We have already seen how Cassiodorus opposes the *fideles* to the *ficti Christiani*.[78] In the exposition of Psalm 100, he comes closest to giving us a positive definition of the term. At the beginning of the psalm, the congregation of the saints had said how it loved the *fideles* and preferred their company, while fleeing the "consort of evil men."[79] Then in the exposition of verse 6, the holy congregation as the speaker of the psalm tells how it prefers the company of "rightly believing men" and saints. These are the "faithful of the earth," who are Christians living throughout the whole world and remaining in the unity of the faith. But the reliable *public* proof of faithful Christians is for them to shine forth in their own life and to reflect this splendor in the conduct of their ministers. Cassiodorus emphasizes that although this applies to the laity, it is especially important that they have priests who do not violate the divine rules.[80]

---

[76] Cf. *supra*, n. 72.

[77] *Expos.* 15.3 (*CChr* 97, 138): " 'Inter illos', hoc est sanctos qui sunt in terra viventium; non inter quoslibet saeculi se ambitione iactantes, sed inter illos tantum qui praedestinati sunt ad regna caelorum; significans innocentes et iustos, inter quos mirae factae sunt voluntates Domini Salvatoris, quando illis oboedientibus et iusta ipsius facientibus, de mortalibus aeternos reddidit, et de terrenis caelestes beneficio suae pietatis effecit."

[78] Cf. *supra*, n. 69.

[79] Cf. *supra*, n. 70. Continuing *Expos.* 100.1 (*CChr* 98, 891): "In prima parte psalmi 'cantare' se dicit 'Domino misericordiam et iudicium' consortiaque refugere pessimorum. Secunda parte fideles se asserit diligere, et cum eis gratissima habitatione versari; ..."

[80] *Expos.* 100.6 (*CChr* 98, 894-895): "Sancta illa congregatio venit ad secundum

In this rather explicit description of the faithful people, the main thrusts in the Augustinian usage of the category *fideles* are clearly enunciated. The term *fideles* applies to all true Christians who prove that they are Christians by the outstanding quality of their life. In this sense, the *fideles* are equivalent to the *iusti* and the *sancti*. As with Augustine, when Cassiodorus employs the term, he thinks of the inner circle of *boni* and not of the *mali*. He can refer to all Christians throughout the world as *fideles*; but by the very fact that he explicitly describes the manifest proof of *faithful* Christians, he implies that there are Christians who are not really *fideles*. They would only be called *fideles* by mistake because they appear as Christians within the communion of the sacraments. Nevertheless, as far as we can see, he does not make use of the term *falsi fideles* as Augustine does.[81] For this reason he does not give the impression that the category *fideles* can also cover the *mali*, even in the sense of *falsi fideles*. Rather he keeps his terminology clear by referring to the *fideles* over against the *ficti Christiani*, who lead a life obviously contrary to that of the *fideles*.

Cassiodorus holds to this clear identification of *fideles* with *iusti* and *sancti* at other places in his commentary. The *fideles* are the virgins led to the king, who conduct themselves in a chaste manner.[82] They are the decor of the church and the living stones from which the heavenly Jerusalem will be constructed.[83] In this latter image, the *fideles* appear to be set apart as a special group within the *Christiani*. It is the peculiar property of the *fideles* to abide

partem et sicut superius abominabiles sibi reddidit infideles, ita nunc recte credentium virorum desiderat habere consortium. Illos enim cordis oculos quos avertebat a pessimis, nunc se profitetur sociare cum sanctis. 'Fideles terrae' dicit, qui per totum mundum habitant Christiani. 'Sedeant' autem 'mecum', id est, in fidei unitate permaneant . . . . Sequitur, 'ambulans in via immaculata, hic mihi ministrabat'. Haec est revera fidelium Christianorum manifesta probatio et sua vita clarescere et ministrorum conversatione relucere, . . . Sed quamvis hoc nec a laicis videatur exceptum, tamen specialiter sacerdotibus probatur impositum, ut tales ministros habeant, qui divinis regulis non repugnent."

[81] Cf. *supra*, n. 49.

[82] *Expos.* 44.15 (*CChr* 97, 413): "Sed quae 'virgines' ante conspectum Domini 'adducuntur'? fideles scilicet et pudica se mente tractantes. Nam quid proderit cuiquam corpus intactum servare, si contingat eam integritatem fidei non habere?"

[83] *Expos.* 68.5 (*CChr* 97, 607): "Scimus 'capillos' nostros ad decorem capitis esse concessos; sic Ecclesiae apostoli sunt tributi, ut, sicut caesaries ornat caput, ita et omnes fideles decorare probentur Ecclesiam." *Expos.* 68.36 (*CChr* 97, 621): " 'Aedificatae sunt' enim 'civitates Iudae', quando Ecclesia catholica per humilitatem piam toto orbe diffusa est. Non enim in aedificiis parietum gaudet Dominus, qui sunt utique vetustate perituri; sed fidelium devotione, hoc est lapidibus vivis, unde Ierusualem futura construitur . . . ."

(*inhabitare*) in future habitations, whereas the dwellers (*habitare*) in the present church are more generally referred to as Christians.[84] The implication for the definition of the *fideles* is clear, although Cassiodorus does not say explicitly in this passage whether he understands *Christiani* to include the *mali*. The term *fideles* can only refer to those Christians who will make it all the way to the heavenly abode and not to those who will drop by the wayside after a temporary stay in the earthly church. As eternal building blocks they will actually become part of the heavenly Jerusalem and not be discarded beforehand as useless. As such the *fideles* must be the predestined saints, whose predestination and righteous life assure them of a place in the celestial structure.

This transition of the *fideles* into eternity fittingly sounds the predominant note when they are paralleled with the *iusti* and the *sancti* on the one hand,[85] and contrasted to the *peccatores* and the *impii* on the other.[86] As *iusti*, they endure hard blows from God in this transitory world so that he can reward them with precious gifts in eternity. And as the sheep at the right hand of Christ (Matt. 25 : 34), they receive the kingdom of the Father held ready for them since the beginning of the world, while sinners are cast into perpetual fire. A more explicit depiction of the *fideles* as the predestined *boni* is hardly possible.

Although Cassiodorus prefers to describe the members of the mini-church in terms of their splendid life and eternal destination, he also refers to *caritas* as the distinguishing mark of the saints and the

---

[84] *Ibid.*: "Sed ne tantum 'civitates', non etiam habitationes futuras adverteres, dicit 'et inhabitabunt ibi'; quod est proprie fidelium 'inhabitare', ubi constanter mentis puritate versantur. Hanc autem Ecclesiam hic habitant Christiani. 'Hereditatem' vero 'adquirunt eam', quando ad Ierusalem illam aeternam Domini miseratione pervenerint." Cf. *Expos.* 121.3 (*CChr* 98, 1150).

[85] *Expos.* 59.5 (*CChr* 97, 532): " 'Ostendit' enim 'dura' *fidelibus* suis, quando martyrum catervas saevis passionibus acquisivit. 'Ostendit' enim in hoc transituro mundo *iustis* suis 'dura', ut reddat in illa aeternitate pretiosa." Cf. *Expos.* 68.1 (*CChr* 97, 605): "... hortans *fideles* ut in Domino debeant confidere, qui Ecclesiam suam de mundi istius adversitate liberavit et *sanctis* suis in ea perenni felicitate prospexit" (Italics mine).

[86] *Expos.* 110.3 (*CChr* 98, 1016): " 'Iustitia' quippe 'eius manet in saeculum saeculi', cum *peccatoribus* dixerit: 'Ite in ignem aeternam, qui paratus est diabolo et angelis eius' [Mt. 25 : 41]. Iterumque 'iustitia eius manet in saeculum saeculi', quando *fideles* advocaverit, dicens, 'Venite, benedicti Patris mei, percipite regnum quod vobis paratum est ab initio mundi' [Mt. 25 : 34]. Sic in utraque parte 'iustitia' Domini perpetua et incommutabilis perseverat." And *Expos.* 110.7 (*CChr* 98, 1017): " 'Veritas' est enim cum *fidelibus* promissa restituit; 'iudicium', quod *impiis* comminatur, quoniam qui hic praecepta eius facere neglegunt, ibi vindictam perpetuam sustinebunt" (Italics mine).

fideles. The whole company of the saints is said to be completely filled with *caritas.* This *caritas* is an essential part of the "peace of Jerusalem," that is, of the *populus fidelis,* which will be received into the eternity of peace at the time of judgment.[87] The *virtus* of Jerusalem, of the *populus fidelis,* is without doubt the peace of the saints which is called *caritas.* Through this they become one and deserve to be the temple of the Creator.[88] In this passage the *sancti* and the *populus fidelis* are treated as equivalent, and the possession of *caritas* is the decisive factor in determining their ability to become the temple of the Lord—i.e. to be built into that heavenly structure of which they are the living stones.

It is more difficult to ascertain in exactly what sense Cassiodorus conceives of this *caritas.* On the one hand, it is comparable to being "strong in moderation" and "outstanding in devoted humility."[89] Here it corresponds to the distinguished moral quality of the life of the righteous saints. It has concrete content in the sense that the *iusti* elect to follow the commandments.[90] On the other hand, *caritas* is certainly understood as love to God as well as the God-like quality present in the saints which enables them to be made into his temple.[91] Here it resembles more the category of a virtue which is possessed, whose possession in turn establishes continuity between God and his true church of *fideles.* It is equivalent to the divine love (*dilectio*) which is present only in true Christians and not in heretics, although they share baptism in common.[92] Cassiodorus speaks elsewhere of *caritas* in this sense, and calls it the supreme virtue of the church. Indeed, to say that the church is clothed with a gold-covered vestment means that she is

---

[87] *Expos.* 121.6 (*CChr* 98, 1154): "Pacificos enim quaerit Dominus: pacificos quaerit et cohors tota sanctorum, qui caritate plenissimi sunt, qui modestia pollent, qui pia humilitate praecelsi sunt. Haec enim et sanctos vult quaerere, quae novit Dominum posse diligere. Sed istam 'pacem' cuius esse dicit? 'Ierusalem' utique, id est populi fidelis, qui tempore iudicii in pacis aeternitate recipitur."

[88] *Expos.* 121.7 (*CChr* 98, 1154): " 'Virtus' quippe ipsius 'pax' sine dubitatione sanctorum est, quae vocatur et caritas; de qua scriptum est: 'Deus caritas est' [I Io. 4 : 16]. Per hanc enim fiunt unum, per hanc templum merentur esse Creatoris; . . ." Cf. Augustine, *Enarr. in ps.* 121.12 (*CChr* 40, 1813): "Per caritatem, hoc est, per virtutem. In quo autem est caritas, fratres? Qui non sua quaerit in hac vita."

[89] Cf. *supra,* n. 87.

[90] *Expos.* 15.11 (*CChr* 97, 141).

[91] Cf. *supra,* notes 87 and 88.

[92] *Expos.* 100.4 (*CChr* 98, 893): " 'Non agnoscebam' dixit, quoniam cum se baptizatos atque signatos asserant, non in eis agnoscitur divina dilectio, qui blasphemi probantur in Domino. Illi enim Christiani veraciter recognoscuntur, qui se fidei pravitate non polluunt."

41

overlayed with the virtue of *caritas*, which outshines the other virtues present in her.[93] *Caritas* is envisioned here as the most prominent emblem of the church of the saints—that same *caritas* which Augustine sets up as the definitive mark of the mini-church.

In summary we can say that Cassiodorus preserves the basic ecclesiological structure of Augustine—the mini-church of saints and *fideles* defined by *caritas* which is mixed with false Christians in the communion of the sacraments. Cassiodorus is especially fond of emphasizing the predestined character of the saints as the side that is turned to God, as well as the high moral quality of their life which they should show to the world. Along with Augustine, he is cognizant of a distinction between the imperfect and the perfect among the saints. He distinguishes among them both in terms of beginners in the faith over against the perfect,[94] and in terms of the possession of complete or incomplete merits and virtues.[95] In spite of this distinction, however, he is concerned to emphasize the need for a sinless quality of life among the *sancti*, and his depiction of them as such tends to call forth a picture of the nearly perfect mass of the predestined filled with merits and virtues marching toward their eternal reward. This group of *sancti*, which is equivalent to the *fideles* for Cassiodorus, is the locus of the church in the most proper sense of the word.

4. The Earlier Medieval Commentaries

As in other areas of theology, the early medieval period attempted to bring order to the terminology used in dealing with ecclesiological problems. There did not always exist uniformity in the application of this terminology, but the tendency was to develop certain explicit categories which could be employed in dealing with ecclesiological

---

[93] *Expos.* 44.10 (*CChr* 97, 410): "Sequitur 'in vestitu deaurato'. Aurum ad caritatis debemus aptare fulgorem, qua virtute circumdata sancta resplendet Ecclesia. Et ne solam ibi intellegeres esse caritatem, 'in vestitu' dicit, 'deaurato', non aureo. 'Deauratum' enim dicimus, quando superducta species auri in aliqua materia glutinatur. Ideo autem supra virtutes alias gratia caritatis apparuit, quia omnia eius fulgor excellit."

[94] *Expos.* 8.3 (*CChr* 97, 90): "Unde infantes et lactentes illi intellegendi sunt, qui propter rudimenta et infantiam fidei escam non capiunt fortiorem, sed doctrina teneriori nutriuntur. Ut iste sit sensus: non solum a perfectis, qui te omnino intellegunt, es laudabilis, sed etiam ab incipientium et parvulorum ore praedicaris."

[95] *Expos.* 110.1 (*CChr* 98, 1014). He even goes so far as to distinguish among the perfect and the more perfect *sancti* and *fideles* in heaven. Cf. *Expos.* 121.5 (*CChr* 98, 1153).

themes. This is true of the exegetical tradition of the period. The men
who edited and expounded the *Glossa*,[96] for example, were forced to
select from, and to some degree systematize, the work of the fathers.
We see this tendency in the preface to the *Glossa* on the Psalms and
to Lombard's commentary, where the members of Christ are neatly
categorized into the perfect, the imperfect, and the *mali*, and where
the terms *numero* and *merito* are borrowed from Augustine to make
this distinction clear.[97] Did the commentators of this period say the
same thing as Augustine and Cassiodorus when they excerpted and
applied their terminology, or was new wine poured into old skins?

Insofar as the distinction between the *boni* and the *mali* is
concerned, the early medieval Psalms commentators hold to the
traditional view of Augustine. For example, the *Glossa*, Lombard and
Hugo take over the Augustinian exposition of *torcularia* (wine presses)
in Psalm 8 to emphasize the simultaneous presence of *boni* and *mali*
in the church until the last judgment.[98] The *Glossa* also adopts the
allegorical interpretation of the vine as the church which Cassiodorus

[96] We consider in this section primarily the *Glossa* on the Psalms (cited *Glo. ord.*
and *Glo. int.*) and its revision and extension by Peter Lombard (cited *Lomb.*). However,
we reckon to this period also the *Postilla* of Hugo of St. Cher (Cardinalis) (cited *Hugo*),
who, according to Miss Smalley (pp. 271ff.), intended his *Postilla* to be a supplement
to the *Glossa*. We have found an illustration of this intention in the exposition of the
83rd psalm (83 : 2): "Potest hoc totum legi allegorice de ecclesia militante, quae in
tabernaculum praesentis militiae pugnat. Et haec expositio est in Glosa unde omittamus
eam." Hugo's sources included not only the fathers and the *Glossa*, but also other
selected 12th and 13th century commentators. It is probable that the *Postilla*, which was
the product of a group of scholars under Hugo, was finished in approximately five years'
time, 1230-35 (Smalley, *ibid.*).

[97] *Glossa* (*prol.*): "Materia: est integer Christus, sponsus et sponsa.... Modus
tractandi. Quandoque agit de Christo secundum quod caput est, aliquando secundum
corpus, aliquando secundum utrunque.... Item de ecclesia tribus modis. Aliquando
secundum perfectos, aliquando secundum imperfectos, aliquando secundum malos: qui
sunt in ecclesia corpore, non mente; numero, non merito; nomine, non numine." The
latter part of this passage, from "Item" on, is found literally in the prologue to Peter
Lombard's commentary except for the omission of "numero, non merito" (*PL* 191, 59).
This is not surprising since Lombard's commentary is a reworking and expansion of the
Glossa, as is his commentary on the epistles of Paul (Smalley, p. 64). For Augustine on
numero/merito, cf. *In Ioh. ev.* 61.2 (*CChr* 36, 481).

[98] For Augustine, cf. *supra*, n. 38, 39. *Glo. ord.* (8 : 1): "Ecclesia dicitur torcular ubi
boni a malis opere ministrorum separantur non loco sed affectu et quasi a tegumentis
purgantur ut frumenta in area a paleis et in torcularibus vina a vinatiis; quae tamen
necessaria erant ut simul nascerentur et crescerent et ad maturitatem pervenirent."
Lomb. (8 : 1; *PL* 191, 121-122). Cf. *Hugo* (8 : 1). Cf. *Glo. int.* (110 : 1): "Hoc dicit fidelis
populus in spe quasi iam sit in angelorum societate. Qui sedebunt super sedes xii.
iudicantes xii. tribus Israel [Mt. 19 : 28], i.e. inter quos iam nullus inquus, sed modo inter
malos gemit ecclesia, qui quando iusti congregabuntur excludentur."

had employed. The vine presents an accurate picture of the church with its ornamentation of the fruit of the saints standing out against the shady leaves of sinners.[99] Following Augustine, the *Glossa* notes that only the *boni* adhere to Christ; the *mali* are allowed to live in the city of God only because the present age is a time of mercy.[100] A good example of the tendency towards clarification and simplicity in the *Glossa* is its explicit application of the Augustinian definition of *praevaricatores* to those who do not do the law of God, "even if they are in the church."[101]

The primary reference of the word "church" in these texts is to the community of the baptized. This is a much clearer and more concrete delimitation of the locus of the church than is the case with Augustine and Cassiodorus, who give the impression that the word is taken properly only for the church of the saints.[102] Hence when the early medieval commentators use the terms "false Christians" or "fictitious Christians," they are referring to Christians whom they consider to be integrally a part of the church, although they are still *mali* as opposed to the *boni*.[103] When Hugo mentions evil Christians and heretics in the same breath,[104] we may assume that the distinction between the two is a genuine one — i.e. that the false Christians really do belong to the church in its basic form as the baptized community.

[99] *Glo. ord.* (79 : 9): "Cas. 'Vineam de Aegypto' per mysticas figurationes quae gesta sunt dicit. Vinea: gens Iudaeorum in typo ecclesiae, quae inter turbas umbratiles peccantium fruge sanctorum ornatur quasi vinea inter folia fructu." Cf. *supra*, n. 68.

[100] *Glo. ord.* (100 : 8): "Augusti. Iam enumeravit quod ei non adhaeserunt nisi boni, quasi: Cur ergo malos in tua civitate tanto tempore tolerasti? Quia tempus est misericordiae." Cf. *Hugo* (100 : 8) and *supra*, n. 43.

[101] *Glo. int.* (100 : 3): " 'Facientes praevaricationes', qui legem dei non faciunt, etsi in ecclesia sint." The Augustinian equivalent is: "et quoscumque intus inveneritis." Cf. *supra*, n. 41.

[102] Our study confirms that what H. Riedlinger says in regard to the interpretation of the Song of Songs in the Anselmian school (p. 115) also applies to the *Glossa* on the Psalms — that is, the eye is directed toward the actual behavior of the members of the baptized community. This leads to a simple application of the word "church" to the baptized community and then to the making of distinctions within this context.

[103] Both the *Glossa* and Lombard give the Augustinian (followed by Cassiodorus) remark to Psalm 59 : 10. *Glo. int.* (59 : 10): "Aug.: 'alienigenae' allophyli, qui ad genus meum non pertinent. Multi enim adorant Christum qui non sunt cum eo regnaturi, i.e. ficti christiani." *Lomb.* (59 : 10; *PL* 191, 557). Cf. *Glo. ord.* (73 : 22): " 'Causam tuam'. Cas.: Dicunt enim: ubi est Deus tuus? Contemptus est a Iudaeis ambulans in terra, et a falsis christianis sedens in coelo."

[104] *Hugo* (41 : 11): "Unde bene coniungit: 'Dum confringuntur ossa mea; exprobaverunt mihi qui tribulant me inimici mei.' Haeretici et mali christiani." *Hugo* (68 : 10): "Sed de opprobriis quae dicunt contra deum haeretici et de iniuriis quas ei faciunt falsi christiani non curant."

If the term "church" has as its locus the community of all baptized Christians, it becomes even more necessary to make precise distinctions between different levels of membership within this community. We have seen how the *Glossa* and Lombard distinguish between the perfect, the imperfect and the *mali*—all of which are conceded to be members of the church and the body of Christ.[105] The categories "perfect" and "imperfect" denote different levels among the *boni* themselves—a distinction already implicit in Augustine.[106] Hugo makes an even finer discrimination among the *boni* in the prologue to his *Postilla* on the Psalms. He refers to three stages of the Christian life: repentance, righteousness and glory. The first stage is that of the "beginners"; the second stage is that of "those who are advancing"; and the third stage is that of the "perfect" or "those who have arrived." He then proceeds to apply the first fifty psalms to the first stage, the second fifty to those who are advancing, and the last fifty to the perfect.[107] Although these three stages refer to the *boni*, the first stage at least does not necessarily exclude sinners. The real *mali*, however, the unrepentant sinners, remain outside all three groups but still in the community of the baptized.

This broadening of the frame of reference, coupled with an explicit denotation of levels of membership, presents a more inclusive picture of the church than we found with Augustine and Cassiodorus. The highlight of this picture is the unashamed inclusion of sinners and *mali* in the church.[108] Accordingly, the outline of the mini-church of

---

[105] Cf. *supra*, n. 97.

[106] Cf. *supra*, n. 30. Augustine also indicates this distinction in his exposition of Psalm 8 : 3. *Enarr. in ps.* 8.5 (*CChr* 38, 50-51): "Bene autem non ait: 'Fecisti', sed: 'Perfecisti laudem'. Sunt enim in ecclesiis etiam hi qui nòn iam lacte potantur, sed vescuntur cibo, quos idem apostolus significat, dicens: 'Sapientiam loquimur inter perfectos' [I Cor 2 : 6]; sed non ex his solis perficiuntur ecclesiae, quia si soli essent, non consuleretur generi humano. Consulitur autem cum illi quoque nondum capaces cognitionis rerum spiritalium atque aeternarum, nutriuntur fide temporalis historiae . . . ." Cassiodorus refers to the possession of different capacities for understanding doctrine (cf. *supra*, n. 94). The *Glossa* and Lombard follow them both on this: *Glo. ord.* (8 : 3); *Lomb.* (8 : 3; *PL* 191, 124).

[107] *Hugo* (*prol.*): "Primus egressus et prima dieta ducit in statum poenitentiae. Secundus egressus et secunda dieta ducit in statum iustitiae. Tertius egressus et tertia dieta ducit in statum gloriae vel ad minus contemplationis divinae. Primus est status incipientium, secundus proficientium, tertius perfectorum seu pervenientium. In hoc triplici statu decantantur psalmi davitici utiliter et decenter. Primam quinquagenam decantant incipientes in primo statu. Secundam cantant proficientes in secundo statu. Tertiam cantant perfecti seu pervenientes in tertio statu."

[108] J. Beumer ("Ekklesiologische Probleme der Frühscholastik," *Sch* 27 [1952], p. 184) maintains that in this period it is generally accepted that faith and baptism make

the *boni* tends to become proportionately more blurred as these finer distinctions are added and the presence of sinners is more positively evaluated.

The haze becomes denser when we consider our key category of *fideles*. In the exposition of Psalm 1, the *Glossa* distinguishes between the kinds of judgment that will be made on the last day and the kinds of men involved in that judgment. Some will judge and not be judged, as the perfect; others will neither judge nor be judged, as the damned *infideles*. Some will be judged and will be saved, as the "mediocre *boni*"; others will be judged and will perish, as the *mali fideles*.[109] Aside from the expected distinction between the perfect and the remaining *boni*, that which immediately catches our eye is the phrase *mali fideles*. The reference of the term *fideles* has been expanded to connote all members of the community of the baptized, so that the *mali* can be referred to as *mali fideles*. The combination of *mali* with *fideles* is indicative of the concreteness of the ecclesiology of this period, where "church," and thereby *fideles*, refer to all baptized Christians, *mali* included.

Nevertheless, there is evidence that the category *fideles* can refer only to the *boni* and not to the *mali* in the traditional sense of Augustine and Cassiodorus. This is particularly true in the case of

one a member of the church. This agrees with what we have seen. But he also maintains (p. 194) that there is a general tendency to put sinners on a lower level in the church. Seen over against Augustine and Cassiodorus, this tendency is more one of appearance than of fact. The concrete reference of the word "church" to the baptized community and the creation of specific levels of membership in this church actually have the effect of assuring the sinner a place in the church, even if at a low level, whereas Augustine, forced by the reproaches of the Donatists, and especially Cassiodorus, tend to concentrate their gaze upon the inner circle of the *boni* and predestined. We see this explicit incorporation of the sinner as a positive tendency, in favor of the sinner so to speak, rather than as a somewhat negative one, as Beumer does.

[109] *Glo. ord.* (1 : 5): "In iudicio quattuor erunt ordines. Alii iudicabunt et non iudicabuntur, ut perfectissimi. Alii nec iudicabunt nec iudicabuntur, ut damnati infideles. Alii iudicabuntur et salvabuntur, ut mediocriter boni. Alii iudicabuntur et pereunt, ut fideles mali." Cf. *Lomb.* (1 : 5; *PL* 191, 65): "Nota quod quatuor ordines in iudicio erunt: Alii namque erunt, qui iudicabunt et non iudicabuntur, ut apostoli, et alii perfectissimi; alii, qui neque iudicabunt, nec iudicabuntur, quia iam iudicati sunt. Sententia enim damnationis eorum toti ecclesiae nota est, ut infideles. Alii iudicabuntur et salvabuntur, ut mediocriter boni. Alii iudicabuntur et damnabuntur ut mediocriter mali ... Duae quippe sunt partes, electorum scilicet atque reproborum; sed bini ordines eisdem singulis partibus continentur .... Professionem vero fidei retinentes, sed professionis opera non habentes, redarguuntur ut pereant, ut mediocriter mali." The *mali fideles* of the *Glossa* are clearly equivalent in Lombard to those who have *fides* without works, whom he denotes as *mediocriter mali* and explicitly as *Christiani falsi* and *falsi fideles* in his Psalms commentary prior to this passage (*PL* 191, 64-65).

Hugo. In his commentary we encounter the definition of the church which we first met in Augustine and which will become increasingly prominent: the *congregatio fidelium*.[110] Interpreting the name Asaph in the title of Psalm 78, Hugo defines the *fideles* as those who are "gathered together in the unity of faith and of good will."[111] On the surface, it appears that Hugo has in mind the whole baptized community as the *fideles*. Nevertheless, when he again expounds the meaning of the *testimonium Asaph* in the title of Psalm 79, he describes it as the "faithful people witnessing to the incarnation of Christ." And when this testimony is described in the title as for "those who will be changed," Hugo sees this as applying to those "who will be changed from unbelief to faith," and "from sin to repentance."[112] The references to the "unity of faith" and to the conversion from "unbelief to faith" imply that the limits of the church are indeed faith and baptism and thus comprehend all baptized Christians. However, the additional restrictions of "good will" and "from sin to repentance" imply that not all of the baptized really profit from the incarnation of Christ, but only the true *fideles* who are genuinely changed from sin to repentance as accomplished both in baptism and penance.

Hugo seems to be thinking very concretely of the life of the

---

[110] Cf. *supra*, n. 47. Hugo is not the first medieval theologian to use this term to describe the church. J. Beumer ("Zur Ekklesiologie der Frühscholastik," *Sch* 26 [1951] pp. 369ff.) gives examples from the twelfth century. For example, Beumer says (p. 369): "Einmal begegnet uns eine Definition der Kirche beinahe in der schulgerechten Form, wenn Nikolaus von Amiens erklärt: 'Ecclesia est congregatio fidelium confitentium Christum et sacramentorum subsidium'" (from *De articulis catholicae fidei*, iv.1 [*PL* 210, 613]). B. Tierney (*Foundations of the Conciliar Theory* [Cambridge, 1955 (reprinted 1968)] pp. 42ff.) gives several early occurrences of the term in the canonistic literature. Well-known is also the definition of Hugh of St. Victor (d. 1141) in *De sacramentis* ii.2.2 (*PL* 176, 417). Hugh sets the *multitudo fidelium* parallel to the *universitas Christianorum* and thus equates the *congregatio fidelium* with the number of baptized Christians: "Quid est ergo ecclesia nisi multitudo fidelium, universitas Christianorum?" M. Grabmann (*Die Lehre des heiligen Thomas von Aquin von der Kirche als Gotteswerk* [Regensburg, 1903], pp. 81-82) notes this occurrence of the term in Hugh of St. Victor, as well as in Moneta of Cremona (cf. *supra*, p. 5) and others, and calls it the "traditionelle allgemeine Begriffsbestimmung ... die wenigstens dem Inhalt nach bei den Vätern in den verschiedensten Variationen vorkommt." The crucial question is, as we have noted, not whether the term *congregatio fidelium* appears or not, but rather how the *fideles* are defined.

[111] *Hugo* (78 : 1): "Ecclesia enim proprie dicitur Asaph, i.e. congregatio; nihil enim aliud est ecclesia quam congregatio fidelium, qui congregantur in unitate fidei et bonae voluntatis."

[112] *Hugo* (79 : 1): "... est 'testimonium Asaph', i.e. fidelis populi testantis Christi incarnationem. 'Pro his', i.e. ad utilitatem eorum, 'qui commutabuntur', de infidelitate ad fidem, de peccato ad poenitentiam."

Christian pilgrim in the context of the sacraments of the church. In the sense that most baptized Christians make repentance for their sins and receive absolution in the sacrament of penance, they can be called *fideles*. The sum of these makes up the *congregatio fidelium*. Elsewhere, however, Hugo indicates more vividly how repentance functions as the mark of the *fideles*. Relying upon Ezekiel 9 : 4 ff., he says that the sign of the *fideles* is the cross of repentance upon their forehead, and those who can exhibit this emblem will not be killed in the day of judgment.[113] Because this cross is the criterion according to which the servants of God are distinguished from the servants of the devil and the guarantee that the *fideles* will survive the slaughter at the last judgment, it can only be the sign of those *fideles* who are, and who remain, *boni*. Does the *congregatio fidelium* encompass all Christians who make repentance, or only those whose repentance is efficacious enough that they will be bypassed by the sword of the Lord?

Given the fact that there are *mali* in the community of the baptized who may not truly repent but who cannot be accurately labeled as such until the last judgment, it may be assumed that all baptized and repenting Christians are *fideles* according to the present state of things.[114] Such a definition of the church as the congregation of the faithful would exclude only the obvious *mali*, i.e. those who refuse to

[113] *Hugo* (73 : 9): "Unde non tantum apostoli, sed et fideles possunt dicere: 'Signa nostra non vidimus'. Haec enim sunt signa fidelium quibus cognoscuntur servi dei a servis diaboli Ezech. [9 : 4]: 'Signa tau super frontes virorum gementium'. Et postea addit: 'Omnem autem super quem videritis tau, ne occidatis etc.' [9 : 6]. Sic erit in die iudicii; super quos invenietur tau, i.e. crux poenitentiae, non occidentur gladio domini." The symbol of the tau, the last letter of the Hebrew alphabet, was frequently interpreted in patristic and early medieval writings as a sign of the cross and the mark of the *fideles*. For a detailed treatment, see Hugo Rahner, *Symbole der Kirche: Die Ekklesiologie der Väter* (Salzburg, 1964), pp. 398ff. and 406ff. Rahner points out that Augustine in his anti-Donatist writings interprets this symbol as an invisible sign of the separation of the *boni* from the *mali (ibid.,* p. 417).

[114] Cf. *Hugo* (121 . 4): " 'Tribus' non omnes, sed 'tribus domini'. Et quae sunt hae determinat 'Testimonium Israel', i.e. quibus est testimonium domini quo cognoscetur quod sunt Israel secundum veritatem. Quod nunc non potest fieri quia paleae mixtae sunt granis et quandoque quod est palea putatur granum et econverso. Sed cum area domini fuerit ventilata, tunc grana a paleis distincte cognoscentur." The justification for such an assumption can also be seen in Hugo's exposition of Psalm 68 : 29: "Let them be deleted from the book of the living." In answer to the exegetical problem of how someone can be deleted from the once for all inscribed book of the living, he says that there is a twofold book—one of "present righteousness" and one of "predestination." Many will be deleted from the first, but none from the second. Thus one could say that all baptized and repenting Christians are *fideles* according to present righteousness, but only those who are not hidden *mali* are *fideles* according to predestination. For a discussion of the role of this distinction before Hugo, see Landgraf, IV/2, pp. 64ff.

repent for their sins. Hugo's explicit definition of the limits of the church shows that this is actually the case. He notes that the limits of the church, which he has just defined as the *congregatio fidelium*, are baptism and penance, and whoever is not within these limits is not within the limits of the church.[115] In the present age the church of the faithful is this comprehensive, although all of these are not "truly" *fideles* who will make the cut-off at the last judgment.

Although the term *fideles* can refer to all baptized and repenting Christians in the present church, we see that the conception of a mini-church of *boni* or true *fideles* still functions for the early medieval commentators. In addition to true repentance (as Hugo establishes it) there is another criterion which sets the *boni* apart in the present age—namely, *caritas*. In this supplementary criterion, we begin to see the scholastic application of this all-important Augustinian mark of the church. Lombard refers to the bond of *caritas* among the brethren,[116] and graphically depicts *caritas* as an essential part of the church.[117] Two thrusts of the Augustinian mark of *caritas* come to the fore here—*caritas* as the bond of unity, and the concrete *caritas* of keeping the commandments, which constitutes the outward expression of the *boni* in the church.

Turning again to Hugo, we see how *caritas* is applied to the definition of the *boni*. Hugo adopts the priority given by Augustine to *caritas* over faith. Without *caritas* faith is dead.[118] Working with the category *fides informis*, Hugo implies further that in the transition from mortal sin to a state of grace (parallel, according to the Psalm

---

[115] *Hugo* (79 : 12): "Isti enim sunt termini vineae domini, i.e. ecclesiae. Incipit enim a flumine baptismi et terminatur in mare poenitentiae. Qui hos terminos non habet non est intra limites ecclesiae."

[116] *Lomb.* (121 : 8; *PL* 191, 1144): "... sed 'propter fratres meos et proximos meos', id est, ut fratres et primi [sic] vinculo caritatis astringantur."

[117] *Lomb.* (67 : 14; *PL* 191, 608): "Vel pennae sunt duo mandata caritatis, in quibus tota lex pendet et prophetae [Mt. 22 : 40]. 'Posteriora dorsi eius', id est dorsum columbae, quod est pars posterior, caritas est ... ita in caritate connectuntur alae Ecclesiae, id est duo praecepta caritatis, quae sunt alae Ecclesiae." Cf. Augustine, *Enarr. in ps.* 67.18 (*CChr* 39, 881). By the time of Perez in the later Middle Ages, the two wings have become explicitly *fides formata* and the hope of heavenly goods: *Perez* (67 : 14): "Et sic ecclesia facta est quasi una columba ornatu virtutum et gratiarum varietate; cuius due ale sunt fides caritate formata et spes bonorum celestium, quibus alis ipsa volat inter duos terminos, scilicet a terra in celum."

[118] *Caritas* is the subject matter of Psalm 41, which is seen as supplementary to the preceding psalm which treats faith. *Hugo* (41 : 1): "In praecedenti psalmo egit de fide. Et quia fides sine caritate mortua est, ideo bene sequitur iste psalmus in quo agit de caritate. ... In hoc psalmo loquitur fidelis solum deum sitiens. Materia de qua loquitur est caritas."

text, with wisdom) this unformed faith becomes faith working through love, because only he is called wise who puts his faith to work.[119] Since the primary access to this state of grace is penance, it is not surprising that Hugo couples the mark of the *fideles* noted above, true repentance, with *caritas*. Of all the members of the church, he says, those make the best showing who are rooted firmly in the solid habit of repentance, in an exemplary way of life and in the fervor of *caritas*. This is the case no doubt because, as Hugo continues, *poenitentia* and *caritas* join man to God.[120] Hugo draws these two elements together with the necessary perseverance in his exposition of the "tribes of the Lord" in Psalm 121 : 4. The sign of the cross, which enables these true Christians to endure to the end, is faith working through love (*fides formata*), the final act of repentance and perseverance.[121]

This examination of Hugo's understanding of the *fideles* confirms that we must reckon with two possible references of the term in this early medieval period. Corresponding to the tendency towards concreteness and the explicit inclusion of *mali* in the church, the *fideles* can cover all baptized and repenting Christians regardless of the fact that *mali* are hidden among them. Hugo has not lost sight of the mini-church, however. The true *fideles* comprehend only the *boni* who are singled out by true repentance, *caritas* and perseverance to the end.[122] The Augustinian conception of an inner circle of *boni* and

---

[119] *Hugo* (110 : 10: "Initium sapientiae timor domini, ..."): "Alii dicunt quod in eis qui convertuntur de infidelitate ad fidem, prima est fides; in eis autem qui de peccato mortali ad gratiam supposita fide informi, timor est prima. Ipse etiam timor praecedit opera fidei secundum quod dicitur Act. ix[: 6], quod Paulus tremens ac stupens dixit: 'Domine, quod me vis facere?' Et secundum hoc possumus dicere, quod sapientia dicitur hic fides operans per dilectionem. Credens enim non dicitur sapiens nisi secundum quod credit operetur."

[120] *Hugo* (79 : 9): "Quinta est quia vinea radicata inter petras, in eminenti loco, in radio solis melius vinum facit. Sic illi de ecclesia qui fundati et firmati sunt in duritia poenitentiae, in eminentia vitae, in fervore caritatis melius docent et operantur ... et poenitentia et caritas coniungunt hominem deo." Cf. *ibid.* (44 : 10): "Vel per 'vestitum' intelliguntur opera sine quibus homo nudus est .... 'Vestitus' ergo 'deauratus' sunt opera in caritate facta, quae ornant ecclesiam ut assistat sponso." Petrus Cantor also emphasizes the importance of *caritas* for the *boni*, the "wheat," in his Psalms commentary (Landgraf, IV/2, p. 88, n. 194).

[121] *Hugo* (121 : 4): " 'Tribus domini', i.e. innocentes et poenitentes ... angeli et sancti .... Et in his omnibus est 'testimonium Israel', scilicet fides operans per dilectionem vel finalis poenitentia. Ezech. ix[: 6]: 'Illos in quibus videritis tau, ne occidatis.' Tau figuram crucis habet et ideo poenitentiam et fidem significat. Item ultima littera est in alphabeto Hebraeorum; ideo perseverantiam designat." Cf. *supra*, n. 113.

[122] Riedlinger (pp. 271f.) quotes a passage from the *Postilla* to Song of Songs 4 : 7 in which Hugo writes: "In quo enim macula est, non est membrum ecclesiae." Riedlinger finds this statement "anachronistisch" after all that has been said before

predestined marked by *caritas* lives on in these true *fideles*. The important thing to note is that no matter how the term *fideles* itself is employed, there remains for Hugo a mini-church of *boni* and *iusti* emblazoned with the cross of repentance and *caritas*.

The retention of this Augustinian conception of a mini-church defined through the *caritas* of her members carries with it the integral connection between ecclesiology and soteriology evident in Augustine himself. This relationship emerges with particular clarity in the *Postilla* of Hugo. In medieval exegesis, the tie between ecclesiological concerns and soteriological understanding finds a natural habitat in two of the four senses of Scripture employed in the fourfold text interpretation — in the allegorical (or mystical) and the moral (or tropological) senses. The allegorical sense applies the text to the church or *fidelis populus*, while the focus of the moral application is the individual Christian or *fidelis anima*. Much of what is said of the former in the collective sense can also be said of the latter in the individual sense. Thus Hugo can often say that a particular text can be interpreted in reference both to the church and to the faithful soul.[123]

This relationship is especially evident when the subject under discussion is the definition of the church in terms of her members. We have already seen an illustration of this above, where in the analogy of the vine — which applies allegorically to the church — Hugo speaks of the repentance and *caritas* of her members and concludes with the soteriological statement that penance and *caritas* join man to God.[124] It is even more clearly expressed where Hugo says explicitly: "The seat of God in the church and in the faithful soul is *caritas*."[125]

Hugo about the membership of sinners in the church and since Hugo obviously refers to the presence of *boni* and *mali* in the church. His explanation is that the above statement applies to the "church in the strict sense" in accord with the traditional exposition of the Song of Songs, which ascribes church membership in the narrow sense only to the *iusti*. This definition in the strict sense applies not only to the *Postilla* on the Song of Songs, however. It also corresponds to our findings in the *Postilla* on the Psalms where the true *fideles*, marked by repentance and *caritas*, correspond to the *iusti* for Hugo. That Hugo can also define the church in this narrow sense while holding to the existence of *mali* in the church is not anachronistic, but rather reflects the two-pronged reference of the terms "church" and *fideles* in this period.

[123] For example, (73 : 3): " 'In sancto,' i.e. in templo dei, quod est ecclesia vel fidelis anima." Also (44 : 11): "Moraliter potest exponi satis eodem modo, ut quod hic ecclesiae dictum est, etiam fideli animae dicatur."

[124] Cf. *supra*, n. 120.

[125] *Hugo* (88 : 14): "Sedile dei in ecclesia et in fideli anima est caritas." The same affirmation could have been made by one of the most important theologians of this

Here ecclesiology and soteriology are as closely related as possible. The most important characteristics of the church *and* of the individual *fidelis* are identical—*caritas* as the seat of God. *Caritas* guarantees the presence of God in the individual *fidelis* as well as in the church of the true *fideles*. It is indispensable for the salvation of the true *fideles* just as it is necessary for the church to be truly the church. *Caritas* establishes continuity between the individual *fidelis* and God as well as between the church and God. This simultaneous function of *caritas*, which is part and parcel of the Augustinian ecclesiological heritage, is embedded in the medieval exegetical method.

The medieval tradition attests to the fact that how one defines the *congregatio fidelium* is directly dependent upon how one defines the individual *fidelis*, and—not to be overlooked—this applies in reverse.[126] It cannot be maintained that one is necessarily dependent upon, or derived from, the other; for ecclesiological and soteriological references exist entirely independent of one another. Therefore, when attempting to define the limits of the church, one must consider both kinds of statements, especially where the element of *caritas* is employed as a distinctive mark of the church in the ecclesiological context and of the individual *fidelis* in the soteriological context. This interrelation becomes even clearer when we pursue our investigation further in the tradition.

5. A Systematic Interlude

We move briefly away from the primary object of our attention, the medieval Psalms commentaries, to consider a text from the *Summa Theologiae* of Thomas Aquinas (d. 1274), who, at least in our time, is a more well-known representative of the Dominican order than the

period, Bernard of Clairvaux. Congar ("L'ecclésiologie de S. Bernard," pp. 143ff.) speaks of Bernard's conception of the church as "an assembly of holy souls." He sees the church primarily as the *ecclesia electorum* or *congregatio iustorum*. The heart of this church, then, is *caritas*, through which these souls are united to Christ as his bride: "Le cœur de l'Eglise, c'est la charité, par laquelle les âmes, répondant à l'élection éternelle que Dieu a faite d'elles, s'unissent à Lui comme ses épouses; l'Eglise n'existe vraiment que dans les saints" (p. 144).

[126] Cf., for example, the close association of *ecclesia* and *anima* in Gerson's *De nuptiis Christi et Ecclesiae* (ed. Glorieux, VI, 198): "Attende conformiter mystice quoniam nubit Deus humanitati in Incarnatione; nubit animae singulari in fide et devotione; nubit Ecclesiae universali in perfecta carismatum omni donatione et in elargitione bonorum tam viae quam patriae." The same coupling of *ecclesia* and *anima* appears on the eve of the Reformation in the *Libellus de executione eterne predestinationis* of Johannes von Staupitz (Nuremberg, 1517), 56 and 112.

first cardinal from that order, Hugo of St. Cher. We consider this text before we pass on to the Psalms commentators of the later Middle Ages because it provides a refreshingly clear insight into the categories which we have attempted to delineate up to this point.

The text under consideration is the third article of the eighth question from Part III of the *Summa*, where Thomas takes up the problem of whether it is proper to say that Christ is the head of all men. The first objection to such an assertion is that Christ is head of his body, and since it is impossible for the *infideles* to belong to the body of Christ, he cannot be the head of all men.[127] The second objection argues that the church for which Christ gave himself has neither spot nor wrinkle (Eph. 5 : 25, 27), and since the spot or wrinkle of sin is found in many of the *fideles*, Christ cannot be the head of all the *fideles* either.[128] It is already evident that the terms *fideles* and *infideles* apply respectively to those within and outside the community of baptized Christians, whose sinful members also rate the name of *fideles*.

After asserting that Christ is the head of all men on the basis of I Timothy 4 : 10 and I John 2 : 2,[129] Thomas proceeds to explain how this can be the case. The basis of his answer lies in the distinction between the natural body of man and the mystical body of the church. In the human body all the members are present simultaneously, but the body of the church embraces men from the beginning to the end of the world. Thus all members of the body of the church are not present at any one instant of time, since some who will later have grace do not yet have it at any one particular moment, when others already possess it. Thomas then distinguishes those members of the mystical body who are "actually" or "in fact" members (*in actu*) from

---

[127] *Summa Theologiae* (cited *ST*) III q.8 a.3 obj.1: "Caput enim non habet relationem nisi ad membra sui corporis. Infideles autem nullo modo sunt membra Ecclesiae, 'quae est corpus Christi,' ut dicitur Eph. 1[: 23]. Ergo Christus non est caput omnium hominum."

[128] *ST* III q.8 a.3 obj.2: "Praeterea, Apostolus dicit, Eph. 5[: 25, 27], quod 'Christus tradidit semetipsum pro Ecclesia, ut ipse sibi exhiberet Ecclesiam gloriosam, non habentem maculam aut rugam aut aliquid huiusmodi.' Sed multi sunt, etiam fideles, in quibus invenitur macula aut ruga peccati. Ergo nec erit omnium fidelium Christus caput."

[129] *ST* III q.8 a.3 sed contra: "Sed contra est quod dicitur I Tim. 4[: 10]: 'Salvator omnium est, et maxime fidelium.' Et I Io. 2[: 2]: 'Ipse est propitiatio pro peccatis nostris; non autem pro nostris tantum, sed etiam pro totius mundi.' Salvare autem homines, aut propitiatorem esse pro peccatis eorum, competit Christo secundum quod est caput. Ergo Christus est caput omnium hominum."

those who are only "potentially" members (*in potentia*). Some who are potentially members will never become members in fact, but those who are actually members can be distinguished according to three levels.[130]

According to these levels, Christ is principally head of those who are actually (*actu*) united to him in glory. Secondly, he is head of those who are in fact (*actu*) united to him through *caritas*. And finally, he is head of those (also *actu*) who are united to him through faith. One group of those who are united to him only potentially (*potentia*) will become members of him in fact (*ad actum reducenda*), and these are members according to divine predestination. But another group of potential members will never become actual members of Christ, i.e. those men who live in the world but are not predestined.[131]

On the basis of these distinctions Thomas can reply to the above-mentioned objections in the following way. In the first place, although the *infideles* are not actually members of the church (and thereby of the mystical body of Christ), nevertheless they are potentially members.[132] By definition then, the *infideles* must encompass those persons outside the baptized community who are predestined to become members of it, as well as those who will never

---

[130] *ST* III q.8 a.3 resp.: "Respondeo dicendum quod haec est differentia inter corpus hominis naturale et corpus Ecclesiae mysticum, quod membra corporis naturalis sunt omnia simul, membra autem corporis mystici non sunt omnia simul: neque quantum ad esse naturae, quia corpus Ecclesiae constituitur ex hominibus qui fuerunt a principio mundi usque ad finem ipsius; neque etiam quantum ad esse gratiae, quia eorum etiam qui sunt in uno tempore, quidam gratia carent postmodum habituri, aliis eam iam habentibus. Sic igitur membra corporis mystici non solum accipiuntur secundum quod sunt in actu, sed etiam secundum quod sunt in potentia. Quaedam tamen sunt in potentia quae nunquam reducuntur ad actum; quaedam vero quae quandoque reducuntur ad actum, secundum hunc triplicem gradum, quorum unus est per fidem, secundus per caritatem viae, tertius per fruitionem patriae."

[131] *Ibid.*: "Sic ergo dicendum est quod, accipiendo generaliter secundum totum tempus mundi, Christus est caput omnium hominum: sed secundum diversos gradus. Primo enim et principaliter est caput eorum qui actu uniuntur sibi per gloriam. Secundo, eorum qui actu uniuntur sibi per caritatem. Tertio, eorum qui actu uniuntur sibi per fidem. Quarto vero, eorum qui sibi uniuntur solum potentia nondum ad actum reducta, quae tamen est ad actum reducenda, secundum divinam praedestinationem. Quinto vero, eorum qui in potentia sibi sunt uniti quae nunquam reducentur ad actum: sicut homines in hoc mundo viventes qui non sunt praedestinati. Qui tamen, ex hoc mundo recedentes, totaliter desinunt esse membra Christi: quia iam nec sunt in potentia ut Christo uniantur."

[132] *ST* III q.8 a.3 ad 1: "Ad primum ergo dicendum quod illi qui sunt infideles, etsi actu non sint de Ecclesia, sunt tamen in potentia. Quae quidem potentia in duobus fundatur: primo quidem et principaliter, in virtute Christi, quae sufficiens est ad salutem totius humani generis; secundario, in arbitrii libertate."

become members in fact. Aquinas thus opts for the interpretation of Augustine's statements in regard to the predestined which maintains that the predestined members who are not yet inside the baptized community will become members of the community because, as Aquinas puts it, they are predestined to become members of the mystical body in fact (*ad actum reducenda*).[133]

Secondly, Thomas' distribution of the actual members according to three levels enables him to meet the second objection that there is sin among the *fideles*. The church will never be completely without spot or wrinkle in its pilgrim state (*in statu viae*), but only when it reaches the fatherland (*in statu patriae*). Nevertheless, there are some who are not stained by mortal sin and these are members of Christ through the "actual union of *caritas*." Others, who are now subjected to mortal sin, are only potentially members of Christ unless they have the *fides informis*, in which case they are actual members in an imperfect sense. They have once imbibed the *fides formata* in baptism or penance and were actual members through *caritas*, but through the heat of mortal sin this *caritas* has evaporated and only an "unformed faith" remains behind. They are the recipients of a certain "vital injection" from the outside in that they believe, just as if a man would lift by external force one of his bodily members which had died.[134]

We have here in summary form a clear delineation of the ecclesiological categories we have dealt with up to this point. Aside from the saints who are in glory, the highest level of membership in the church is through the union of *caritas*. This corresponds to the disposition of Augustine's ecclesiology where the *boni* are united and set apart through *caritas*, but it is expressed in specifically scholastic terms as we found in somewhat vaguer form with Hugo. The true *fideles*, who are marked by repentance and *caritas* for Hugo, correspond to those members who for Thomas are united to Christ

---

[133] Cf. the discussion *supra*, pp. 23ff.

[134] *ST* III q.8 a.3 ad 2: "Ad secundum dicendum quod esse Ecclesiam 'gloriosam, non habentem maculam neque rugam', est ultimus finis, ad quem perducimur per passionem Christi. Unde hoc erit in statu patriae: non autem in statu viae, in quo 'si dixerimus quia peccatum non habemus, nosmetipsos seducimus', ut dicitur I Io. 1[: 8]. Sunt tamen quaedam, scilicet mortalia, quibus carent illi qui sunt membra Christi per actualem unionem caritatis. Qui vero his peccatis subduntur non sunt membra Christi actualiter, sed potentialiter: nisi forte imperfecte, per fidem informem, quae unit Christo secundum quid et non simpliciter, ut scilicet per Christum homo assequatur vitam gratiae; 'fides' enim 'sine operibus mortua est', ut dicitur Iac. 2[: 20]. Percipiunt tamen tales a Christo quendam actum vitae, qui est credere: sicut si membrum mortificatum moveatur aliqualiter ab homine."

through the actual union of *caritas*. It should be noted that even those members at the highest level are not free from all venial sins, but only free from mortal sin. As a result we can scarcely say that the medieval tradition conceives of a group of sinless members at the core of the church. The Augustinian restriction on the absence of sin in the *boni* to the absence of sin against *caritas* is preserved by Thomas in terms of the actual union through *caritas* of those members unstained by mortal sin.[135]

The remaining members of the baptized community possess only the *fides informis*; these Thomas describes earlier in his reply as united to Christ only through faith (*per fidem*). This category corresponds to the group which have been called *mali* up to this point. They are not truly members of Christ and, expressed in other terminology, they belong to the church only *numero, non merito*. This group is, so to speak, fluid, since if they repent and their faith is formed again through *caritas*, they become members at the inner level. In this case they do not remain *mali*, but will join the ranks of the *boni* and *iusti* not to be cut off at the last judgment.

A further clarification for us arises from Thomas' inclusion of this group among the *fideles*. The term *fideles* is clearly used by Thomas to denote all baptized Christians who are actually members of the mystical body in contrast to all *infideles* outside the baptized community who are only potentially members of this body. This is a natural development of the terminology used in the *Glossa* which speaks of *mali fideles*. When Thomas explicitly calls the church the *congregatio fidelium*,[136] we know that he is referring to all baptized Christians who are "actually" united to Christ. This is not immediately

---

[135] Cf. *supra*, pp. 32f. The absence of mortal sin is frequently the sign of the spotless character of the bride in the exposition of the Song of Songs (see Riedlinger, *passim*). Thomas treats this theme in his commentary on Psalm 44, where the *sponsa Christi* is the church. According to the traditional parallel, the *anima* is also the *sponsa Christi*, which, Thomas says, is united to God through *caritas* (in *Quaest. disp. de carit.* q.1 a.12 obj.24; Grabmann, pp. 252-253). Here in the *Summa*, however, Thomas concedes to sinners a more secure position in the church (*per fidem informem*) than he does in his *Sentences* commentary, where they belong only *aequivoce* to the church (III *Sent.* d.13 q.2 a.2; Grabmann, pp. 108-109).

[136] *ST* III q.8 a.4 ad 2: "Ad secundum dicendum quod Ecclesia secundum statum viae est congregatio fidelium: sed secundum statum patriae est congregatio comprehendentium. Christus autem non solum fuit viator, sed etiam comprehensor. Et ideo non solum fidelium, sed etiam comprehendentium est caput, utpote plenissime habens gratiam et gloriam." The church as *congregatio fidelium* includes all those *fideles* which are described in note 134 above, i.e. all those who are "actually" united to Christ as members of the baptized community.

transparent in Hugo because of his identification of the *fideles* with those Christians who are marked by *caritas* and repentance. Since Hugo tends to define the *fideles* as parallel to the *iusti* and *boni* in the sense of Augustine, it remains unclear as to whether he would also attribute the name *fideles* explicitly to the *mali*, even though the term appears to cover the *mali* insofar as they are hidden among the *boni* in the present age. Thomas leaves no doubt, however, that the category *fideles* does include the *mali*.

This broader usage of the term *fideles* will become the standard meaning of the word in most of the medieval literature. Occam (d. 1349), for example, will define the church as the *congregatio fidelium* in the broadest and most concrete sense possible. In order to be a member of this church which includes *boni* and *mali*, it suffices that one be baptized, not declare himself expressly against the faith, and so observe the external rites that one appears to belong to the church.[137] And in the medieval concept of *christianitas*, not only the baptized members of the church are called *fideles*, but all the subjects of a ruler as well, who are presumed, of course, to belong simultaneously to the church.[138] From this point on, we have to reckon basically with the broad meaning of the *fideles* as equivalent to the baptized.

A further point to note on the basis of this text from Thomas is the widest possible reference of the term, body of Christ. Such is definitely not the case with Augustine, who limits membership in the body of Christ to the *boni*. Yet, in the *Glossa* the *mali* are already reckoned members of the church as the body of Christ, and here Thomas expands it to include all men, even those potential members who are not among the baptized regardless of whether they are predestined to become actual members or not.[139] The mystical body of Christ can be said to encompass all men, but the basic sense of the

[137] Lagarde, p. 46. For Occam, the terms *fideles, catholici, christiani* and *credentes* are synonymous (*ibid.*, p. 44). Oberman points out that Biel also understands the church as the *congregatio fidelium*, following Occam in emphasizing the inclusion of laymen in the church (*The Harvest of Medieval Theology* [rev. ed., Grand Rapids, 1967], p. 419).

[138] See Walter Ullmann, *The Individual and Society in the Middle Ages* (Baltimore, 1966) pp. 9, 24. Lagarde (pp. 49ff.) notes that for Occam the *congregatio fidelium* denotes those living under the double aspect of religious and political authority.

[139] For the development of the doctrine of the church as the mystical body of Christ as it grew out of the Eucharistic discussions, see E. Kantorowicz, *The King's Two Bodies* (Princeton, 1957), pp. 194ff. For the association of the terms *corpus mysticum* and *congregatio fidelium* and their employment in canonistic thought, see Tierney, pp. 132ff. Here both terms were used in the broad sense to refer to all baptized Christians.

word "church" remains for Thomas the *congregatio fidelium*—the community of the baptized in unity.

This inclusion of the *mali* in the congregation of the faithful and the extension of the body of Christ to all men represent departures from the Augustinian definition of these terms. Nevertheless, the Augustinian ecclesiological structure itself remains intact. There exists for Thomas, as for Hugo, a mini-church of *boni fideles* within the baptized community even though this external community is designated as the congregation of the faithful. This mini-church retains its Augustinian badge of *caritas* as evidence that it is not guilty of mortal sin.[140] Furthermore, the Augustinian priority of *caritas* over faith is preserved insofar as *caritas* mediates a closer actual union with Christ than plain (unformed) faith. For faith to be worthy of attaining this degree of union, it must be adorned with precisely this *caritas*.

In spite of the recasting of this essentially unchanged structure into scholastic molds, we see a consensus forming around the concept of a mini-church marked by *caritas* at the heart of the baptized community. The occurrence of this pattern in a representative systematic theologian such as Thomas reinforces similar findings in

---

[140] According to Mersch (Vol. II, pp. 235ff.), the basic twofold distinction made by Thomas between the actual members of Christ according to *caritas* and according to *fides informis* is not the only possible distinction to be found in this period. It is possible even to lose *fides* but keep the external profession of religion and be designated "more removed members." The distance increases if one falls into schism or is excommunicated, and in this case one may be considered "outside." Heretics and the damned are totally excluded. We are interested, however, in the basic twofold distinction within the *fideles* determined by the presence or absence of *caritas*. P. Fehlner points to this same distinction in Bonaventure's ecclesiology (*The Role of Charity in the Ecclesiology of St. Bonaventure* [Rome, 1965], p. 36). Those who have *caritas* are members of the church *actu*, whereas the baptized Christian in a state of sin can potentially acquire *caritas* and thus belongs to the church only *potentia* (for Thomas still *actu*). Fehlner notes that Bonaventure also regards *caritas* as the bond of ecclesiastical unity (*ibid.*). Thus he is forced to discuss the same problem which we have treated in regard to Augustine: how can *caritas* be the mark of unity (*boni* and *mali* in the church of the sacraments) as well as the mark of the *boni* alone. Fehlner solves the dilemma by maintaining that "Bonaventure's view of charity is primarily centered around the uncreated gift of charity, or the person of the Holy Spirit," and thus "for Bonaventure to affirm that charity is the essence of church unity is for him to affirm the presence of the Holy Spirit, wherever, whenever, and whatever degree and state of the Church or mystical body of Christ is actualized" (*ibid.*, p. 41). More important than this possible solution, however, is the visible influence of Augustine's ecclesiology, which is the source of the dilemma. For further occurrences of this distinction between membership *per fidem informem* and *per fidem formatam* in the systematic tradition, see J. F. Stockmann, *Joannis de Turrecremata O.P. vitam eiusque doctrinam de corpore Christi mystico* (diss. Fribourg, Bologna, 1952) p. 75.

the Psalms commentaries of such successors of Augustine as Cassiodorus and Hugo. Whether or not we can establish the existence of such a consensus for all of our medieval Psalms commentators depends upon the outcome of our investigation into the Psalms exegesis of the later Middle Ages.

6. The Later Medieval Commentators

What new developments, if any, emerge in Lyra, Paul of Burgos, Perez and Faber Stapulensis in regard to our theme—*congregatio fidelium*? As one reads these commentaries, there is no question that the term *fideles* has established itself as the primary denotation of the members of the church. And yet, even though we have reached relative clarity in regard to the twofold reference of this category—to the entire community of the baptized in unity or to the *boni* alone—the case is not yet completely closed.

Nicholas of Lyra. — In accord with our supposition for this period that the term *fideles* has the broadest connotation possible, Lyra implies that the *fideles* can denote both those who belong to the church only *numero* as well as those who belong *numero et merito*, i.e. both those who belong to the total number of the baptized as well as to the *boni* alone.[141] The matter is complicated, however, by Lyra's moral application of certain psalms to the individual *fidelis* "who is a member of Christ."[142] The same moral application is made to the *devotus fidelis*; this modifier implies that he is referring only to that *fidelis* who is *numero et merito* in the inner circle of the *boni*. This *devotus fidelis* is described in the context of Psalm 41 as he who considers this life a prison and longs for the heavenly city.[143] It is hard

---

[141] *Lyra*[m] (68 : 36): " 'Quoniam deus salvam faciet Sion', id est ecclesiam militantem. 'Et aedificabuntur civitates Iudae', id est congregationes plebis christianae quae aedificantur in moribus et fide. 'Et inhabitabunt ibi', scilicet illi qui fideles sunt non solum numero sed etiam merito. 'Et haereditate acquirent eam', id est ecclesiam in qua iam sunt secundum statum ipsius militantis et acquirent eam secundum statum ipsius triumphantis; est enim unica ecclesia tamen duos habens status." *Lyra*[m] denotes the moral exposition of Lyra.

[142] *Lyra* (8: end of literal expos.): "Moraliter autem posset exponi psalmus iste, qui est de Christo capite ut visum est, de quolibet fideli qui est membrum Christi."

[143] *Lyra*[m] (41 : 1): "Moraliter potest exponi de quolibet devoto fideli qui considerans hanc vitam esse captivitatem suspirat ad civitatem coelestem, sicut Paulus Phil. i[: 23]: 'Desiderium habens dissolvi et esse cum Christo.' " Cf. *Lyra* (15: end of lit. expos.): "Moraliter autem posset exponi psalmus iste de quolibet fideli qui est membrum Christi expectans resurrectionem futuram et positionem sui ad dexteram cum aliis electis secundum quod habetur Matthei xxv[: 33ff.]."

to imagine that this *fidelis* could be one of the *mali* in the external church of the sacraments. What are the consequences of these epithets, *devotus* and "member of Christ," for the definition of the *fidelis*?

If we approach the description of the *fidelis* from the aspect of his being a member of Christ, we are confronted immediately with Lyra's understanding of the church as *corpus mysticum*. There are two basic options open to him: either to define the body of Christ in the narrow sense of Augustine or in the broader sense of Thomas. It appears that Lyra opts for the broader interpretation. At the beginning of his moral interpretation of Psalm 8, Lyra says that the psalm is able to be interpreted mystically in reference to the mystical body which is the church in *both* of its states: the militant church and the triumphant church.[144] Although such a definition does not include the "potential" members of Thomas outside the baptized community, it certainly embraces the total community of the baptized plus the saints already in the heavenly city. Since this statement of Lyra follows directly upon his references to every *fidelis* who is a member of Christ,[145] the conclusion is unavoidable that the *fidelis* can be every member of the baptized community. The broad reference of the *corpus mysticum* over against the inner circle of the *boni* is also indicated in his exposition of Psalm 15 where Lyra opposes the *corpus mysticum*, taken for the church gathered from the Gentiles, to the number of the elect.[146]

Thus in the consideration of the attribute *devotus* and the predicate "member of Christ," we find an apparent contradiction insofar as the locus of the *fideles* is concerned. When we hear of the devoted *fidelis*, we are forced to think in terms of the *boni*; on the other hand, if we inquire as to his status in the *corpus mysticum*, we find that the *fidelis* could be any member of the baptized community.

The solution has to lie in the same direction as it does with Hugo. The explicit Augustinian emphasis upon the simultaneous existence of *boni* and *mali* in the church of the baptized has become an implicit assumption in the medieval commentaries which only occasionally

---

[144] *Lyra*[m] (8 : 1): " 'Domine, dominus noster.' Sensus litteralis huius psalmi est de triumpho Christi sed mystice potest exponi de suo corpore mystico quod est ecclesia, cuius est duplex status: militans et triumphans."

[145] Cf. *supra*, n. 142.

[146] *Lyra*[m] (15 : 1): "Licet autem moraliter posset exponi de quolibet christiano qui est de numero electorum, videtur tamen mihi exponendus magis proprie de corpore Christi mystico accepto pro ecclesia de gentibus collecta."

turns up in explicit form. The category *fideles*, which originally denoted only the *boni* and was given in the form of *mali* or *falsi fideles* when it was employed to cover the *mali*, has become so common that it refers to all members of the baptized community without pinpointing the *mali* as *mali fideles*. If we were able to ask one of these commentators who the *fideles* really are, we would certainly receive the answer that they are the members of the baptized community. But if we pressed the matter, our commentators would agree that only the *boni* are truly *fideles*. Since the *mali* are mixed with the *boni* in the present, however, they speak in general of the *fideles*, except when they occasionally make the distinction *numero* or *merito*, or otherwise have reason to differentiate more carefully.[147]

It often happens, therefore, that the *fideles* are described specifically in terms of the *boni* and yet appear to include all baptized Christians.[148] The medieval commentators see no particular contradiction in this, since all baptized Christians — seen from the outside — have equal opportunity to make it to the heavenly fatherland, and if there are *mali* or reprobate among them, they will not make it anyhow, whether they are mistakenly called *fideles* or not.

When the chips are down, however, our commentators do not hesitate to say what is required in order for the *fideles* to become true *fideles* and *boni* and thus survive the hazardous journey to the heavenly Jerusalem. Lyra refers to the citizens of the cities of Judea, which are the churches, as the *fideles* who are united in faith and *caritas*, and maintains that the *fideles* dwell there *numero et merito*,

---

[147] Tierney (pp. 202f.) indicates how in the fourteenth and fifteenth centuries, the definition of the church as the *congregatio fidelium* became the predominant one in canonistic thought over against the various definitions of the thirteenth century canonists where *ecclesia* was also defined as the bishops alone, the cathedral chapter, the clergy of a diocese, etc. Especially interesting is the quote he gives from Guido de Baysio (d. 1313), where the church is defined *either* as the *collectio sanctorum* or the *catholicorum collectio*, reflecting both the broad and narrow meanings of the term *fideles* (Tierney, p. 203).

[148] For example, *Lyra* (15 : 6): " 'Etenim haereditas etc.', id est ecclesia fidelium quae vocatur haereditas Christi, sicut scribitur in persona domini Hiere. 51[: 19] 'Qui fecit omnia ipse est et Israel sceptrum haereditatis eius; dominus exercituum nomen eius.' " See *WA* 55/I, 117. 1ff. for a discussion of the interpretation of the *haereditas Christi* in the tradition. The so-called "transitive" interpretation, where the heredity is given as the church, goes back to Cassiodorus, who describes it as the predestined saints (cf. *supra*, n. 73). Hugo expressly interprets it as the *boni*: *Hugo* (15 : 6): "Vel transitive potest legi sic: 'Dominus est pars haereditatis meae', id est bonorum qui sunt haereditas Christi." Thus, when Lyra describes the heredity as the *ecclesia fidelium*, one is tempted to conclude that he has the *boni* in mind, although the formulation could cover the whole communion of the sacraments.

since, paraphrasing Augustine, *"caritas* alone makes the division between the sons of perdition and the sons of the kingdom."[149] The reference to the inhabitants of the "churches" in general would imply that the *fideles* in the broad sense are intended, but Lyra does not hesitate to define precisely what *fideles* he means—namely, those united in faith and *caritas* and dwelling in the churches *numero et merito*. Of course, he is cognizant of the presence of evil men mixed in with these true *fideles*, but his gaze is directed only at the latter, although he speaks in general of the inhabitants of the churches.

Thus as we see with Hugo and most clearly with Thomas, a broad connotation of the *fideles* does not preclude a restriction on the number of these *fideles* who are *boni* and truly *fideles*. The *fidelis* who commits mortal sin, and thus loses *caritas* while retaining only an unformed faith, does not cease to be called *fidelis*; but it is necessary to have his faith "reformed" through *caritas* in order for him to recover his status as truly *fidelis*. The church as the congregation of all the baptized *fideles* in unity remains the broad frame of reference in which the true *fidelis* forms his faith through *caritas*. Nevertheless, the mini-church of true *fideles* distinguished by the mark of *caritas* remains.

Jacobus Perez of Valencia. — The same restriction of a portion of the *fideles* to the *boni* and the righteous is evident in the Psalms commentary of the Spanish bishop, Perez of Valencia. True, he also works from a broad frame of reference. The "whole Christian religion" is called the congregation of the righteous insofar as it is the congregation of all the faithful. These are defined in the broadest possible way by participation in the sacraments and the *fides quae*.[150]

---

[149] *Lyra* (68 : 36-37): " 'Et aedificabuntur civitates Iudae.' Quia apostoli aliique discipuli de monte Sion missi sunt ad praedicandum per orbem universum, ubi per eos constitutae sunt et ordinatae ecclesiae, quae dicuntur civitates eo quod civitas est civium unitas; ibi autem uniebantur fideles in fide et caritate .... 'Et inhabitabunt ibi.' Fideles Christi. 'Et haereditate etc.' Quia decedentibus primis alii quasi haereditarie succedunt eis. 'Et semen servorum eius,' i.e. Christi et vocantur hic eius servi sui discipuli, quorum semen, i.e. imitatores eorum, possident ecclesias per orbem. 'Et qui diligunt nomen eius', existentes in caritate. 'Habitabunt in ea', numero et merito, quia sola caritas dividit inter filios perditionis et regni." Cf. *supra*, n. 58.

[150] *Perez* (110 : 1): "Et nota quod tota religio christiana dicitur congregatio iustorum inquantum est adunatio omnium fidelium. Sed dicitur consilium iustorum inquantum omnes in ea congregati conveniunt et consentiunt in unam fidem et unum baptisma, et omnes venerantur in hoc sacramentum et cetera sacramenta ecclesiastica et credunt omnibus xii. articulis fidei." Werbeck (p. 111) points out that Perez understands *fides*

At the same verse he gives a similar definition and opposes this *ecclesia fidelium* to the congregation of the reprobate Jews, Saracens and heretics, that is, to all *infideles* who are outside the communion of the sacraments.[151] We could hardly ask for a clearer statement on the scope of the *fideles* as including all baptized Christians in unity.

Perez is naturally familiar with the distinction between the *boni* and the *mali* in the church. The *mali* (or *falsi*) *Christiani* and the heretics are of the same breed, and Perez hardly distinguishes between them in assigning both to the left hand of the church over against the *catholici* and *boni christiani* who stand on the right.[152] It is hardly conceivable that these *mali Christiani* can be called *fideles*, especially when he equates the *fideles* with the *iusti* and the *sancti* at other points in his commentary.[153] This equation with the *iusti* would imply that even in the broad definitions given above, the *congregatio iustorum* which is the *congregatio fidelium* hardly includes evil Christians, since their comrades in arms, the heretics, are explicitly excluded from that assembly.

What Perez is really after becomes clearer when we consider the place of predestination in his ecclesiological structure. Strongly influenced by Augustine,[154] he makes more reference to the role of predestination than we have found in any of the commentators since Cassiodorus. We can even go so far as to speak of a church of the

primarily as *fides quae creditur*, i.e. as the articles of faith which are to be believed, as in this text.

[151] *Perez* (110 : 1): "Et hoc faciam in consilio et congregatione iustorum, i.e. fidelium, quasi dicat, licet confessio mea non sit credenda et acceptanda in congregatione Iudeorum, reproborum et sarracenorum et hereticorum, tamen recipietur apud fideles, quia hoc sacramentum eucharistie de quo intendo predicare et cantare recipietur in tota ecclesia fidelium et celebrabitur."

[152] *Perez* (88 : 12-13): "... et aquilo qui sunt heretici et falsi christiani et frigidi. Et invenitur mare, scilicet persecutiones. In hebreo habetur: 'Aquilonem et dextrum tu creasti,' quia in ecclesia invenitur dextrum et sinistrum. Dextrum sive meridionale sunt catholici sive boni christiani; sinistrum ecclesie sunt heretici et mali christiani. Illos enim permittit deus in ecclesia; istos autem creat per gratiam."

[153] *Perez* (88 : 6): "... in ecclesia sanctorum, id est omnium fidelium." Cf. *Perez* (121 : 2): "Nam ego previdi in spiritu qualiter 'pedes nostri erant stantes in atriis tuis', id est qualiter omnes iusti et fideles debemus habitare in te, hic per gratiam, in futuro per gloriam."

[154] Werbeck (pp. 52ff.) has pointed to the strong influence of Augustine on Perez. He is the most-cited authority in the Psalms commentary, although there is explicit reference to only one of the anti-Donatist writings, *De unico baptismo*, where the same passage is cited on five different occasions. Perez was also a member of the same order as Luther (Augustinian Hermits). These two factors alone are enough to arouse even superficial interest in his possible influence on Luther. Cf. *supra*, Introduction, n. 5.

predestined in Perez. He maintains that Christ congregated into the church *only* those whom the Father had predestined in eternity, and indeed makes this the predominant theme in his exposition of Psalm 15. This church is composed of the righteous *alone*, the congregation of spiritual and holy men, in contrast to carnal and impious men.[155]

Perez is also concerned to emphasize that this church of the predestined includes the *fideles* of both the Old and the New Testament, from Adam until the last *electus*. This is the church, or *corpus mysticum, adam mysticus, homo mysticus*, or city of God, as he embellishes the Augustinian terminology for this phenomenon with his own special terms.[156] The question how this church of the predestined can be reconciled with the church of the present time encompassing both *boni* and *mali* is solved in the same way as with Hugo: God has to engage in double bookkeeping. Those who are predestined according to the eternal purpose are inscribed with indelible ink in the book of predestination. This book is already closed. In the second book, a book of running accounts (*secundum praesentem dispositionem*), the names of the *fideles* are constantly being entered or erased according to whether a particular *fidelis* is momentarily in a state of grace or has fallen into sin.[157] In the end,

---

[155] *Perez* (15 : 3): "Ex quibus patet quod filius ex tempore vocavit et iustificavit et redemit et gratificavit et magnificavit quos pater ab eterno predestinavit et hos solos Christus in ecclesiam congregavit, ceteris in suis carnalibus desideriis et mundanis adinventionibus permanentibus; tota ergo voluntas et desiderium et conatus Christi fuit voluntatem patris adimplere quos ipse predestinaverat redimere et iustificare." Cf. (15 : 4); (15 : 6).

[156] *Perez* (76 : 1): "... et ideo diffinitur corpus mysticum ecclesiasticum, quod est multitudo fidelium Christum expectantium sive in fide et spe Christi viventium, incipiens ab Adam usque ad ultimum electum. Et eadem est diffinitio ipsius ecclesie. Nam corpus mysticum et ecclesia convertuntur sicut dictum est in prologo. Et sic Adam cum tota posteritate sua fidelium dicitur corpus mysticum sive Adam mysticus, sive homo mysticus, sive ecclesia, sive civitas dei, sive populus dei." Cf. *Perez (prol.* tr.3 c.2 cl.7).

[157] *Perez* (68 : 29): "Nam unus liber dicitur divine predestinationis secundum eternum propositum, et tunc nihil aliud est nisi divina voluntas beneplaciti que ab eterno proposuit gratiam iustis preparare; et eos elegit et in suo libro ascribendos et iustificandos proposuit. In quo libro ab eterno primo fuit scriptus Christus homo et virgo Maria et omnes apostoli et iusti. Secundus liber dicitur liber vite secundum presentem dispositionem; et iste est conscientia cuiuslibet iusti disposita per gratiam. Et iste liber non est in deo nisi obiective inquantum deus prospicit in anima iusti similitudinem sue bonitatis, per quam iustus est deo gratus et acceptus secundum presentem dispositionem. Et de isto libro multi noviter delentur per peccatum et in eo noviter scribuntur per novam gratiam .... Differt ergo liber vite secundum eternum propositum a libro vite secundum presentem dispositionem, nam ille est solum in deo, iste autem in conscientia hominis." For Hugo, cf. *supra*, n. 114.

of course, the books must balance out, i.e. the names which appear among the *iusti* in the second book at the last judgment will be identical with the names in the book of predestination. In the present age, however, this system of double bookkeeping allows Perez to speak both of a fixed church of the predestined and of a church including *boni* and *mali* where the number of the *iusti* is always fluid. Thus the *fideles* can appear both as the predestined *iusti* and as the total number of baptized Christians, many of whom are constantly oscillating between *iusti* and *mali*.

With Perez, therefore, we find the same twofold reference as with our other commentators after Cassiodorus. The *fideles* can denote all members of the baptized community because the *mali* remain sufficiently camouflaged in the present state of the church. In this sense, the *fideles* have the broad reference which we find in Thomas and which is also present with Lyra. Nevertheless, Perez would agree that the true *fideles* are equivalent to the truly *boni* and *iusti*, the *electi*, who are predestined to the heavenly Jerusalem and who will emerge with clarity when the time is ripe.

Faber Stapulensis. — It is important to keep this double reference of the *fideles* in mind when we endeavor to determine the locus of the *populus fidelis* in the *Quincuplex Psalterium* of the French humanist Faber Stapulensis (d. 1536). He is consistent with the tradition in employing the term very frequently, but on the whole his exposition is only sparsely dotted with any kind of precise explanations or definitions of this or any other ecclesiological category. This is unfortunate, since it would be especially interesting for our investigation of Luther to see what effect this influential work had upon the young biblical professor at work on his first major lecture course.

The clues we have indicate that Faber is cognizant of the two-pronged reference of the category *fideles*. He speaks of Zion, the *ecclesia fidelium,* as the steadily expanding "congregation of the peoples" who avow and profess God.[158] He also pits the *populus fidelis* against the *infideles*. As we have seen, this normally implies the

---

[158] *Faber*[e] (68 : 36): "Quoniam deus salvam faciet Sion et edificabuntur civitates Iude.' Quoniam pater meus salvabit ecclesiam fidelium et multiplicabuntur et accrescent congregationes populorum deum agnoscentium et confitentium." We use the following notation for citing texts from different parts of Faber's exposition: *Faber*[t] = *titulus*; *Faber*[e] = *expositio continua*; *Faber*[a] = *adverte*. The verse numbers which Faber uses do not correspond to the standard Vulgate enumeration. We give only the Vulgate enumeration in accordance with our procedure.

convergence of the *fideles* with the entire baptized community—
especially, as the case is here, when the *fideles* are explicitly contrasted with the pagans, Turks and *infideles*.[159] In the allegorizing
interpretation of Psalm 113, Faber interprets the "house of Israel"
as the *universus populus fidelis,* which has been enlightened with
knowledge of the true God, and "the entire holy people."[160]

The broad connotation of the *populus fidelis* can be seen as the
natural result of Faber's hermeneutical concern. Faber's complete
absorption of any kind of traditional literal sense into the spiritual
sense[161] tends to concentrate interest on Christ and the church as
self-evident speakers of the psalm rather than objects of detailed
interpretation.[162] The *populus fidelis* is, so to speak, a given for Faber,
which functions in the interpretation of the psalm but which itself
does not need interpreting. It represents automatically the church in
its most basic meaning—the baptized community. Thus Faber is more
interested in employing the *populus fidelis* as an interpretive category
than in analyzing its nature or calling attention to fine points in its
make-up.

Nevertheless, this hermeneutical hindrance does not totally exclude
any definitive remarks on the *fideles.* The *sancti* of Psalm 15 are
described as the "pure and unstained faithful."[163] God himself is the
lover of the "faithful and those trampling vices underfoot."[164] And in

---

[159] *Faber*ᵃ (73 : 20): "Hic itaque populus fidelis in spiritu precatur dominum ut
attendat ad sanctum evangelium quo per universum orbem publicetur et cognoscatur.
Quia terre replete sunt tenebris ignorantie cognitionis, habitationes inique offuse
obruteque sunt illis tenebris, quia habitationes inique tot per universam ferme terram
paganorum, turcarum, et infidelium replete tenebris terrestribus, erroribus terrenis,
depravationibus divine legis et heresibus." Cf. *Faber*ᵗ (101): "Psalmus deprecatio ecclesie,
id est populi fidelis, infidelium calamitate pressi ad Christum dominum. Propheta in
spiritu populum fidelem orantem inducit."

[160] *Faber*ᵃ (113): "Quia hec eductio populi Hebraici de Aegypto per Mosen fuit
figura liberationis generis humani de potestate principis tenebrarum. Ideo psalmus ad
allegoriam tractus facile sue restituitur veritati. Domus Israel: universus populus fidelis
qui ad veri dei agnitionem est illuminatus, et cuncta plebs sancta. Domus Aaron: pars
sacerdotalis et universi rei sacre ministri."

[161] *Faber (praefatio):* ". . . et videor mihi alium videre sensum, qui scilicet est
intentionis prophetae et spiritus sancti in eo loquentis. Et hunc literalem appello, sed
qui cum spiritu coincidit." See Preus, pp. 137ff., for a more detailed analysis.

[162] Thus the *populus fidelis* appears in the title of many psalms as the prophetically
intended speaker. Cf. *supra,* n. 159.

[163] *Faber*ᶜ (15 : 3): " 'Sanctis' . . . fidelibus puris et incoinquinatis qui sunt in orbe
terrarum eius."

[164] *Faber*ᶜ (83 : 9): ". . . Deus amator fidelium et vitia calcantium, precibus meis
inclina favorem tuum."

66

the exposition of Psalm 100 : 6, Faber presents Christ delivering the following oration:

> 'My eyes are toward the faithful of the earth, etc.' I affectionately look out for those who faithfully receive the commandments of God on earth, that they might share with me the kingdom of my father. He who was keeping the law of God in singleness and purity of mind was my obedient servant.[165]

It is improbable that the faithful here refer to the *mali*. This does not mean that the *fideles* are described as sinless or that the church is regarded as a sinless entity. The terminology is rather reminiscent of Augustine, who, in the exposition of the same psalm, speaks of a "time of mercy" and the consequences of transgressing the law.[166] Without discoursing upon the scholastic requirement of *caritas,* Faber pictures the *fideles* as abiding faithfully by the law of God. Although there are certainly sinners among the true *fideles,* he speaks in a deceptively simple manner of the church as this faithful group of pure, "law-abiding" Christians. Once again we encounter statements on the *fideles* as *boni* transposed upon, and entwined with, depictions of the *ecclesia fidelium* as the baptized community.

The mark of caritas.—Insofar as Faber emphasizes the concrete conduct of the *fideles* in keeping the commandments and "trampling vices underfoot," he forms a notable exception to the later medieval commentators who insist upon *caritas* as the mark of the true *fideles.* We recall, for example, the exclusive role given to *caritas* by Lyra in defining those *fideles* who dwell in the church *numero et*

---

[165] *Faber*^{c} (100 : 6): " 'Oculi mei ad fideles terre, ...' Affectus animi mei et providentia ad fideliter mandata dei suscipientes in terra, ut mecum participes sint in regno patris mei; observans in simplicitate et puritate mentis legem dei, ille mihi famulabatur et obsequium prestabat." In the sense of Augustine, those who transgress the commandments will be exterminated at the second coming of Christ. *Faber*^{c} (100 : 8): "In adventu meo exterminavi omnes impios orbis, ut extirparem de regno dei universos qui mandata dei prevaricantur aut contemnunt."

[166] Cf. *supra,* notes 41 and 43. Cf. *Faber*^{a} (100 : 8): "Ultimo versu ... ut legimus, primo adventui applicari potest. Nam in primitiva ecclesia universa ferme exterminata est idolatria et per baptismum omnes peccato mortui, ut resurgerent iustificati in civitate domini, monte Sion et tabernaculo dei cum hominibus. Verum ut sacer Hieronymus traduxit: de secundo adventu recte intelligi potest; cum in ipsis exordiis ipsoque futuri seculi diluculo dicturus est peccatoribus et impiis: 'Discedite a me maledicti in ignem eternum, qui paratus est diabolo et angelis eius' [Mt 25 : 41]. Ergo in utroque adventu delentur peccatores, sed in primo per correptionem et iustificationis vivificationem, in secundo vero per secundam mortem et eternam condemnationem."

merito and who will make it as "sons of the kingdom."[167] For Lyra it is the *fides formata* by which the faithful are led into the militant church,[168] and *caritas* is the form of the other virtues which make up the vestment of the church and the soul.[169] Indeed, the *fideles* move from one of these virtues to the other as they accumulate grace on their journey toward the blessed vision.[170]

This traditional interplay between ecclesiology and soteriology is carried almost to extremes by Perez. After holding that the church is called a sparrow because it flies to heaven on the wings of faith and *caritas*,[171] Perez gives a detailed account of the grades by which the faithful ascend to a state of perfection in this life and arrive in heaven. The grades of virtue are contained in the grace of the sacraments and, together with the *fides articulorum* and the understanding of the divine law, they are the means by which Christ the lawgiver enables us to reach the fatherland.[172] After identifying these grades as the *fides quae*, the hope of future glory and good works done in *caritas*, Perez concludes that the Christian having met these requirements is truly righteous and works according to the righteousness of faith formed by hope and *caritas*.[173] At the end of his exposition, he maintains that no one is able to see God in glory, unless he acquires merits through the exercise of virtues in this life.[174]

---

[167] Cf. *supra*, note 149.

[168] *Lyra*^m (42 : 3): " 'Et adduxerunt in montem sanctum tuum,' id est ecclesiam militanten per fidem caritate formatam." Cf. *Burgos* (83 : 6 *Additio* 2): " 'Semitae in cordibus suis.' Fides enim formata proprie sunt semitae tendendi in divinam cognitionem et amorem."

[169] *Lyra*^m (44 : 10): " 'Astitit regina.' Descripta sponsi conditione ponitur hic consequenter descriptio sponsae, scilicet ecclesiae suae, cum dicitur: 'Astitit regina,' i.e. ecclesia quae stare debet per virtutis eminentiam et non iacere per pusillanimitatem. Ideo subditur: 'A dextris tuis', i.e. in prosperitate virtutis. Ideo subditur: 'In vestitu', scilicet virtutum quae sunt vestes animae. 'Deaurato', scilicet caritate quae est forma virtutum." Cf. Cassiodorus to the same verse, *supra*, n. 93.

[170] *Lyra* (83 : 8): " 'Ibunt de virtute in virtutem', semper proficiendo in augmento gratiae donec perveniant ad terminum visionis beatae."

[171] *Perez* (83 : 4): "Ecclesia etiam passer dicitur inquantum per fidem et caritatem volat in celum."

[172] *Perez* (83 : 5-8): "Unde notandum quod Christus legis dator duo dedit nobis, quibus possemus ad illam patriam pervenire, scilicet gratiam et veritatem. Gratia est virtus sacramentorum qua purgamur a peccatis et adiuvamur et preservamur et penitentiam agimus. Veritas autem est fides articulorum et intelligentia legis divine. Sed ista gratia continet in se quosdam gradus virtutum per quos fideles ascendunt in statum perfectionis in hac vita usque in celum."

[173] *Ibid.*: "Et tunc christianus dicitur vere iustus et operatur secundum iustitiam fidei formate spe et caritate."

[174] *Perez* (83: *conclusio*): "Quarta conclusio quod nemo potest videre deum deorum

Nowhere in the exegesis of the Psalms is the medieval soteriological structure worked out more clearly in conjunction with ecclesiology than in Perez. This is nicely illustrated by his exposition of Psalm 44 where he discusses the three nuptials of Christ—the incarnation, reconciliation and glorification. Instead of treating the nuptial of reconciliation as the marriage of Christ with the individual soul as we might expect, Perez says that it is the marriage of Christ with the *church*.[175] The vestments of Christ (verse 9) in this nuptial are the distilled aromas of holiness and doctrine and the myrrh of passion, and they exist for the benefit of the *fideles* in the church in this mystical union:

> The myrrh of passion flowed from the robe of Christ, and its potency was captured and deposited in the ivory cases of the ecclesiastical sacraments. In like manner, from these cases the church constantly pours forth the ointment made out of the myrrh and distilled aromas of the passion of Christ in order to heal all the infirmities and wounds which sin has inflicted. Christ takes great delight in these ointments because they lead to the reconciliation of the faithful.[176]

The mystical union turns out in practice to be a sacramental union between Christ and the *fideles,* where the sacraments of the church form the indispensable middle link. In the justification and salvation of the *fideles* effected through these sacraments, the church functions as the go-between. This is again indicated in the tenth conclusion to Perez' exposition of Psalm 44, where *caritas* as the gold veneer on the vestments of the church is brought into direct connection with the variety of virtues, sacraments and diverse orders in the church.[177] Through the sacraments the *fidelis* has access to the *caritas*-embellished virtues that enable him to progress as a truly righteous member of the *congregatio fidelium* toward the longed-for glory.

---

in Syon superiori nisi per exercitium virtutum acquirat merita in hac vita et in hoc loco lachrymarum ubi deus voluit opera esse meritoria et penitentiam fructuosam."

[175] *Perez* (44 : 9): "Secunde fuerunt nuptie reconciliationis in quibus Christus univit sibi totam ecclesiam in unitate mystica."

[176] *Ibid.*: "... qualiter a vestimentis humanitatis Christi fluxit illa myrrha passionis, cuius virtus fuit recepta et reposita in domibus et capsis eburneis ecclesiasticorum sacramentorum; a quibus capsis iugiter ecclesia educit unguentum ex myrrha et cassia et gutta passionis Christi confectum ad sanandas omnes infirmitates et vulnera peccatorum, in quibus unguentis Christus valde delectatur propter reconciliationem fidelium."

[177] *Perez* (44: *conclusio*): "Decima conclusio quod vestimenta ecclesie Christi deaurata sunt per caritatem et circundata varietate virtutum et sacramentorum et diversorum ordinum et graduum ministrorum et prelatorum ecclesie."

If *caritas,* which embroiders the church and adorns the other virtues, is received through the sacraments of which presumably most of the *fideles* partake, does there exist for Perez as for his predecessors a mini-church of true faithful marked by *caritas*? On the one hand, Perez certainly speaks in terms of such a group. For example, he asserts that since Christ is righteous and innocent and pure, he loves those who are the same. In fact, Christ teaches this purity, *caritas* and faithfulness in the Gospels by his own words and example. Here Perez brings *caritas* and *fidelitas* together in such a way that *caritas* as the mark of the *fideles* (= *iusti*) cannot be far from his mind.[178] He is even bold enough to describe explicitly those whom Christ excludes from his society, all of whom are certainly guilty of sinning against *caritas.*[179] In opposition to these Christians caught in the quagmire of mortal sin, all the righteous faithful who have been innoculated against such sin by the injection of *caritas* in the sacraments form a mini-church marked by this caritas, as long as they are not reinfected by mortal sin.

On the other hand, the emphasis on an ascent through grades of virtue allows plenty of room for different levels of membership within the congregation of the faithful. There exist various degrees of purity among the *fideles,* and, of course, sinners are not excluded from the communion of the sacraments. Perez includes sinners within the scope of the church whether he denotes the church as *corpus mysticum* or as *ecclesia fidelium.* For example, in the church there are pure, healed, and infirm members:

> Again, one ought to note that just as the church as mystical body has three distinct eras, so it has three kinds of members. Some are pure like the Virgin Mary, who never sinned, and on whose account that statement is valid for the whole church: "My beloved possesses a flawless beauty" [Songs of Songs 4 : 7]. And some members are already healed, for whom the following is verified: "I buckled under the blows so that I almost fell, but the Lord caught me up" [Ps. 117 : 13]. And some are infirm, who still struggle along under some sin. In reference to these one can truly say: "Heal me, O Lord, because I am infirm" [Ps. 6 : 3]. Thus many statements

---

[178] *Perez* (100 : 6): "Cum ergo Christus sit iustus et innocens et purus ut dictum est, ergo diligit iustos et puros et hanc puritatem et caritatem et fidelitatem docet in lege evangelica exemplo et doctrina."

[179] *Perez* (100 : 5): "Octo ergo conditiones excludit Christus a societate sua, i.e. ab hereditate et gratia et merito et gloria, scilicet iniustos, prevaricatores legis, pravos corde, scilicet malitiosos vel hypocritas, et rebelles a voluntate Christi, et detractores proximorum, et superbos et avaros."

apply validly to the whole church because they apply to one kind of member or another; wherefore the reader ought to pay close attention.[180]

Or the different members can be more precisely designated as sinners, converted penitents, those who are still progressing and those who are already perfect.[181] Finally, much more in the sense of Thomas, Perez distinguishes three *atria* of the church of the faithful: those having *fides informis*, those who have faith with some hope, and those who work through faith formed by hope and *caritas*.[182]

These last three texts are appropriate ones on which to conclude our look at the later medieval commentators. At the end of the text translated above, Perez indicates the difficulty which we ourselves have encountered in trying to circumscribe accurately the locus of the *congregatio fidelium*. The church embraces various kinds of members, and individual texts apply respectively to these different members, although each text is no less true for the church as a whole. Perez' admonition to pay close attention is just as important for our analysis of the commentators' text as it was for the commentators' analysis of the Psalm texts. The last text from Perez is indicative of the problem. It presents us explicitly with the *fideles* in the broadest possible sense of the word, where it includes not only the *iusti* but also those who are still sinners and have only unformed faith. At the same time, a portion of these *fideles* are singled out at the inner-most level as possessing the decoration of *caritas*.[183] We can maintain

---

[180] *Perez* (*prol.* tr.3 c.2 cl.7): "Iterum est notandum quod sicut ista ecclesia sive hoc corpus mysticum habet tria distincta secula, ita etiam tria genera membrorum. Nam quedam sunt pura sicut est virgo Maria que nunquam peccavit, pro qua de tota ecclesia verificatur illud: 'Tota pulchra est amica mea.' Et quedam sunt membra iam sanata, pro quibus verificatur illud: 'Impulsus eversus sum, ut caderem, sed dominus suscepit me.' Et quedam sunt infirma que adhuc in aliquo peccato laborant. De quibus verificatur illud: 'Sana me domine quoniam infirmus sum.' Et sic multe locutiones verificantur de tota ecclesia ratione alicuius membri; quare advertat lector." Riedlinger (p. 374) notes that in his commentary on the Song of Songs Perez maintains that the only time the church was truly without blemish was after the footwashing at the Last Supper. Then Judas had already left and the church consisted of 120 pure men and women—the virgin Mary, the apostles and disciples, Mary Magdalena and the other women.

[181] *Perez* (118 : 176): "Quia in ecclesia sunt simul quattuor status, scilicet peccatorum, et conversorum penitentium, et proficientium, et perfectorum."

[182] *Perez* (133 : 1): "Unde nota quod ecclesia fidelium habet tria atria, scilicet fidem, spem et caritatem. Nam quidam habitant tantum in primo atrio, scilicet habentes fidem informem. Alii in secundo quia habent fidem cum aliqua spe sed non operantur per caritatem. Alii, scilicet iusti, habitant in tertio atrio ecclesie, scilicet operantes per fidem formatam spe et caritate, et isti possunt bene laudare et benedicere dominum."

[183] Another significant theologian of this period from the Augustinian order, Johannes von Staupitz (d. 1525), sees in *caritas* the decisive mark of membership in the

---

with confidence that a mini-church of true *fideles* remains clearly recognizable in this level of membership marked by *caritas.* These members are the *iusti,* the *boni* and, in the last analysis, for the later medieval commentators also the true *fideles.*

7. *Caritas*-ecclesiology

This chapter hardly needs a summary in the usual sense of the word. The two-pronged reference of the phrase *congregatio fidelium* has been emphasized over and over again. In the medieval Psalms commentaries which we have investigated, the word *ecclesia* has been used to denote the community of baptized Christians in unity as well as a mini-church within this community which is composed only of the *boni,* the *iusti,* and the *electi.* The category *fideles* has been broadened from its original reference to the *boni* alone (as with Augustine and Cassiodorus) to include all members of the community of the sacraments. This expansion is at least partially the result of the insistence of Augustine that it is impossible to distinguish accurately between the *boni* and the *mali* prior to the final judgment. Thus the whole communion of the sacraments can be called the *congregatio fidelium* according to the state of present righteousness, although according to God's predestination only the true *fideles* and righteous make up this church.

The keynote of this chapter, which gives unity and clear definition to the above-mentioned aspects, is Lyra's version of the Augustinian statement which we have cited more than once: "*Caritas* alone makes the division between the sons of perdition and the sons of the kingdom."[184] This text sums up the most important finding of our study to this point. *Caritas* is the mark of the true *fideles* who dwell in the church *numero et merito* and will enter the kingdom of heaven as the triumphant church. It is not membership in the outward church of the sacraments which assures one of a seat in the kingdom, but, apart from God's hidden predestination (or precisely in accord with it),

---

church for those who have grace and therefore are members of Christ (*Staupitz, Tübinger Predigten. Quellen und Forschungen zur Reformationsgeschichte,* Vol. VIII, ed. G. Buchwald and E. Wolf [Leipzig, 1927], p. 232): "Item qui graciam habet, membrum est Christi, quoniam ecclesiae dei in unitate caritatis unitus, ..." Johannes Turrecremata (d. 1468) identifies the innermost level of membership in the church as that *per unitatem fidei formatae* (Stockmann, *Joannis de Turrecremata* ..., pp. 81ff.).
[184] Cf. *supra*, notes 58, 149.

membership in the circle of *iusti* or true *fideles* through the possession and manifestation of *caritas*.

Caritas thus functions as the mark par excellence of the true *congregatio fidelium*. Regardless of the changes which the understanding of *caritas* itself undergoes, this mark continues to embody the Augustinian ecclesiological heritage to the medieval exegesis of the Psalms.[185] Decisive for our commentators is the Augustinian conception of a church of the *boni* marked by *caritas*. Insofar as this is true, we can speak of a basic *caritas*-ecclesiology which is visibly operative in most of the commentaries we have studied, and we can label their understanding of the true *congregatio fidelium* with this term. This interpretive phrase expresses a consensus of opinion among our commentators in regard to the existence of such a mini-church marked by *caritas*, in spite of the ambivalent connotation of the term *fideles*.

Lyra's statement is also prototypal because it indicates the persistence of the Augustinian connection between ecclesiology and soteriology in these commentaries. The text from Lyra can be supplemented (and complemented) by the clear formulation of Hugo: "The seat of God in the church and in the faithful soul is *caritas*."[186] Our caption, *caritas*-ecclesiology, is also valid in this respect. The true *fideles* at the heart of the church are precisely the *iusti*, who have been rehabilitated through *caritas* and are now marching in virtue toward perfect wholeness in the kingdom of heaven. What can be said of the true *fideles* as individuals can be applied corporately to the true

---

[185] The influence of Augustine on medieval ecclesiological thought has often been noted, e.g. by Beumer ("Zur Ekklesiologie ...," p. 374) in relation to early scholastic ecclesiology: "Kein Theologe dieser Epoche hat sich dem Einfluß des hl. Augustinus auf dem Gebiet der Lehre von der Kirche vollständig entziehen können, und bei vielen läßt er sich nicht allein in der großen Gedankenführung der Ekklesiologie, sondern auch bis in die letzten Formulierungen hinein verfolgen. Darin besteht ein Kennzeichen, das bei der Ekklesiologie des 12. Jahrhunderts nicht übersehen werden kann: sie ist augustinisch." In his development of this theme, however, Beumer totally neglects the one aspect in which we see the main influence of Augustine: the definitive mark of *caritas* for the true *fideles* or *boni* at the inner level of the church. Thus we cannot agree with Merzbacher when he writes in regard to medieval ecclesiology (p. 277): "Mit der Zeit rückten nämlich die Theologen des öfteren von der Definition Augustins 'Ecclesia est universalis congregatio iustorum' merklich ab."

[186] Cf. *supra*, n. 125. This relationship is important not only for our commentators, but also for the "systematic" tradition and throughout the Middle Ages. H. A. Oberman emphasizes that the doctrine of justification in Gabriel Biel gravitates not toward Christology, but toward ecclesiology, and gives a text from the *Collectorium* which shows clearly that the infusion of *caritas* means simultaneously for Biel justification and incorporation into the church *numero et merito*. (*Harvest*, pp. 120f. and 121, n. 31).

congregatio fidelium — in particular, the decisive character of the mark of *caritas*. And yet, one kind of statement is never totally absorbed by, or dependent upon, the other. The two spheres of ecclesiology and soteriology remain clearly defined even if they do overlap.

The phrase, *caritas*-ecclesiology, points to this close relationship, as well as to the place of the sacraments in this ecclesiological structure. The indispensable *caritas* is received through the sacraments, in practice especially through penance and the Eucharist. Even if the sacraments have enjoyed quite varying degrees of emphasis in our commentaries, their importance is to be assumed from Hugo on.[187] This sacramental emphasis reaches its peak in the commentary of Perez, but even in his case we cannot generalize and say that he represents a conception of the church primarily as *Heilsanstalt*. The sacraments function in intimate connection with his understanding of the church as the congregation of the faithful.

The best interpretive category remains: *caritas*-ecclesiology. This term sums up the most significant aspects of our commentators' understanding of the *congregatio fidelium*, and will help imprint these features on our mind as we pursue our study.

---

[187] If Ratzinger is right in connecting the Augustinian emphasis on *caritas* at the inner level with the developing penitential practice in the church, then the sacramental factor cannot be ignored with Augustine (cf. *supra*, n. 23). W. Jetter (*Die Taufe beim jungen Luther* [Tübingen, 1954], pp. 23f.) points to the importance of penance for Augustine. It overshadows baptism for him and lies in the direction of a new "Gnadenmedizin," although it is not yet sacramentalized. Although Jetter sees the importance of the *vinculum caritatis* for the inner circle of the *boni* and the *iusti* in Augustine's ecclesiology (p. 19), he does not make any connection between this and penance. However this may be, the Augustinian ecclesiological heritage does not lie in the handing over of a sacramental structure, but in the establishment of *caritas* as the mark of the *boni* regardless of how this *caritas* is acquired. Our Psalms commentators take over the latter almost unanimously while they vary in the importance they attribute to the sacraments. This consensus forms the most suitable platform from which to launch a comparison with Luther. Therefore we are not in a position to agree with E. Altendorf (*Einheit und Heiligkeit der Kirche* [Berlin und Leipzig, 1932], p. 172) when he plays off the "hierarchical-papal" structure of medieval ecclesiology against Augustine and then contrasts Luther only against this background, while implying a direct line between Luther and Augustine: "In der nachaugustinischen mittelalter-lich-scholastischen Lehre von der Kirche hat die Einheit ihren Grund nicht mehr in der Liebe, sondern in der Stiftung der einheitlich, hierarchisch verfaßten Kirche, in deren monarchischem Haupte, dem Papste, die Einheit der Kirche ihren sichtbaren Ausdruck findet. Dieser hierarchisch-papalistischen Einheitstheorie setzte Luther die alle äußere Organisation negierende Vorstellung der einen katholischen Kirche entgegen, die an allen Orten und zu allen Zeiten über die Erde hin ausgebreitet ist unter dem einen Haupt Christus in Einheit des Glaubens und der Liebe." The investigation into Luther's ecclesiology must rather take account of the consensus which we have found in the medieval exegesis of the Psalms beginning with Augustine.

CHAPTER II

ECCLESIA MILITANS ET TRIUMPHANS

1. *Ecclesia Militans: Imago Triumphantis*

The material under consideration in this chapter is immediately related to our discussion of the congregation of the faithful. After all, the goal of every true *fidelis* in the militant church, or *congregatio fidelium*, is to become a member of the triumphant church—i.e., to enjoy at last the blessed vision of the saints in heaven. The matter which concerns us here, however, is not to define the *fideles* or the *congregatio fidelium* as such, but rather to call explicit attention to an important dimension of the ecclesiological structure already delineated. Precisely because the goal of every pilgrim in the militant church is to reach that church triumphant, these two states of the church are never far apart in the thinking of our commentators. The way in which they define the true church of the *fideles* is influenced by the picture they have of the destination of these *fideles*, i.e. the church triumphant. As these commentators view the present church of the faithful, they have one eye simultaneously on the *ecclesia triumphans*.

It is no secret that the categories *ecclesia militans* and *ecclesia triumphans* are well-known and closely connected in medieval ecclesiological thought. Lyra, for example, writes succinctly that the mystical body of Christ is the church having two states: one militant and the other triumphant.[1] Hugo gives us a more detailed description of these two states of the church and depicts the transient life of the pilgrim in the militant church while striving for a place in the church triumphant:

> "In the place of the admirable tabernacle," that is, of the militant church, whose locus is Christ because it is founded in Christ. The militant church is called a "tabernacle" because those who are serving God receive there food and shelter for their journey. . . . Or "in the place of the tabernacle,"

---

[1] Cf. *supra*, Ch. I, n. 144. The terms appear explicitly for the first time in the second half of the twelfth century, according to Christine Thouzellier, "Ecclesia militans," in *Études d'histoire du droit canonique dédiées à Gabriel Le Bras*, Vol. II,(Paris, 1965),pp. 1410, 1415ff. She locates the first occurrence of *ecclesia militans* in the *Historia scholastica* of Peter Comestor (d. 1179) published in 1168.

that is, into the church itself, where Christ dwells with his faithful; for he is not to be found anywhere else. Nor will I stop there, but I will keep on going "up to the house of God," that is, to the triumphant church. . . . For now the righteous man travels toward this house in hope; eventually, however, he will make it all the way home.[2]

The church of the sacraments where Christ dwells with the faithful is to be admired, but it is not the ultimate goal of the journey of the faithful pilgrim. It is like a highway with many roadside rest areas where the true *fidelis* receives sufficient rest and nourishment to continue his journey toward his final destination in the triumphant church.

In the above passage we encounter one of the ways in which the two states of the church are related. Existence in the militant church is characterized as existence in hope (*in spe*), while existence in the triumphant church is "actual existence," "real existence," existence in fact (*in re*). These terms express an essentially negative relationship between the two states of the church. Existence *in spe* has a negative cast to it. The medieval understanding of existence in hope is that of a mean between two extremes: the hope of mercy or glory on the basis of merits on the one hand, and the fear of judgment on the other.[3] Life *in spe* in the militant church is definitely uncertain existence and inferior to the existence *in re* in the triumphant church. When the militant church is dubbed the inferior house of the Lord over against the superior house of the triumphant church, we can take these adjectives as indicative both of location and of significance.[4]

This element of discontinuity between the two states of the church is also expressed in terms of the contrast between grace and glory. Using the imagery of the dove for the church, Perez notes that the

---

[2] *Hugo* (41 : 5): " 'In locum tabernaculi admirabilis', id est ecclesiae militantis, cuius locus est Christus, quia in Christo fundata est. Dicitur autem ecclesia militans tabernaculum, quia in ea peregrinantes et militantes deo pascunt et cubant. . . . Vel 'in locum tabernaculi', id est in ipsam ecclesiam quae est locus in quo Christus cum fidelibus habitat. Nec extra locum istum invenitur. Nec ibi sistam, sed pertransibo. 'Usque ad domum Dei', id est ecclesiam triumphantem. . . . Ad hanc domum transit in praesenti vir iustus spe, in futuro autem transiet re."

[3] E.g. *Hugo* (100 : 1): "Dicit ergo quilibet fidelis: 'Psallam', id est bona opera faciam, sperans misericordiam et timens iudicium. Sed quia non placent deo opera de genere bonorum, nisi omnia mala opera relinquantur. . . ." For texts out of the systematic tradition, see R. Schwarz, *Fides, spes und caritas beim jungen Luther*, (Berlin, 1962), pp. 424ff. (Exkurs 5).

[4] *Hugo* (121 : 1). Cf. *Lyra* (83 : 11): " 'In domo dei mei', i.e. in ecclesia militante quae est domus dei inferior, sicut ecclesia triumphans est domus dei superior." Cf. the following note.

76

fideles are conveyed from the church here below in grace to the glory of the church above.[5] The faithful are kept alive by grace in the militant church until they can bask in the glory of the triumphant church. There is only "imperfect participation" in God through grace in the militant church, but in the triumphant church there is full participation in glory.[6] When Lyra explains how the church as the bride stands at the right hand of Christ, he first envisions her as the triumphant church standing beside Christ in the goods of heavenly glory. In a similar way, he says, the militant church stands beside Christ in the goods of grace, "which are the best possible goods of the present life."[7]

What we have characterized as a negative relationship or discontinuity between these two states of the church would scarcely be formulated so sharply by the medieval commentators themselves. In fact, existence *in spe* and *per gratiam* in the militant church is the only means by which the *fideles* can make it to the triumphant church. Since the triumphant church is the more excellent state of the church and the goal to be strived for, the *fideles* in the militant church must conform themselves as much as possible to the perfect state of existence awaiting them in the church triumphant. Precisely because of the inherent discontinuity between *spes* and *res*, and between grace and glory, the medieval commentators endeavor to establish as much continuity as possible between the two states of the church so that the *fideles* may smoothly pass from one to the other.

Such continuity does not have to be artificially manufactured by the medieval commentators. The early Christian conviction that the present life in the Spirit is a downpayment (Eph. 1 : 13-14) of the life to come soon finds expression in ecclesiological categories. Augustine speaks of the church as a "heap of testimony" to the life to come since she scorns the life in this world.[8] He calls those blessed who abide in

---

[5] *Perez* (67 : 14): "Alio modo termini inter quos volat ista columba sunt due ecclesie, scilicet ista inferior per gratiam et superior per gloriam. Nam ista columba semper volat ferendo et vehendo fideles ab ista ecclesia et hereditate ad illam superiorem...."

[6] *Burgos* (121 : 3): "Quae quidem Hierusalem secundo loco hic intellecta potest intelligi de ecclesia militante, in qua deus participatur per gratiam, licet imperfecte. Vel altius de ecclesia triumphante, in qua deus participatur plene per gloriam."

[7] *Lyra* (44 : 10): " 'Astitit regina', scilicet ecclesia Christi sponsa. 'A dextris tuis', i.e. in potioribus bonis eius. Quod patet de ecclesia triumphante, quae est cum Christo in bonis coelestis gloriae. Similiter de militante quae astat ipsi Christo in bonis gratiae, quae sunt maxima bona praesentis vitae." Cf. *Hugo* (44 : 10): " 'Regina', ecclesia sponsa. 'A dextris tuis', in potioribus bonis aeternis, iam in spe sed non adhuc in re."

[8] *Enarr. in ps.* 59.13 (*CChr* 39, 764): "Si enim bellare vellet ecclesia et gladio uti,

77

the church—although it is the place of wandering, yearning and pressure—because they will possess the heavenly Jerusalem without such anxiety and pressure.[9]

It is Cassiodorus, however, who emphasizes real continuity between life in the present church and the life to come in the heavenly city. In commenting on Psalm 41 : 5, Cassiodorus writes:

> It is clear why the *fidelis* poured out his soul, namely "because he was entering into the place of the tabernacle," that is, into the present church. For there, even as he was entering, he was bemoaning all the more the fact that the Jerusalem had not come which the Lord promised to his saints. For one naturally desires more eagerly what one hopes for when one already sees something like it.[10]

This idea of a similarity between the present church and the heavenly Jerusalem is taken up by the early medieval commentators. In the *Glossa*, the statement of Cassiodorus is formulated in terms of the present church as the hope of the coming Jerusalem,[11] while Lombard speaks more explicitly of the present church as "a certain image and outward appearance of the future Jerusalem."[12]

---

videretur pro vita praesenti pugnare; quia vero contemnebat vitam praesentem, ideo factus est acervus testimonii de vita futura." Yves Congar maintains that for the church fathers the spiritual world is a world in which things receive their *vérité* from above, because those "things above" manifest a superior order, both in terms of decision or purpose, and in terms of disposition or hierarchy ("L'ecclésiologie de S. Bernard," p. 150). He is thinking here of the influence of Greek philosophy on the thought of the fathers, esp. on that of Origen, and we can certainly add, Augustine. In another work, Congar points out that the early church conceived of herself as a "supra-temporal reality" ("Ecclesia ab Abel," p. 80). Such a philosophical orientation facilitates the concept of a basic continuity between the earthly and the heavenly church.

[9] *Enarr. in ps.* 83.8 (*CChr* 39, 1152): "Sed hic nidus est, et hic peregrinatio, et hic suspirium, et hic tritura, et hic pressura, quia hic torcular: quid est autem quod desiderat? quod concupiscit? quo it? quo tendit desiderium nostrum? quo nos rapit? Hic positus illa meditatur, positus inter tentationes, positus inter pressuras, positus in torcularibus, suspirans in superna promissa; quasi quid ibi acturus, iam praemeditatur gaudia futura. 'Beati', inquit, 'qui habitant in domo tua'. Unde beati? quid habituri? quid acturi? . . . Possident Ierusalem caelestem sine angustia, sine pressura, sine diversitate et divisione limitum: omnes habent eam, et singuli habent totam. Magnae illae divitiae."

[10] *Expos.* 41.5 (*CChr* 97, 382): "Sequitur etiam cur in se effuderit animam suam; scilicet, 'quoniam ingrediebatur in locum tabernaculi'; hoc est in Ecclesiam praesentem. Ibi enim dum ingrederetur amplius plorabat, amplius gemebat adhuc differri illam Ierusalem, quam sanctis suis Dominus repromisit. Necesse est enim vivacius desiderare quod exspectatur, quando eius quaedam similitudo conspicitur."

[11] *Glo. int.* (41 : 5): " 'Tabernaculum'. Cas.: i.e. praesentem ecclesiam quae est spes future Hierusalem, quae dum videtur amplius illa desideratur, et amplius in ista gemit usque ad domum dei non captus desideriis seculi."

[12] *Lomb.* (41 : 5; *PL* 191, 417): "Id est, in praesentem Ecclesiam, quae est quaedam imago et species futurae Ierusalem, quae, dum videtur, amplius illa desideratur, et

Cassiodorus himself uses such terms. He calls the *populus fidelis* a "certain image of the age to come,"[13] and pictures it standing at the right hand of God when he will have changed its tribulation into rejoicing.[14] He interprets the "seed of Christ" as those who have believed faithfully in him and in whom the future kingdom is sown. Drawing on his characteristic moral definition of the *fideles* as the *sancti*, he affirms that they are the ones who will endure into eternity.[15] Finally, Cassiodorus makes clear that in spite of all the differences between the earthly and the heavenly city, it is still one *populus fidelium*:

> He added, "as a city," as if he wanted to show that it indeed has the likeness of a city. For although every city gets its name from its citizens, it is more accurately called a city if its citizens are of the same mind. Now this city under consideration contains indiscriminately all kinds of people; but the coming city accepts without doubt only the perfect. The present city is shaken by opposing forces; the coming one rejoices in constant security. The former is full of people repenting; the latter knows no tears. The present city believes in hope; the one to come will see God face to face. And thus it happens that, although now two cities exist, in the future there will be only one faithful people.[16]

This affirmation of continuity in face of all the inherent discontinuity between the cities is the predominant feature of the relationship between the militant and triumphant churches.

amplius in ista gemit. Ideo dicit ingrediar in locum tabernaculi, quia extra locum tabernaculi huius aliquis quaerens Deum errat."

[13] *Expos.* 110.1 (*CChr* 98, 1015): "Unde hic profusa laetitia exsultat populus fidelis, quamdam imaginem futuri saeculi designans, ubi voces istae continuae sunt et laudes Domini devota mente concelebrant." Cf. *Glo. int.* (110 : 1): "Hoc dicit fidelis populus in spe quasi iam sit in angelorum societate."

[14] *Expos.* 59.7 (*CChr* 97, 532-533): "Populus ille fidelium, divinis iam virtutibus subiugatus, secundam partem supplicationis ingreditur, deprecans ut Dei virtus tribulationes eorum in gaudii alacritatem convertat. Et bene precatur populus iste ut 'salvus fiat dextera', quia in ipsa parte staturi sunt, qui perpetua felicitate gaudebunt."

[15] *Expos.* 88.37 (*CChr* 98, 814): " 'Semen' Christi sunt omnes qui ei fideli mente crediderint; quia in ipsis futurum regnum seminatum est, quod ventura messis ostendat, sicut et in vigesimo primo psalmo ipse dicit: 'Semen meum serviet illi' [Ps. 21 : 31]. 'Manebunt' ergo sancti 'in aeternum', qui in excellenti ac beata conversatione demorantur. Unde illos proprie 'manere' non dicimus qui a regno Domini respuuntur."

[16] *Expos.* 121.3 (*CChr* 98, 1150): "Addidit, 'ut civitas', quatenus similitudinem civitatis in illa esse monstraret. Nam cum omnis civitas dicatur a civibus, verius tamen illa civitas dicitur, quae unanimes cives continere monstratur. Scire autem debemus quod ista quae nunc agitur, continet indiscretos populos atque permixtos; illa vero quae futura est, solos recipit sine dubitatione perfectos; ista contrarietatibus quatitur, illa iugi securitate laetatur; ista plena paenitentium, illa nescia lacrimarum; ista spe credit, illa Deum facie ad faciem videt, eoque fit ut, cum duae civitates sint, unus tamen populus futurus credatur esse fidelium."

The keynote for this continuity in the later medieval commentaries is struck by the affirmation of Lyra that the militant church ought to conform itself to the triumphant church.[17] Paul of Burgos sets up a threeway comparison between the earthly Jerusalem, the militant church and the triumphant church. For him the "material" Jerusalem is the image of the church militant, while the latter—on the basis of Dionysius' *De ecclesiastica hierarchia*—is the image of the triumphant church.[18] Burgos is especially interesting for the way in which he carries through this comparison: first with reference to the worship of God and the members of the communities, and secondly, with reference to the respective judicial authority in the communities:

> Fourth in order, he shows how the earthly Jerusalem corresponds proportionately to the militant church, and the church militant to the heavenly one. There are principally two ways: the first pertains to the worship of God, and the second to the direction of the neighbor. Concerning the first, he says: "There the tribes went up, the tribes of the Lord." Proper worship of God includes the profession of true faith and the confession of divine praise, and the tribes of Israel were certainly exhibiting both. . . . "The testimony of Israel to confess the name of the Lord." This worship also thrives in the church militant where the tribes of the Lord, namely the *fideles*, daily ascend through grades of virtues in order to profess their faith and offer the confession of praise. It flourishes even more, however, in the heavenly Jerusalem, to which only the elect ascend who are truly the tribes of the Lord. And they witness perfectly to the excellence of God because they see him face to face. . . .

[17] *Lyra*^m (88 : 6): " 'Et veritatem tuam in ecclesia', scilicet militante quae se debet triumphanti conformare."

[18] *Burgos* (121 : 3): "Est tamen verum quod Ierusalem materialis, cum cultus divinus ibi vigeret, fuit figura ecclesiae militantis, et ipsa ecclesia militans secundum Dionysium de ecclesiastica hierarchia est figura coelestis ecclesiae." Congar ("L'ecclésiologie de S. Bernard," p. 150) notes that Bernard speaks in terms of the heavenly church as exemplified in the earthly church, possibly under the influence of Dionysius' *De ecclesiastica hierarchia*. He sees this as a direct continuation of the philosophical orientation of the ecclesiology of the fathers (cf. *supra*, n. 8) and speaks of its influence on medieval thought before the coming of "naturalism" with the works of Aristotle. The influence of Dionysius (the Pseudo-Areopagite, c. 500) persists throughout the Middle Ages, as we see here with Burgos. For a brief survey of the concept of the similarity between the earthly and heavenly churches in patristic and medieval thought with special attention to the relationship between the celestial and earthly hierarchies and the influence of Dionysius, see Ray C. Petry, *Christian Eschatology and Social Thought* (New York and Nashville, 1956), pp. 173ff. and esp. 177ff. Fehlner (p. 17) describes the similarity between the earthly and heavenly churches as fundamental for understanding the ecclesiology of Bonaventure. The thought of Dionysius also influences the reform ecclesiology of Gerson, who regards it as necessary that the militant church be governed on the model of the triumphant church. See G. H. M. Posthumus Meyjes, *Jean Gerson: Zijn Kerkpolitiek en Ecclesiologie* ('s-Gravenhage, 1963), pp. 168, 229, 232,

Concerning the direction of the neighbor he says: "Because the seats sit there in judgment." Whatever questions and doubtful cases arose in the divine law were settled in the earthly Jerusalem. . . . This practice flourishes in the militant church, where cases pertaining to the faith and activities of the faithful are settled universally and principally by the highest pontiffs, . . . whose authority is founded upon the house of David, namely upon Christ saying to Peter: "Feed my sheep" [John 21 : 17] . . . . However, this applies most of all to the triumphant church, and chiefly at the final judgment. Wherefore the Savior [Matt. 19 : 28] says to the apostles: "You also will sit upon twelve thrones, judging the twelve tribes of Israel." The twelve thrones signify the perfection of the tribunal, namely all those judging, who are the perfect, just as the twelve tribes all those to be judged.[19]

Several interesting points emerge in this text. Aside from the outward conformity of genuine worship of God in the three ecclesiastical communities, Burgos expresses an implicitly positive relationship between the historical tribes of Israel offering true worship to the Lord, the *fideles* of the militant church and the *electi* of the triumphant church. The positive comparison between the first two groups will occupy our attention in the upcoming chapter. Meanwhile it is obvious that Burgos is more interested in the similarity between the *fideles* advancing in virtue in the church militant and the *electi* in the church triumphant. It is not going too far to assume that those true *fideles* who complete their progress in virtue turn out to be

---

[19] *Burgos* (121 : 4): "Consequenter quarto ostendit in quibus Hierusalem illa materialis correspondet proportionabiliter militanti et etiam ecclesia militans coelesti. Et sunt duo principaliter: quorum primum pertinet ad cultum dei, secundum vero ad directionem proximi. De primo autem dicit: 'Illic enim ascenderunt tribus, tribus domini.' Illud enim proprie pertinet ad cultum dei, quod ad protestationem verae fidei et confessionem divinae laudis pertinet, quae quidem testificabantur seu protestabantur tribus Israel, . . . 'Testimonium Israel ad confitendum nomini domini.' Qui quidem cultus praecipue viget in ecclesia militanti ubi tribus domini, scilicet fideles, quotidie ascendunt per gradus virtutum ad testimonium fidei expressius exhibendum et offerendum confessionem laudis. Perfectius autem iste cultus viget in Hierusalem coelesti ad quam ascendunt soli electi qui sunt vere tribus domini, et testificantur dei excellentiam perfecte per claram eius visionem. . . . De secundo autem dicit: 'Quia illic sederunt sedes in iudicio.' In Hierusalem enim materiali determinabantur quaecunque questiones et dubia in lege divina exorta. . . . Quod praecipue viget in ecclesia militante ubi causae pertinentes ad fidem et operationem fidelium determinantur universaliter et principaliter per summos pontifices . . . cuius summi pontificis auctoritas fundatur super domum David, scilicet supra Christum dicentem Petro: 'Pasce oves meas', Iohannis ultimo [21 : 17]. . . . Ad ecclesiam autem triumphantem hoc maxime pertinet et praecipue in iudicio finali, unde salvator Matthei xix[: 28] ait apostolis: 'Sedebitis et vos super sedes duodecim iudicantes duodecim tribus Israel.' Ubi per duodecim sedes intelligitur perfectio tribunalis, scilicet universitas iudicantium, qui sunt omnes perfecti, sicut per duodecim tribus universitas iudicandorum. . . ."

also the *electi*, who see God with unhindered vision in the church triumphant. In this way, Burgos fills out with more scholastic terminology the affirmation of Cassiodorus that, although there are two cities, there is only one faithful people. At the same time he works out the conformity between the two states of the church which Lyra demands.

Not only does Burgos seek to establish continuity between the two states of the church on the basis of the kinds of worship and worshippers in the three communities, but he also draws the ecclesiastical tribunal into his schema. He attributes to the Pope supremacy in the order of jurisdiction in the militant church and sets this supremacy parallel to the judicatory activity of Christ, the apostles and the *perfecti* at the last judgment. This parallel function of the Pope in the militant church with that of Christ and his co-judges in the church triumphant is not to be underestimated. The concept of the militant church as the image and figure of the triumphant church receives here its most concrete application. The authority of the Pope does not depend alone upon proof texts from Scripture but also derives its validity from the structural similarity between the two states of the church. The judicial mandate of the Pope is built into the church by virtue of his representation of Christ in the militant church. As a result, the immediate activity of Christ is implicitly reserved for the last judgment, when he, together with the apostles and *perfecti*, will make the final selection of members for his church triumphant.[20]

[20] Burgos certainly regards Christ as the chief justice at the last judgment and the *perfecti* only as co-judges. The references to the *universitas iudicantium* and *iudicandorum* are taken from IV *Sent.* d.47 c.2 (as Burgos notes), where the same verse (Matt. 19 : 28) is quoted as proof that the *sancti* will judge with Christ: "Non autem solus Christus iudicabit, sed et Sancti cum eo 'iudicabunt nationes' [Sap. 3 : 8]. Ipse enim Apostolis ait: 'Sedebitis et vos super sedes duodecim, iudicantes duodecim tribus Israel.' " Cf. *Glo. ord.* (121 : 1): "Primo gaudet se monitum ire ad Hierusalem ubi sancti securi et cum domino iudicabunt." In contrast to this, the commission of Christ to Peter (John 21 : 17) does not offer to the Pope the position of co-judge with Christ in the militant church, but rather legitimates his authority as vicar of Christ, i.e. judging in place of Christ in the militant church. This implicit relegation of Christ to the last judgment and the triumphant church is congruent with the conception of Christ as judge in late medieval theology. Cf. Oberman, *Harvest*, pp. 319f. The similarity between the militant and triumphant churches is used more explicitly by other medieval theologians as an argument for the papal monarchy in the militant church. For example, Thomas writes in *Summa contra Gentiles* IV, 76: "Ecclesia militans a triumphanti Ecclesia per similitudinem derivatur. . . . In triumphanti autem Ecclesia unus praesidet, qui etiam praesidet in toto universo, scilicet Deus. . . . Ergo et in Ecclesia militante unus est qui praesidet universis." Cajetan builds his sermon to the second session of the

Perez also develops the idea of the militant church as the image of the church triumphant and, as we suspected above, actually sees fundamental continuity between existence in grace in the former and existence in glory in the latter. In the preface to his exposition of Psalm 121, he writes that the prophet rejoices in the splendor of Jerusalem because the earthly city (the militant church) in which the righteous live in grace is the image of the heavenly city above where they will dwell in glory.[21] The actual link between the two states of the church is the *iusti* themselves. Because they live in a state of grace in the church militant, they will dwell in glory in the church triumphant. Because they praise God here in the present church, they will praise him in the future Jerusalem. And it is in this present church that they are deemed worthy of passing over into the triumphant church. Precisely because of this continuity in the life of the *iusti* in both states of the church, the militant church can be called an image of the triumphant church.

The fundamental question remains, however, how this continuity between the *iusti* in grace and in glory can be established. The problem can also be formulated in the following way. What is it that the righteous in a state of grace in the church militant possess that will accompany them on their journey to the triumphant church and will abide with them there? If we consider the virtues which the righteous in the state of grace possess, the answer quickly becomes apparent. The *spes* which describes life in the present church cannot exist in the triumphant church, because existence there is existence *in re*, and no longer existence *in spe*. *Fides* cannot be the mark of the righteous in the heavenly Jerusalem because there they will see God "face to face" and not merely "believe in hope." Only *caritas* remains and, as we might have expected, *caritas* becomes the decisive link in the chain

---

Lateran Council (1512) around this argument for the papal monarchy, although he passed over this argument of Thomas in his ecclesiological work of 1511, *Auctoritas Papae et Concilii seu Ecclesiae Comparata*. See Gerhard Hennig, *Cajetan und Luther* (Stuttgart, 1966), pp. 21, 35ff. Petry notes that Bonaventure and Nicholas of Cusa use similar argumentation (pp. 186f. and 189).

[21] *Perez* (121 : 1): "... propheta expectans possessionem et statum huius civitatis que est ecclesia militans per gratiam et triumphans per gloriam, propter quattuor eius magnificentias letatur iam in spe et commendat ipsam in quattuor magnificentiis. Primo quia omnes iusti habitant in ea, hic per gratiam et in futuro per gloriam. Secundo quia ista civitas Hierusalem militans hic per gratiam est imago superioris triumphantis per gloriam. Tertio quia omnes isti qui ascendunt in istam ecclesiam ad laudandum deum per gratiam laudabunt ipsum in superiori per gloriam. Quarto quia in hac ecclesia iudicantur et lucrantur premium omnes iusti pro illa gloria."

that ties the *iusti* in the militant church to the church triumphant. Turning to our commentators, we find this to be the case. The way is prepared by Augustine, who speaks of the cultivation of *caritas* in the present church in preparation for the perfect *caritas* of the eternal city. The princes of the church are intent upon *caritas* in the present age so that, liberated from this captivity and enlightened with perfect *caritas* in eternity, the bride of Christ might see herself perfectly and not only through a veil.[22] In this explicitly ecclesiological context, Augustine emphasizes the importance of *caritas* to the earthly city in order that she might reign with God in eternity where she will be illuminated with perfect *caritas*. It is this *caritas* which is able to abide in both cities, and thus it alone is able to become the mark of continuity between them.

Such continuity is the direct result of the function of *caritas* as the unifying force of the mini-church of the *boni*—for Augustine, the body of Christ. This relationship is best exhibited in the summary of a passage from Augustine, given both by Lombard and the *Glossa*, in which *caritas*, by uniting the body to Christ on earth, is able to lift it to heaven with the glorified Christ. Through *caritas* we are united to Christ so that with him we are, as it were, one Christ. Therefore, when Christ ascends on high clothed with his church, he can only ascend insofar as he is one with us. For "through *caritas* he is with us on earth; through *caritas* we are with him in heaven."[23] *Caritas* functions as the transportation link between earth and heaven because it forms the bond between Christ and his members in both locations. Only those members of the mystical body who are joined to Christ on earth

---

[22] *Enarr. in ps.* 44.33 (*CChr* 38, 517): "Ipsi enim civitati, cui alius psalmus cantat: 'Gloriosa dicta sunt de te, civitas Dei' [Ps. 86 : 3] ipsi sponsae Christi, ipsi reginae filiae regis, et coniugi regis; quia principes eius sunt memores nominis eius in omni generatione et generatione, id est, quamdiu transeat hoc saeculum, quod multis generationibus agitur, gerentes pro illa caritatis curam, ut de isto saeculo liberata in aeternum Deo conregnet; propter hoc eidem ipsi confitebuntur populi in aeternum, conspicuis et manifestis illic cordibus omnium perfecta caritate luminosis, ut se universam plenissime noverit, quae hic in multis suis partibus occulta sibi est."

[23] We give the text according to the *Glo. ord.* (122 : 1): "Per caritatem namque multi unus homo sunt qui a finibus terrae clamat. Et per eamdem Christo unimur ut cum ipso quasi unus Christus sumus, secundum quod ipse dicit in evangelio: 'Nemo ascendit in coelum nisi qui descendit de coelo, filius hominis qui est in coelo' [Io. 3 : 13]. Descendit quidem caput; ascendit idem cum corpore, scilicet ecclesia, vestitus quam sibi exhibuit sine macula et ruga [Eph. 5 : 27]. Solus ergo ascendit qui nobiscum unus est. ... Cum illo ergo ascendit qui cum illo unus esse voluit. Per caritatem nobiscum est in terra; per caritatem cum illo sumus in coelo." Cf. Lombard to the same verse (*PL* 191, 1145) and for Augustine, *Enarr. in ps.* 122.1 (*CChr* 40, 1814).

84

through *caritas* are able to rise with him to heaven where they remain bound to him through the same *caritas*. Because *caritas* functions horizontally as the cohesive force of the body of Christ, it executes a vertically-directed function in bringing the members of the mystical body into heaven.

The most explicit expression of the necessity of *caritas* as the link between the militant and triumphant churches is contained in a text from an anonymous thirteenth century commentary on the Pauline epistles cited by Landgraf. It demonstrates the reasoning behind the choice of *caritas* as the necessary link:

> Question: through what are the members united with the head, since the head had neither hope nor faith. Reply: the church militant becomes the church triumphant; therefore it is the same church and the same union. Indeed unity ought to be established in the church through that which is common to both the militant and the triumphant churches. This common factor is *caritas*, which will not be exhausted. The other virtues, however, will pass away. So I Cor. 13 [: 13]: "Now faith, hope, *caritas* remain, these three, but the greatest of these is *caritas*."[24]

In this text the ecclesiological and soteriological spheres overlap one another as completely as possible. The question posed by the commentator is both ecclesiological and soteriological. We can reformulate it in terms of both spheres. How are Christians really united to Christ and thus saved by him? Or, what is the bond between the head and members of the mystical body which is the church? The problem arises from the generally accepted medieval axiom that Christ possessed neither faith nor hope—an axiom that functions in the background of all medieval soteriological thought. If Christ had neither of these, then only *caritas* remains to join members to their head.

Actually, this much would have answered the question quite satisfactorily; the author could have quoted his passage from First Corinthians and stopped there. The amazing thing is that the anonymous commentator introduces the relationship between the two states of the church to solve the problem. The question he could have answered quite simply in soteriological terms is answered instead in

---

[24] Landgraf, IV/2, p. 94, n. 229: "Queritur, quid est illud, per quod uniuntur membra cum capite, cum caput non habuerit spem neque fidem. Responsio: Ecclesia militans fiet triumphans. Et ideo eadem est ecclesia et eadem unio. Unitas utique debet esse in ecclesia per id, quod ecclesie commune est militanti et triumphanti. Hec autem caritas est, que non evacuabitur. Alie autem virtutes evacuabuntur. Unde I Cor. xiii: 'Nunc autem manent fides, spes, caritas, tria hec, maior autem horum est caritas.' "

explicitly ecclesiological terms. It is not simply because *caritas* abides forever that it is the link between Christ and his members, but because *caritas* is the one element that is common to the militant and triumphant *churches*. The answer is indicative of the importance which ecclesiological considerations have for the soteriological sphere of medieval thought, and the resulting extremely close relationship between the two spheres.[25] In addition, it is indicative of the importance which the relationship between the two states of the church has upon the formulation of what we have called the medieval "*caritas*-ecclesiology"—the emphasis upon *caritas* as the mark of the true *fideles*.

This last text we have quoted does not come from one of our medieval Psalms commentaries. Nevertheless, it expresses the rationale behind the establishment of *caritas* as the connection between the two states of the church which we have seen indicated by Augustine, Lombard and the *Glossa*, and which is also expressed by our later medieval Psalms commentators. A good example of the latter is the passage in which Lyra makes his definitive statement concerning *caritas* as the divider between the sons of perdition and the sons of the kingdom. The statement appears in Lyra's exposition of Psalm 68 : 36-37—a passage which Lyra interprets first in terms of the militant church and then in terms of the triumphant church. This formulation of the decisive role of *caritas* pertains, of course, to the militant church. But Lyra goes on to interpret verse 37 in terms of the triumphant church as follows: " 'And they who love his name will dwell in her,' because in the heavenly city is perfect *caritas*."[26] The *caritas* which distinguishes the sons of the kingdom in the militant church abides as perfect *caritas* in the church triumphant. When one

---

[25] Preus (p. 116) points to the significance of the absence of faith and hope in Christ for tropological exegesis in the Middle Ages. It must teach primarily *caritas* and obedience when Christ is the model and in this way *caritas* becomes determinative for soteriological considerations. This absence is also significant for medieval ecclesiological thought when one moves from tropology to allegory in order to define the link between head and members. However, as we have shown, there exists already a "*caritas*-ecclesiology" for our medieval commentators which is not dependent upon, nor derived from, the role of *caritas* in tropological exegesis. In the text under discussion, we see how this *caritas*-ecclesiology reacts upon the soteriological sphere and confirms the importance of *caritas* already present there.

[26] *Lyra* (68 : 37): " 'Et qui diligunt nomen eius habitabunt in ea', quia in civitate coelesti est caritas perfecta." Cf. *Burgos* (121 : 6): "Non poterat habere accessum nisi per veram caritatem, ex qua pax perfecta coelestis attingitur ... est abundantia pacis quae in solis habentibus caritatem habetur. Impiis enim non est pax." Cf. *supra*, n. 22 for *caritas perfecta* in Augustine.

considers the latter part of the statement, then it is clear why *caritas* is the divider of the church militant—it transports the sons of the kingdom into the perfect *caritas* of the triumphant church.

An amplification of this function of *caritas* occurs in the conception of different grades or positions in the church triumphant according to the different grades of *caritas* or merits. Not only is there a simple continuity of *caritas* between the two states of the church, but the correspondence is so exact that the quality of one's *caritas* or merits in the militant church affects one's rank in the triumphant church. Lyra says in his moral exposition of the same verse that the grades of mansions in the heavenly city are distinguished according to the grades of *caritas*.[27] He also maintains that participation in God in the heavenly Jerusalem is more or less participation according to the diversity of one's merits.[28] Perez notes that God prepares diverse mansions for the elect in the kingdom of heaven according to the measure and grace of each one's merits.[29] The continuity between the two states of the church has become specialized to the highest degree possible.

The image-relationship between the church militant and the triumphant church fits well into the ecclesiological structure which we have characterized as "*caritas*-ecclesiology." Not only is it a component part of the structure, but it also exerts a considerable influence upon the definition of the *fideles* themselves. For this reason we can speak of a *caritas*- and *imago*-ecclesiology in our medieval Psalms commentaries. Because *caritas* is *the* virtue which can survive in both states of the church, and because it can exist both in Christ

---

[27] *Lyra*ᵐ (68 : 37): "'Et qui diligunt nomen eius habitabunt in ea.' Gradus enim mansionum supernae civitatis distinguuntur secundum gradus caritatis."

[28] *Lyra*ᵐ (121 : 3): "'Hierusalem quae aedificatur ut civitas.' Sicut enim civitas materialis constituitur ex diversis statibus hominum, sic superna Hierusalem ex distinctis ordinibus angelorum et hominum ad eosdem ordines assumptorum. 'Cuius participatio eius in idipsum', id est in idem et unum. Deus enim est omnibus beatitudinis obiectum, plus tamen et minus participatum secundum diversitates meritorum." Hugo notes that a variety of rewards exists in the triumphant church *in re* just as in the militant church *in spe*: *Hugo* (44 : 10): "Item varietas praemiorum quae in ecclesia triumphante sunt in re, in militante autem sunt in spe."

[29] *Perez* (15 : 5): "Ita ergo pariter deus secundum funiculum et propositum sue voluntatis ab eterno predestinavit et preparavit diversas mansiones suis electis in regno celorum, quas postea filius distribuit eisdem electis per ipsum vocatis et iustificatis, et hoc fecit secundum mensuram et gratiam meritorum uniuscuiusque." Cf. *Lyra* (83 : 4): "'Altaria tua domine virtutum', i.e. angelorum; supple sunt illa in quibus quietatur appetitus humanus. Et vocat hic altaria electorum diversa consortia secundum varia eorum merita."

and in his members, *caritas* comes to be the most important mark of the *fideles* making their pilgrimage in the militant church toward the heavenly Jerusalem. It does what faith and hope cannot do—bridge the gap between earthly and heavenly existence and carry the individual *fidelis* as well as the *congregatio fidelium* to their life in the church triumphant. In this way the continuity and correspondence between these two states of the church become key elements in the ecclesiological thought of the medieval Psalms commentators.

2. *Semper Ascendere*

To fill out our picture of the continuity between the two states of the church, it is instructive to take a closer look at the life of the *fideles in spe* in the militant church. We recall from our discussion of the *congregatio fidelium* that one of the characteristics of the life of the *fideles* marked by *caritas* is the constant increase in virtue and merits.[30] And in this chapter we have seen that the continuity in *caritas* between the militant and triumphant churches leads to a conformity between the righteousness and merits of their respective members. Because this conformity in *caritas* and in merits is the determining factor in the transition from one state of the church to the other, the overriding concern of the pilgrim in the militant church is to advance and increase constantly (*iugiter* or *semper*) in virtue in order to conform his *caritas* here as much as possible to that of the heavenly city. Perez sums up this progress of the *viator* in virtue: "The righteous ascend from virtue to virtue and through grades of virtue from this Zion here below to the Zion above, where they will see the God of gods in glory."[31]

The necessity of advancing in virtue and *caritas* is consonant with existence *in spe* in the militant church. In spite of the constant progress made in the church militant, existence there is never equal to life in the church triumphant, but is always existence *in spe* as opposed to *in re*. Nevertheless, as we have seen, existence *in spe* is only valid if the necessary merits are present which justify this hope.[32] Therefore, the *fidelis* must constantly strive to acquire

---

[30] Cf. *supra*, Ch. I, notes 170 and 172.

[31] *Perez* (83 : 8): "Quasi dicat quod iusti de virtute in virtutem et per gradus virtutum ascendunt ab hac Syon inferiori in Syon superiorem in qua vident deum deorum per gloriam."

[32] Cf. *supra*, n. 3. The basic medieval text for this view is Lombard, III *Sent.* d.26 c.1: "Est enim [spes] certa exspectatio futurae beatitudinis, veniens ex Dei gratia et ex meritis praecedentibus vel ipsam spem, quam natura praeit caritas, vel rem speratam,

these merits in order to ensure that his hope has a firm basis and does not degenerate into empty presumption. By making these merits possible, *caritas* becomes the prerequisite for possession of a valid hope, and, in so doing, establishes itself as the link between the two states of the church. The element of hope is not cancelled out. Life *in spe* is a sign of not yet having passed over into, not yet having, the *caritas perfecta*. At the same time, however, there cannot be existence *in spe* at all without the prior possession and constant increase of *caritas*.

This existence *in spe* is characteristic of life in the militant church even for our earliest commentators, before it is expanded to include progress in virtue and *caritas* in more explicitly scholastic terms. We recall how Jerome maintains that it is necessary for the *sanctus* daily to advance, "forgetting those things which are behind and stretching out toward those things that lie ahead" (Phil. 4 : 13).[33] Augustine makes clear that God's promises are not to be expected in this life:

> For "all his commandments are trustworthy." He does not renege; he will produce what he has promised. Nevertheless, his promises are not to be expected here, not to be hoped for here, but "they are confirmed for eternity in truth and righteousness." And it is only right that one works here and will rest from his labor there, because "he has sent redemption to his people." From what else are they redeemed, except from the captivity of this wandering? There is no rest anywhere, therefore, unless it be sought in the heavenly fatherland.[34]

This life is for work; only in the fatherland are we able to rest in peace. Citing the example of Paul, which is behind Jerome's statement above, Augustine maintains no one can say that he has reached the longed for goal in this life. If Paul was still running, how can we claim to have finished the race?[35]

---

id est beatitudinem aeternam: sine meritis enim aliquid sperare, non spes, sed praesumtio dici potest." Note especially how *caritas* is said to precede *spes* by nature.

[33] Cf. *supra*, Ch. I, n. 6.

[34] *Enarr. in ps.* 110.7 (*CChr* 40, 1624): " 'Fidelia', enim 'omnia mandata eius'; non fallit, exhibet quod promisit. Non tamen quod promisit, est hic exspectandum, non hic sperandum; sed 'confirmata' sunt 'in saeculum saeculi, facta in veritate et iustitia'. Hoc est verum et iustum, ut hic laboretur, illic requiescatur, quia, 'Redemptionem misit populo suo'. Unde autem redimuntur, nisi a captivitate peregrinationis huius? Non ergo requies nisi in caelesti patria requiratur."

[35] *Enarr. in ps.* 83.4 (*CChr* 39,1149): "Nullus autem in hac vita pervenisse se dicat. Quis enim potest tam perfectus esse quam Paulus? Et ait tamen, 'Fratres, ego me non arbitror adprehendisse; unum autem, quae retro oblitus, in ea quae ante sunt extentus, secundum intentionem sequor ad palmam supernae vocationis Dei in Christo Iesu' [Phil. 3 : 13-14]. Vides Paulum adhuc currere, et te iam existimas pervenisse?"

Life *in spe* in the present church for Augustine necessarily calls for tribulation. His interpretation of *torcularia* (wine presses) in Psalm 83 as the churches or tabernacles of this age affords ample opportunity to expand upon the necessity of *pressura* and *tribulatio* in this life. The speaker in Psalm 83 is the body of Christ, whose members are situated now in *torcularia*. These are the "pressures of temptation" to which the body is now subjected, but it longs for those tabernacles where all pressure will be lifted.[36] Thus when the body of Christ rejoices, it can rejoice now merely *in spe*. Only in those future tabernacles will it be able to rejoice *in re*. Nevertheless, it *can* rejoice now *in spe* and tolerate all the pressures of the wine press because it is certain that it will enter the eternal tabernacles promised to it. This is what Paul means when, in Romans 12 : 12, he immediately follows up the phrase "rejoicing in hope" with "patient in tribulation."[37] Although life in the churches of the present time is full of wandering, longing and pressure, they who dwell in the house of the Lord will possess the heavenly Jerusalem without anxiety and pressure.[38]

Tribulation does not only have a negative connotation. Its presence in the church also serves a positive function:

> That which is called happiness in human affairs ought to be feared more than misery. Misery brings forth much good fruit out of tribulation, but happiness corrupts the soul with perverse security and gives room to the devil, the tempter.[39]

Tribulation keeps the *fidelis* awake and prevents him from becoming deluded by a false sense of security. It does not allow him to slack up in his striving for a place in the fatherland. Tribulation is an essential

[36] *Enarr. in ps.* 83.1 (*CChr* 39, 1146): "Propterea torcularia nominantur ecclesiae Dei huius temporis." And in the same psalm, *Enarr. in ps.* 83.5 (*CChr* 39,1150): "Talis est qui cantat in hoc psalmo. Quis est? Corpus Christi. Quis est iste? Vos, si vultis; . . . Ergo in pressuris tentationum constituti, edamus hanc vocem, et praemittamus desiderium nostrum: 'Quam dilectissima sunt', inquit, 'tabernacula tua, Domine virtutum!' Erat in tabernaculis quibusdam, id est, in torcularibus; sed desiderabat alia tabernacula, ubi nulla pressura est."

[37] *Enarr. in ps.* 83.6 (*CChr* 39, 1150): "Quod ait apostolus: 'Spe gaudentes'. Ibi iam re gaudebit, modo adhuc spe. Ideoque qui spe gaudent, quia certi sunt se accepturos, tolerant in torculari omnes pressuras. Propterea et ipse apostolus cum dixisset: 'Spe gaudentes', quasi his loqueretur, qui iam in torculari sunt, addidit statim: 'In tribulatione patientes.' "

[38] Cf. *supra*, n. 9.

[39] *Enarr. in ps.* 68, s.1.1 (*CChr* 39, 901): '. . . ipsa quae in rebus humanis vocatur felicitas, plus sit timenda quam miseria; quandoquidem miseria plerumque affert ex tribulatione fructum bonum, felicitas autem corrumpit animam perversa securitate, et dat locum diabolo tentatori."

part of the life *in spe* because it keeps that hope alive. In fact, "if you think you do not undergo tribulation, you have not yet begun to be Christian."[40]

Cassiodorus underscores and amplifies this positive contribution of tribulation. When the church of God is trampled underfoot, the merits of the saints previously unnoticed in easy times become visible. The pressure of the *torcular* increases holiness and leads directly to the heavenly reward and eternal rest.[41] The faithful Christian is pressed into shape by these *torcularia* and desires to reach the heavenly Jerusalem where he will not be weighed down by tribulations but will enjoy secure blessedness.[42] On the basis of this spiritual conditioning, the *fidelis* is in a position constantly (*semper*) to advance, constantly to ascend with the help of the Lord toward heaven.

Cassiodorus stresses the positive effect of tribulation in enabling the *fidelis* to become holier. He marches ever higher by constantly (*semper*) advancing in the overcoming of vice and increasing in virtue.[43] The concept of virtue itself, however, does not yet have the specialized sense of infused and acquired virtues which make up the *habitus* of the medieval *viator*. Augustine lays the foundation for

[40] *Enarr. in ps.* 55.4 (*CChr* 39, 680): "Nemo sibi dicat: Fuerunt tribulationes apud patres nostros, apud nos non sunt. Si putas te non habere tribulationes, nondum coepisti esse christianus. Et ubi est vox apostoli: 'Sed et omnes qui volunt in Christo pie vivere, persecutiones patientur' [II Tim. 3 : 12]? Si ergo non pateris ullam pro Christo persecutionem, vide ne nondum coeperis in Christo pie vivere. Cum autem coeperis in Christo pie vivere, ingressus es torcular; praepara te ad pressuras, sed noli esse aridus, ne de pressura nihil exeat."

[41] *Expos.* 83.1 (*CChr* 98, 767): "Sic Ecclesia Dei cum afflictionibus persecutionibusque conteritur, declarantur merita sanctorum, quae quietis temporibus cognita non fuerunt. Istius ergo torcularis pressura sanctificat, contritio meliorat, cuius labor caelestis fructus est et poena praesens requies sempiterna." Tribulation leads to the hope of eternal life on the basis of Romans 5 : 3-5. Cf. *Expos.* 59.10 (*CChr* 97,534-535): " 'Olla spei' tribulatio significatur, sed illa quam in hoc mundo sanctissimi sustinent Christiani, quae ad spem vitae eternae, Domino praestante, porrigitur, sicut dicit apostolus [Rm. 5 : 3-5]." Also cf. *supra*, n. 14.

[42] *Expos.* 83.2 (*CChr* 98,768): " 'Quam amabilia sunt tabernacula tua, Domine virtutum!' Filius Core spiritali fecunditate regeneratus et torcularibus Ecclesiae competenter expressus, ad futuram Ierusalem desiderat pervenire: in qua iam nulla sint pondera tribulationum, sed beatitudine secura, imperturbata felicitate potiatur."

[43] Cf. *Expos.* 83.6 (*CChr* 98, 770): "Utique illi beato cui est auxilium a Domino, 'ascensus' est 'in corde', quia semper proficit, semper ascendit et quantum Dominus praestat auxilium, tanto altius elevatur ad caelum. Tale est enim (verbi causa) quod dicimus, cum vicerit quis auxilio Domini libidinem, ascendit primum gradum; cum dominatus fuerit superbiae, salit alterum; dum superaverit avaritiam, subit tertium; et tot gradibus evehitur quot vitiis fuerit absolutus." Cf. *Expos.* 121.4 (*CChr* 98, 1152): "Et ut caelestem esse cognosceres, addidit, 'ascenderunt'. Ad quam beati semper ascendunt, quoniam iugi exercitatione proficiunt."

this specialization by interpreting Psalm 83 : 8 ("They will go from virtue to virtue") as the transition from the four classical active virtues (*prudentia, iustitia, temperantia, fortitudo*)—which he understands as given through grace—to the final *virtus* of contemplating God.[44] When a more detailed soteriological schema is projected on this basis, the way is cleared for scholastic formulations of the progress in virtue in our medieval commentators.[45]

In his *Postilla* Hugo, as Cassiodorus, emphasizes the role of tribulation in the justification of the saints. In vivid terms he describes what it means to say that the church is an "ivory house." This "frigid ivory" is the *castitas* of the saints, and, just as ivory begins to shine when it is polished and chiseled into shape, so the saints are refined through tribulation and engraved with a variety of virtues so that they serve as examples of the mortification of the flesh, humility and faith to the *minores* in the church.[46] Carnal men can be made spiritual only with great difficulty and the way to heaven passes through many tribulations. But it is precisely this tribulation which acomplishes the transition from "guilt to grace" and from "exile to the fatherland," because it engraves the saints with a variety of virtues.[47] Thus the road to heaven is paved with these diverse virtues[48] and itself constitutes

---

[44] *Enarr. in ps.* 83.11 (*CChr* 39, 1157-1158). By interpreting the first part of the verse, "Benedictionem dabit legislator," as the giving of grace after the law, Augustine already sets up the progress in virtue as a direct result of the reception of grace. *Ibid.*: "Adveniet gratia post legem; ipsa est benedictio. Et quid nobis praestitit ista gratia et benedictio? 'Ambulabunt a virtutibus in virtutem.' "

[45] However, Augustine does not conceive of existence *in spe* as based upon confidence in man's own merits. *Spes et merita* do not belong together for him since *spes* is hope in the promise of God alone: *Enarr. in ps.* 88, s.1.1 (*CChr* 39, 1220): "Et nemo in hoc saeculo robustus est, nisi in spe promissionis Dei; quantum enim adtinet ad merita nostra, infirmi sumus; quantum ad eius misericordiam, robusti sumus."

[46] *Hugo* (44 : 9): "Domus etiam Christi dicitur ecclesia ... Et dicitur ecclesia domus eburnea quia per ebur frigidum intelligitur castitas sanctorum. Et quia sicut ebur primo obscurum est, sed limis et serris et scopulis lucidum fit, postea caelatur et sculpitur, sic sancti per tribulationes fiunt puriores et varietate virtutum quasi insculpuntur. Est ergo sensus verborum quae dicuntur hic, quod per exempla sanctorum habent minores ecclesiae carnis mortificationem, humilitatem et fidem."

[47] *Hugo* (59 : 1): "... et difficile fiunt carnales homines spirituales et etiam per multas tribulationes oportet intrare in regnum coelorum [Act. 14 : 21] ... Intentio est ostendere beatam esse tribulationem et amplectendam, per quam fit commutatio de culpa ad gratiam, de exilio ad patriam." Cf. *Hugo* (79 : 9): "Quia vinea tormento fructificat. . . Sic ecclesia tribulationibus et oppressionibus magis magisque fructificavit."

[48] *Hugo* (83 : 8): "Iter istud figuratum fuit in itinere filiorum Israel, quo per diversas deserti mansiones pervenerunt ad terram promissionis. Per diversas enim mansiones de quibus habetur Numer. xxxiii. significantur diversae virtutes. Per terram promissionis aeterna patria designatur."

constant progress in virtue. Speaking in more scholastic terms—and yet within the framework of Augustine's interpretation of the same verse—he explains that, although the virtues themselves are infused simultaneously with grace, the actual progress in virtue must be understood in terms of the working out of these virtues.[49]

The formulations of our later medieval commentators on this matter are familiar to us.[50] It is appropriate, however, to call attention to a passage from Perez' interpretation of Psalm 83, in which he sets up a threeway comparison between the "old law," the "evangelical law" and the fatherland above. The old law is the field and vine which provide the raw materials for the threshing floor and wine press of the evangelical law. In like manner, the evangelical law (= New Testament existence or church) is the field and the vine for the fatherland above, because here meritorious fruits are extracted from the press and in the day of judgment the grain is separated from the chaff and the wheat from the tares, i.e. righteous men from the midst of the *mali*. Perez continues: "And thus the heavenly fatherland will be the end of this evangelical wandering and labor; for just as here we gather the fruits of grace, so there we gather the fruits of glory."[51] Perez understands the present church as the place of gathering merits (the fruits of grace) through labor and tribulation and establishes direct continuity between this and the gathering of the fruits of glory in the fatherland.

A passage from an anonymous thirteenth century Dominican commentary on the Song of Songs sheds more explicitly ecclesiological light on our subject. The biblical text is again that important verse 8 from Psalm 83 and the authority for the interpretation of the text is, unsurprisingly, Pseudo-Dionysius. Drawing on the latter's understanding of the correlation between the earthly and the heavenly hierarchy, the commentator notes that in *caritas*, the form of merits,

---

[49] *Hugo* (83 : 8): " 'De virtute in virtutem', i.e. de actu unius virtutis in actum alterius virtutis. Non enim de ipsis virtutibus intelligi potest cum omnes simul infundantur cum gratia."

[50] Cf. *supra*, pp. 68ff. and 87.

[51] *Perez* (83 : 1): "Item ulterius est notandum quod sicut lex vetus fuit ager frugum sive vinea sive peregrinatio respectu nove legis, et lex evangelica est area et torcular et terminus quietis illius; ita pari modo lex evangelica est ager et arbor et vinea et peregrinatio respectu superioris patrie. Nam ex hac vinea continue colliguntur et extorquentur fructus meritorum et in die iudicii triturabitur messis et separabitur granum a paleis et frumentum a zizania et universaliter mali de medio iustorum. Et sic patria celestis erit finis evangelice peregrinationis et laboris; nam sicut hic colligimus fructus gratie, ita ibi colligimus fructus glorie."

there can be no standing still, but only a constant progressing from good to better. Following the line of interpretation given since Augustine, he maintains that the text first treats grace—as he interprets the word *benedictio* in the text—and then progress in virtue. The virtues themselves are the stages in the life of the *fideles* in the church: those starting out in true penance, those advancing in the active life through external works, and those perfect through contemplation.[52] The transition from active virtues to contemplation in the Augustinian sense is adapted to the three levels of membership in the church and subsumed under the scholastic understanding of the working out of merits on the basis of infused *caritas*.

This text sums up nicely our discussion of the life *in spe* of the *fideles* in the militant church. This life is characterized by constant progress in virtue under the banner of hope toward the church triumphant. This progress in virtue is in turn an advancing in *caritas*, i.e. constantly establishing and perfecting this element of continuity between the two states of the church, continually extending the bridge over which the *fideles* pass from the one to the other. We encounter again the way in which ecclesiology and soteriology overlap for our commentators. The required conformity between the two states of the church demands that the *fideles* in the militant church make optimal use of the soteriological means at their disposal—*caritas* and the variety of virtues—in order to be properly attired for their entry into the triumphant church. And yet this life remains life *in spe*. The steady striving and progress in virtue are necessary so that the *fideles* do not presume that they have already reached the triumphant church.

For our commentators tribulation and pressure function both to prevent this presumption and false security from arising and to mold the *fideles* into holy (*sancti*) and righteous (*iusti*) travellers from one state of the church into the other. Augustine gives preference to the first function of tribulation. Nevertheless, he simultaneously lays the

---

[52] Riedlinger, p. 293, n. 21: " 'Benedictiones dabit legislator, ibunt de virtute in virtutem, videbitur Deus deorum in Sion' Ps. [83 : 8]. Beatus Dionysius in libro de caelesti hierarchia dicit, quod omnis res beatificabilis et perfectibilis eo est beatior et perfectior, quo ei, qui universaliter perfectus est, per accessivas illuminationes est propinquior et similior. Et ideo divina providentia congrue disposuit, ut in forma meritorum, scilicet in caritate, non sit status, sed continuus in bonis profectus. ... Et est ordo congruus, ut primo agatur de gratia et post de progressu virtutum; sine gratia enim progredi non contingit. Et appellantur hic virtutes status incipientium, proficientium et perfectorum. Et consistit status incipientium in detestatione peccati per veram paenitentiam, status vero proficientium in exercitio vitae activae per operationem, status autem perfectorum in speculari dulcedine per contemplationem."

groundwork for the notion that advancing in virtue is essential to the journey of the faithful. His successors in the exegesis of the Psalms take up this aspect of his thought and build the idea of steady progress in virtue into their conception of the continuity between the two states of the church. The *semper ascendere* becomes an essential component of their *caritas-* and *imago*-ecclesiology.

CHAPTER III

ECCLESIA ET SYNAGOGA

We pursue the investigation into the ecclesiology of our medieval Psalms commentaries by directing our attention to a different set of problems, all of which revolve around the relationship of the church to the Jews or the synagogue. This is indeed the first task that faced the primitive church—to defend itself, a child of the synagogue, over against those Jews who had not come to believe in Christ as the expected Messiah and who continued to press the claim of being God's chosen people. This confrontation forms the setting for the church's initial pondering of its own nature—that is, the setting for its first ecclesiological thinking. And since the Jewish people have remained a unique, living and lively entity alongside the church until the present day, the relationship between the two peoples has always played a key role in the church's self-analysis.

From the side of the church this confrontation has assumed a twofold form, which W. Seiferth designates as that of the *concordia* or *altercatio* between the synagogue and the church.[1] The *concordia* stresses the continuity of God's revelation in both testaments and allows both the synagogue and the church to retain their integrity as God's peoples, even though the church and the New Testament are the fulfillment and the revelation of the veiled promises made to the synagogue in the Old Testament. The *altercatio* emphasizes the superiority of the church over the synagogue by discounting the positive picture of the *concordia* and painting an almost entirely negative picture of the synagogue and the Jewish people.

The exposition of the Psalter has frequently served as the setting for this confrontation. As the favorite Old Testament book of the church, it provides abundant material for arguments over passages which are interpreted as referring to the promised Messiah (having come or not come in Christ) and to the people of God (the synagogue or the church). However, it is not the only biblical book which plays a role in this confrontation. The Epistle to the Romans with its explicit

---

[1] Seiferth, pp. 33ff. and 56ff. The *concordia* is that of the *Concordia Veteris et Novi Testamenti*. The *altercatio* takes its name from the tract, *Altercatio ecclesiae et synagogae*, falsely attributed to Augustine (Seiferth, pp. 56ff.; see also *Kirche und Synagoge*, Vol. I, p. 100).

references to the Jews and Israel is the most influential source for the discussion of the church-synagogue relationship by the early church fathers.[2]

Of course, we are not attempting to give a complete history of this confrontation, but it is important to keep in mind as we turn to our medieval Psalms commentators that neither the problem nor many of the attempts at solutions are totally new. Nevertheless, the Psalms commentators under consideration treat the relationship between church and synagogue in great detail, and this treatment affords valuable insight into their understanding of the church.

1. Altercatio Synagogae et Ecclesiae

We turn first to evidence of the *altercatio* in our medieval commentators, where the Jews or the synagogue are seen primarily in a negative light over against the church. The references are legion, and so we deal only with selected passages which indicate the way in which our commentators picture the synagogue in this unfavorable light, and what consequences this has for their understanding of the church.

The most obvious reproach against the Jews is their refusal to believe in Christ. The synagogue is rejected in favor of the believing church, or as Augustine puts it, the daughter-in-law (the church from the Gentiles) is divided against her mother-in-law (the synagogue).[3]

---

[2] See Schelkle, "Kirche und Synagoge in der frühen Auslegung des Römerbriefes," pp. 282ff. Elements of both the *concordia* and the *altercatio* are present in these commentaries, although the *altercatio* tended to prevail with time. Referring to the verdict of the fathers concerning Israel's guilt, Schelkle observes: "Also auch hier, wie so oft, ist die Sprache der späteren Kirche strenger als die der früheren" (*ibid.*, p. 291). However, Congar's remark concerning Bernard's attitude — that he is both generous and severe with the synagogue — is typical for most medieval authors, our commentators included ("L'ecclésiologie de S. Bernard," p. 151).

[3] *Enarr. in ps.* 44.12 (*CChr* 38, 502-503). Seiferth (pp. 52f.) calls attention to the importance of Psalm 44, along with the Song of Songs, for the idea of the marriage between Christ and the church. In maintaining that Augustine influences the connection of this theme with the rejection of the synagogue, he refers explicitly to this passage: "Die *unio mystica* ist mit der Blindheit und der Verwerfung der Synagoge eng verbunden. An dieser Verbindung hat Augustin schöpferischen Anteil ..." (p. 52). The Jews referred the Song of Songs to the relationship between God and the people of Israel (Riedlinger, p. 26). When the church is seen as the bride of Christ, here as well as in Psalm 44 and other passages, the natural consequence is the rejection of Israel and the substitution of the church for the synagogue. A notable exception is the commentary of Lyra on the Song of Songs. In treating the *ecclesia universalis* as bride, he sees the first six chapters of the Song of Songs as referring to the people of Israel, and chapters seven and eight to the history of the church up to Constantine (Riedlinger, pp. 371ff.).

97

The origin of Christ in the synagogue makes the reference to the synagogue as the mother of Christ quite natural. While the identification has positive significance for the synagogue, it is still necessary to account for the mutual rejection of Christ and the synagogue, the estrangement between Christ and his mother. The pericope which depicts Christ's encounter with his mother and brothers [Mk. 3 : 33] serves as a parable of this estrangement between Christ and the synagogue and, consequently, between the bride of Christ, the church from the Gentiles, and her mother-in-law, the synagogue. This bride did not consent to carnal circumcision, that is, to the "old sacraments" to which her mother-in-law, the synagogue, had adhered. The allegorizing is carried further. As the mother and brothers of Jesus remained outside the house where Jesus was teaching, so the contemporary Jews remain outside the church where Christ is still teaching. Not only is the original rupture between the church and the synagogue explained, but the transition is also made from the historical synagogue to the contemporary Jews, an identification which will become at times tragic for the Jews in the Middle Ages.[4]

These facets of the *altercatio* mentioned by Augustine recur in the Psalms commentaries of his successors. Cassiodorus speaks both of the blood ties of Christ to the synagogue and his estrangement from it. Christ calls the Jews "brothers," but he became an outsider to them when they did not believe in him. These Jews were also the "sons of his mother," but they were certainly not true sons, because if they had been true sons, they would have received Christ not as a stranger, but as a beloved brother.[5] Hugo mentions how the Jews heard the words of Christ and saw his miracles, but still did not believe. In fact, the people of the Jews had "donkey ears," namely stiff

---

[4] Especially during the Crusades when the zeal of some Crusaders and Crusade-preachers against the Moslem occupation of the Holy Land overflows into a sometimes equal hatred for the contemporary Jews in the Holy Land and in Europe as destroyers of the holy places and successors to the "killers of Christ." See Seiferth, pp. 101ff. and *Kirche und Synagoge*, Vol. I, pp. 111ff.

[5] *Expos.* 68.9 (*CChr* 97, 609): "Iudaeos hic appellat 'fratres', qui erant ei sanguinis vicinitate coniuncti: quibus 'extraneus factus est', quando ei credere noluerunt. ... Adiecit 'et hospes filiis matris meae. Hospitem' dicimus quemlibet domum nostram ad tempus habitantem, qui non nomine consanguinitatis, sed tamquam peregrinus excipitur. 'Matrem' vero suam Synagogam dicit, de qua ortus est, dum in iudaea gente nasci dignatus est. 'Filios' ergo 'matris' ipsos dicit, quos superius dixit et 'fratres'. Sed isti 'filii', si fuissent veri, non ut 'hospitem' habuissent, sed ut fratrem carissimum suscepissent Dominum Christum."

and heavy.[6] He also interprets Psalm 68 : 9 ("And a stranger to the sons of my mother") in reference to Christ and the synagogue. Christ explains that he sustained the reproach of the synagogue on account of the church to be built.[7] To this church taken from the Gentiles Christ gave his heredity—faith or the kingdom of heaven—when the Jews became reprobate.[8]

Perez makes some very explicit statements concerning Christ's rejection of the synagogue. The Messiah loved the church ("this city") more than the old synagogue.[9] It was necessary for Christ to repudiate the synagogue and to abolish the old law in order that he might give the new law. In turn, it is appropriate for the Jews to receive his new doctrine, believe in him, see his miracles, and obey and follow him by leaving the synagogue and the "oldness" of the Law.[10] In fact, the entire synagogue with all of its ceremonies died and was buried with Christ. It could not rise with Christ, however, because only the "evangelical truth" rose with Christ. This truth had been prefigured, to be sure, in those old ceremonies, but they were first brought to fulfillment in Christ.[11]

The common theme which runs through all these expressions of the *altercatio* is the rejection of the Jews because they did not believe in Christ. Important here is the role of *fides* as the decisive factor in this rejection and the succession of the Gentiles to the church. It is

---

[6] *Hugo* (44 : 11): "Sed quia multi Iudaei audierunt verba praedicationis Christi et viderunt mirabilia quae fecit, qui tamen non crediderunt. ... Sed quia populus Iudaeorum aures habebat asinas, scilicet erectas et graves...."

[7] *Hugo* (68 : 9-10): " 'Et peregrinus filiis matris meae', synagogae, i.e. Iudaeis. ... Et ostendit causam quare talia sustinebat, videlicet propter ecclesiam dei construendam. Unde dicit: 'Quoniam zelus domus tuae', i.e. amor de domo tua, i.e. ecclesia aedificanda."

[8] *Hugo* (110 : 7): " 'Ut det illis haereditatem gentium', scilicet fidem vel regnum coelorum, quod Iudaeis reprobatis datum est gentibus in haereditatem."

[9] *Perez* (86 : *conclusio*): "... messias diligit istam civitatem magis quam veterem synagogam."

[10] *Perez* (44 : 12): "Ex supradictis apparet et inferuntur quattuor conclusiones. Prima quidem est quod Christus rex messias in suo adventu debebat repudiare et abdicare synagogam et abolere legalia et dare novam legem et declarare legem veterem per hoc quod ait: 'Audi, filia et vide et inclina aurem tuam et obliviscere populum tuum et domum patris tui.' Quasi dicat: audi novam doctrinam sponsi et crede sibi et vide eius miracula et obediendo sequere eum dimittendo synagogam et vetustatem legis et mores antiquorum."

[11] *Perez* (83 : 1): "Unde dictum est psal. xlix. quod tota synagoga simul cum omnibus cerimonialibus mortua et sepulta fuit cum Christo, et non surrexit cum Christo nisi sola veritas evangelica figurata per illa cerimonialia, inquantum omnia fuerunt impleta in Christo."

99

not a matter of distinguishing between the true and false *fideles* in the already established church. Rather the distinction to be made is between the members of the baptized community, the *fideles* in the broadest sense, and the *infideles*, in this case the unbelieving Jews. All the *fideles* are assumed to possess faith, at least in the sense of believing in Christ and the articles of faith. As we know, when a further distinction becomes necessary, *caritas* or *fides formata* assumes the role of divider between "the sons of perdition and the sons of the kingdom." In drawing the line between the synagogue and the church, however, faith in Christ plays the decisive role:

> From what purification is the Jew excluded? From faith. For we live out of faith [Gal. 3 : 11] and concerning faith it was said: "Cleansing their hearts with faith" [Acts 15 : 9]. And because only faith in Christ [*fides Christi*] purifies, by not believing in Christ they forfeit their chance of becoming clean.[12]

By repudiating the *fides Christi*, the Jews become impure and lose their claim upon God's promises.

It is a short step from the rejection of the Jews because of their unbelief to the charge that they are hostile (*inimici*) to the church—the last example of the *altercatio* we wish to discuss. Whenever the word *inimicus* occurs in the Psalms, it is commonly interpreted as referring to the Jews. In his exposition of Psalm 8, Faber interprets "enemies" in the plural as the priests, scribes and Pharisees, and then the phrase "enemy and avenger" as the Jewish people, "which in the persecution of Christ the Lord appeared to be the defender of God and avenger of the Mosaic law."[13] This passage is obviously a reference to the role of the Jews in the crucifixion of Christ, which is one of the reasons for the frequent designation of the Jews as "enemies." We find other references to the responsibility of the Jews for the crucifixion, for example, in the interpretation of Psalm 68 : 2 ("The waters have entered up to my soul"). This passage is interpreted almost unanimously by our commentators as referring to the crucifixion of Christ

[12] *Enarr. in ps.* 88, s.2.7 (*CChr* 39, 1240): "A qua ergo emundatione dissolvitur Iudaeus? A fide. Ex fide enim vivimus; et de fide dictum est: 'Fide mundans corda eorum'; et quia sola fides Christi mundat, non credendo in Christum soluti sunt ab emundatione."

[13] *Faber* (8 : 3): " 'Propter inimicos tuos': sacerdotes, scribas et phariseos. 'Inimicum et ultorem': Iudaicum populum qui videbatur in persecutione Christi domini defensor dei et mosaice legis ultor." Cf. *Lyra* (8 : 3): "Populum Iudaicum Christum persequentem, qui fuit eius inimicus." And Cass., *Expos.* 88.11 (*CChr* 98, 806): " 'Inimicos' autem dicit infideles Iudaeos, qui per innumeras gentes Christi Domini virtute dispersi sunt...."

by the Jews—i.e., to the separation of his soul from the body.[14] The designation of the Jews as "enemy" is not only connected with the crucifixion of Christ but also more generally with their rejection of him: in that they defend the Father alone and thus dishonor the Son, they do not honor the Father either.[15] At the same time, not only the Jews are designated as enemies, but, according to Lombard, "all those who say things contrary to the dispensation made in the Crucified One."[16] The *Glossa* makes the identical statement and then gives two examples: the heretic who impugns true faith and the philosophers who impugn true wisdom.[17] The heretics are mentioned parallel with the Jews as enemies of Christ and the church.[18] This parallel is not only formulated in general terms, but occasionally the Jews are lined up with a particular heresy, e.g. when Cassiodorus accuses them together with the Donatists of appropriating to themselves the universal claim of the catholic church.[19]

The Jews come to serve as a model for all the enemies of the church, especially the heretics. Augustine expands the parallel further to include false Christians:

[14] Selected examples: Cassiodorus, *Expos.* 68.2 (*CChr* 97, 605): "Quapropter populus ille iudaicus 'usque ad animam' Domini Salvatoris 'intravit', quando eum crucifigere scelerata mente praesumpsit." *Hugo* (68 : 2): " 'Quoniam aquae,' scilicet populi Iudaeorum insipidi... 'Intraverunt usque ad animam meam', i.e. praevaluerunt contra me usque ad hoc quod tollunt animam meam crucifigendo me." *Glo. ord.* (68 : 2) in dependence on Augustine: " 'Aquae', id est, turbae quae praevaluerunt occidere Christum." *Lyra* (68 : 2): "Et ideo haec littera potest intelligi de capite Christo, quia persecutiones Iudaeorum intraverunt usque ad animam eius, i.e. usque ad separationem animae a corpore." Cf. also *Brev. in ps.* (100 : 8; *PL* 26, 1126): "Iudaei hunc versum audientes, et sequentes litteram occidentam, et desiderantes sanguinem fundere, si quis praevaricatus fuerit de lege, interficiunt eum. Siquidem non sunt contenti occisione prophetarum, sed et ipsum Dominum crucifixerunt." And *Perez* interprets Psalm 68 : 9 in terms of the Jewish leaders and carries Jesus' estrangement from his own people as far as the crucifixion (68 : 9).

[15] *Lomb.* (8 : 3; *PL* 191, 124): "Iudaeus enim inimicus est Dei, dum Patrem solum defendit, quia qui non honorificat Filium, non honorificat Patrem [Io. 5 : 23]."

[16] *Lomb.* (8 : 3; *PL* 191, 124): "Inimici sunt generaliter omnes, qui dispensationi per crucifixum factae contraria dicunt."

[17] *Glo. ord.* (8 : 3): "Inimici sunt omnes qui dispensationi per crucifixum factae contraria dicunt. Defensores videntur haeretici fidei, philosophi sapientiae, cum tamen et illi fidem et hi sapientiam veram impugnent." Cf. Aug., *Enarr. in ps.* 8.6 (*CChr* 38, 51).

[18] *Brev. in ps.* (79 : 9; *PL* 26, 1057): "Iudaeis atque haereticis, qui in circuitu Ecclesiae obstrepunt, nosque impugnant."

[19] *Expos.* 8.2 (*CChr* 97, 90): " 'In universa' vero 'terra', quia totum per mundum eius religio sancta dilatatur, nec erit aliqua patria, ubi catholica non laetetur Ecclesia. Quapropter desinant Iudaei vel Donatistae sibi specialiter vindicare quod ad universitatem magis pervenisse cognoscunt." Cf. *Glo. ord.* (8 : 2).

Who are the enemies of the church? the pagans? the Jews? The evil
Christians live worse than all of these. . . . Seeing, therefore, the multitude
of those leading despicable lives in the church, he says, "I have become
a scandal to all my enemies." The *mali* live worse in my sacraments than
those who have never entered the church.[20]

In the same vein Augustine maintains that the Jews sinned less by
crucifying Christ while he was still on earth than those who scorn him
sitting in heaven, namely the heretics and those who bring scandal
upon the church by leading evil lives.[21] In his anti-Donatist tract, *De
baptismo*, Augustine identifies the adulteress in Hosea 2 : 1-13 with
the pseudo-Israelites, whom the pseudo-Christians, the heretics and
the schismatics imitate.[22]

Hugo offers an interesting variation on the parallel between the
inimical Jews and some of their successors. In the context of his
remarks on the Jews, the heretics and the false Christians in his
exposition of Psalm 68, he makes a bold comparison between the
leaders of the synagogue who tormented Christ and the *clerici*
and *praelati* who still persecute Christ today (*hodie*) by oppressing
the righteous and simple and polluting the church.[23] Such a corre-

---

[20] Quoted by B. Blumenkranz in German translation in *Kirche und Synagoge*, Vol.
I, p. 95. The Latin text: *Enarr. in ps.* 30.ii, s.2.6 (*CChr* 38, 206): "Qui sunt inimici
ecclesiae? Pagani, Iudaei? Omnibus peius vivunt mali christiani. . . . Adtendens itaque
multitudinem male viventium in ecclesia, 'super omnes', inquit, 'inimicos meos factus
sum opprobrium'. Peius, inquit, vivunt mali in sacramentis meis, quam qui ad illam
nunquam accesserunt." With *mali christiani* Augustine certainly means the *mali* still
nominally in the catholic communion and not the Donatists, as Blumenkranz interprets
them.

[21] *Enarr. in ps.* 68, s.2.6 (*CChr* 39, 922): "Minus enim peccaverunt Iudaei cruci-
figentes in terra ambulantem, quam qui contemnunt in caelo sedentem. Quod ergo
fecerunt Iudaei, ut in escam quam iam acceperat darent bibendum amarum illum
potum, hoc faciunt qui male vivendo scandalum inferunt ecclesiae: hoc faciunt haeretici
amaricantes." Cf. *Glo. ord.* (73 : 22): "Cass. Dicunt enim: ubi est deus tuus? Contemptus
est a Iudaeis ambulans in terra, et a falsis christianis sedens in coelo."

[22] *De bapt.* iii.19.26 (*PL* 43, 151): "Quae est illa mulier adultera, quam Osee propheta
designat, quae dixit: 'Ibo post amatores meos, qui mihi dant panes meos et aquam
meam, vestes meas et linteamina mea, et universa quae mihi condecent' [Os. 2 : 5]?
Licet quidem hoc et de praevaricatrice Iudaeorum gente intelligere, sed tamen quos
alios imitantur pseudochristiani (hoc enim sunt omnes haeretici et schismatici), nisi
pseudo-Israelitas? Erant enim et veri Israelitae. . . ." Cf. Chapter I, n. 17 for the
continuation of this text and elaboration upon the *pseudo-christiani* and *antichristi*.

[23] *Hugo* (68 : 21): "Quia sicut Annas et Caiphas pontifices tribulaverunt dominum
persequendo eum, ita hodie clerici et praelati tribulant eum persequendo iustos et
simplices et polluendo ecclesiam." Vercruysse (pp. 47f. and 71) wonders if Luther's
criticism of the leaders of the synagogue could be a foretaste of his coming criticism
of the church hierarchy. We see here with Hugo that this approach had already been
taken, although the content of the respective criticisms is yet to be explored.

spondence is no longer a harmless comparison with the church's enemies outside its walls, but carries the thrust right to the heart of the church itself. Beginning in the same century, the Franciscan Spirituals would compare their persecution by the "church of the Pope" or the "church of the clerus" in a much more radical way with the suffering of Christ and his persecution at the hands of the original synagogue.[24]

The *altercatio* between synagogue and church can become a powerful weapon in the hands of those who reflect the negative glare of the synagogue back upon the church itself. The themes of the *altercatio* recur often, and generally they make the church look good as it defines itself in terms of its faith in Christ over against all unbelieving Jews and their successors. The church finds in the Jews a model for all its enemies, both internal and external. But the church also acknowledges that it is the successor of God's Old Testament people and that there exist continuity and *concordia* between them. This attitude leads to important insights into the church's understanding of itself as expressed by our Psalms commentators.

2. *Concordia Synagogae et Ecclesiae*

We can delineate three basic approaches to the *concordia*, three fundamental ways in which the synagogue is pictured in a positive light. First, and most obvious, is the concentration upon those Jews who were converted at the time of Christ and were joined with the converted Gentiles to form the church. Second is the projection of the church back into the Old Testament, so that certain spiritually enlightened members of the Jewish people, primarily the patriarchs and the prophets, are regarded as members of the church. And thirdly, there is the attribution of certain positive characteristics to the synagogue or Jewish people itself apart from a direct connection with the church.

The church from the Jews and Gentiles. —The most graphic picture of the composition of the church out of both converted Jews and Gentiles is given by Augustine: the image of a corner joined by two walls. One wall originates in circumcision and is composed of those Jews who believed. The other wall comes from the Gentiles and meets the wall from the Jews in the cornerstone who is Christ himself (Eph. 2 : 20). For Augustine, the truth of God is fulfilled (that is, the

[24] Ernst Benz, *Ecclesia Spiritualis* (Darmstadt, 1964), pp. 273, 302f., 341f.

103

fulfillment of his promise) in those Jews who believed, while the conversion of some Gentiles was due solely to his mercy.[25]

Augustine maintains that those Jews who were made Christians are Jews in the truest sense, whereas the other Jews who did not believe deserved to lose even the name. Thus "the true Judea is the church of Christ, believing in that king who came from the tribe of Judah through the Virgin Mary."[26] Following Paul he notes that the "church coming from the Gentiles" is the wild olive branch which is grafted onto the root in place of the branches broken off on account of unbelief (Rom. 11 : 17ff.).[27] And finally, Augustine describes the formation of the church through the conjunction of the two peoples with the metaphor of one flock and one pastor. In this context, the one flock is formed when the "faithful people from the Gentiles," the "other sheep not of this fold," are joined to the "faithful people from the Jews," the "lost sheep from the house of Israel."[28]

These themes are echoed by the commentators subsequent to Augustine. Hugo succinctly describes the foundation of the church in the conversion of the Gentiles and of "certain Jews."[29] Capitalizing on the meaning of the name "Joseph" as "increase," Hugo refers the name to the believing people of the Gentiles, which has expanded and

---

[25] *Enarr, in ps.* 88, s.1.3 (*CChr* 39, 1221-1222): "Ergo impleta est veritas Dei in iis, qui ex Israelitis crediderunt, et venit unus paries de circumcisione applicans se ad lapidem angularem [Eph. 2 : 20]. Sed ille lapis angulum non faceret, nisi alium parietem ex gentibus susciperet. Ille itaque paries tamquam proprie pertinet ad veritatem, iste autem alius ad misericordiam." Also *Enarr. in ps.* 76.17 (*CChr* 39, 1063). The *Glossa* uses this image in connection with another verse of the same psalm: *Glo. ord.* (88 : 13): " 'Thabor', Iudaei ad quos primum lumen venit. 'Hermon', gentes quae prius fuerunt anathematizatae. 'In nomine tuo exultabunt', coniunctis in angulari lapide duobus parietibus."

[26] *Enarr. in ps.* 75.1 (*CChr* 39, 1037): "Illi ergo verius Iudaei, qui christiani facti sunt ex Iudaeis; ceteri Iudaei qui in Christum non crediderunt, etiam nomen ipsum perdere digni fuerunt. Iudaea ergo vera, Christi ecclesia est, credens in illum regem qui venit ex tribu Iuda per virginem Mariam. . . ."

[27] *Enarr. in ps.* 72.2 (*CChr* 39, 987): "Ergo de radice patriarcharum dicit fractos quosdam ramos propter infidelitatem, et insertum ibi oleastrum, ut esset particeps pinguedinis olivae, id est, ecclesiam ex gentibus venientem."

[28] *Enarr. in ps.* 77.3 (*CChr* 39, 1068): "Neque dedignari nos oportet, immo gratias ineffabiles agere, quod sumus oves manuum eius, quas praevidebat cum diceret: Habeo alias oves quae non sunt de hoc ovili; oportet me et ipsas adducere, ut sit unus grex et unus pastor' [Io. 10 : 16], iungendo scilicet fidelem populum gentilium fideli populo Israelitarum, de quibus prius dixerat: 'Non sum missus nisi ad oves quae perierunt domus Israel' [Mt. 15 : 24]. Nam et congregabuntur ante eum omnes gentes, et separabit eos sicut pastor oves ab haedis."

[29] *Hugo* (8 : 3): "Et conversio gentium et quorundam Iudaeorum in quibus constituta est ecclesia."

been joined by the "believing people of the Jews," with the result that the church herself has increased.[30] Through the apostles God has led these sheep from the desert of unbelief into the flock of the *fideles*. Faber uses the same metaphor in speaking of the convergence of the Gentile and Hebrew peoples into one flock and fold.[31]

The coming of the believing Jews into the church is also expressed in terms of the synagogue which is to be converted. For example, Faber interprets Psalm 106 as "divine praise containing prophecy concerning Christ the Lord, the redeemed people, and the synagogue which is to be converted to saving faith."[32] And Lyra understands the phrase *propter inimicos meos* in Psalm 68 : 19 not only negatively in terms of the Jews who did not believe, but also "for the sake" of those Jews who are to be converted after they have heard of the resurrection of Christ, like the three thousand who believed Peter's Pentecost proclamation (Acts 2).[33]

The succession of the Jews to the church is facilitated by their role as the heredity of the Lord. This endowment is a favor that the merciful Lord did not grant to other nations. Only when the Hebrew people "became infirm" by not believing in the Lord Savior, has the Lord "perfected his heredity" by admitting the other nations into the "fullness of belief."[34] The Gentiles were only allowed to become members of the church because at least a portion of the Jews did not believe in Christ, although they were his unique heredity from the beginning. The key to the positive worth of the Jews is, in all these

---

[30] *Hugo* (79 : 2): " 'Israel', scilicet populum Iudaeorum. .... 'Ioseph', i.e. populum credentem de gentibus significatum per Ioseph, qui interpretatur augmentum, et populus gentium auctus et adiunctus est populo Iudaeorum credenti, et ita sunt augmentum ecclesiae. Deduxit dominus has oves per apostolos de deserto infidelitatis ad gregem fidelium."

[31] *Faber* (101 : 23): ". . . ut populi gentium et Hebreorum in unum gregem et ovile unum conveniant."

[32] *Faber* (106 : 1): "Psalmus: laus divina de Christo domino, de populo redempto, de synagoga ad fidem salutaris convertenda continens prophetiam."

[33] *Lyra* (68 : 19): " 'Propter inimicos meos', id est propter Iudaeos, quod dupliciter exponitur. Uno modo de Iudaeis obstinatis, ut per resurrectionem Christi confundantur. Alio modo de convertendis, ut audita Christi resurrectione convertantur, sicut legitur Act. ii. quod praedicante Petro Christi resurrectionem multi conversi sunt ad fidem, et ibidem subditur, 'et appositae sunt in die illa animae circiter tria milia' [Act. 2 : 41]."

[34] *Expos.* 67.10 (*CChr* 97, 589-590): "Denique sic sequitur: 'segregans Deus hereditati tuae', quia non hoc Dominus aliis gentibus dedit, quod tunc hebraeo populo miseratus indulsit. 'Hereditas' enim ipsius fuit populus Hebraeorum, sicut legitur: 'Et facta est portio Domini populus eius, Iacob funiculus hereditatis eius' [Dt. 32 : 9]. Haec si ad tempus 'infirmata est', Domino Salvatori minime credendo, 'perficit hereditatem' suam, quando gentes reliquas in supplementum credulitatis admittit."

texts, their belief in Christ and subsequent membership in the church. This applies specifically to those Jews at the time of Christ who made the right decision. Their predecessors, however, are also given a chance to belong to the church.

The church in the Old Testament.— According to Yves Congar, the idea that the church claims members for herself before the coming of Christ originates in the anti-Jewish polemic of the fathers. If this is the case, it seems strange that we include this topic in our discussion of the *concordia* between the synagogue and the church. It is, however, precisely the continuity of the church with Israel which is favored by the three-pronged counterattack of the early church against the Montanists, the Marcionites and the Manichaeans—all of which debased the Old Testament—as well as by direct efforts of the early church to undermine the claim of the Jewish people to be the exclusive custodian of God's revelation.[35] And this continuity is established primarily by projecting the church itself back into the Old Testament to include the patriarchs, the prophets, and all the righteous of the Old Testament. If this slights the integrity of these Israelites as Old Testament people, nevertheless such is not intended by the early fathers, nor by our commentators, who take up the same theme in their exposition of the Psalms.

Congar uses the term *ecclesia ab Abel* to characterize the inclusion of the Old Testament righteous in the church of the elect, which began with Abel and will exist until the last *electus* fills out the number of the predestined. Although theologians prior to Augustine considered the Old Testament righteous as belonging to the church,[36] Augustine appears to have been the first to speak of the beginning of the church of the elect with the righteous man Abel who was killed by his impious brother.[37] This theme emerges in the *Enarrationes*, where, for example, Augustine expands the limits of the church as far as possible both spatially and temporally:

[35] Congar, "Ecclesia ab Abel," p. 80.
[36] *Ibid.*, pp. 80-81.
[37] Congar (*ibid.*, pp. 84ff.) notes that the texts which deal with the *ecclesia ab Abel* date from 412 and the years following. He connects them with the beginning of Augustine's reflections on the two cities theme. Here we have to supplement what we said in Chapter I (*supra*, pp. 23ff.) about the close relationship between the predestined and the visible church to include the righteous of the Old Testament in the church of the predestined. Far from considering these Old Testament righteous apart from the church, Augustine projects the church back into the Old Testament.

The body of this head [Christ] is the church, which is found not only in this region, but is both here and extends throughout the whole world; nor does it exist only at this point in history, but it runs from Abel himself to the end of the world and includes all those who will be born and who will believe in Christ—the whole people of the saints belonging to one city. This city is the body of Christ, whose head is Christ.[38]

The church which began with Abel is simultaneously the body of Christ and is defined by Augustine as the body of all those throughout the extent of space and time who believe in Christ.

This would imply that the Old Testament righteous also believed in Christ even though they lived before the incarnation, and to a certain extent were Christians themselves. Augustine does not hesitate to make such a far-reaching assertion. In speaking of the patriarchs as the anointed (*christi*) of the Lord, Augustine asks whether they were not also Christians (*christiani*):

> And thus anointed, even if hiddenly, are they not already Christians? For although the flesh of Christ came from them, nevertheless, Christ was before them—which he himself told the Jews: "Before Abraham was, I am" [John 8 : 58]. Moreover, how did they not know him or believe in him, since for this reason they were called prophets, because they were proclaiming the Lord beforehand, though hiddenly. Wherefore he himself says plainly: "Abraham desired to see my day, and he has seen it and rejoiced" [John 8 : 56]. For no one, either before his incarnation or afterwards, is reconciled to God apart from faith which is in Christ Jesus, as was accurately defined by the Apostle: "God is one, and there is one mediator between God and man, the man Jesus Christ" [I Tim. 2 : 5].[39]

Because the patriarchs believed in Christ, they can be called Christians, and Augustine implies that this is possible for all men living before the incarnation who possessed such faith. In this respect,

---

[38] *Enarr. in ps.* 90, s. 2.1 (*CChr* 39, 1266): "Corpus huius capitis ecclesia est, non quae hoc loco est, sed et quae hoc loco et per totum orbem terrarum; nec illa quae hoc tempore, sed ab ipso Abel usque ad eos qui nascituri sunt usque in finem et credituri in Christum, totus populus sanctorum ad unam civitatem pertinentium; quae civitas corpus est Christi, cui caput est Christus." For Cain and Abel as the fathers of all the *iniqui* and *iusti* respectively, see *Enarr. in ps.* 48, s. 2.11 (*CChr* 38, 574).

[39] *Enarr. in ps.* 104.10 (*CChr* 40, 1542): "An ideo christi, quia etiamsi latenter, iam tamen christiani? quamvis enim caro Christi ex illis, tamen Christus ante illos, quod et Iuadeis respondit, dicens: 'Antequam Abraham fieret, ego sum.' Quomodo autem hunc illi ignorarent, aut in eum non crederent; cum propterea prophetae dicerentur quia licet occultius, tamen Dominum praenuntiabant? Unde aperte ipse dicit: 'Abraham concupivit videre diem meum, et vidit, et gavisus est.' Non enim quisquam praeter istam fidem quae est in Christo Iesu, sive ante eius incarnationem, sive postea, reconciliatus est Deo; cum sit ab Apostolo veracissime definitum: 'Unus enim Deus, et unus mediator Dei et hominum, homo Christus Iesus.' "

there is really no difference between those *fideles* or *iusti* who lived before Christ and we who live after him. They believed in Christ who was to come and were healed by their faith in him, whereas we believe in Christ who has come and are reconciled by this same faith. All these *fideles* form one church, one city, one body of Christ reaching across the span of time.[40]

On the basis of these texts in particular, Congar maintains that Augustine arrives at the position which the Scholastics also adopt: the Old Testament righteous were Christians. He points to the important fact that the bond between the Old Testament and the New Testament *fideles* is not an historical one, but rather a spiritual bond.[41] Those who live spiritually and believe in Christ, regardless of whether they live before or after the incarnation, belong to the church and are members of his body. Thus the historical integrity of the Old Testament people as such is ignored, and their positive value lies only in their proleptic possession of the *fides Christi.*

The Scholastics were not the first writers after Augustine to project the church back into the Old Testament. Our Psalms commentators do the same—which is to be expected considering the occurrence of the theme in the *Enarrationes* themselves. This projection does not always take the explicit form of the *ecclesia ab Abel*, however. Cassiodorus, for example, asks explicitly, if there are two testaments and only one law, why should we hesitate to assert that both the "old

[40] *Enarr. in ps.* 36, s. 3.4 (*CChr* 38, 370): "Dominus enim ipse in corpore suo, quod est ecclesia, iunior fuit primis temporibus, et ecce iam senuit. Nostis, et agnoscitis, et intellegitis, quia in hoc positi estis, et ita credidistis, quia caput nostrum Christus est; corpus capitis illius nos sumus. Numquid soli nos, et non etiam illi qui fuerunt ante nos? Omnes qui ab initio saeculi fuerunt iusti, caput Christum habent. Illum enim venturum esse crediderunt, quem nos venisse iam credimus; et in eius fide et ipsi sanati sunt, in cuius et nos; ut esset et ipse totius caput civitatis Ierusalem, omnibus connumeratis fidelibus ab initio usque in finem, adiunctis etiam legionibus et exercitibus angelorum, ut fiat illa una civitas sub uno rege, et una quaedam provincia sub uno imperatore, felix in perpetua pace et salute, laudans Deum sine fine, beata sine fine." We recall that the Old Testament *iusti* can also possess *caritas.* Cf. *supra*, Ch. I, n. 35.

[41] Congar, "Ecclesia ab Abel," p. 86: "Augustin, lui, arrive à cette conclusion que nous verrons les scolastiques reprendre très fermement: les justes de l'Ancien Testament étaient des chrétiens. C'est en toute vérité qu'ils appartenaient à l'Eglise. Entre celle-ci et l'ordre ancien auquel l'Evangile a mis fin, la coupure n'est pas proprement historique, mais spirituelle: les fidèles qui vivent charnellement dans l'Eglise appartiennent au vieux testament, et les justes qui, sous le régime de la Loi, ont vécu spirituellement au nouveau testament. De l'un à l'autre testament, le progrès est spirituel; il peut s'accomplir ou, au contraire, ne pas s'accomplir dans chaque âme, à quelque temps de l'Economie qu'elle appartienne."

and the new church compose the one bride of Christ acquired by his precious blood"?[42] Under the "old church," Cassiodorus understands those who before the coming of the Lord believed in him "with a holy faith," as he puts it elsewhere.[43] The *Glossa* appears to make no distinction between the *fideles* of the Old and the New Testament in affirming that all of them will be glorified with a "twin blessedness" after the destruction of death.[44]

Through the image of the vine our commentators affirm the continuity of God's people in both testaments and envision the church as present before the incarnation. Although Augustine places the origin of the vine in the Jewish people and accents its unity and continuity with the Jewish people through Christ, the Apostles and the first believers,[45] he does not apply his *ecclesia ab Abel* category to this particular biblical image. In fact, by speaking of the one vine of the Jewish people as the seed of Abraham and the root onto which the wild olive branch (the Gentiles) is grafted, he actually retains the integrity of the Old Testament people as such, at least in terms of historical continuity.[46] Cassiodorus acknowledges the origin of the vine in the Hebrew people, but he is anxious to make an allegorical application to the church instead of an historical one. Thus the vine becomes a *typus* of the church, the origin of the congregation of faithful peoples.[47]

[42] *Expos.* 8.1 (*CChr* 97, 89): "Nam si vetus et novum recte dicitur testamentum, cum tamen unius lex esse doceatur, cur asserere dubitemus antequam et novam Ecclesiam unam esse Domini Christi sponsam pretioso sanguine conquisitam?"

[43] *Expos.* 110.6 (*CChr* 98, 1017): "'Annuntiavit', manifestum fecit, populo suo scilicet christiano, quem redemit sanguine pretioso. Sed hoc illi prophetiae spiritu dicunt, qui ante adventum Domini in eum sancta fide crediderunt. 'Dedit' autem 'eis hereditatem gentium', quando Ecclesiam catholicam de cunctis nationibus vivis lapidibus fabricavit. Ipsa est 'hereditas' quae promissa est Abrahae: 'Multiplicabo semen tuum sicut stellas caeli et sicut arenam quae est ad oram maris' [Gn. 22 : 17]."

[44] *Glo. ord.* (88 : 37): "... quia fideles tam novi quam veteris testamenti post mortis occasum gemina beatitudine glorificabuntur, et inde testis fidelis in coelo, id est Christus."

[45] *Enarr. in ps.* 79.9 (*CChr* 39, 1115): "Sed tamen prima gens Iudaea fuit ista vinea. Gens autem Iudaea usque ad mare, et usque ad flumen regnavit. ... Videamus ergo testimonium Asaph; quid factum est primae vineae, quid est exspectandum secundae vineae, imo eidem vineae; ipsa est enim; non enim altera est. Inde Christus salus ex Iudaeis, inde Apostoli, inde primi credentes, et pretia rerum suarum ante pedes apostolorum ponentes; inde omnia haec."

[46] *Enarr. in ps.* 79.12 (*CChr* 39, 1116-1117): "Non aliam institue, sed hanc perfice. Ipsum est enim semen Abraham, ipsum est semen in quo benedicuntur omnes gentes: ibi est radix, ubi portatur oleaster insertus."

[47] *Expos.* 79.9 (*CChr* 98, 743): "Vineam enim dicit Hebraeorum gentem, quam positam in typo constat Ecclesiae, unde fidelium nata est congregatio populorum."

The *Glossa*, in turn, takes up both of these emphases: the historical continuity of the vine in Christ, the Apostles and the other righteous of which Augustine speaks, as well as the typological approach of Cassiodorus.[48] Hugo notes that Cassiodorus treats the vine "both literally and mystically concerning the church"; and, while Hugo constructs his own extensive typological comparison between the natural vine and the church, he also devotes a separate literal interpretation to the historical synagogue.[49] As a result, in the exposition of verse 15 of Psalm 79 ("And visit this vine and perfect it"), Hugo can employ the Augustinian continuity approach, where the vine begun in the Jews is perfected in the Gentiles; or, as the church alone, the vine is perfected by the remnant of the Jews which will be saved at the end.[50]

Even when the vine is interpreted by the preceding commentators as originating in the Jewish people, it receives positive worth only insofar as it is related to the church—either in terms of historical continuity or as a *typus* of the church. With Lyra, however, the historical vine is completely subsumed under "the one church of both the Old and New Testaments," the *ecclesia ab Abel*.[51] This application of Augustine's category to the image of the vine is facilitated by one of the homilies of Gregory the Great (d. 604), which worked its way

---

Expos. 79.13 (*CChr* 98, 744): "Istius vineae quae a iudaico populo ducit originem, miratur cur fuerit eversa munitio, hoc est, Domini subtracta defensio."

[48] *Glo. ord.* (79 : 10): "Et hoc est quod alibi dicitur: 'Et dominabitur a mari usque ad mare et a flumine usque ad terminos orbis terrae' [Ps. 71 : 8] quod non gentes Iudaeorum. Et non est altera, sed eadem vinea, inde Christus, inde apostoli, inde et alii iusti etsi aliqui rami fracti." Cf. *supra*, Ch. I, n. 99.

[49] *Hugo* (79 : 9): " 'Vineam. . .' Secunda pars, in qua agit de ecclesia sub typo vineae. Sed notandum quod Cassiodorus legit istos sex versus et ad litteram et mystice de ecclesia, ut sit hic differentia inter synagogam et ecclesiam. De synagoga ergo ad litteram primo transcurramus." There follows as the separate literal sense a history of the Jewish people up to the destruction by Titus.

[50] *Hugo* (79 : 15): " 'Et visita', gratia cooperante, ut procedat de virtute in virtutem. 'Vineam istam', scilicet ecclesiam. 'Et perfice eam', de reliquiis Israel quae in fine salvae fient. Vel quae inchoata est de Iudaeis, perfice de gentibus, non aliam inchoa."

[51] *Lyra* (79 : 1): " 'Qui regis Israel etc.' Ad intellectum huius psalmi sciendum quod una est ecclesia veteris et novi testamenti quae frequenter in veteri et novo testamento dicitur vinea dei. Unde dicit Greg. homel. vii. super evangelium: 'Quis vero patrisfamilias similitudinem rectius tenet quam conditor noster, qui regit quos condidit et electos suos in hoc mundo possidet quasi subiectos dominus in domo; qui habet vineam suam, scilicet ecclesiam, quae ab Abel iusto usque ad ultimum electum qui in fine mundi nasciturus est, quot sanctos protulit quasi tot palmites misit.' Asaph igitur processum huius vineae in spiritu sancto praevidens scripsit hunc psalmum, in quo primo describit statum huius vineae ante Christi adventum et secundo post eius adventum."

into the common tradition.[52] For Lyra, this church from Abel has produced as many saints as the vine has sprouted branches. He regards the entire psalm as depicting the procession of this vine both before and after the advent of Christ. Although he notes that the church prior to the advent is properly called the synagogue, Lyra nevertheless subsumes the *synagoga* under the category *ecclesia*.[53]

This form of the *concordia* is known not only to the later Psalms commentators. Thomas projects the church back into the Old Testament. For him, the church in the Old and New Testaments is one church.[54] In the passage from the *Summa Theologiae* discussed above,[55] we intentionally omitted the third objection to the statement that Christ is the head of all men and the rebuttal to this objection. According to the objection, Christ compares to the sacraments of the old law as a body to its shadow. Since the fathers of the Old Testament were paying allegiance to these sacraments in their own time, they could not belong to the body of Christ and Christ cannot be the head of all men.[56] In his rebuttal, Thomas maintains that the fathers of the Old Testament were not insisting upon the legal sacraments as things in themselves (*res*), but as images and shadows of things to come. After showing that the same *motus* is involved in regard to the image as well

[52] *Hom. in Evang.* 19 (*PL* 76, 1154): "Regnum coelorum homini patrifamilias simile dicitur, qui ad excolendam vineam suam operarios conducit. Quis vero patrisfamilias similitudinem rectius tenet quam conditor noster, qui regit quos condidit, et electos suos sic in hoc mundo possidet, quasi subiectos dominus in domo?. Qui habet vineam, universalem scilicet Ecclesiam, quae, ab Abel iusto usque ad ultimum electum qui in fine mundi nasciturus est, quot sanctos protulit, quasi tot palmites misit. Hic itaque paterfamilias ad excolendam vineam suam mane, hora tertia, sexta, nona et undecima operarios conducit, quia a mundi huius initio usque in finem ad erudiendam plebem fidelium praedicatores congregare non destitit."

[53] *Lyra* (79 : 9): " 'Vineam'. Hic consequenter describitur processus ecclesiae ante Christi adventum, quae proprie nomine dicitur synagoga; et primo describitur processus in prosperitate, secundo in adversitate, ibi 'Ut quid destruxisti'. Circa primum dicit: 'Vineam' id est populum Israel dei cultorem, Esa. v [: 7]: 'Vinea Domini exercituum domus Israel est.' " Although Lyra describes the church before the advent of Christ in terms of the historical synagogue, it remains essentially *church*. He also interprets the Song of Songs in this way. Cf. *supra*, n. 3.

[54] *ST* III q. 8 a.6 obj. 1: "Sed una est Ecclesia in novo et in veteri Testamento." This statement is made as a generally accepted premise on which he bases an objection. The rebuttal does not challenge the authenticity of this premise, but also takes it for granted.

[55] Cf. *supra*, pp. 52ff.

[56] *ST* III q.8 a.3 obj. 3: "Praeterea, sacramenta veteris Legis comparantur ad Christum sicut umbra ad corpus, ut dicitur Col. 2 [: 17]. Sed Patres veteris Testamenti sacramentis illis suo tempore serviebant: secundum illud Hbr. 8 [:5]: 'Exemplari et umbrae deserviunt caelestium.' Non ergo pertinebant ad corpus Christi. Et ita Christus non est caput omnium hominum."

111

as to the *res*, he concludes that, by observing the legal sacraments, the *antiqui patres* were annexed to Christ by the same faith and love by which we (= post-advent Christians) are brought to him. As a result, they were belonging to the same body of the church to which we adhere.[57]

At another point in the *Summa* where Thomas discusses the relationship of the new law to the old, he maintains that some living under the Old Testament possessed the *caritas* and grace of the Holy Spirit. These privileged few were expecting primarily spiritual and eternal promises; and in this respect, they were "belonging to the new law."[58] Again, those in the Old Testament who were acceptable to God through faith were belonging already to the New Testament, for they were not being justified apart from faith in Christ, who himself is the author of the New Testament.[59] In spite of the unity of faith in both testaments, however, Old Testament faith had a different "status" from New Testament faith. The Old Testament faithful were believing that which would come (*futurum*), while we believe that which has been accomplished (*factum*).[60]

[57] *ST* III q.8 a.3 ad 3: "Ad tertium dicendum quod sancti Patres non insistebant sacramentis legalibus tanquam quibusdam rebus, sed sicut imaginibus et umbris futurorum. Idem autem est motus in imaginem, inquantum est imago, et in rem: ut patet per Philosophum, in libro *de Memoria et Reminiscentia*. Et ideo antiqui Patres, servando legalia sacramenta, ferebantur in Christum per fidem et dilectionem eandem qua et nos in ipsum ferimur. Et ita Patres antiqui pertinebant ad idem corpus Ecclesiae ad quod nos pertinemus."

[58] *ST* I-II q.107 a.1 ad 2: "Fuerunt tamen aliqui in statu veteris testamenti habentes caritatem et gratiam Spiritus Sancti, qui principaliter expectabant promissiones spirituales et aeternas. Et secundum hoc pertinebant ad legem novam."

[59] *ST* I-II q.107 a.1 ad 3: "Illi autem qui in veteri testamento Deo fuerunt accepti per fidem, secundum hoc ad novum testamentum pertinebant: non enim iustificabantur nisi per fidem Christi, qui est auctor novi testamenti." In view of this and the above texts from Thomas, the following statement of Preus is misleading (p. 121): "With Lombard and those who followed him, such as Bonaventura and Thomas, justification could not occur until the time of Christ, because that is the time of the appearance of grace and *caritas* (which makes the moral law work spiritually); with Perez, the suggestion is that justification could already occur for the Old Testament fathers on the basis of the future, promised Christ." On the contrary, justification of the Old Testament fathers can occur through faith (where *caritas* is not excluded) in Christ for any theologian, such as Augustine and Thomas, who projects the *church* back into the Old Testament. The Old Testament fathers are regarded as belonging to the New Testament—yet before the time of Christ. Perez is no different in our estimation (cf. the discussion *infra*, pp. 126ff.).

[60] *ST* I-II q.107 a.1 ad 1: "Ad primum ergo dicendum quod unitas fidei utriusque testamenti attestatur unitati finis: dictum est enim supra quod obiectum theologicarum virtutum, inter quas est fides, est finis ultimus. Sed tamen fides habuit alium statum in veteri et in nova lege: nam quod illi credebant futurum, nos credimus factum."

112

These Old Testament fathers were, of course, a minority among the Old Testament people, and they were righteous only insofar as they were already perceiving, living by, and believing in the New Testament and its author, Christ. Thus they belonged to the church, or better, the church was already present in them. That which joined them to the church was the unity of faith in Christ which could be enjoyed and utilized in the Old Testament, insofar as they were already believing in Christ who was to come. This is a faithful rendering of the Augustinian affirmation of one church and one faith in both testaments.[61]

Perez gives a concise summary of the themes surrounding the one church in both testaments:

> And therefore Gregory, in his homily on the vine, says that there was always one vine and one church from Adam and Abel up to the last predestined, whose branches and members were all the elect of both testaments. And thus Adam and Abel and Abraham were already members of Christ and citizens of this city. For though Christ was not yet incarnate, nevertheless he was already being believed, because faith is that which joins the members to their head.[62]

All the elements are present: the *ecclesia ab Abel* (also *ab Adam*), the one vine, the one church, the membership of the patriarchs and Old Testament righteous in the church, and the one faith in Christ which makes them members. The church completely subsumes the synagogue into itself, and the *concordia* between synagogue and church is attained through the projection of the church back into the Old Testament. This absorption of the synagogue by the church deprives it of any positive historical significance of its own. In fact, it is more appropriate to speak of a union of the synagogue and the church than of a *concordia*.

---

[61] Cf. *supra*, notes 38-40. Also *Enarr. in ps.* 50.17 (*CChr* 38, 612): "... et ita a sanctis patribus dispensatio susceptae carnis futura credebatur, sicut a nobis facta creditur. Tempora variata sunt, non fides." The faith of the Old Testament fathers is not only a *fides implicita*, but includes belief in some of the most important articles of faith, especially the Christological ones: the incarnation, passion, resurrection and ascension of Christ. See J. Beumer, "Die Idee einer vorchristlichen Kirche bei Augustinus," *MThZ* 3 (1952), p. 166.

[62] *Perez* (*prol.* tr.3 c.2 cl.7): "Et ideo dicit Grego. homelia de vinea quod ab Adam et Abel usque ad ultimum electum semper fuit una vinea et una ecclesia, cuius palmites et membra fuerunt omnes electi utriusque testamenti. Et sic Adam et Abel et Abraham iam erant membra Christi et cives huius civitatis. Nam licet Christus nondum esset incarnatus, tamen iam erat Christus creditus quia fides est illa que compaginat membra suo capiti."

The positive estimate of the synagogue.— At this point one could ask whether the Psalms commentators had anything positive to say about the synagogue as an Old Testament people. Such a positive estimation would have to form the basis for any real *concordia* between church and synagogue, where the synagogue does not lose its identity in the church and prematurely assume New Testament character. The answer to this question depends upon the hermeneutical stance of our authors, that is, how they understand the literal sense of the Psalter and how seriously they take the historical Old Testament situation in which the Psalms were composed, as well as the Old Testament people who composed them and about whom they sing.[63] As one might suspect, the interest of our commentators is not primarily directed to the Old Testament setting itself; thus, whatever favorable appraisal is made of the Old Testament people in their own right tends to be tempered with a negative judgment measured by the standard of the New Testament people.

This attitude goes back to Augustine himself. He defines the synagogue as those who were worshipping God devotedly (*pie*), but nevertheless on account of earthly things, on account of the goods of this present life.[64] The word "nevertheless" (*tamen*) is the key word here. True, this synagogue was better off than other peoples, insofar as it sought these temporal goods from God and not from demons. Except for a few prophets, however, whose gaze could discern beyond these earthly goods the heavenly and eternal kingdom, the members of the synagogue were attentive only to the worldly favors which they had been promised and granted by God. They did not understand the spiritual *res* signified by these earthly goods; thus, they did not imagine there was anything better which God could give to those who were loving and serving him.[65] The synagogue as a whole

---

[63] See Preus for a very clear discussion of medieval hermeneutics, in which he deals with a number of our commentators. We do not recount all his conclusions in our study. Suffice it to say he concludes a basic inability of the medieval authors to deal with the Old Testament in a manner which allows it to retain its historical integrity. It tends rather to remain in the shadow of the New (cf. Preus, pp. 269f.).

[64] *Enarr. in ps.* 72.6 (*CChr* 39, 990): "Synagoga ergo, id est, qui Deum ibi pie colebant, sed tamen propter terrenas res, propter ista praesentia."

[65] *Ibid.*: "Sunt enim impii qui praesentium rerum bona a daemonibus quaerunt; hic autem populus ideo melior erat gentibus, quod quamvis praesentia bona et temporalia, tamen ab uno Deo quaerebat, qui est creator omnium, et spiritalium, et corporalium: cum ergo illi pii secundum carnem adtenderent, id est, illa synagoga quae erat in bonis, pro tempore bonis, non spiritalibus, quales erant ibi prophetae, quales pauci intellectores regni caelestis, aeterni; ergo illa synagoga animadvertit quae acceperit a

114

is cast in a negative light in spite of its devotion to God, and Augustine's interest is concentrated on those who were able to understand what was behind the Old Testament figures. These Israelites with the extraordinary depth perception are the real heirs of the New Testament, as opposed to all the other "carnal Israelites" to whom God gives the earthly Jerusalem—which is only Old Testament, belonging to the old man.[66]

In spite of these limitations, Augustine concedes a degree of positive worth to the synagogue in its devotion to God at its own level. This inherent positive worth can be traced in our other commentators, although certainly not in abundance, and often tempered by reservations. Cassiodorus maintains that although God creates and disposes all things, he is said to have created the Jews in a special way (*specialiter*); he gave them the law and the prophets and performed miracles on their behalf. They learned proper faith and worship of God through Moses, and remained the heredity of the Lord as long as they were serving him with a pure spirit.[67] The *Glossa* picks up this theme of the special creation of the Jews.[68] And Hugo even speaks of the "sanctification" of the people; they were made holy in the promised land by worshipping the true God.[69] Hugo makes this comment in the course of his historical interpretation of Psalm 113. We find a similar expression in the literal exposition of

Deo, et quae promiserit Deus populo illi, abundantiam rerum terrenarum, patriam, pacem, felicitatem terrenam; sed in his omnibus figurae erant; et non intellegens quid ibi lateret in rebus figuratis, putavit hoc pro magno dare Deum, nec habere melius quod dare posset diligentibus se et servientibus sibi."

[66] *Enarr. in ps.* 110.8 (*CChr* 40, 1624): "Dedit quidem Deus Israelitis carnalibus terrenam Ierusalem, 'quae servit cum filiis suis' [Gal. 4 : 25], sed hoc Vetus Testamentum est, ad veterem hominem pertinens. Qui autem ibi figuram intellexerunt, haeredes etiam tunc Novi Testamenti exstiterunt; quoniam 'quae sursum est Ierusalem libera est, quae est mater nostra' [Gal. 4 : 26] aeterna in caelis."

[67] *Expos.* 73.2 (*CChr* 98, 673): " 'Congregatio' enim Iudaeorum evidenter ipso adiuvante praevaluit, cum eos sub aegyptio populo crescere faciebat et quando placuit miraculis insignibus liberare dignatus est. Nam cum omnes 'creet' atque disponat, Iudaeos quasi specialiter 'creasse' dicitur, quibus et legem dedit et prophetas contulit et miracula magna concessit. 'Ab initio' dixit, fidei scilicet culturaeque prolatae, quam per Moysen populus accepit hebraeus. Sequitur 'liberasti virgam hereditatis tuae'. 'Hereditas' Domini fuit populus Iudaeorum, quamdiu ei puro animo serviebat." The phrase "as long as" (*quamdiu*) indicates that there is more to come. In fact, Cassiodorus continues this psalm with an account of the falling away of the Jews from Christ and the prophecy of their return in the end.

[68] *Glo. ord.* (73 : 2): " 'Possedisti', Cas. vel creasti; et si omnes creat et disponit, Iudaeos tamen specialiter, quibus legem et prophetas dedit."

[69] *Hugo* (113 : 2): " 'Sanctificatio', ... id est populi Iudaeorum, qui in terra promissionis sanctificatus est colendo verum deum."

115

Lyra.[70] He calls the Jews a devoted people, who were firmly hoping to be liberated from the Babylonian captivity.[71] The sons of Israel are God's elect, whom he chose to become his special people.[72] Lyra also admits the rabbinic interpretation of "lilies and roses" in Psalm 44: these are the sons of Israel who were excelling all other peoples in faith and worship of the one God.[73] All the same, he affirms that this psalm speaks *literally* of Christ and the church, and in the course of his literal exegesis compares the exterior glory of the synagogue unfavorably with the interior glory of the church.[74] As a result of this concentration upon the church, the positive evaluation of the synagogue fades into the background.

Thus it is difficult for our commentators to speak positively of the synagogue without simultaneously pointing out its disadvantages over against the church. A good example is the way in which Faber concedes that the synagogue had a grace of its own coming from above, by which it was living in expectation of the Messiah. But he cannot stop there. He immediately overshadows this concession with a double affirmation of the superiority of the abundant grace which the church received.[75] The temptation of using the synagogue as a foil against which to enhance the glory of the church is too great in most cases to allow the Old Testament people to stand on their own feet

---

[70] Preus (pp. 67ff.) points to the double literal sense in Lyra's hermeneutic: the historical sense of the Old Testament and the New Testament normative literal sense where the OT *res* immediately signify NT *res*. Lyra's focusing on the history of the Old Testament people in the first "literal sense" is the setting for his positive statements on the Jews.

[71] *Lyra* (41 : 6): " 'Quare tristis'. Hic consequenter ponitur aliquale solatium quod surgebat ex hoc quod populus devotus firmiter sperabat ab illa captivitate liberari."

[72] *Lyra* (88 : 4): " 'Electis meis', id est filiis Israel quos elegi in populum peculiarem."

[73] *Lyra* (44 : 1): ". . . quia secundum Hebraeos per lilia vel rosas hic intelliguntur filii Israel qui alios populos in fide excellebant et cultu unius dei; et in psalmo isto exprimitur prosperitas filiorum Israel quae fuit praevisa in spiritu a filiis chore."

[74] *Lyra* (44 : 1): ". . . propter quod psalmus iste loquitur ad litteram de rege immortali Iesu Christo qui est vere deus latria adorandus et de sua sponsa ecclesia tanquam de regina." And (44 : 12): " 'Et concupiscet etc.', quia Christus rex delectatur in cultu spirituali ecclesiae, quae est pulchrior quam cultus exterior synagogae in auro templi et similibus consistens." And (44 : 14): " 'Omnis gloria etc.' Gloria enim ecclesiae consistit in ornatu interiori charismatum et virtutum et non in magno apparatu exteriori, sicut sinagoga gloriabatur in parietibus templi deauratis et vasis aureis et caeteris pretiosis in ministerium templi deputatis."

[75] *Faber*[a] (132 : 2): "Et sequenti versu ros caelestem et desuper advenientem gratiam significat, qua synagoga in expectatione Messie sancti sanctorum vegetabat ac vivebat. Sed ecclesiam Christus dominus multo amplius benedixit et sanctificavit quam unguentum illud veteris legis Aaron et synagoge sacerdotes. Multo uberiorem vivificantem gratiam contulit quam ros ille gratie sue veteri olim elargitus synagoge."

and function as an independent partner in the *concordia*. The gaze of our commentators is drawn rather to those Jews who joined the church at the time of Christ or who could be reckoned members of the church already in the Old Testament period. The church remains the dominant partner in the *concordia*.

3. Synagoga Fidelis

We gain further insight into the positive evaluations of the synagogue by examining a series of texts which cluster around the interpretation of the name *Asaph*, who is given as the author of Psalms 49 and 72-82.[76] Augustine keynotes the theme by observing that through translation from the Hebrew and transliteration from the Greek, Asaph is interpreted *synagoga*, and thus the voice of Asaph speaking in the psalm is the voice of the synagogue.[77] He simultaneously gives this interpretation a positive connotation by admonishing his hearers not to think of the synagogue always in terms of those Jews who killed the Lord, but to remember there were "rams" (*arietes*) among them of whom we are sons. The rams turn out to be not the whole Old Testament people before the advent of Christ, but rather the apostles and Paul—that is, those Jews who were most outstanding among the first believers in Christ.[78]

This interpretation of Asaph as synagogue comprises the same basic group which we have met as the first expression of the *concordia*—the first Jewish converts to Christianity.[79] In his exposition of the title to Psalm 72 (*Psalmus Asaph*), Augustine also mentions the remaining positive evaluations of the synagogue with which we have dealt. The

[76] According to I Chronicles 16 : 4ff., Asaph was the chief of the ministers appointed by David to sing thanks to the Lord before the ark of the covenant. Also according to I Chronicles 25 : 1, Asaph was one of David's chief ministers of music. Our commentators are aware of the historical factor, of course. Cf. *Brev. in ps.* (77 : 1; *PL* 26, 1014): "Asaph unus fuit de chorodidascalis, sicut fuerunt et filii Core, et Idithun, et caeteri."

[77] *Enarr. in ps.* 72.4 (*CChr* 39, 988): "Cuius vox est psalmus? 'Asaph'. Quid est: 'Asaph'? Sicut invenimus in interpretationibus ex lingua hebraea in graecam, et ex graeca nobis in latinam translatis, 'Asaph' synagoga interpretatur. Vox est ergo synagogae." The Hebrew verb אסף means "to gather" and is given by the Greek συνάγω (= to bring together), the noun form of which is συναγωγή.

[78] *Ibid.*: "Sed tu cum audieris synagogam, noli continuo detestari quasi interfectricem Domini. Erat quidem illa synagoga interfectrix Domini; nemo dubitat; sed memento de synagoga fuisse arietes, quorum filii sumus. Unde dicitur in psalmo: 'Afferte Domino filios arietum' [Ps. 28 : 1]. Qui inde arietes? Petrus, Iohannes, Iacobus, Andreas, Bartholomaeus, et ceteri apostoli. Hinc et ipse primo Saulus, postea Paulus."

[79] Cf. *supra*, pp. 103ff.

117

first evaluation concerns those "over-perceivers" (usually the prophets) who were capable of discerning that God had promised heavenly, eternal *res*, and should be worshipped on account of these and not only for the sake of earthly goods.[80] Augustine asks whether only the prophets (represented by the person of Asaph), or not also some of the people, had this extraordinary depth perception:

> Is therefore "the understanding of Asaph" to be taken in such a way that Asaph alone is understood, or should it be taken figuratively, so that the synagogue is intended, that is, the same people to whom it is said: "Attend, my people, to my law"? Why then does he reproach that same people through the prophet saying, "Israel has not known me, and my people has not understood" [Is. 1 : 3]? But certainly some of the people were understanding, having faith which afterwards was revealed not to belong to the letter of the law, but to the grace of the Spirit. For they must have had the same faith which they were able to foresee and foretell would be revealed in Christ, especially since the old sacraments signified future ones. Did the prophets alone have this faith, and not also the people? Certainly those who took the prophets at their word were being helped by the same grace, so that they might understand what they were hearing.[81]

Not only the prophets, therefore, but also those Jews who trusted the foresight of the prophets were able to perceive the fulfillment in Christ. This group, who already possessed the New Testament faith

[80] Cf. *supra*, n. 65 ("prophetae ... pauci intellectores"). Cf. *Enarr. in ps.* 72.1 (*CChr* 39, 986): "... illi ergo populo primo adhuc carnali, ubi pauci prophetae intellegebant et quid desideraretur a Deo, et quando haberet publice praedicari, praenuntiaverunt futura haec tempora, et adventum Domini nostri Iesu Christi."

[81] We begin the Latin text a few lines earlier. *Enarr. in ps.* 77.2 (*CChr* 39, 1066-1067): " 'Adtendite', inquit, 'populus meus, legem meam.' Quem hic credamus loqui nisi Deum? Ipse enim legem dedit populo suo, quem liberatum ex Aegypto congregavit, quae congregatio proprie synagoga nuncupatur, quod interpretatur Asaph. Utrum ergo ita dictum est: 'Intellectus Asaph', quod ipse Asaph intellexerit, an figurate intellegendum, quod eadem synagoga, hoc est, idem populus intellexerit, cui dicitur, 'Adtendite, populus meus, legem meam'? Quid est ergo quod eumdem populum per prophetam increpat, dicens: 'Israel autem me non agnovit, et populus meus non intellexit' ? Sed profecto erant etiam in illo populo qui intellegerent, habentes fidem quae postea revelata est non ad legis litteram, sed ad gratiam Spiritus pertinentem. Non enim sine ipsa fide fuerunt, qui eius in Christo futuram revelationem praevidere et praenuntiare potuerunt; cum et illa vetera sacramenta significantia fuerint futurorum. An soli prophetae habebant hanc fidem, non et populus? Immo vero etiam qui prophetas fideliter audiebant, eadem adiuvabantur gratia, ut intellegerent quod audiebant." Preus (p. 45) rightly calls attention to the division of the OT people into two camps—the carnal, ordinary folk who do not know what is going on, and the spiritual elite who have the special "intellectus" and really do not belong to the Old Testament anymore. That which he notes in connection with Bonaventura and Lombard, however, is already explicit in Augustine.

whose fulfillment they foresaw, is properly called synagogue. The theme of the one faith in both testaments, which Augustine emphasizes in connection with the *ecclesia ab Abel*, emerges here in his positive evaluation of the synagogue.

The devoted worship of the whole synagogue, which forms the third positive evaluation of the Old Testament people, appears in Augustine's exposition of the title of Psalm 72—that is, when he is discussing the interpretation of Asaph as synagogue.[82] Thus all three types of positive evaluation discussed in the previous section appear in the course of Augustine's dealing with the interpretation of Asaph as synagogue. This is decisive for the definition of the *synagoga fidelis*, which, to be sure, Augustine himself does not mention, but which becomes the *terminus technicus* for designating the positive descriptions.

As far as we could determine in the course of our investigation, the term *synagoga fidelis* originates with Cassiodorus. He employs it to make more precise the meaning of Asaph as synagogue, that is, to explain how a part of the synagogue could function as the speaker of psalms which point to the coming of Christ:

> We ought to see the faithful synagogue of the Lord speaking here, which believed that Christ would come and received his advent with glorious expectation. This faithful synagogue contained the patriarchs and the prophets, Nathaniel, and even the apostles themselves, as well as others who were believing sincerely and devotedly.[83]

In this text, two of the above-mentioned groups are accounted for: the patriarchs and prophets of the Old Testament who already believed in and expected Christ, and the first New Testament believers from the Jews. Cassiodorus elaborates upon this composition of the faithful synagogue at other points in his commentary. In his exposition of Psalm 77, Cassiodorus interprets Asaph as the faithful synagogue and then asserts that those Old Testament righteous who had the proper *intellectus* cannot be regarded as "strangers to our

---

[82] Cf. *supra*, n. 64.
[83] *Expos.* 49.1 (*CChr* 97, 440): "Huius enim nominis significatio, quae apud Hebraeos semper est plene mysteriis, indicat Synagogam quae in hoc psalmo loquitur. Sed hic illa fidelis Domini Synagoga intellegenda est quae et venturum Christum credidit, et adventum eius gloriosa exspectatione suscepit: in qua fuerunt patriarchae, prophetae, Nathanael, ipsi quoque apostoli et reliqui sincera devotione credentes." Asaph denotes the *synagoga fidelis* because the title says *Intellectus Asaph*. Cf. *Expos.* 77.1 (*CChr* 98, 709): "Asaph vero diximus hebraea lingua Synagogam significare, latine collectionem. Sed quia intellectum praemisit, fidelem· hic Synagogam loqui posse declaravit. Exprobrare enim malis nequeunt, nisi corda fidelium."

119

faith," since they understood their obedience to the commandments as spiritual.[84] The prophets also possessed this faith, because they were not righteous unless they believed what they were foretelling concerning the advent of the Lord.[85] When Cassiodorus explains the significance of Asaph in the title of Psalm 78, he does not explicitly attach the adjective *fidelis* to the synagogue. But it cannot be far from his mind when he says that those living before the time of Christ—"the prophets, patriarchs and the people already devoted to Christ"—can hardly be conceived of as foreign (*alieni*) to Christians, when the former sparkled so brightly with the Lord's grace.[86] Finally, Asaph signifies that synagogue whose members were alive at the coming of Christ and deserved to see him in the flesh.[87]

The primary reference of the term *synagoga fidelis* is to that part of the Old Testament people who perceived the coming of Christ beforehand and believed in him, as well as to those Jews who received him when he came. Both had faith in Christ and were essentially New Testament people, who, wholly in the sense of Augustine, already belonged to the church. But Cassiodorus also interprets Asaph simply as the synagogue which was worshipping the Lord, although, when they began to see evil men prosper, they fell victim to some bad theologizing.[88] This is the limited positive evaluation of the synagogue given by Augustine in his exposition of Psalm 72, which is here taken

---

[84] Cf. the preceding note. *Expos.* 77.1 (*CChr* 98, 710): " 'Populus meus' illos profecto significat qui eius mandatis oboedientes fuerunt. Non enim aut prophetae, aut alii iusti a nostra fide dici potuerunt alieni, qui actus illos primi temporis spiritaliter acceperunt, . . ."

[85] *Expos.* 77.3 (*CChr* 98, 711): " 'Patres' suos Moysen dicit et alios prophetas veteris testamenti, qui de Domini adventu multa locuti sunt et illuminati praedicaverunt, quod et iste fieri praevidebat. Iusti enim non essent, nisi probarentur credere quae dicebant."

[86] *Expos.* 78.1 (*CChr* 98, 732): " 'Psalmus Asaph'. Sicut saepe diximus, haec significatio nominis ad actus illos pertinet qui ad mandata Domini gratiamque referuntur. Asaph vero Synagogam significat, quae tamen catholicae convenire possit Ecclesiae. Neque enim Christianis alieni credendi sunt, qui gratiae dominicae claritate fulserunt. Adde prophetas, patriarchas et populum illum iam Christo devotum ante tempora christiana."

[87] *Expos.* 81.1 (*CChr* 98, 757): "Ponitur enim hic 'Asaph', quod indicat Synagogam, quae Dominum Salvatorem corporea quoque praesentia meruit intueri, quando dignatum est Verbum caro fieri et in gratiam nostrae vivificationis occidi."

[88] *Expos.* 72.1 (*CChr* 98, 660): "Asaph Synagogam significare hebraea lingua testatur, quae Dominum quidem colebat; sed videndo florere malos, in pessimas cogitationes inciderat." This bad theologizing, literally "worst kinds of thoughts," refers to the attitude that, if the evil prosper without worshipping the true God, then what advantage is there in this worship. In other words, they were thinking only *carnaliter* (cf. the following note).

120

over by Cassiodorus.[89] He also affirms that Asaph, as the synagogue, addresses the faithful Jews (*fideles Iudaeos*) and thereby designates where the name of the Lord is made known through the declaration of his powers.[90] If we include these two interpretations of Asaph under the category of *synagoga fidelis*, all three positive appraisals of the synagogue emerge as possible meanings of the term.

The *synagoga fidelis* finds its way into the early medieval commentaries by way of Cassiodorus. The term does not appear in the *Breviarium in Psalmos* attributed to Jerome, but that does not hinder the *Glossa* from adopting Jerome's translation of Asaph as synagogue and then affixing the interpretation of Cassiodorus that Asaph is the faithful synagogue expecting Christ.[91] In two other cases the *Glossa* employs the term to interpret the name Asaph, but then elaborates its meaning on the basis of Augustine. Evidently, the editor of the *Glossa* borrows the term itself from Cassiodorus and, realizing that the groundwork for the interpretation has been laid by Augustine, goes to the latter for the definition. In one case, the *synagoga fidelis* is that which worshipped God devotedly, though for the sake of earthly goods.[92] This is the limited positive interpretation which Augustine gives to the synagogue in its own right. In the other case, the *intellectus* of Asaph is emphasized, so that the *synagoga fidelis* represented in Asaph understands that which is narrated in the psalm "internally" and not only *in figura*.[93] This latter attribution of the

---

[89] Cf. *supra*, n. 65. *Enarr. in ps.* 72.6 (*CChr* 39, 990): "Adtendit, et vidit quosdam peccatores, impios, blasphemos, servos daemonum, filios diaboli, viventes in magna nequitia et superbia, abundare rebus talibus terrenis, temporalibus, pro qualibus rebus ipsa Deo serviebat; et nata est cogitatio pessima in corde, quae faceret nutare pedes, et prope labi a Dei via. Et ecce ista cogitatio in populo erat Veteris Testamenti; utinam non sit in carnalibus fratribus nostris, cum iam aperte praedicatur felicitas Novi Testamenti!"

[90] *Expos.* 75.1 (*CChr* 98, 691): "'Asaph', cuius vocabulum interpretari diximus Synagogam, in prima parte dirigentes, id est, fideles alloquitur Iudaeos: designans ubi nomen Domini factum sit virtutum declaratione notissimum."

[91] *Brev. in ps.* (49 : 1; *PL* 26, 968): "Asaph interpretatur congregatio." *Glo. ord.* (49 : 1): "'Psalmus Asaph'. Hiero. Asaph latine congregatio, graece synagoga; quae fidelis hic loquitur, quae Christum expectat, per quam magis confutantur increduli Iudaei." For the interpretation of Asaph as *synagoga fidelis* without further elaboration, see the *Glo. int.* on Psalms 72, 74, 75, 76, 78.

[92] *Glo. ord.* (72 : 1): "Loquitur Asaph, i.e. synagoga, sed fidelis, quae pie deum coluit, licet propter terrena quae a deo non a daemonibus ut gentes quaerebat."

[93] *Glo. ord.* (77 : 1): "'Intellectus Asaph'. Aug. Quia haec narrata interius intelligenda sunt, non modo in figura. Intellectus igitur Asaph est quod intellexit synagoga, sed fidelis." This juxtaposition of *interius* and *in figura* refers to a discussion by Augustine in the exposition of this same psalm (*Enarr. in ps.* 77.1 [*CChr* 39, 1066]

intellectus to the faithful synagogue stands in the line of the more frequent emphasis of Augustine and Cassiodorus on that part of the Old Testament people who perceived and believed in the coming Christ.

Peter Lombard treats Asaph as the faithful synagogue in more detail. After identifying the historical person of Asaph and explaining the etymology of the name, he maintains that in Psalm 49 the synagogue is speaking "according to the faithful part which expected Christ," and that the unbelieving Jews are refuted by this faithful portion. At the same time, this faithful part treats both advents of Christ, enticing with the first and instilling fear with the second.[94] This formulation is taken from Cassiodorus and fits into that group of positive evaluations of the synagogue which attributes to the faithful part special insight into the coming of Christ.

A similar formulation in Lombard describes the voice of Asaph as the voice of the synagogue "according to the grain and not according to the chaff." The faithful part of the synagogue has the *intellectus Asaph*, that is, it understands that the sacraments and promises of the Old Testament are different from those of the New. The sacraments of the Old Testament were only promising salvation, while those of the New actually confer it. The promises of the former were merely promises of earthly things, while those of the New Testament promise eternal goods. The faithful synagogue realized that truth would come when the figures were removed and that eternal and not temporal *res* were to be sought.[95] This truth is that the promise of God would be

and *ibid.* 77.3 [*CChr* 39, 1069]). The distinction means that the *synagoga fidelis* not only recognizes that the things narrated in the psalm are figures, but it also perceives the *res* underneath the figures, i.e. that which will happen to the church in the New Testament. Cf. the continuation of the passage in the *Glo. ord.*: "vel quod spiritualiter debet intelligere; quae enim mystice tunc, i.e. figuraliter, eadem modo in re." Cf. *Lomb.* (77 : 1; *PL* 191, 723).

[94] *Lomb.* (49 : 1; *PL* 191, 473-475): "Sicut supra diximus, Asaph cum aliis multis praefectus fuit cantoribus in tabernaculo Domini, de quo in titulis psalmorum plerumque fit mentio, tum pro officii reverentia, tum pro nominis interpretatione. Asaph enim Hebraice, Latine congregatio, Graece synagoga interpretatur, quae secundum partem fidelem hic loquitur quae Christum exspectavit, per quam magis confutantur increduli Iudaei... agit etiam de utroque adventu Christi; per primum blandiens, per secundum terrens. Et est sensus tituli: 'Psalmus' iste attribuitur 'Asaph', id est synagogae fideli, in cuius persona loquitur hic Propheta. ..."

[95] *Lomb.* (73 : 1; *PL* 191, 681-683): "Asaph ergo, id est Synagogae, quae tantum de Iudaeis proprie dicitur, vox est hic; sed secundum grana, non secundum paleas. Synagogae vero data est lex, quae quidem a Deo per Mosen data est, per Christum vero gratia et veritas facta est. ... In lege vero et prophetis tria erant, scilicet praecepta, sacramenta, promissa ... sacramenta non eadem, quia illa tantum promittebant, haec

fulfilled in Christ, and thus the function of the faithful synagogue as represented by Asaph is to lead the Jews to Christ, lest they ruin their faith and hope in Christ which they have in expectation of the promise of God.[96]

For Lombard the *synagoga fidelis* has become almost entirely that part of the Jews which properly discerned the eternal character of the promises of God and their fulfillment in Christ. True, Lombard quotes Augustine and the *Glossa* to the effect that Asaph represents the synagogue which was worshipping God devotedly for the sake of earthly goods.[97] His main emphasis, however, is upon the enlightened part of the Old Testament people, the *synagoga fidelis*, which prophesies against the remaining Jews.[98] Thus he enhances the split within the Jewish people which is characteristic of two of the three positive evaluations of the synagogue.

---

dant salutem. Promissa non eadem, quia ibi terrena primo animalibus promittebantur; hic aeterna, spiritualibus. .... Hic est 'intellectus Asaph', id est, in hoc psalmo aperitur quid fidelis Asaph intelligat, ... scilicet quod venit veritas figuris ablatis, et quod aeterna, non temporalia quaerenda sunt." Preus (p. 40) has found the same distinction between the promises and sacraments of the two testaments in the *Sentences* (III d. 40 c. 3) and mentions the similarity to Augustine's thought. He concludes, however, that this distinction formulated in the *Sentences* became the standard for scholasticism and "also played a prominent role in commentaries on the Psalms." The reverse is more likely the case: the distinction found in the *Sentences* originated in the Psalms commentaries of Augustine and Lombard. In this case we can trace the distinction back to the *Enarrationes.* Cf. *Enarr. in ps.* 73.2 (*CChr* 39, 1005-1006). What Preus has shown in regard to the "hermeneutical divide" between the Old and New Testaments (i.e. the necessity of the New Testament to understand correctly the Old) is directly related in the Psalms commentaries to the perception of the enlightened part of the Old Testament people—i.e., the *synagoga fidelis.*

[96] *Lomb.* (74 : 1; *PL* 191, 697): "Psalmus iste contra tumorem superbiae medicinam humilitatis apportat, in quo Christus ostenditur verus Deus, et verus homo, iudex vivorum et mortuorum: ut Iudaei credant, et non corrumpant fidem et spem suam in Christum; sed Dei promissionem certa fide exspectent. Et hoc dicit 'Asaph,' id est fidelis synagoga. Et est sensus: 'Psalmus' iste, qui monet ad bene operandum, est 'cantici,' quia agit de remuneratione aeterna, qui est 'Asaph,' id est fidelis Synagogae, hoc agit 'ne' tu, O Iudaee, vel quicunque, 'corrumpas' vel 'disperdas,' id est ne violes spem, quae habetur in promissione Dei. ..." Cf. *Lomb.* (75 : 1; *PL* 191, 703-704): "Contra hos loquitur hic Asaph, id est fidelis Synagoga, confutans eos hic, quibus nomina gloriae dicit ablata. Et ad alios translata, quae sunt Iudaea, Israel, Salem, Sion, et nihil boni posse sine Christi gratia probantur. Et est sensus: 'Psalmus' iste 'Asaph,' id est fidelis Synagogae attribuitur, quae hic loquitur dirigens nos in 'finem,' id est in Christum. ..."

[97] *Lomb.* (72 : 1; *PL* 191, 669): "His autem carnalibus deficientibus quae Deus subtraxit, ut quaererentur ea quae occulta in illis tegebantur, loquitur Asaph, id est Synagoga, sed fidelis, quae et ante pie coluit Deum; licet propter terrena, quae quidem a Deo quaerebat, non a daemonibus ut gentes."

[98] Cf. *supra*, nn. 93, 95, 96.

The *synagoga fidelis* is mentioned in connection with Asaph by two more of our commentators.[99] Hugo omits reference to the whole synagogue which was worshipping God devotedly for the sake of earthly goods and comes right to the point which followed this assertion in Augustine and his successors. Asaph represents the faithful people who understand that the figures would pass away and that truth would come, and that eternal things are to be sought instead of temporal goods.[100] He also inserts a reference to the fathers of the Old Testament. The assembly of those fathers who longed for Christ is the proper understanding of Asaph.[101] In fact, Asaph is the faithful people testifying to the incarnation of Christ.[102] This could refer either to the faithful wing of the Old Testament people, as in the previous references, or it could refer to those Jews who actually saw the incarnation and believed in Christ. In another place, Hugo interprets the synagogue in the latter sense—as the faithful synagogue which praises God for the sake of eternal goods after having been "converted from the Jews."[103] As we have noted, this interpretation covers those Jews who actually became members of the church. As a result, it is not difficult for Hugo to designate Asaph mystically as the church on the basis of the general meaning of Asaph as *congregatio*.[104]

The *synagoga fidelis* prophesies not only concerning the first advent of Christ but also concerning his second advent.[105] Its perspective spans the whole earthly existence of the church and is not confined to the first coming of Christ. Thus Hugo emphasizes even more strongly than his predecessors the New Testament perception of the

---

[99] Hugo and Faber. The strict separation between the literal and moral interpretation in Lyra leads him to refer only to the historical person of Asaph. We will treat below the reason for the absence of the term in Perez (cf. *infra*, pp. 137f.).

[100] *Hugo* (73 : 1): "Et hic est 'intellectus Asaph', id est fidelis populi, qui intelligit quod transierunt figurae et quod veritas venit et quod aeterna quaerenda sunt, non temporalia."

[101] *Hugo* (79 : 5): " 'Servi tui', Asaph, per quem intelligitur cetus sanctorum patrum desiderantium Christum."

[102] *Hugo* (79 : 1): "Psalmus iste dirigens nos 'in finem', Christum, est 'testimonium Asaph', id est fidelis populi testantis Christi incarnationem."

[103] *Hugo* (72 : 1): "Iste psalmus attribuitur 'Asaph', id est, fideli synagogae, quae de Iudaeis conversa deum laudat pro aeternis."

[104] *Hugo* (76 : 1): "Asaph enim interpretatur collectio aut congregatio. Et Idithum interpretatur transiliens eos. Et significat utrumque ecclesiam fidelium in unam Christi fidem et amorem collectam et unitam."

[105] *Hugo* (74 : 1): " 'Asaph', fidelis synagogae. ... Item in praecedenti psalmo egit propheta de salute data per gratiam in primo adventu; in isto autem agit de salute danda per gloriam in secundo adventu."

124

synagoga fidelis and has little trouble moving to a direct interpretation of Asaph as the congregation of the New Testament faithful.

The last mention of the *synagoga fidelis* which we have encountered is found in Faber's exposition of Psalm 79:

> . . . a song of Asaph. This psalm concerns Christ the Lord and the faithful synagogue seeking his advent. The prophet, speaking in the spirit, introduces the holy people yearning to God for the arrival of the Messiah.[106]

Faber gives a slightly different coloring to the faithful synagogue in this text. Asaph himself does not directly represent the faithful synagogue, and therefore the faithful synagogue does not have the immediate insight of the prophet into the New Testament events. Rather, the *synagoga fidelis* is represented in its Old Testament setting as yearning and asking for the coming of the Messiah. It knows that the coming Messiah will be Christ, but the passage is not sufficiently specific to determine if Faber would attribute to the synagogue a complete New Testament faith in him, as Augustine did to the Old Testament people heeding the testimony of the prophets. Nevertheless, some New Testament insight is attributed to the faithful synagogue here;[107] for this reason the passage remains in the mainstream of interpretation of the category—namely, that part of the Old Testament people who were already perceiving, believing in and expecting the coming Christ.

Up to this point in our discussion of the *concordia* between synagogue and church, we have delineated the various positive evaluations of the Old Testament people by our commentators. These evaluations are epitomized in the rubric *synagoga fidelis*, which refers primarily to that part of the synagogue which understands that God's promises are to be fulfilled in Christ and already believes in him and expects him.

The emphasis can vary, however, within this general definition.

---

[106] *Faber* (79 : 1): " 'Ad victoriam pro liliis testimonium Asaph canticum.' Psalmus de Christo domino et fideli synagoga adventum domini postulante. Propheta in spiritu inducit populum sanctum pro adventu messie ad deum suspirantem."

[107] The synagogue knows explicitly what to ask for: Cf. *Faber* (79 : 20): "Domine deus celestium agminum dirige nos ad te, largire nobis ut videamus Christum tuum, ut eius agnoscamus adventum et sic salvi, liberati et redempti a malarum potestatum captivitate evademus." *Faber* (79 : 4): " 'Deus converte nos et ostende faciem tuam et salvi erimus.' Conditor et creator noster fac nos ad te fide converti et conspiciendum nobis prebe filium tuum, consubstantialem nativam et veram tue substantie imaginem, quam si spiritu si fide, ut par fasque est, viderimus, redimemur ac salvabimur."

125

Some of our commentators stress the fact that the Old Testament *fideles* already belonged to the church and possessed the *fides Christi* of the New Testament church (most clearly Augustine in his concept of the *ecclesia ab Abel*). A corollary of this view is the application of the *synagoga fidelis* to those Jews who lived to see the coming of Christ in the flesh, believed in him, and were taken up into the church. A more restrained form of this interpretation asserts that the Old Testament *fideles* had insight into the figurative character of the old sacraments and promises and knew therefore to expect eternal *res* from God's promises and new sacraments which would actually confer salvation. If this is not explicit possession of the *fides Christi*, it is the next best thing. In an even more restrained manner, Faber emphasizes the expectant yearning of the *synagoga fidelis* from within the Old Testament situation for the coming of Christ. Finally, the other way in which the *synagoga fidelis* is taken seriously as the Old Testament people—as worshipping God devotedly for the sake of earthly rewards—functions only as a foil against which to emphasize the necessity of seeking eternal *res* from God.

The question to be asked at this point is what effect these evaluations of the synagogue have upon our commentators' view of the church, or, in other words, how is the *concordia* between synagogue and church actually worked out? In most of the above cases the answer is clear. Insofar as the church itself was already present in the Old Testament *fideles* (or rather, insofar as the faithful synagogue was already church), the identity of the two peoples forms the *concordia*. Here one proceeds from the given fact that the church had the *fides Christi* and the ability to perceive the promises of God as promises of eternal rewards. In this case, the church functions as a model for the faithful synagogue, which actually becomes part of the church itself, instead of vice versa. The "vice versa" is the other possibility, i.e. that the synagogue taken seriously in its Old Testament setting serves as a model for the church. The forward-looking posture of the church is then based on the unfulfilled character of the synagogue in its "deprived" pre-incarnation situation. We must now take a look at one of our commentators who has been regarded as moving in this direction.

4. Perez on Synagogue and Church

In the section of his illuminating study of medieval hermeneutics devoted to Perez, J. S. Preus outlines two modes of interpretation of the Old Testament which Perez employs, and illustrates these with reference to the function of the Old Testament fathers in each mode. In the first case, the *antiqui patres* are taken seriously as Old Testament people living under the promise of Christ and, as such, serve as models for Christians living under the promise of the second advent of Christ. In the second case, the Old Testament fathers are only figures of Christ, and thus not they, but Christ himself, becomes the model for Christians in the New Testament state of existence.[108] Preus finds examples of both lines of interpretation in the prologue to the Psalms commentary of Perez and points out how, if the second line of interpretation is followed, "tropological exegesis will always concentrate on the virtues of *caritas*, humility and obedience, rather than on faith or hope." The implication for the formation of Reformation theology is clear, although not explicitly mentioned by Preus.[109]

We are in full agreement "in theory" with the preceding distinction worked out by Preus, but we are convinced *neither* that the first possibility of interpretation is so clearly enunciated in Perez, *nor* that the hints of such a possibility in Perez are so unparalleled in the medieval tradition as Preus would lead us to believe.[110] How the Old Testament people should be related to the New Testament faithful is not only a hermeneutical problem; the question is equally ecclesiological in nature, i.e. how the synagogue is related to the church.

---

[108] Preus, p. 113. We quote the whole passage for the sake of clarity: "If the reality of their [the OT fathers] existence under the promise of Christ is emphasized, as well as their hope, expectation, and petition for the fulfillment of these promises, these figures emerge as subjects of real theological interest, living in hope and expectation of the future, rather than appearing merely as carnal (the victims of the prophet's duplicity). They can also serve the interpreter as models and examples for Christians: the exegete can move directly from literal explication to tropological (or moral) application.

"If, however, the *figurative* character of the Old Testament fathers is the focus of attention, the results are quite different: not the fathers' expectation and hope, but the figurative or typological similarity of their words and actions to Christ's words and actions is brought out; and they serve the interpreter as figures of Christ (whatever else they were then becomes irrelevant to the interpretation). The exegete in this case moves from literal (now meaning 'unedifying') to allegorical exposition, that is, from Old Testament events to those of the New. The next natural step is tropology, in terms of *imitatio Christi*."

[109] *Ibid.*, p. 116. Preus by no means claims that Perez was a Reformation theologian *in occulto*. He is quite clear in maintaining that the second line of interpretation predominates in Perez (p. 112).

[110] *Ibid.*, p. 112: "This idea of promise could, if developed, significantly alter the *predominant notions* of the Old Testament's theological value, . . ." (Italics mine).

When we examine Perez from the ecclesiological standpoint, the situation looks a bit different.

Perez certainly describes the Old Testament *fideles* as living constantly in the desire for, and expectation of, the advent of Christ.[111] In the course of his commentary, as well as in the prologue, Perez maintains that the promise made to the fathers was disposing them to faith and that in this faith they were being justified and saved.[112] But such an affirmation does not necessarily mean for Perez that the Old Testament faithful serve as models for the New Testament people disposed to faith by the promise of their glorification at the second advent of Christ. In fact, Perez follows up the affirmation just mentioned with the statement that the Lord has "disposed all the mysteries of the incarnation and passion and resurrection through figures," which are the same mysteries he prepared in truth and fulfilled for his faithful in the New Testament.[113] In other words, the faith of the Old Testament fathers was acquired through special insight into the *figura* of the Old Testament, which, in turn, signified the *res* of the New Testament (i.e. what would actually happen—namely, the incarnation, passion and resurrection of Christ). The promise of these *res* is fulfilled by their appearance in Christ and are received by the New Testament people as complete; the promise is not paralleled by a further promise to the New Testament faithful. The promise to the fathers, which looked so "literal" at first glance, is really an accomplice in effecting a depreciation of the literal sense of

[111] *Perez* (8 : 1): "Secundo est notandum quod totum desiderium patriarcharum et prophetarum et fidelium veteris testamenti fuit scire virtutes et perfectiones et videre effectus nominis dei adonai. . . . Ideo omnes patriarche et prophete desiderabant tanto tempore videre adventum Christi."

[112] *Perez* (88 : 4): "Nam promissio facta Abrahe, Isaac et Iacob et Moysi fuerunt quedam dispositiones, ut illi ponerent spem suam in Christo futuro. Unde per illas promissiones disponebantur ad fidem, in qua fide iustificabantur et salvabantur." Cf. Preus, p. 114, n. 28.

[113] *Perez* (88 : 4): "Et ideo dicit: Tu domine dixisti mihi per revelationem: 'Ego disposui testamentum electis meis', scilicet patribus veteris testamenti disposui per figuras omnia mysteria incarnationis et passionis et resurrectionis et eadem preparavi in veritate et complevi fidelibus meis in novo testamento." Similarly, the fathers were desiring not only Christ, but the "evangelical truth" hidden in the old law. *Perez* (44 : 14): "Totum etiam hic potest referri ad legem Moysi et ad totam scripturam veteris testamenti cuius veritas non consistit in littera exteriori, sed in sensu spirituali interiori; que quidem lex vetus est quasi tunica et vestis sub qua latet evangelium sive veritas evangelica. Et sic gloria veteris legis est veritas evangelica latens ab intus in fimbriis aureis, et hanc veritatem et gloriam interiorem legis desiderarunt omnes patres veteris testamenti et hanc concupivit et acceptavit et predicavit Christus."

the Old Testament and enhancing the *signum-res* schema—precisely what Preus is trying to avoid.

The pivotal question to be raised, however, is whether Perez really understands the fathers of the Old Testament, disposed to faith in the coming Christ, as Old Testament people in their own right or as already proleptically members of the church. Consider the following extensive passage from Perez' exposition of Psalm 76:

> We should note that the promise of the advent of Christ in the flesh for the purpose of freeing the entire human race was the cause of faith and *caritas* and hope in all the patriarchs and prophets of the Old Testament. This promise was first given to Adam, according to Augustine in his work, *Cur Deus homo.* The prophet says that the advent of the Lord from the Virgin was promised to the first man so that, even if he should be sad because of his momentary misery, nevertheless he might rejoice already from afar over his own cure and that of his posterity. For this reason Adam, although he was expelled from the joys of paradise, began to have faith on the basis of the promise made to him concerning the coming redemptor, Christ. And on the basis of this faith he was moved to the *caritas Christi,* and on the basis of such a firm faith, a firm hope for the coming Christ welled up in him. And Abel attained this faith and hope, and Seth and Enosh and Enoch and Noah and Abraham, etc. So we can say that faith and hope began with Adam as a result of the promise made to him, and it was passed down to his faithful offspring. But it increased in each one of these patriarchs and prophets according to the measure in which each one had special revelation of the advent of Christ. For Abel had this special revelation and Enosh began to call upon the name of the Lord, and Noah and finally Abraham, to whom was made a special promise. And the same can be said of Isaac and Jacob and the other patriarchs and prophets in whom faith and hope always intensified as new revelations and promises came.[114]

---

[114] *Perez* (76 : 1): "... est advertendum quod promissio adventus Christi in carnem ad liberandum genus humanum fuit causa fidei et caritatis et spei omnibus patriarchis et prophetis veteris testamenti, que quidem promissio primo facta fuit ipsi Ade, secundum quod ait Aug. libro Cur deus homo. Unde dicit quod primo homini promissus est adventus domini ex virgine, ut si de instanti miseria doleret, tamen de suo sueque posteritatis remedio iam de longinquo gauderet. Unde Adam, licet esset expulsus ab illa felicitate, tamen ex promissione ipsi facta de Christo redemptore futuro incepit habere fidem. Et ex fide motus est ad caritatem Christi, et ex tali firma fide resultavit in eo firma spes adventus Christi. Et hanc fidem et spem secutus est Abel et Seth et Enos et Enoch et Noe et Abraham etc. Et sic est dicendum quod fides et spes incepit ab Adam ex promissione ipsi facta. Et sic descendit in totam eius posteritatem fidelium. Sed crevit in unoquoque ipsorum patriarcharum et prophetarum secundum quod unusquisque habuit specialem revelationem de Christi adventu. Nam specialem revelationem habuit Abel, et Enos incepit invocare nomen domini, et Noe et Abraham, cui facta est specialis promissio. Et sic est dicendum de Isaac et Iacob et ceteris patriarchis et prophetis, in quibus semper crevit fides et spes propter novas revelationes

If we stop at this point, we are aware that something is present in this description which is not kosher Old Testament. First of all, the promise of Christ is not just the cause of faith and hope in the patriarchs and prophets—which could be interpreted as true Old Testament response to the promise—but it is also the cause of *caritas* in them. The possession of *caritas* is, of course, the exclusive possession of the New Testament people in a state of grace, i.e. of the church. Thus the patriarchs and prophets already manifest New Testament characteristics.

Secondly, we notice in the above passage that, at least for all the righteous after Adam, this faith and hope increased according to special revelation of the advent of Christ. In other words, they were able to understand the New Testament mysteries enshrouded in the Old Testament letter, and thus were not really in the darkness of the Old Testament pre-advent situation. These two factors alone would lead us to think that Perez regards the Old Testament patriarchs and prophets as New Testament people. In fact, he continues the above exposition as follows:

> And all of these make up the mystical body of Christ in that they lived in hope and faith of the coming Christ. And we can define the ecclesiastical mystical body in this way: the multitude of the faithful either expecting Christ or living in the faith and hope of Christ, beginning from Adam and extending to the last elect. And the definition of the church is the same. For the mystical body and the church are interchangeable terms, as we said in the prologue. And thus Adam with all his faithful offspring is called the mystical body, or the mystical Adam, or *homo mysticus*, or church, or city of God or people of God according to Augustine in Book XV of *De civitate dei.* ...[115]

et promissiones." The work *Cur Deus homo*, which Perez cites as stemming from Augustine, is of unknown authorship. Passages from this work attributed to Augustine appear in the extensive medieval concordance to the works of Augustine, *Milleloquium S. Augustini*, begun by Augustinus Triumphus of Ancona (d. 1328) and completed by his pupil, Bartholomaeus of Urbino (d. 1350). Perez found in this concordance the passage to which he refers in this text and at seven other points in his commentary. See Werbeck, *Jacobus Perez von Valencia*, pp. 61ff.

[115] *Ibid.* (continuation of the preceding text): "Et sic omnes isti sunt corpus mysticum Christi eo quod vixerunt in spe et fide Christi futuri. Et ideo diffinitur corpus mysticum ecclesiasticum, quod est multitudo fidelium Christum expectantium sive in fide et spe Christi viventium, incipiens ab Adam usque ad ultimum electum. Et eadem est diffinitio ipsius ecclesie. Nam corpus mysticum et ecclesia convertuntur sicut dictum est in prologo. Et sic Adam cum tota posteritate sua fidelium dicitur corpus mysticum sive Adam mysticus sive homo mysticus sive ecclesia sive civitas dei sive populus dei secundum Aug. xv. de civi. ..."

What really underlies Perez' understanding of promise and faith in the Old Testament fathers is not a new hermeneutical principle, but the "old" refrain of the *ecclesia ab Abel* (or *ab Adam*). Perez refers to the prologue of his commentary where he speaks explicitly of the *ecclesia ab Adam*:

> Just as in both testaments there remains only one Christ who is believed and one law, so there was always one church, one city of God and one mystical body from Adam until the judgment. . . . Just as the unity of a city, therefore, depends on the unity of the law, so the unity of the church and the mystical body arises from the unity of one law and one faith and one head, that is, of Christ believed. And so in both testaments we should consider there to be only one head who is Christ believed, and one faith and one church or one mystical body, whose head always was and always remains Christ.[116]

What Perez is after is not a comparison between the people of the Old Testament and those of the New, but rather the essential identity of both peoples in the one church of both testaments. He even speaks of the church according to the state of each testament. The church according to the state of the Old Testament was desiring the advent of Christ, but the church according to the state of the New Testament has received him.[117] The divergence between the two states is that of promise and fulfillment; no parallel exists between the two people in regard to living under a promise. In fact, because the church lives under the same faith and *caritas* of Christ, it remains in essence the same from Adam until the last judgment, differing only according to diverse states, ages and degrees of perfection.[118]

---

[116] *Perez (prol.* tr. 3 c. 2 cl. 7): "Sicut ergo in utroque testamento semper unus est Christus creditus et una lex, ita semper fuit una ecclesia et una civitas dei et unum corpus mysticum ab Adam usque ad iudicium. . . . Sicut ergo unitas civitatis sumitur ab unitate legis, ita et unitas ecclesie et corporis mystici sumitur ab unitate unius legis et unius fidei et unius capitis, id est Christi crediti. Et sic in utroque testamento est considerandum unum caput qui est Christus creditus et una fides et una ecclesia sive unum corpus mysticum cuius caput semper fuit et semper est Christus."

[117] *Ibid.*: "Nam totum tempus veteris legis fuit tempus significandi et figurandi et desiderandi, sed tempus nove legis fuit tempus adimplendi et verificandi et recipiendi promissiones. Unde quando dicitur in Canticis: 'Osculetur me osculo oris' [Ct. 1 : 1], verificatur de ecclesia secundum statum veteris testamenti quia tunc desiderabat adventum Christi sponsi sui. Sed cum postea dicitur: 'Quesivi quem diligit anima mea et inveni et tenui nec dimittam illum' [Ct. 3 : 1, 4], tunc verificatur de ecclesia secundum istum statum ilico post adventum Christi prout ipsum recepit."

[118] *Perez* (5 : 1): "Ex quo patet quod sola ecclesia est hereditas domini ab Adam et Abel usque ad ultimum electum, ut ait Aug. et Grego. Que quidem ecclesia licet sit una essentialiter ab Adam usque ad iudicium, eo quod vivit sub una fide Christi et caritate, tamen differt accidentaliter secundum diversos status et diversa secula et secundum minus perfectum et magis perfectum."

Preus sees in the *una fides* a result of the *promissio* hermeneutic, i.e. the Old Testament people and the New Testament people were both living in faith in the promises of a coming Christ.[119] This unity of faith is deceptive, however, and must be handled with care. First of all, if the comparison between the two peoples is such that the Old Testament people were responding in faith to the promise of the first advent of Christ, while the New Testament people were responding in faith to the promise of his second advent, then their faith is not identical in regard to its *object*, since it differs according to the different advents expected. Rather, the former *fides* is parallel to the latter in terms of their *orientation* toward the promise of a future event. On the other hand, if the promise of Christ to come in the first advent disposes the Old Testament fathers to faith in that Christ in whom also the New Testament people have faith as the one who *has already come*, then the *same advent* and the *same Christ* are the objects of faith of both peoples, or as Perez puts it, it is the *una fides* of the *una ecclesia*. In this case, the *fides* of both peoples is identical in its object, but not in its orientation. The *una fides* in terms of its object (Christ believed) is only possible where the Old Testament and New Testament people form the *una ecclesia*, and not where the Old Testament people are taken seriously as Old Testament people and serve as models for the New Testament people.

We recall in this context that the *una fides* is an integral part of the Augustinian understanding of the *ecclesia ab Abel*—the essential factor by which the *ecclesia* is projected back into the Old Testament.[120] This *una fides* means for Augustine that the object of faith of both the Old Testament righteous and the New Testament righteous (i.e. the whole *ecclesia ab Abel*) is the one Christ who is believed. The faith of both states of the church is identical in its object. Thomas states this explicitly and explains that, although there exists unity of faith in both states according to its object, nevertheless (in our terms) the orientation of the faith in each state was different (*habuit alium statum*): the Old Testament faithful were believing *futurum*, while the New Testament people believe *factum*.[121]

---

[119] Preus, p. 116: "The way of *promissio*, however, will bring to expression the idea that the faith of the Old Testament fathers was the same as ours: ..."

[120] Cf. *supra*, notes 40 and 61. We mention here also the observation of Y. Congar on the *una fides* of Augustine and its influence on later authors ("Ecclesia ab Abel," p. 89): "*Una fides*. La grande affirmation augustinienne est devenue un principe commun de la théologie latine."

[121] Cf. *supra*, n. 60.

Such is the way Perez conceives of the *una fides* — in terms of its object (*Christus creditus*) and not in terms of its orientation. In order to support his desire to see a real parallel in the *fides* of the Old and New Testament people within a *promissio* hermeneutic, Preus would have to show that Perez sees the identity of the *fides* of both peoples in terms of its orientation, and not in terms of its object, that is, that both the Old and New Testament people were believing *futurum*. In this case, the object would not be the same (two different advents), but rather the orientation (i.e. each people believes in a future coming of Christ). The fact is, however, that Perez' thought is controlled by the *ecclesia ab Abel* (*Adam*) category, and thus he envisions the unity of faith of both the Old and New Testament peoples in the traditional sense of identity of object, and not of orientation.

Preus supports his view with the following passage from Perez:

> For even though Christ had not yet been incarnated, yet he was already believed ... for all those fathers of the Old Testament accepted no promises except with us ... For the same faith in Christ which saves us saved them also, since they were believing and accepting as future that same Christ whom we believe has now come, and whom we receive. And in such faith they were being saved.[122]

When we put this text in context, however, and fill in the omissions, it is clear that Perez is thinking of the *ecclesia ab Abel*. The whole "context" runs as follows:

> And therefore Gregory, in his homily concerning the vine, says that there was always one vine and one church which extends from Adam and Abel up to the last elect. And thus Adam and Abel and Abraham were already members of Christ and citizens of this city. For even though Christ had not yet been incarnated, yet he was already believed, because faith is that which binds members to their head. And Augustine says that the whole church of the faithful is one *homo mysticus*, who in Adam was expelled from the earthly paradise, but whom God handed over to Christ to be healed. Thus this *homo mysticus* wandered through faith in the first testament until it reached Christ, in whom and from whom it receives the promises with us, as the Apostle says [Hebr. 11 : 39-40]. For all the fathers of the Old Testament accepted no promises except with us. From

---

[122] Preus, pp. 116-117. He gives the Latin text in note 33 (*prol.* tr. 3 c. 2 cl. 7): "Nam licet Christus nondum esset incarnatus, tamen iam erat Christus creditus ... Quia omnes illi patres veteris testamenti non acceperunt repromissiones nisi nobiscum ... Nam eadem fides Christi que salvat nos salvavit et illos, quia quem nos credimus iam venisse, et quem recipimus, illum et eundem Christum, ipsi credebant et expectabant futurum. Et in tali fide salvabantur."

this it is clear according to the Apostle that there is one church and one faith in Christ in both the New and the Old Testaments. For the same faith in Christ which saves us saved them also, since they were believing and accepting as future that same Christ whom we believe has now come, and whom we receive. And in such faith they were being saved.[123]

It is not the Old Testament fathers as genuine Old Testament people who have the same faith and have received the same promises as we, but rather the whole *ecclesia ab Adam* (also named collectively by Perez *homo mysticus*). The Old Testament fathers received the same promises as we have received and possessed the same faith because they were members of the one church which spans both testaments. The point is that we (i.e. New Testament people) have received the promises and thus believe *factum* what the Old Testament faithful believed *futurum*. The *una fides* of both testaments is identical in regard to its object (Christ), and not in its orientation.[124] Therefore, the

[123] *Perez* (*prol.* tr. 3 c. 2 cl. 7): "Et ideo dicit Grego. homelia de vinea quod ab Adam et Abel usque ad ultimum electum semper fuit una vinea et una ecclesia, cuius palmites et membra fuerunt omnes electi utriusque testamenti. Et sic Adam et Abel et Abraham iam erant membra Christi et cives huius civitatis. Nam licet Christus nondum esset incarnatus, tamen iam erat Christus creditus quia fides est illa que compaginat membra suo capiti. Et sic dicit Aug. quod tota ecclesia fidelium est unus homo mysticus cuius caput a paradiso terrestri in Adam, quem hominem deus remisit ad Christum ut sanaretur ab eo. Et sic iste homo mysticus peregrinatus est per fidem in primo testamento usquequo pervenit ad Christum in quo et a quo accepit nobiscum repromissiones, ut ait apostolus ad Hebreos xi. quia omnes illi patres veteris testamenti non acceperunt repromissiones nisi nobiscum. Ex quo patet secundum apostolum quod una est ecclesia et una fides Christi novi ac veteris testamenti. Nam eadem fides Christi que salvat nos, salvavit et illos, quia quem nos credimus iam venisse, et quem recepimus, illum et eundem Christum, ipsi credebant et expectabant futurum. Et in tali fide salvabantur." Cf. *supra*, notes 116 and 118 for the *una ecclesia* and the *una fides*.

[124] Compare the following passages in which the *una ecclesia* in both testaments is based upon the *una fides* in regard to its *obiectum* or *fundamentum* which is Christ. *Perez* (117 : 4): "Ex supradictis patet quod sicut una est ecclesia veteris et novi testamenti quantum ad fundamentum fidei Christi, eo quod una est fides omnium, ita est una domus Israel et una domus Aaron novi ac veteris testamenti ratione fidei Christi secundum istum modum loquendi. Nam quod illi tractabant in figura, nos tractamus in re et veritate ut dictum est. Sed est differentia quod nos sumus filii Israel secundum promissionem et veritatem promissam. Iusti autem et fideles illius temporis erant filii secundum carnem et etiam secundum promissionem inquantum expectabant salvari per Christum futurum. Et sic vivebant in fide Christi futuri, quem iam recepimus." Note the difference in orientation of the *fides* expressed in the last line: "And thus they were living in faith in the coming Christ, *whom we have already received*" (italics mine). Notice also how this presupposes a *figura-res* hermeneutical structure. Further, *Perez* (*prol.* tr. 3 c. 2 cl. 7): "Item per eandem rationem habuerunt eandem fidem nobiscum de Christo et ecclesia quia quod credimus preteritum et presentem, ipsi crediderunt et expectarunt futurum. ... Item sicut fuit una fides, ita fuit unum obiectum fidei qui est Christus." Note again the same object, but a different orientation.

134

faith of these Old Testament members of the *una ecclesia* cannot serve as a model for the New Testament people in terms of believing *futurum*. The *una fides* in the traditional sense, which remains unchanged for Perez, is not a result of a new *promissio* hermeneutic, where both peoples are seen as living under the promise of an advent of Christ.

Perez' persistence in seeing the Old Testament fathers as part of the whole *una ecclesia ab Adam* prevents him from setting them up as a model for the New Testament people. This limitation applies also to the two-advent structure which Preus values so highly. Preus writes: "There are passages in the prologue in which Perez refers to the concrete people of Israel living under the promise," and then quotes the following passage to show how the concrete Old Testament people living under the promise of the first advent serve as a model for the New Testament people living under the promise of the second advent:

> All the fathers and faithful of the Old Testament were stretching toward Christ, in order that they might receive the promises in him, and consequently, they were saved more through faith in Christ than through works of the law. For they were not carrying out the works of the law except in professing faith in the future Christ. Second one must notice that just as God handed Adam and all the faithful of the Old Testament over to Christ, in order that they might be redeemed by him in the first advent, so also Christ hands his own people over to the second advent, that they might be glorified by him. For just as through the first advent redemption is promised to the faithful through Christ, so to us, now redeemed, glory and beatification are promised through the same Christ in his second advent. For already redeemed, we stretch toward Christ in order to be glorified, for we expect him to return to the marriage feast, as is plain in the whole Gospel story.[125]

Let us compare this passage with two other texts in which Perez utilizes the two-advent structure. In the first passage Perez writes:

[125] Preus, pp. 113-114. The Latin text, p. 114, n. 28 (*prol.* tr. 3 c. 1): "Omnes patres et fideles veteris testamenti tendebant in Christum, ut in eo acciperent repromissiones, et per consequens magis salvati sunt per fidem Christi quam per opera legis, quia non exercebant opera legis nisi protestando fidem Christi futuri. Secundo est notandum quod sicut deus remisit Adam et omnes fideles veteris testamenti ad Christum ut ab eo redimerentur in primo adventu, ita Christus remisit suos ad secundum adventum ut ab eodem glorificarentur. Nam sicut per primum adventum promissa est fidelibus per Christum redemptio, ita nobis iam redemptis promissa est per eundem Christum in ii. adventum gloria et beatificatio. Iam enim redempti tendimus in Christum ut glorificemur, expectamus enim eum a nuptiis reversurum ut patet per totum discursum evangelicum."

Therefore, this *homo mysticus* journeyed from the foundation of the world up to the halfway point, the first advent of Christ, that it might be healed and reconciled to God. But now it journeys from the first advent through the evangelical law up to its final destination in the second advent, that it might be glorified.[126]

The second text is formulated in the following way:

It is essential to note that the church of God has three states, namely two in the present and one in the future which is called the state of glory. The first state is called the age of the law, of shadow, figure, the state of captivity, wrath, righteousness, ignorance and night. The second state is called the state of truth, of evangelical light, liberty, grace, mercy, wisdom and day. In the first state all the old fathers were desiring the second state. And we who are in the second state desire the third, namely to be dissolved and to be with Christ in glory. And therefore, just as through the first advent of Christ the first state was changed into the second, so through the second advent of Christ the second state of the church will be changed into the third.[127]

The two-advent structure for Perez is directly dependent upon his understanding of the *ecclesia ab Adam* in both testaments. The two advents function as dotted boundary lines between the three states of the *one* church, as the second text indicates. There is a certain parallel between the first and second states in that both the Old Testament fathers (the Old Testament state of the church) and the New Testament people (the New Testament state of the church) are desiring the state of the church which is ahead of them. But both texts make it clear that the *una ecclesia* (also called *homo mysticus*) of both testaments is the basis of the two-advent structure. The Old Testament fathers are not concrete Old Testament men to

---

[126] *Perez (prol.* tr. 3 c. 2 cl. 7): "Ideo iste homo mysticus peregrinatus est a principio mundi usque ad primum adventum Christi tanquam ad medium ut sanaretur et deo reconciliaretur. Sed modo peregrinatur a primo adventu per legem evangelicam usque ad secundum adventum tanquam in finem ultimum ut glorificetur." *Homo mysticus* is a collective term for the *ecclesia fidelium* as Perez explicitly says (cf. *supra*, n. 123).

[127] *Perez* (76 : 11): "... est valde advertendum quod ecclesia dei habet tres status, scilicet duos in presenti et unum in futuro qui dicitur status glorie. Primus status dicitur status legis et umbre et figure et captivitatis et ire et iustitie et ignorantie et noctis. Secundus status dicitur status veritatis et luminis evangelici et libertatis et gratie et misericordie et sapientie et diei. Tertius autem dicitur status glorie et premii. In primo statu omnes patres antiqui desiderabant statum secundum. Et nos qui iam sumus in statu secundo desideramus tertium, scilicet dissolvi et esse cum Christo in gloria. Et ideo sicut per primum adventum Christi primus status mutatus est in secundum, ita per secundum adventum Christi secundus status ecclesie mutabitur in tertium." Perez also divides the history of the church since Adam into four stages according to different schemes. Cf. *Perez* (73 : 16) and (118 : 176).

the extent that they, totally apart from the church, serve as models for New Testament Christians, but rather they all belong to the *una ecclesia.*

Preus concludes finally that "by momentarily shifting the *definiens* of justification from grace and *caritas* to faith in Christ—from present *res* to faith in the future—Perez has hit on a way to see people as 'justified' before the establishment of the Church and the implementation of her justifying ordinances, the sacraments."[128] We maintain that this justification of the Old Testament fathers is not effected "before the establishment of the church," since Perez considers the Old Testament fathers to be members of the *ecclesia ab Adam* all along. In addition, these fathers possess not only faith (and hope) in Christ, but also the New Testament grace (*caritas*) of the church.[129] They are members of the *una ecclesia* just as New Testament Christians, and thus cannot function as concrete Old Testament models for the latter within a *promissio*, two-advent structure. Further, although their faith is a believing *futurum*, it cannot function as a model for a parallel faith of the New Testament people, because as members of the "one church" with the "one faith" in Christ having come in the flesh, the New Testament people believe *factum.*

We find further confirmation of our belief that Perez consistently thinks in terms of the *una ecclesia* of both testaments in the absence of any mention of the *synagoga fidelis* in his commentary. We have observed that the faithful synagogue can take on certain New Testament or "church" characteristics such as special insight into the coming of Christ, but the employment of the term *synagoga fidelis* itself implies that the Old Testament *fideles* are taken seriously to some extent as Old Testament people. The perfect expression of this would occur if the *synagoga fidelis* were to be understood as trusting in God's promise of the Messiah without a New Testament understanding of exactly who that Messiah would be. We have not encountered such a pure specimen in any of our commentators; rather, the primary interpretation comprises the prophets who were foreseeing the coming of Christ and the people who were believing them.

If Perez were working at least partially on the basis of a *promissio*

---

[128] Preus, p. 122.
[129] Cf. *supra*, n. 114.

hermeneutic, the category of the *synagoga fidelis* would have offered a golden opportunity for him to treat the Old Testament *fideles* in their Old Testament situation. Or even if he had employed it in the traditional way (i.e. with some New Testament character), it would have given more Old Testament character to the Old Testament *fideles*. The fact is, however, that Perez does not need the term at all, because he utilizes the *ecclesia ab Abel* category to the fullest extent by quite openly assigning the Old Testament faithful to the church and, in this way, projecting the church back into the Old Testament.

When Perez expands upon the interpretation of Asaph, only the church comes into play.[130] There is no positive mention of the synagogue in this connection. In his exposition of Psalm 121 : 4-5, Perez does speak of the "tribes of the Lord" as the "true sons of Israel who received the Messiah," i.e. those Jews who became Christians. This reception of Christ is the testimony of Israel which all the *fideles* receive who accept Christ, and only these *fideles* can ascend into the heavenly Jerusalem.[131] Christians then are the spiritual tribes of the Lord who profess the testimony of Israel by believing in Christ.[132] The parallel between the true sons of Israel and "we Christians" is simply that between the first Christians and their successors, and has nothing to do with the pre-advent Old Testament people or a comparison between such a people and later New Testament Christians.

---

[130] First in the context of explaining the significance of the names of the various authors of the Psalms: *Perez* (72 : 1): "Nam inquantum ecclesia Christi est congregata ex omnibus fidelibus, figuratur per Asaph, qui interpretatur electio seu congregatio." At the beginning of the exposition of Psalm 79, Perez maintains that Asaph is only the singer of the psalm, and not the author, and represents the whole church according to the interpretation of his name—which "whole church" suffered and suffers three periods of persecution beginning before the advent of Christ. *Perez* (79 : 1).

[131] *Perez* (121 : 4): "Unde notanter dicitur tribus domini quia non omnes tribus et generationes ascendunt in Hierusalem sed solum tribus domini. Unde tribus domini dicuntur veri filii Israel qui receperunt Messiam... Qui ergo non receperunt Christum non sunt veri filii Israel quia non receperunt testimonium eius nec prophetiam verificant nec affirmant ... Ideo fideles qui Christum recipiunt, recipiunt verum testimonium Israel et faciunt testimonium ipsi Israel de veritate. ... Ergo soli fideles ascenderunt illuc in Hierusalem celestem ad confitendum nomini domini in testimonium Israel."

[132] *Perez* (121 : 5): "Ita nos christiani qui sumus tribus domini spirituales regenerati per apostolos continue ascendimus in Hierusalem militantem ad confitendum et prebendum testimonium, i.e. fidem Israel, nomini domini qui est Iesus Christus. Nam credendo in Christum et exhibendo ipsi latriam confitemur testimonium Israel, id est, sequimur fidem et testimonium quod Israel prebuit et predixit et previdit de Christo."

We have found in Perez, then, no hint of a truly positive evaluation of the Old Testament people in the darkness of the pre-advent situation. The point of our extensive discussion of Preus' interpretation is to show that, regardless of Perez' somewhat intriguing remarks on *promissio* and the two advents, his assignment of the Old Testament *fideles* to the *una ecclesia* of both testaments prevents Perez from utilizing a *promissio* or two-advent structure hermeneutically in such a way that the faith of the concrete Old Testament *fideles* can become a model for Christian faith. What is seen as identical, *una fides* in the *una ecclesia*, can hardly be distinct enough for one part to become the model for the other. The presence of both people in one church causes their faith to be identical in object (Christ believed), though different in orientation (*futurum* vs. *factum*). What is needed, however, for Old Testament faith to be the model for New Testament faith is a different object (two advents) and the same orientation (believing *futurum*).

The failure of Perez to set up the synagogue as a positive model for the church is typical for our medieval commentators. We have observed how their picture of the church controls for the most part the favorable appraisals conceded to the synagogue. For the commentators who employ the *ecclesia ab Abel*, this positive estimation consists in annexing the Old Testament faithful to the church which stretches over the entire course of human history. For those who prefer the *synagoga fidelis*, the *synagoga* is endowed with various degrees of New Testament ecclesiological insight and grace, so that it can discern the fulfillment of God's promises in Christ. The *concordia* between synagogue and church does not contribute any innovations to the definition of the *fideles* in the church, but rather extends the historical scope of the church to include the Old Testament *fideles*. The Old Testament righteous, in turn, serve as models for New Testament Christians only insofar as they exhibit the faith and *caritas* of *fideles* in the church—which they already are. We can speak only of a quantitative alteration of the ecclesiology of our commentators in this regard, and not of qualitative innovations.

The synagogue in its own historical setting does, however, exercise direct influence on their ecclesiology in the framework of the *altercatio*. The unbelieving Jews serve as models for the enemies of the true *fideles*—heretics and evil Christians. Although we have not found extensive elaboration upon this theme in our commentaries, this parallel enhances the split between the true and false *fideles* in the church and could be exploited to draw even more sharply the demarcation line between them. The same applies to the *synagoga fidelis.* If it were to lose at least some of its New Testament gloss and could function in its unhewn form as the company of genuinely Old Testament faithful, it could also contribute to the definition of its New Testament counterparts—the true *fideles* in the church. Our commentators thus open up tantalizing possibilities for a more fruitful encounter between synagogue and church—possibilities, however, on which they fail to capitalize in full.

PART TWO

MARTIN LUTHER: DICTATA SUPER PSALTERIUM
(1513-1515)

CHAPTER IV

VARIATIONS ON THEMES BY HOLL AND GRISAR

How does one begin to filter out Martin Luther's understanding of the nature of the church from the wealth of material which he compiled in the years 1513-1515 in conjunction with his first lectures on the Psalms?[1] For the researcher who is attempting to get a grip on this material, there exists an ample but not overwhelming supply of works which provide a full option of starting points. The problem with these works is that they also provide a plethora of possible conclusions about Luther's ecclesiology in the *Dictata* which are by no means compatible with one another and which therefore only add to the confusion of the researcher approaching the *Dictata* for the first time. Nevertheless, in order to get one's bearings on the problems involved, it is necessary to take a serious look at the literature on Luther's early ecclesiological development.[2]

All subsequent research into Luther's early ecclesiology has composed variations on the basic themes sounded in the controversy between Karl Holl and Hartmann Grisar in the early part of this century. Grisar had maintained in 1912 that Luther's "new" views on the nature of the church were only emergency measures undertaken in order to justify his break with the Roman Church when the latter did not embrace his new teaching on justifica-

---

[1] Luther began his lectures on the Psalms in August of 1513 and completed this first series of lectures in October, 1515. However, two sections of the exposition of Psalms 1 and 4 (*WA* 3, 15.13-26.18 = *WA* 55/II, 1.1-24.2 and *WA* 3, 39.21-60.7 = *WA* 55/II, 46.15-85.26) were prepared in 1516 for a printing which never appeared. See Erich Vogelsang, *Der junge Luther*, Vol. V of *Luthers Werke in Auswahl* (3rd ed., Berlin, 1963), p. 40 and the same, "Zur Datierung der frühesten Lutherpredigten," *ZKG* 50 (1931), pp. 116ff. Along with the *Dictata* itself, we take into consideration in Part II the *Adnotationes Quincuplici Psalterio adscriptae* (*WA* 4, 466-526), notes which Luther made to the commentary of Faber Stapulensis especially at the beginning, but also throughout his work on the *Dictata* (Vogelsang, *Der junge Luther*, p. 38).

[2] Summaries of the literature can be found in Christa Tecklenburg Johns, *Luthers Konzilsidee in ihrer historischen Bedingtheit und ihrem reformatorischen Neuansatz* (Berlin, 1966), pp. 165ff.; Gerhard Müller, "Ekklesiologie und Kirchenkritik beim jungen Luther," *NZSTh* 7 (1965), pp. 101ff., and "Neuere Literatur zur Theologie des jungen Luther," *KuD* 11 (1965), pp. 341f.; and in Joseph Vercruysse, *Fidelis Populus*, pp. 5ff.

tion.[3] In order to refute this assertion, Holl, in 1915, launched his own investigation into the development of Luther's teaching on the church and came to two famous conclusions. First, there existed a necessary (one could say "cause and effect") relation between Luther's new understanding of justification and his new understanding of the nature of the church.[4] Since Holl viewed Luther's new understanding of justification as already formulated in the *Dictata*, he was able to draw his second momentous conclusion: namely, that the understanding of the nature of the church which Luther had formulated in the *Dictata* was precisely the view which he held for the rest of his life.[5]

There are actually two questions involved in this dispute which are not easily separated from one another. The first question concerns the date at which Luther's new ecclesiology was "complete" or "essentially there." The second question directs itself to the specific theological locus or to the larger theological context in which the ecclesiology of Luther was developed. For those, such as Grisar, who wish to interpret Luther's new understanding of the church merely as a reaction to his rejection by Rome, it is most convenient to sever Luther's thinking on the nature of the church from his new understanding of justification, the Word or other aspects of his soteriological thought. On the other hand, as we see with Holl, one effective way of arguing for the existence of a new ecclesiology in Luther's works before 1517 is to maintain that Luther's ecclesiological innovations are directly related to his developing soteriological thought, and especially to his new understanding of justification.

How did the subsequent variations sound which later researchers

---

[3] Hartmann Grisar, *Luther*, Vol. III: *Am Ende der Bahn* (1st & 2nd ed., Freiburg, 1912), p. 775: "Erst als die alte Kirche nicht zu seiner neuen Lehre herübertrat, sondern sie streng zu verurteilen sich anschickte, entschloß er sich unter großem inneren Kampfe zur Losreißung; und eben um diesen Schritt bei sich zu rechtfertigen und nach außen zu decken, bildete er seine neuen Ansichten über Wesen und Begriff der Kirche nach und nach aus." Specifically, Grisar saw Luther's "new idea of the church" first formulated in his *Sermon von dem Bann* which goes back to 1518 (*ibid.*; for the dating of this sermon, see O. Clemen ed., *Luthers Werke in Auswahl*, Vol. I [6th ed., Berlin, 1966], p. 213).

[4] Karl Holl, "Die Entstehung von Luthers Kirchenbegriff (1915)," *Gesammelte Aufsätze zur Kirchengeschichte*, Vol. I: *Luther* (7th ed., Tübingen, 1948), p. 289: "Seine Rechtfertigungslehre war es, die unmittelbar auch seine neue Auffassung der Kirche hervortrieb."

[5] *Ibid.*, pp. 298-299: "Das ist ein vollkommen fertiger, in sich abgerundeter Gedankenzusammenhang. Es ist derjenige Kirchenbegriff, den Luther zeitlebens vertreten hat."

composed on the primary themes of that first dispute? On the Protestant side, Ernst Kohlmeyer maintained in 1928 that, notwithstanding striking outward continuity, the "decisive inner changes" were already present in 1513 in Luther's understanding of the church, changes to which he would adhere the rest of his life.[6] In his history of dogma, Reinhold Seeberg affirmed that the *Grundlinien* of Luther's ecclesiology were already present in his commentaries on the Psalms and the Letter to the Romans (1515-1516).[7] Johannes Heckel, in turn, dealt with the development of Luther's ecclesiology in connection with Luther's understanding of ecclesiastical law. He came to the conclusion that at the time of the Ninety-Five Theses, Luther stood at the end of the same road that he had already embarked upon in his first Psalms lectures.[8] These researchers were all in agreement with Holl that the decisively new elements in Luther's ecclesiology were present in the *Dictata super Psalterium* from the years 1513-1515.

They were also in agreement with Holl in regard to the theological context in which Luther's ecclesiology took shape. Kohlmeyer and Seeberg noted the importance that the Word assumed for Luther in the *Dictata* in place of the sacraments as the means of grace and justification.[9] Heckel emphasized the simultaneous development of the new understanding of justification and the nature of the church and attributed this to Luther's struggle to understand properly the sacrament of penance.[10] Summing up in 1950 the development of Luther's ecclesiology, Albrecht Oepke brought together in one sentence the essence of the two main arguments of Holl:

---

[6] Ernst Kohlmeyer, "Die Bedeutung der Kirche für Luther," *ZKG* 47 (1928), p. 470: "Denn es ist, wenn wir uns dem Sachlichen zuwenden, der traditionelle scholastische Kirchengedanke, der uns in Luthers Anfängen unverkennbar entgegentritt, obgleich sich schon 1513 die entscheidenden inneren Veränderungen des Kirchenbegriffs vorfinden, an denen Luther sein Leben lang festhielt." F. Kattenbusch, writing about the same time as Kohlmeyer, gave his stamp of approval to Holl's conclusions ("Die Doppelschichtigkeit in Luthers Kirchenbegriff," *ThSK* 100 [1927/28], pp. 214ff.).
[7] Reinhold Seeberg, *Lehrbuch der Dogmengeschichte*, Vol. IV, 1 (6th ed., Darmstadt, 1959), p. 344: "... so liegen auch die Grundlinien seines Kirchenbegriffes schon in der Erklärung der Psalmen und des Römerbriefs vor."
[8] Johannes Heckel, *Initia iuris ecclesiastici Protestantium*. In *Sitzungsberichte der Bayerischen Akademie der Wissenschaften*, Philosophisch-historische Klasse, Jahrgang 1949, Heft 5 (München, 1950), p. 34: "Mit dem Thesenanschlag steht Luther am Ende eines Wegs, den er schon in der Psalmenvorlesung von 1513-15 betreten hatte."
[9] Kohlmeyer, p. 471 and Seeberg, Vol. IV, 1, p. 345. Holl had emphasized the same point (pp. 292ff.).
[10] Heckel, *Initia ...*, p. 12.

145

... that Luther's thesis of the invisibility of the church is present already in the first lectures on the Psalms, thus before the collision with Rome, and that it grows organically out of the newly bestowed knowledge of God, Christ and justification.[11]

The conclusions of Holl had dominated Protestant research into Luther's early ecclesiology up to this point.

Although Roman Catholic researchers after Grisar showed little evidence of being directly influenced by him, the outcome of their investigations differed from his only in degree and not in kind. W. Wagner went his own way in 1937 in researching Luther's understanding of the church as *corpus mysticum*. In reference to the *Dictata*, he admitted that Luther saw the significance of the ecclesiastical hierarchy in the proclamation of the Word rather than in the dispensing of the sacraments. According to Wagner, this demonstrates the "insufficiency" of Luther's understanding of the church as *corpus mysticum*, while at the same time it hints at a new, independent conception of this traditional image of the church.[12] Nevertheless, he was certain that Luther's new ecclesiology had not been expressed in terms of the *corpus mysticum* category in the first Psalms commentary.[13] In contrast to this, Luther's statements on the *corpus mysticum* from the period of the indulgence controversy show that he understood the church as *corpus mysticum* exclusively in terms of the *communio sanctorum*.[14]

Other Catholic researchers have admitted the existence of certain "new" elements in Luther's ecclesiology before the outbreak of the indulgence controversy. At the same time, however, they have emphatically attributed to that controversy the decisive role in forcing Luther to take at least the final steps in formulating his ecclesiology. Hubert Jedin maintains that Luther first "drew the consequences" of his new theology for his ecclesiology when the indulgence controversy catapulted him into the limelight.[15] In the process of tracing the words

---

[11] A. Oepke, *Das Neue Gottesvolk* (Gütersloh, 1950), p. 410: "... daß Luthers These von der Unsichtbarkeit der Kirche schon in der ersten Psalmenvorlesung, also vor dem Zusammenstoß mit Rom, vorliegt und daß sie hier organisch aus der neugeschenkten Gottes-, Christus- und Rechtfertigungserkenntnis herauswächst."

[12] Wilhelm Wagner, "Die Kirche als Corpus Christi mysticum beim jungen Luther," *ZKTh* 61 (1937), pp. 49-50.

[13] *Ibid.*, p. 52: "Eines bleibt sicher: Jedenfalls ist die protestantische Auffassung von der Kirche in der ersten großen Schrift Luthers noch nicht in die Sprache des Corpus Christi mysticum übersetzt worden."

[14] *Ibid.*, p. 54.

[15] Hubert Jedin, *Geschichte des Konzils von Trient*, Vol. I: *Der Kampf um das*

and deeds of Luther in regard to the calling of a council, A. Ebneter concedes that many elements of Luther's new ecclesiology were already present prior to 1518-1519, but he asserts even more strongly that they could only be welded together and come to the fore after he had denied the divine right of the papacy and the authority of a council.[16] With a nod to Wagner, he declares that only ignorance of patristic thought and medieval mysticism could delude one into thinking that Luther's new ecclesiology was already complete in the *Dictata*.[17] E. Iserloh categorically insists that Luther's doctrine of the church—which, in his opinion, never was a definition of the essential nature of the church—was developed in the course of his battle against the papal hierarchy.[18] And even in a work which does not pertain directly to Luther's ecclesiology, Harry McSorley dares to remark offhand that Luther worked out no ecclesiology in the course of his theological development on the basis of which he opposed the Pope, since "Luther did not separate himself from the Church of the Catholic theologians, but from the Church of the papacy."[19]

All these attempts to depict Luther's ecclesiology as the result of his open battle with the papacy stand squarely in the tradition of Grisar. They are frequently accompanied by the argument that Luther was not confronted by a unified medieval ecclesiology. As a result, he did not run up against a particular ecclesiology, but rather against the Church

Konzil (2nd ed., Freiburg, 1951), pp. 137-138: "Er wurde sich der Tragweite seiner theologischen Anschauungen erst bewußt und zog die Konsequenzen für den Kirchenbegriff erst, als ihn der Ablaßstreit mit einem Schlage in den Mittelpunkt des öffentlichen Interesses stellte und ihn zum Führer einer gewaltigen Bewegung machte."

[16] Albert Ebneter, "Luther und das Konzil," *ZKTh* 84 (1962), p. 20: "Nachdem das Papsttum *ex jure divino* und die bindende Autorität des Konzils erschüttert war, konnte sich Luthers neuer Kirchenbegriff, von dem viele einzelne Momente schon vorhanden waren, erst ganz durchdringen."

[17] *Ibid.*, p. 20, n. 130: "Es sei rundweg ein Fehlurteil — nur aus Unkenntnis der Vätertheologie und der mittelalterlichen Mystik erklärlich — wenn manche Autoren meinen, daß Luthers Kirchenbegriff in der 1. Psalmenvorlesung sozusagen schon 'fertig' war."

[18] E. Iserloh, J. Glazik and H. Jedin, *Reformation, Katholische Reform und Gegenreformation.* Vol. IV of *Handbuch der Kirchengeschichte* (Freiburg, Basel and Wien, 1967), p. 226: "Diese seine Lehre von der Kirche hat Luther entwickelt im Kampf gegen die hierarchisch gefestigte Papstkirche." Also p. 223: "Im Sinne einer Wesensbestimmung hat Luther keinen neuen Kirchenbegriff aufgestellt."

[19] Harry J. McSorley, *Luthers Lehre vom unfreien Willen* (München, 1967), p. 247: "... denn Luther trennte sich nicht von der Kirche der katholischen Theologen, sondern von der Kirche des Papsttums. Es waren nicht die Theologen, die er den Antichristen nannte, sondern der Papst. Er kam zu diesem Schluß nicht durch sorgfältige ekklesiologische und historische Argumente; diese waren für sein Urteil, der Papst sei der Antichrist, nur zweitrangig."

itself, which he endeavored to reform on the basis of Scripture and his new soteriological conception.[20] This argument helps pave the way for the Grisar thesis that the developing ecclesiology of Luther is severed from his emerging theology as a whole and from his new soteriological understanding in particular; and thereby minimal significance is attributed to the role that Luther's ecclesiology played in the period before the indulgence controversy and even thereafter.

While subsequent Catholic research has served mainly to confirm the conclusions of Grisar, more recent Protestant research into Luther's ecclesiology has deviated somewhat from the strict Holl interpretation. This deviation consists mainly in the denial that the mature ecclesiology of Luther was already present in the *Dictata super Psalterium* (1513-1515). Holsten Fagerberg takes the middle road between Protestant and Catholic research tendencies in affirming that Luther was more dependent on the medieval tradition than Holl wanted to concede, and yet, more than Catholic researchers wanted to admit, had given his concept of the church already in the *Dictata* those features which were to remain permanent for him.[21] The fact that Luther still accepted the hierarchical structure of the church as it existed showed that his concept of the church was not yet fully ripe. And yet, with his principle of the authority of Scripture and faith, Luther's views contained the "explosives," as he puts it, with which Luther could blast his own way when the hour had come.[22]

H. J. Iwand regards the decisive breakthrough in Luther's ecclesiology as occurring in his lectures on Romans (1515-1516).

---

[20] Hubert Jedin, "Ekklesiologie um Luther," p. 28: "Auch Luther will das Christentum als Kirche. Er findet keine geschlossene Ekklesiologie vor, er stößt sich aber begreiflicherweise an der Gestalt der Kirche, die ihn umgibt. Er will sie vom Schriftprinzip her und auf der Grundlage seiner Heilslehre reformieren. Beides kann die katholische Kirche nicht annehmen. So entsteht die Kirchenspaltung." Cf. Iserloh, *Handbuch*, Vol. IV, p. 9: "Die Unsicherheit war besonders groß hinsichtlich des Kirchenbegriffs. . . ." We have presented in Part I evidence which substantially refutes this assertion.

[21] Holsten Fagerberg, "Die Kirche in Luthers Psalmenvorlesungen 1513-1515," *Gedenkschrift für D. Werner Elert*, ed. by F. Hübner (Berlin, 1955), pp. 109-110: "Eine erneute Prüfung des Materials läßt erkennen, daß Luther, mehr als es Holl zugibt, von älterer Tradition abhängt, aber auch mehr als katholische Forscher zugestehen, dem Kirchenbegriff die Züge gegeben hat, an denen er während seiner späteren theologischen Wirksamkeit festhielt."

[22] *Ibid.*, p. 118: "In den Psalmenvorlesungen liegt noch nicht Luthers endgültige Anschauung vor, was sich u.a. in seinem Akzeptieren der kirchlichen Hierarchie zeigt, aber mit dem Prinzip von der Autorität der Schrift und dem Glauben enthalten sie den Sprengstoff, womit Luther sich seinen eigenen Weg bahnen sollte, wenn die Stunde gekommen war."

Although the struggle over the true church first broke out when Luther appealed to the authority of the Word of God over against the authority of the Church,[23] in the lectures on Romans Luther had already overcome with his *simul* the Catholic understanding of sanctification.[24] In contrast to this new dialectical understanding, the concept of *sanctus* and *iustus* in the *Dictata* was still "undialectical."[25] Gerhard Müller comes to the same conclusion when he compares the lectures on Romans with the *Dictata*. While in the *Dictata* sinners were only "guests" in the church, in the lectures on Romans the *veri fideles* remained themselves sinners.[26] Therefore, Luther's ecclesiology receives a "new accent" in the lectures on Romans which goes back to his new understanding of sin and grace.[27]

These more recent Protestant investigations into Luther's ecclesiology disagree with Holl insofar as they do not consider Luther's ecclesiology to be fully developed in the *Dictata*. But they are still in basic agreement with Holl's second conclusion that Luther's new understanding of the church is intimately related to certain aspects of his new soteriological understanding, either to the primacy of the Word or to the relation between sin and grace—aspects which were present before the first open clash with the papacy.

Wilhelm Maurer has approached the subject somewhat differently and introduced the important angle of Luther's hermeneutic directly into the discussion. He consciously rejects the temptation to determine to what degree Luther's concept of the church in the *Dictata* was "Catholic" or "Protestant," but rather limits himself to

---

[23] H. J. Iwand, "Zur Entstehung von Luthers Kirchenbegriff," *Festschrift für Günther Dehn*, ed. by W. Schneemelcher (Neukirchen, 1957), p. 150.

[24] *Ibid.*, p. 153: "Denn damit ist das bisherige für die katholische Kirche ebenso bezeichnende wie entscheidende Verständnis von Heiligung und Heiligen-Dasein in der Wurzel unmöglich gemacht."

[25] *Ibid.*, p. 152.

[26] Gerhard Müller, "Ekklesiologie und Kirchenkritik . . .," p. 114.

[27] *Ibid.*, p. 115: "Luthers Ekklesiologie erhält also schon in der Römerbriefvorlesung, gemessen an den *Dictata*, einen neuen Akzent, der auf sein neues Verständnis von Sünde und Gerechtigkeit zurückgeht." Cf. Müller, "Die Einheit der Theologie des jungen Luther," *Reformatio und Confessio: Festschrift für D. Wilhelm Maurer* (Berlin and Hamburg, 1965), p. 49: "In der Ekklesiologie werden erst in der Römerbrief-vorlesung Konsequenzen aus der neuen Beschäftigung mit den Fragen nach Sünde und Gnade gezogen." In his study of Luther's view of church history, John Headley contented himself with the remark that at the time of the early lectures on the Psalms, Luther had not yet developed his concept of the church, nor had he broken with Rome and come to final awareness of himself as a reformer (*Luther's View of Church History* [New Haven and London, 1963], p. viii).

investigating certain facets of the theme "Church and History" in the *Dictata*.[28] He comes to the conclusion that Luther's early ecclesiology must be seen in relation to his Christology, and that for Luther as well as for Scholasticism, ecclesiology really belongs under the heading of Christology.[29] In making such an identification, Maurer not only emphasizes the *corpus mysticum* and its hermeneutical function; he also points out how the allegorical interpretation of a Scripture passage, which pertains to the church, is closely related to the tropological sense, which pertains to the individual Christian.[30] Whether or not one regards the *corpus mysticum* as the undergirding link between Christ (in the prophetic-literal sense) and the Christian (in the tropological sense) in Luther's employment of the fourfold interpretation of Scripture,[31] Maurer has pointed to the important relationship between Luther's hermeneutical procedure and his ecclesiological development—a connection which definitely goes beyond Holl.

[28] Wilhelm Maurer, "Kirche und Geschichte nach Luthers Dictata super Psalterium," *Lutherforschung heute*, ed. Vilmos Vajta (Berlin, 1958), p. 85.

[29] *Ibid.*, p. 100: "Es gibt also eine Geschichte der Kirche nur, weil und soweit die Kirche *Leib Christi* ist. Indem Luther diese biblische Aussage aufnimmt und in den Mittelpunkt seiner Ekklesiologie stellt, schließt er sich an die Tradition an. ... Die Ekklesiologie ist ein Teil der Christologie — das gilt für die Hochscholastik ganz besonders, das gilt aber, wie wir gesehen haben, auch von dem Luther der ersten Psalmenvorlesung." Cf. Maurer, "Luthers Anschauungen über die Kontinuität der Kirche," *Kirche, Mystik, Heiligung und das Natürliche bei Luther: Vorträge des Dritten Internationalen Kongresses für Lutherforschung* (Göttingen, 1967), p. 105: "Der Zusammenhang von Christologie und Ekklesiologie bildet einen durchgehenden Zug in Luthers Theologie."

[30] Maurer, "Kirche und Geschichte . . .," p. 96: "Es darf aber dabei nicht außer acht gelassen werden, daß auch die allegorische Deutung im engeren Sinne, die das Christus-geschehen auf die Kirche als den Leib Christi bezieht, mit der tropologischen aufs engste zusammenhängt." Maurer is, of course, by no means the first to realize the importance of Luther's employment of the fourfold sense for his ecclesiology. Nevertheless, Luther's use of the allegorical application and the ecclesiological consequence of this application received only passing attention after E. Vogelsang's emphasis upon the primacy of the tropological sense in the *Dictata* and its key role (in his opinion) in Luther's Reformation discovery (*Die Anfänge von Luthers Christologie nach der ersten Psalmenvorlesung*, Berlin and Leipzig, 1929). For example, G. Ebeling mentions the allegorical sense and the doctrine of the church, but he prefers to treat in detail the tropological sense ("Die Anfänge . . .," p. 227). Against this background, Maurer was admonishing Luther researchers not to forget the importance of Luther's hermeneutical presuppositions for his ecclesiology, and that means not altogether neglecting the allegorical sense.

[31] Maurer (*ibid.*) does not express a direct preference either for the *corpus mysticum* as the link between Christ and the Christian, or for a direct connection via the tropological application: "Der einzelne ist Glied Christi, sofern er Glied seines Leibes, der Kirche, ist und umgekehrt." Such neutrality was not to hold the day, however. Cf. our discussion, pp. 170ff.

In an article published shortly after Maurer's work on the *Dictata*, W. J. Kooiman emphasizes even more pointedly that Luther's new ecclesiology must be sought in his handling of the fourfold interpretive schema[32] and concludes that Luther's interpretation of Scripture must lead to a strongly "Christological ecclesiology." As a result, the doctrines of justification and of the church are as closely related as possible.[33] In a recent dissertation, Theophil Steudle has renewed this emphasis upon the intimate relationship between ecclesiology and Christology; in doing so, he explicitly regards justification and Christology as inseparable.[34] Steudle's systematic viewpoint leads him to structure his entire dissertation on this basis and results in the most expanded treatment to date of Holl's thesis that Luther's ecclesiology is a logical consequence of his new understanding of justification.

In the most recent and comprehensive study of Luther's ecclesiology in the *Dictata*, Joseph Vercruysse also notes the importance of Luther's hermeneutical procedure for his early ecclesiology.[35] Vercruysse professes no intention of trying to determine whether Luther's ecclesiology in the *Dictata* was still Catholic or already Protestant. Rather, he wishes to proceed completely objectively ("phenomenologically") and simply present what Luther had to say about the church in his first Psalms commentary.[36] Although he recognizes the need for comparing what Luther said about the church with the ecclesiological material in the medieval Psalms commentaries which Luther used in his preparation, he himself has no intention of

---

[32] W. J. Kooiman, "Het brongebied van Luthers ecclesiologie," *Ecclesia*, Vol. I ('s-Gravenhage, 1959), p. 99.

[33] *Ibid.*, p. 104: Luther's exegesis of Scripture "moest leiden tot een in sterke mate christologische ecclesiologie. De leer van de justificatio en die van de kerk hangen ten nauwste samen."

[34] T. Steudle, *Communio sanctorum beim frühen Martin Luther* (unpublished Th. D. diss., Mainz, 1966), p. 46: "Das Kommen Christi ist conditio sine qua non für jede Gemeinschaft. M.a.W.: Die Ekklesiologie wie auch die Rechtfertigung haben bei Luther ihren Grund in der Christologie. Andererseits bedeutet dies die Zugehörigkeit der Christologie zur Ekklesiologie und Rechtfertigung." And *ibid.*, p. 48: "Ekklesiologie ist notwendig Christologie und umgekehrt." Steudle devotes relatively little attention to the *Dictata*.

[35] *Fidelis Populus*, pp. 11ff. Concrete examples on pp. 78 and 82.

[36] *Ibid.*, p. 4: "Unsere Hauptsorge war nicht, zu erfahren, ob Luther in dieser Zeit *noch* einen katholischen oder *schon* einen reformatorischen Kirchenbegriff hatte. Unser Ziel war ebensowenig, in eine Diskussion mit der Sekundärliteratur über diesen Gegenstand einzutreten. Wir haben nichts zu beweisen; wir wollen nur sehen und begreifen. Wir gehen *phänomenologisch* vor. . . ."

151

treating either that material or the ecclesiology of the later Luther.[37]

It is, therefore, unfortunate that Vercruysse casts a distracting shadow over his otherwise useful work by drawing conclusions at the end of his study which the main body of his book does not support and which tend to align him with the Grisar interpretation. Ecclesiological questions are pressed upon Luther because of the succeeding events and in conjunction with these events Luther gradually (*nach und nach*) constructs a new ecclesiology. True, Luther appropriates certain elements which had been present in his early writings, but the important thing is that Luther rejects in the name of the Gospel the concrete Church which he had earlier accepted. Vercruysse puts the traditional emphasis on the indulgence controversy as the "catalyst" in Luther's development, and then proceeds to separate Luther's ecclesiology from his new doctrine of justification.[38] In addition to these premature conclusions, Vercruysse imposes an artificial "sacred history" (*heilsgeschichtlich*) structure on Luther's ecclesiology in the *Dictata*.[39] Although this may be one way to bring order out of Luther's manifold statements on the church, such a structure is foreign to the material itself. Because of these unsupported conclusions and the renunciation of any effort at interpretation, Vercruysse's work must be regarded as a useful compendium of Luther's ecclesiological statements in the *Dictata* and not as an interpretive study which advances our knowledge of where Luther stood in his ecclesiological development during his first Psalms lectures.

Regardless of the various conclusions which previous researchers have drawn in reference to Luther's early ecclesiology, especially in the *Dictata*, and regardless of the procedure employed by them, one thing

[37] *Ibid.*, p. 1: "Wir möchten nicht untersuchen, welches Erbgut Luther in seinem ersten Psalmenkommentar verarbeitete, wo er von seinen Vorgängern und der traditionellen Auslegung abhängig ist, wo er erneuert.... Wir behandeln also weder die Vor- noch die Nachgeschichte, so dringend nötig beide Untersuchungen auch wären."

[38] *Ibid.*, p. 203: "Es kommt uns so vor, als ob die Ekklesiologie für Luther *erst in seinem Streit gegen die Ablässe* wichtig würde, wo er selbst immer persönlicher *mit der konkreten Kirche* konfrontiert wird.... Die Fragen werden ihm durch die *Ereignisse und Vorfälle aufgedrängt. Nach und nach* wird der Reformator eine neue Ekklesiologie aufbauen.... Die konkrete Kirche, die er früher akzeptierte, weist er jetzt *im Namen des Evangeliums* ab. Der Ablaßstreit wirkt als Katalysator. Seine Ekklesiologie ist *nicht logische Konsequenz* seiner Rechtfertigungslehre" (emphasis ours to indicate those phrases which have been heard before in Catholic research). Vercruysse also appeals to the disunity in medieval ecclesiology (*ibid.*, pp. 203-204) in order to sidestep the question whether Luther's ecclesiology in the *Dictata* was Protestant or Catholic.

[39] *Ibid.*, p. 4.

is common to them all: they have made no concentrated effort to compare Luther's ecclesiological utterances in the *Dictata* with the ecclesiological categories found in the medieval Psalms commentaries which Luther himself used.[40] Only through such a comparison can we obtain a clearly focused picture of what Luther is saying about the church in the *Dictata*, and whether or not it is essentially new or traditional as seen over against the preceding Psalms exegesis. Such a comparison forms the basis of our approach to Luther's ecclesiology in the *Dictata*. This procedure cannot avoid contributing further variations to the basic themes sounded by Holl and Grisar. They have raised the fundamental questions to be asked of Luther's ecclesiology. Nevertheless, by approaching the *Dictata* from the perspective of the medieval Psalms commentaries, we have introduced new themes which round out the composition as a whole and give it a more definitive structure.

In a sense, we also will be imposing an artificial disposition upon Luther's utterances on the nature of the church. This is the case, however, because our aim is *neither* merely to represent objectively what Luther said about the nature of the church in the *Dictata nor* to make a mechanical comparison between Luther and the tradition at certain carefully selected Psalms texts. Rather, we are interested in comparing the definition of key ecclesiological concepts and categories in the respective Psalms commentaries in order to determine whether Luther is saying something significantly new about the nature and structure of the church and what implications any "new" insights might have for his subsequent theological and reforming activity. As we examine Luther's treatment of the same themes which were handled by the medieval exegetes of the Psalms, we have a concrete basis of definitive terms with which to work.

For the moment we pass over the specific elements in which previous researchers have seen the newness of Luther's ecclesiology over against the medieval tradition. They will be dealt with in the course of our investigation. We stress once more, however, that there existed a consensus among the majority of our medieval Psalms commentators regarding the treatment of most of the themes which we have studied so far: a consensus regarding the existence of the mini-church of true *fideles* marked by *caritas*; the image-relation-

---

[40] Several of the researchers have made isolated comparisons, of course. E.g. Wagner, pp. 39ff. and Vercruysse, pp. 102 and 129.

ship between the militant and triumphant churches; the Jews and their successors as enemies of the church; and the implementation of the *concordia* between synagogue and church by attributing New Testament ecclesiological characteristics to the synagogue either in the form of the faithful synagogue or the *ecclesia ab Abel.* Therefore, we should be able to make a judgment as to where Luther stayed within the bounds of this consensus and where he went his own way in regard to these themes. It is essential that our procedure be that of examining these themes and the categories employed in their treatment. The relationship of Luther's ecclesiology to his hermeneutical presuppositions and his developing doctrine of justification will thus be handled in the course of our investigation and will not form the starting point for our study of the *Dictata.*

CHAPTER V

CONGREGATIO FIDELIUM

1. Traditional Themes

We recall that the medieval exegetes of the Psalms denoted the members of the church most frequently as the *fideles*, the faithful. It should come as no surprise that Luther, too, uses this term in the most general way to describe the church and its members. For him, the word *ecclesia* is synonymous with the expression "the faithful people."[1] He calls all members of the church "the faithful" (*fideles*)[2] and speaks of churches, in the sense of individual parishes, as "congregations of the faithful."[3] When he wishes to distinguish the members of the church from the unbelieving Jews and heretics, he refers to the "faithful people" separated from the latter through faith.[4] This nomenclature is fully compatible with traditional usage, where faith as belief in Christ differentiates the members of the baptized community from those unbelievers who stand outside—prime examples of which are the Jews and heretics.

Luther also identifies the *fideles* closely with the apostles and their fellow Christians in the early church. At the beginning of Psalm 59, the prophet speaks in the person of the faithful people, "chiefly of the primitive church."[5] The apostles, martyrs and "all the faithful in the whole church" are designated as new creatures in Christ through the Holy Spirit, who, though great before God, appear weak, foolish, mean

---

[1] *WA* 55/I, 116.10 (*Gl.* to Ps. 15 : 6): "... 'etenim hereditas mea' Ecclesia sive plebs fidelis. ..." *WA* 55/II, 120.12f. (*Sch.* to Ps. 15 : 5): "... 'hereditatem meam mihi,' i.e. populum fidelem, Ecclesiam meam. ..." Although Luther certainly had the *Expositio* of Cassiodorus before him as he worked on Psalm 15 (cf. *WA* 55/II, 117.11 and 55/I, 116.17), he does not explicitly define *hereditas* here as the *electi* (*supra*, Ch. I, n. 73). He does explain the word *praeclaris* with *apostoli* and *electi*, but seems content to leave the more general phrasing of *populus fidelis* for *hereditas* (cf. Lyra, *supra*, Ch. I, n. 148). Also *WA* 3, 335.12: "... 'super rosis' vel liliis, de fidelibus vel Ecclesia, ..."
[2] *WA* 3, 520.24 (*Gl.* to Ps. 75 : 12): "... 'omnes' fideles eius in Ecclesia. ..."
[3] *WA* 4, 25.12ff. (*Sch.* to Ps. 86 : 2): "Sed constat, quod annunciatio fit in Ecclesiis, parochiis, congregationibus fidelium, ergo ipse sunt porte Zion. Quia per illas ingreditur omnis salvandus."
[4] *WA* 4, 441.3f. (*Gl.* to Ps. 140 : 10): "... 'peccatores' increduli Iudei et heretici: 'singulariter' per fidem ab eis separatus 'sum ego' solus populus fidelis, ..."
[5] *WA* 3, 335.31: "Loquitur propheta in persona populi fidelis Christi praecipue primitivae Ecclesiae, ..."

and abject before men.[6] The apostles and the "faithful peoples" are paired in the context of their preaching activity and presented by Luther as the proper interpretation of the *iusti*.[7] In these passages, Luther appears to have in mind all members of the early church without distinction.

Although the *fideles* can refer categorically to all Christians in the baptized community, Luther does employ the term in contexts where it appears to apply more specifically to Christians in a state of grace. In his exposition of Psalm 44, Luther interprets the spices named there (i.e. the ointment prepared from these spices) as that grace which is diffused among all the faithful of Christ.[8] Further, the *fideles* are those who have been truly "changed" through Christ and reborn. In fact, "all of us are changed through grace in this life from sin into righteousness, from flesh into spirit, from the letter and shadow of the law into the life and light of the Gospel. . . ."[9]

A further indication that Luther uses the term *fideles* to denote such an inner circle is his traditional equation of the *fideles* with the *iusti* and the *sancti*. In the *glossae* to Psalm 36, Luther interprets "those who will inherit the earth" on one occasion as the *veri Christiani*. In this text he identifies the *iustus* as "Christ and his own." Later in the same *glossae*, the *iusti* are explicitly construed as the *fideles* who will inherit the earth.[10] The categories *iusti, fideles* and *veri Christiani*

---

[6] *WA* 4, 240.26ff. (*Sch.* to Ps. 110 : 2): "Ista opera sunt creature nove create in Christo per spiritum sanctum . . . Et sunt ipsi Apostoli, martyres, omnesque fideles in tota Ecclesia . . . Valde enim magni sunt, non corpore aut coram mundo, sed virtutibus et sapientia coram deo, et mirabiles, quod infirmi, stulti et abiecti et humiles sunt coram hominibus . . . Ergo 'Magna opera domini' sunt ipsa Ecclesia fidelium."

[7] *WA* 4, 85.14f. (*Gl.* to Ps. 92 : 3): " 'Elevaverunt' aperte predicaverunt et confidenter 'flumina' Apostoli et populi fideles, . . ." *WA* 3, 294.18f. (*Gl.* to Ps. 51 : 8): ". . . 'iusti' Apostoli et fideles omnes. . . ."

[8] *WA* 3, 260.18ff. (*Sch.* to Ps. 44 : 9): "Que res significabat, quod Ecclesia et omnis populus Christi spiritualiter ungendi erant gratiis, donis et virtutibus. . . . Myrrha ergo et gutta et casia, id est unguentum ex illis confectum, id est gratia per talem confectionem significata, in omnibus fidelibus Christi diffusa est." Cf. Perez' interpretation of the same verse in terms of the sacraments (*supra*, Ch. I, n. 176).

[9] *WA* 3, 254.14ff.: "Et sic volunt pro fidelibus intelligi, qui vere sunt commutati per Christum et alterati et renati ac iterum geniti . . . Ideo omnes nos [corr: *WA* 55] immutamur hic per gratiam de peccato in iustitiam, de carne in spiritum, de litera et umbra legis in vitam et lucem Evangelii, et post hec de corruptione in incorruptionem, de ignominia in gloriam eternam." Hugo speaks of the faithful people as changed from sin to repentance (*supra*, Ch. I, n. 112).

[10] *WA* 3, 207.7ff.: " 'Quia benedicentes' quales sunt solum veri Christiani verbo et opere 'ei' iusto, qui est Christus et suis, 'haereditabunt terram' viventium hic et in futuro." And *WA* 3, 208.12: " 'Iusti autem' fideles Christi 'haereditabunt terram' viventium ut supra." The *ut supra* in the latter text clearly refers to the first text.

must be running on parallel tracks in Luther's mind. In reference to the famous passage from Psalm 68 concerning the "book of the living," Luther maintains that the righteous who will be "written in heaven" are the *fideles*.[11] He also groups the righteous and the faithful in regard to their flexible receptivity to the truth and their rigid stance against all falsehood in contrast to the Jews, heretics and their imitators who are just the opposite.[12]

Luther makes a similar identification between *sancti* and *fideles*.[13] In the *glossae* to Psalm 88, Luther interprets the "church of the saints" from two sides: once in contrast to the "church of the impious" and once as the *fideles*.[14] The contrast with the *impii* points to the traditional parallel of the *sancti* with the *boni*, which Luther then expands to include the *fideles*. The catch-phrase *ecclesia* or *communio sanctorum*[15] is, however, not immediately to be taken as indicative of a "Reformation" ecclesiology in the *Dictata*. This parallel between the *sancti* and the *fideles* within the core of the church is in itself traditional. The deciding factor is the definition of these categories.[16]

As we have seen, Luther does not reserve the category *fideles* for an inner circle of true Christians or saints. Not only the members of the mini-church may be called *fideles*, but all the baptized as well. Insofar as he uses the term to cover all members of the baptized

---

[11] *WA* 3, 414.24-415.1 (*Gl.* to Ps. 68 : 29): " 'Deleantur de libro viventium' effectu ostendantur non esse scripti in libro vite: 'et cum iustis' fidelibus meis 'non scribantur' in coelis." Unlike the tradition, Luther avoids any reference to the predestined (cf. *supra*, Ch. I, nn. 75 and 157).

[12] *WA* 3, 513.18ff. (*Sch.* to Ps. 74 : 4): "Iusti et fideles Christi ad omnem veritatis normam sunt mollissimi et liquidissimi, ad normam autem falsitatis rigidissimi et inflexibiles. Econtra Iudei ad omnem normam mendacem liquidissimi, ad normam autem veritatis rigidissimi et obstinatissimi: similiter heretici et omnes capitosi et singulares."

[13] *WA* 3, 146.27 (*Gl.* to Ps. 25 : 6): "... 'inter innocentes' fideles et sanctos, ..." Cf. *WA* 4, 422.9 (*Gl.* to Ps. 131 : 9).

[14] *WA* 4, 37.22f. (*Gl.* to Ps. 88 : 6: "... 'in ecclesia sanctorum,' non autem in Ecclesia impiorum, qui potius negant eam." And *ibid.*, 37.28-38.1: "... 'in concilio' Ecclesia 'sanctorum' fidelium."

[15] For the *communio sanctorum*, cf. *WA* 3, 389.26ff.

[16] Luther provides us with the traditional definition of *sanctus* in the *Dictata*: *WA* 3, 178.10f.: "Notandum quod 'sanctus' in scriptura significat, quem theologi Scolastici dicunt 'in gratia gratificante constitutum.' " On the other hand, he speaks of the *sancti* also in those terms which we believe to be a new definition of the *fideles* (see p. 168). The passages containing references to the *ecclesia sanctorum* and *communio sanctorum* are themselves difficult to categorize. The important thing to note, however, is that the traditional parallel between the true *fideles* and the *sancti* will lead Luther to redefine the *sancti* when he redefines the *fideles*. Then the way is clear for later formulations of the true church as the *communio sanctorum*.

157

community, Luther can name the members of the church *fideles* even when they sin. When this happens, they retain the *fides informis* (and *spes informis*) and hold on to Christ as if they were fringes on the outer edge of the garment of the church.[17] And yet, even though the whole church—the *mali* as well as the *boni*—is shaken when the faithful sin, God's covenant with his people does not become invalid as it did in Old Testament times.[18] The important thing is for the *fideles* to persevere in grace so that sin might not reign in them, as Luther, drawing on an Augustinian formulation, phrases it.[19] Making further use of traditional terminology, he maintains that among the faithful there are tares as well as wheat; nevertheless, the tares are still in the church.[20] Indeed, the sinner is in obedience to the church and under its yoke. Luther describes such sinners as "infirm," who sin out of fragility because they are still strong in the flesh and weak in the spirit.[21]

Clearly, therefore, Luther gives the term *fideles* the same twofold reference as the Psalms commentators before him—to denote on the one hand the inner circle of *boni* and *iusti*, i.e. those who are in a state of grace and have the *fides formata*, and on the other hand, all members of the baptized community, including those *mali* who have sinned and fallen out of the state of grace and retain only the rudiments of faith. The above passages afford us no reason to doubt

---

[17] *WA* 3, 495.14ff. (*Sch.* to Ps. 73 : 3): "Sed non sic in fidelibus etiam peccantibus: qui saltem fidem informem, spem quoque eodem modo retinent et sic velut ultima fimbria eum adhuc tenent, quam diu sunt in hac vita."

[18] *WA* 4, 41.27ff. (*Gl.* to Ps. 88 : 35): "Unde et quando peccant fideles, tota Ecclesia flagellatur, mali cum bonis, sed non irritum fit pactum. Olim autem etiam si pauci peccassent, solvebatur pactum, quia fundatum erat in operibus eorum." For Luther's understanding of *pactum* in relation to this passage, cf. H. A. Oberman, "Wir sein pettler. Hoc est verum," *ZKG* 78 (1967), pp. 247f.

[19] *WA* 3, 153.15ff. (*Gl.* to Ps. 27 : 9): " 'Salvum fac populum tuum' fidelium 'domine et benedic' ut augeantur, 'hereditati tuae,' qui sunt heredes tui et coheredes mei: 'et rege eos' ut perseverent in gratia, ne peccatum in eis regnet 'et extolle' finaliter 'illos usque ineternum.' " Cf. Aug., *Enarr. in ps.* 41.9 (*CChr* 38, 466).

[20] *WA* 4, 418.30ff. (*Gl.* to Ps. 128 : 6): "Manipuli sunt populi fidelium, in quibus adhuc multe sunt palee et non totum est grana: sunt tamen in Ecclesia. Iudei vero nec manipuli sunt, quia nullo modo in Ecclesiam colliguntur, et omnes pertinaciter increduli."

[21] *WA* 3, 610.18f. (*Sch.* to Ps. 79 : 14): "Porcus enim domesticus est peccator in obedientia et iugo Ecclesie, sed sylvester et ferus est extra Ecclesiam." And *WA* 3, 446.22ff. (*Sch.* to Ps. 69 : 4-5): "Sane 'infirmos' ibi sine dubio dicit eos, qui peccant in Ecclesia ex fragilitate. Qui adhuc sunt fortes in carne et mundo, infirmi autem in spiritu, licet non sint sapientes in carne, quia sciunt veritatem humilitatis et fidei, sed peccant ut dixi ex infirmitate carnis."

this traditional bifurcate reference. In effect, we are confronted initially with those *fideles* in a state of grace, the true *fideles*, as opposed to the false or apparent *fideles* who live only on the fringes. This formulation stands in accord with the tradition.[22]

The basis for this twofold reference of the category *fideles* is the same as that in the tradition—the acceptance of the existence of *mali* as well as *boni* in the church. Luther makes use of the traditional interpretation of the wine press (*torcular*) as tribulation and pressure, and applies it as his predecessors had done to the process of distinguishing the good from the bad in the church.[23] Even the *impii* are in the church for a while, although they cannot inhabit the church as true heirs.[24] The simultaneous existence of grain and chaff in the church poses a stumbling block for heretics, because they see only the chaff and willfully conclude that the church is totally evil since they alone wish to be regarded as good.[25] Luther argues for the necessity of authority in the church by maintaining that if we were all *boni* and perfect, we would already be saved or at least merely waiting on our salvation. But since we are evil (!), or at least mixed, it is necessary that there be powers in the church who exercise judgment and correction.[26] Luther's refusal to exclude the *mali* from the church has

---

[22] We would therefore make more precise the formulations of W. J. Kooiman ("Het brongebied ...," p. 107) where he refers to the "faithful" and the "unfaithful" living together in the church. Not the *infideles*, but rather the false *fideles* (whom Kooiman also mentions) are the opponents of the true *fideles* in the baptized community.

[23] *WA* 3, 610.29ff. (*Gl.* to the title of Ps. 80): "Torcular ps. 8 expositum est pro passione Christi. Ita nunc secundum Augustinum hoc loco mystice pro passionibus et pressuris sanctorum exponitur. In quibus probantur boni et mali: sicut oleum et amurca in oliva per torcular discernuntur, ita et per tribulationes et pressuras probantur et distinguuntur." For the tradition, *supra*, Ch. I, nn. 38-40, 98.

[24] *WA* 3, 351.4ff. (*Gl.* to Ps. 60 : 5): "'Inhabitabo' sicut heres et particeps 'in tabernaculo tuo' Ecclesia tua, quod non contingit impiis 'in saecula' sine fine, licet ad tempus in eo sint."

[25] *WA* 3, 445.8ff. (*Sch.* to Ps. 69 : 4-5): "Heretici autem propriissime velle malum Ecclesie dicendi sunt. Quia imponunt ei falsitatem et colluviem vitiosorum et malorum Christianorum: et ita ex paucitate malorum [*sic*] omnes concludunt esse malos. Quia plurimum vident palearum in area, totum sine ullo grano paleam esse audacter affirmant. Ac sic sibi tantum bona, Ecclesie autem mala volunt, id est voluntatem habent, et vellent, ut soli boni putentur, Ecclesia autem in omnibus mala reputetur. Nec enim possunt ipsi boni videri, nisi Ecclesiam malam, falsam et mendacem asserant."

[26] *WA* 4, 405.7ff. (*Sch.* to Ps. 121 : 5): "Si enim omnes boni essemus et perfecti, salvi essemus et tantummodo salvandi, non autem iudicandi et damnandi. Nunc quia mali sumus, vel saltem mixti, necesse est potestatem esse, que iudicet, arguat et corripiat." Luther's affirmation, which he hastily qualifies, that "we are evil" indicates the penetration of his thought by the *semper peccamus* idea, which we have yet to examine, but which here almost demolishes the *boni/mali* structure. See pp. 236ff. Luther also

led him, like his fellow exegetes before him, to give the *fideles* their traditional double reference: to the *boni* alone as *iusti*, and to the *boni* and *mali* together.[27]

2. The New Definition of the *Fideles*

Although we find this traditional double reference in the *Dictata*, Luther tends to speak more frequently of the *fideles* in terms which would identify them only with the *boni*. For example, the faithful and the unbelievers are paralleled respectively with the *boni* and the *mali*.[28] The *fideles* are often set over against not only the Jews and the heretics, but also over against their comrades-in-arms, the evil Christians. The only way that God can save the faithful people is to destroy those who oppress them, namely the heretics and all impious Christians, especially those in high office, who impede truth and righteousness in the church as the Jews did in the synagogue.[29] The Jews, heretics, Moslems and all proud men transgress the law and the way of truth, but this is not the case (*non sic ... non sic*) with "the church and the *fideles*."[30] Those who are truly Christians and *fideles* are "immaculate" though still *in via*, while the Jews and heretics are

uses the categories of the *corpus Christi verum* or *simulatum*, which was Augustine's improvement over the *corpus bipertitum* of Tyconius (*supra*, Ch. I, n. 20). Luther applies the terms, except on one occasion, to the Jews and the church. Cf. *WA* 3, 552,21ff. (*Gl.* to Ps. 77 : 12) and *WA* 3, 612.17ff. and 612.29f. (*Gl.* to Ps. 80 : 17 and 80 : 14).

[27] Kohlmeyer correctly observes that the double reference in Luther's statements on the church corresponds to the Augustinian-scholastic tradition, and that the decisive factors lie within the "spiritual concept of the church" ("Die Bedeutung ...," p. 470). What these factors are remains to be seen.

[28] *WA* 4, 235.31f. (*Sch.* to Ps. 109 : 5): "Quoad incredulos est dies ire, quoad fideles est dies gratie, sicut et in futuro erit dies glorie bonis, dies ire malis."

[29] *WA* 4, 93.4ff. (*Sch.* to Ps. 93 : 1-2): "Neque enim salvare populum fidelem aliter potest quam ut ulciscens deprimat eos, qui populum seducunt et perdunt ... Quia illi exaltati sunt et impediunt veritatem et iustitiam, ipsi non introeunt in regnum coelorum et introeuntes prohibent, ac per hoc Christus humiliatur. Quare petit, ut exaltetur. Sic enim contra Hereticos quoque et omnes impios Christianos, maxime maiores, orandum est, ut dominus ultionum exaltetur. Quoniam similia faciunt in Ecclesia, que illi in synagoga."

[30] *WA* 4, 136.26ff. (*Sch.* to Ps. 100 : 3): "Quia faciunt declinationes seu prevaricationes a lege et via veritatis ad suam viam et propriam legem ... Hoc primum Iudei, deinde heretici, tandem Maomet et omnes superbi. Quia vetus homo et caro, cum in superbiam sui sensus erigitur, proponit etiam sibi iniquum idolum sapientie sue, quo fit pertinax et immansivus: ... Non sic Ecclesia et fideles non sic." This passage had traditionally been interpreted as referring to prevaricators both inside (for Luther = *superbi*) and outside the community of the baptized: by Augustine (*supra*, Ch. I, n. 41) and the *Glossa interlinearis* (*supra*, Ch. I, n. 101). Only Luther, however, refers explicitly to the *fideles* in this context where the *boni* are intended.

authors of their own righteousness, remaining defiled in this life.[31]

While the previous contrasts indicate that the true *fideles* correspond to the *boni* because of their opposition not only to the Jews and heretics but also to the *mali*, this in itself does not represent any departure from the tradition. The decisive factor is the way in which Luther defines these true *fideles*. In those passages in which the *fideles* assume a sharper profile in their own right, a discrepancy between Luther's definition and that of the tradition begins to manifest itself. Toward the end of the *Dictata*, Luther gives an explicit, positive definition of the true *fideles*: "Hence it is clear that he [the prophet] speaks of creatures created in the spirit through faith, who are his [Christ's] *fideles*."[32] But this characterization is by no means confined to the latter part of the lectures. Already in the *glossae* to Psalm 44, Luther maintains that the proximity of the faithful is not one of flesh and blood as in normal human relationships, but rather a proximity of the same spirit and faith.[33] The same definitive marks of *fides* and *spiritus* turn up in other contexts where Luther mentions the *fideles*. God is known in the individual *fideles* "through faith and in the spirit." And in contrast to the Jews, heretics and *mali* who desire temporal things, the faithful people seek "spiritual things, which are given to us primarily in faith and the Gospel."[34]

In the *scholion* to Psalm 26 : 5 ("He has hidden me in his tabernacle"), Luther expands upon the characterization of the *fideles* as hidden "in faith and the spirit":

> "Tabernacle" is the church or the body of Christ; yet at the same time it is the church mystically understood. And in this [tabernacle] is hidden

[31] *WA* 4, 280.32ff. (*Gl.* to the summary of Ps. 118): "Prophetice primo est descriptio populi fidelis in Christo futuri contra pharisaicas corruptelas. Et sic proprie loquitur de iis, qui [corr: *WA* 55] in via sunt, sed immaculati, contra eos, qui sunt in via, sed maculati: illi vere Christiani et fideles, isti autem sue iustitie auctores, ut Iudei et heretici." One must add here the *superbi* to the Jews and heretics. They are the subject of the moral interpretation in the following lines.

[32] *WA* 4, 450.33f. (*Gl.* to Ps. 144 : 9): "Hinc patet, quod de creaturis in spiritu per fidem creatis loquitur, qui sunt fideles eius."

[33] *WA* 3, 252.37ff. (*Gl.* to Ps. 44 : 15): "Proximitas enim secundum homines est eiusdem sanguinis et carnis, sed proximitas fidelium est eiusdem spiritus et fidei: unde canitur: Quia unus spiritus et una fides erat in eis." Cf. *ibid.*, 19f.

[34] *WA* 3, 268.23ff. (*Gl.* to Ps. 47 : 4): " 'Deus' Christus cum patre et spiritu sancto, vel quod ipse sit Deus, qui [corr: *WA* 55] est rex magnus 'in domibus eius' i.e. fidelibus singulis et omnibus 'cognoscetur' per fidem et in spiritu." And *WA* 4, 376.6ff. (*Sch.* to Ps. 118 : 147): "... sed temporalia desiderantes: ut usque hodie Iudei et heretici et mali ... Sed fidelis populus spiritualia querit, que sunt in fide et evangelio nobis donata maxima, ..."

every *fidelis*. This "being hidden" should not be understood carnally . . . but as follows: man is said to be inward and hidden in that he does not live worldly and carnally — namely, because he withdraws from the life, customs and conversation of the world. . . . Therefore, "to be hidden" is nothing else than not to concur with those living carnally. . . .

The "hidden" character of the church is thus faith itself or the spirit, which is the same, because the *fideles* live in faith and the spirit, i.e. in the knowledge and love of invisible things. Carnal men do not live in faith, but in the thing itself [*in re*], not in the spirit, but in the flesh. Therefore, they are not hidden, but rather out in the open; they are all wrapped up in visible things. And note that the church has no protection out in the open in visible matters, but in those things it is left to the capriciousness of tyrants and evil men, although now the leaders of the church would like most of all to be defended in the open place of the devil's tabernacle, i.e. of the world, in visible matters. But the church is protected in spiritual matters to such an extent that it cannot be deprived of them nor suffer any harm in these affairs, because they are the invincible and eternal, spiritual goods of faith.[35]

The *fideles*, who in this passage constitute the body of Christ, live in the spirit and in faith insofar as they orient themselves around invisible things, i.e. the spiritual goods of faith as opposed to the things of this world. They are "hidden," not in the sense that they cannot be seen, but rather in the sense that they do not live like men who orient themselves around, and are wrapped up in, the things of this world. The hidden character of the church does not apply so much to the persons of the *fideles* themselves as to their orientation in faith and the spirit, which are intangible entities, and yet whose possession leads to a way of life that is actually quite visible. This orientation, this life in faith and the spirit directed toward invisible, spiritual goods, is the mark of the true *fideles*. Insofar as this life in faith is concerned, the true *fideles* are always protected by God,

---

[35] *WA* 3, 150.16ff.: " 'Tabernaculum' est Ecclesia vel corpus Christi, quod tamen mystice etiam est Ecclesia. Et in isto absconditur quilibet fidelis. Que absconsio non debet intelligi carnaliter, . . . sed sic quia homo dicitur interior et absconditus eo quod non vivit seculariter et carnaliter. Scilicet quod subtrahit sese a vita, moribus et conversatione mundi . . . . Igitur 'Abscondi' est nihil aliud nisi non concurrere cum viventibus carnaliter, . . . 'Absconditum' ergo Ecclesie est ipsa fides seu spiritus, quod idem est. Quia in fide et spiritu vivunt, id est in cognitione et amore invisibilium. Sicut carnales non in fide, sed in re vivunt et non in spiritu, sed in carne. Ideo non sunt in abscondito, sed in manifesto, volvuntur in rebus visibilibus. Et nota, quod Ecclesia protegitur non in manifesto in rebus visibilibus, immo in illis derelinquitur ad voluntatem tyrannorum et malorum, licet nunc pontifices maxime defendi velint in manifesto tabernaculi Diaboli, id est mundi, in visibilibus rebus. Sed in spiritualibus defenditur, ita quod illa non possunt ei auferri aut noceri in eis, quia sunt invicta et eterna bona spiritualia fidei."

although in worldly matters they may be subject to tyrants and the *mali*.[36]

Luther treats further the spiritual and hidden character of the true *fideles* in his discussion of the meaning of *abyssus* in the *scholion* to Psalm 32 : 7. He interprets the *abyssi* as the faithful of Christ because they are "spiritual and deep and hidden before men of the world." Then switching his terminology from *fideles* to *sancti*, Luther discusses the distinction between *aquae* and *abyssi*. The *sancti*, he says, are "waters" according to the body in the sense that they are congregated into the church and exist there in a quite obvious place where, as the congregation of the saints, they are manifest to the world. According to the spirit, however, they are *abyssi*, founded in hidden, invisible things which they cannot see but only believe. This is what it means for the "*abyssi* to be put in treasures": the *fideles* or *sancti* are made firm and founded by faith in invisible things, things which are believed, which Luther defined earlier as the mysteries of faith and the sacraments.[37] Once again it is not the faithful themselves who are invisible, but rather their foundation through faith in the invisible mysteries which are the object of faith. Their orientation around these invisible, spiritual goods determines their spiritual character as well.

The second chapter of I Corinthians is operating in the above *scholion*, where, in connection with the *abyssi*, Luther thinks immediately of the *profunda Dei* which only the Spirit of God knows and has revealed to us (I Cor. 2 : 10). In fact, in the *glossa* to the same

---

[36] Note here (and in n. 29 above) Luther's criticism of the leaders of the church, which puts them more on the side of the *mali* than on the side of the true *fideles*, and the opposition of their stance to the absolute invisibility of life in faith and the spirit.

[37] *WA* 3, 183.25ff.: "Abyssi autem sunt aque profunde, que videri nequeunt. Est enim ipsa profunditas seu altitudo aquarum. Sunt autem ipsi fideles Christi, quia sunt spirituales et profundi et absconditi coram Hominibus mundi. ... Quia ergo etiam profunda dei per spiritum sanctum scivit secundum apostolum 1. Corin. 2[: 10] recte vocantur abyssi seu profunditates aquarum. Has ergo abyssos ponit in thezauris, id est occultis vel absconditis, que sunt mysteria fidei et sacramenta Ecclesie. Ponuntur, id est fide fundantur in illis, nam Ecclesia et bona eius sunt thezaurus appellata a Christo Matth. 13[: 44]. ... Ubi videtur significare, sanctos appellari aquas secundum corpus et secundum animam abyssos. Et secundum corpora quidem congregari in utrem, Ecclesiam scilicet, velut certum locum et cognitum et visum: quia utique sanctorum congregatio seu Ecclesia manifesta est secundum carnem, ubi et quando sunt. Sed secundum spiritum ponuntur in thezauris, id est occultis, ita ut nec ipsi adhuc videant ea, in quibus ponuntur, sed tantum credunt: ponuntur enim et fundantur in invisibilibus, que nullus hominum videre potest, credere autem potest. Et hoc est poni, id est fide firmari in absconditis, id est credibilibus."

verse, Luther explicitly identifies the *abyssus* with the *homo spiritualis* of I Cor. 2 : 15, who "judges all things and is judged by no one."[38] Thus, Luther is setting the true *fideles* equal to the *homines spirituales*, who know the depths of God which the Spirit has revealed to them. For Luther, however, this means that the *fideles* as spiritual men pierce these depths by faith. They cannot see them with the naked eye, but only believe in them. The true *fideles* are spiritual and hidden because they believe the invisible things of God and orient their lives toward those things in which they are founded by faith. From the "depths of God" which are mentioned in I Corinthians, we know that it is these invisible things which for Luther are "hidden," and not so much the *fideles* themselves. Yet, the hiddenness of these objects of their faith imparts a hidden trait to their character because the fideles establish their lives on these invisible entities. They live in the spirit and in faith.[39]

This portrayal of the true *fideles* living in faith and the spirit does not refer to some quality which is in them, some possession of theirs, but to the foundation and orientation of their existence—namely, in the invisible things of God. Here we see emerging a definition of the true *fideles* which is quite different from that of the medieval Psalms exegesis. Regardless of what latent connection there may have been in Luther's mind between the *fides* of which he is speaking in these passages and the traditional *fides caritate formata, caritas* as such can no longer be regarded as the mark of the true *fideles* for him. The infused grace of *caritas*, which forms the soul anew, is quite different from the *fides* which directs one toward the invisible things of the spirit and upon which the true *fidelis* is founded and toward which he is oriented.[40] *Fides*, a different *fides* from the *fides formata*, is

---

[38] *WA* 3, 179.11f.: ". . . 'abyssos' spirituales homines, quia omnes iudicant et ipsi a nemine iudicantur 1. Cor. 2." Cf. *WA* 3, 202.23ff. (*Sch.* to Ps. 35 : 7: "Iudicia tua abyssus multa") where reference is made to Psalm 32.

[39] Cf. *WA* 3, 166.36ff.: "Quia etsi secundum corpora, quibus mundo erant manifesti, conturbati sunt ab eis, non tamen secundum spiritum, quo erant eis absconditi in Deo, sed salvi semper fuerunt in fide et spiritu." For the identification of the *fideles* with the *homines spirituales* of I Cor. 2 : 15 and the mark of faith, see further *WA* 3, 148.38ff.: "Et ideo vocantur fideles absconditi, i.e. spirituales, qui omnia iudicant et a nemine iudicantur 1. Cor. 2." *WA* 3, 166.15ff.: " 'Abscondes eos in abscondito' fide, qua vident faciem tuam, et tamen ipsi a nemine iudicantur, cum omnia iudicent, . . ."

[40] The opposition between *fides* and *res*, as it is expressed in n. 35 above and n. 46 below, also points to the incompatibility between *fides* and *caritas* as the defining marks of the *fideles*. See our discussion, pp. 204ff. For Luther's understanding of faith in the *Dictata*, cf. R. Schwarz, *Fides, spes und caritas beim jungen Luther* (Berlin, 1962), pp. 134ff., and for our discussion here esp. 147ff.

beginning to replace *caritas* as the mark of the true *fideles*. Therefore, we disagree strongly with J. Vercruysse when he maintains that Luther's definition of the church as the community of the faithful, who are united to Christ through faith, is the "most traditional definition that there is."[41] *Fides*, which is not the *fides formata*, leads to a completely different definition of the church from that of the exegetical tradition based on *caritas*.

Let us examine further preliminary evidence of the role of faith as the mark of the *fideles*. There are a number of passages in which Luther maintains that Christ is present in the *fideles* through faith. Christ remains both God and man eternally not only in his own person, but also in his faithful through faith.[42] Christ lives and reigns in the *fideles* through faith during the whole time of grace (i.e. between the incarnation and his second coming).[43] In the *scholion* to Psalm 9 : 1, after describing the *fideles* as spiritual virgins hidden in faith, Luther maintains that faith is the "spiritual virginity" by which we are wedded to Christ, as opposed to the Jews and evil Christians who are accused by the prophets of fornication (i.e. unbelief).[44] When

---

[41] *Fidelis Populus*, p. 205: "In dieser Perspektive ist die Kirche Gemeinschaft der Heiligen oder Gläubigen, ein Volk, die Gemeinschaft aller, die durch den Glauben mit Christus vereinigt leben. Diese Definition ist die traditionellste, die es gibt." The following statement of J. Heckel, though not in regard to the *Dictata*, must also be made more precise (*Lex charitatis. Abhandlungen der Bayerischen Akademie der Wissenschaften*, Phil.-hist. Klasse, Neue Folge, Heft 36 [München, 1953], p. 104): "Aber wer fidelis und infidelis ist, entscheidet sich bei ihm—anders als im kanonischen Recht—nicht nach der Zugehörigkeit zur Taufgemeinschaft, sondern zur Glaubensgemeinschaft; maßgebend ist nicht die Mitgliedschaft in der ecclesia universalis, sondern spiritualis." First, Luther also uses the category *fideles* in reference to the entire baptized community. Secondly, at least one medieval tradition—the exegetical—also spoke of an inner circle of true *fideles*, although defined by *caritas*. Luther is not different because he limits the *fideles* to the inner circle of the *boni*, but because he defines them differently—namely, in terms of faith.

[42] *WA* 3, 467.23ff. (*Sch.* to Ps. 71 : 5): "Tamen in utroque, permanet [Christus] nunc ineternum, tam scilicet deus quam homo permanens in seipso: et in fidelibus suis talis per fidem."

[43] *WA* 4, 417.8ff. (*Gl.* to Ps. 127 : 5): "... 'et videas' [Christus] in tuis fidelibus habitans 'bona Ierusalem' Ecclesie tue: 'omnibus diebus vitae tuae' toto tempore gratie, quo vivis et regnas in eis per fidem." Cf. *WA* 55/I, 32.11 (*Gl.* to Ps. 5 : 8): "... 'ego autem' Scil. in populo meo habitans per fidem. ..."

[44] *WA* 55/II, 104.7ff.: "... Iuventus seu Spirituales virgines et adolescentule, que sunt omnes fideles Christi ut Psal. 44[: 15]: 'adducentur regi virgines.' ... Vocantur autem 'mystice', 'arcane' vel 'abscondite' virgines ad differentiam exterioris et carnalis virginitatis, quia sunt in tabernaculo fidei, ut Psal. 29 [30 : 21; cf. 26 : 5]: 'Abscondes eos in abscondito tabernaculi tui,' i.e. in fide Ecclesie tue, 'a contradictione hominum' ... Unde Quia fides est spiritualis virginitas, per quam desponsamur Christo, ... Ideo Iudei et mali Christiani in prophetis semper arguuntur de fornicatione, i.e. incredulitate."

we compare these statements of Luther with the assertion of Hugo, for example, that the seat of God in the *fideles* is *caritas*,[45] all indications point to the fact that Luther is altering the link between God and the *fideles* from *caritas* to *fides*.

Faith also plays a decisive role in the following characterization of the true *fideles* as "expecting" God's salvation:

> And this is the peculiar property of the faithful people, namely to expect. ... For what good would it do to live in faith and hope in the beginning, and then because of the tedium to break down before the end and return to visible things, in which one can live only for present realities without faith and hope. For this is the property of impious and unbelieving men who are unable to grasp invisible and eternal things.[46]

The contiguity of faith and hope in this concise definition brings the character of *fides* as the defining mark of these faithful into clearer focus. The invisible things toward which faith and hope are directed are described by the Psalm text, namely, God's salvation. The attitude of hoping and expecting this salvation indicates that *fides* is not directed inward to its adornment by the internal quality of *caritas*. Rather, it turns the faith of the *fideles* outward toward that which is beyond them, ahead of them, awaiting them, that which cannot yet be seen, in contrast to visible things of this life around which the impious and unbelievers orient themselves. They can only be believed, hoped for and expected, and this attitude of faith is the *proprium* of the faithful people, not as an internal quality or virtue, but expressive of a stance, a posture, a foundation in that which is outside of itself.

A few lines later Luther asserts in reference to the same *fideles* that "those who are expecting are fixed and suspended in heaven; therefore, when either prosperity or adversity comes, they are not moved, but remain steady expecting other things."[47] Elsewhere we find the *fideles* portrayed as "heavenly." They will be established in mercy and mercy in them, and God gives to them a heavenly and spiritual

---

[45] *Supra*, Ch. I, n. 125.

[46] *WA* 4, 388.10ff. (*Sch.* to Ps. 118 : 166: "I was expecting your salvation, O Lord, and I have loved your commandments"): "Et hoc proprium est fidelis populi, scl. expectare, ... Nam quid prodesset in fide et spe vivere tantum pro principio, et tedio frangi ante finem ac redire ad visibilia, in quibus sine fide et spe, sed re et presentia vivitur? Hoc est enim impiorum et incredulorum, qui sapere nesciunt invisibilia et eterna: ..."

[47] *Ibid.*, 17ff.: "Qui autem expectant, sunt in celo fixi atque suspensi: ideo veniat [corr: *WA* 55] adversitas sive prosperitas, non moventur, sed permanent expectantes alia."

mercy.[48] This "heavenly" character of the *fideles* indicates that they are founded in something which is outside of themselves, namely in the mercy of God. Suspended, as it were, above earthly, visible things in this mercy, they believe and expect that God will preserve his mercy in respect to them regardless of what may come and deliver the awaited salvation. This kind of faith-orientation in the spiritual, invisible mercy and salvation of God is the hallmark of the true *fideles* for Luther.

Caught up in his new understanding of the true *fideles*, Luther applies it to other categories which had traditionally been synonymous with these *fideles*. In the *scholion* to Psalm 110 : 1, Luther maintains that the "council of the righteous" is the "spiritual convent of the *fideles*," which is composed only of the "truly righteous" although it exists bodily among those not "truly righteous" in the baptized community. They have the same sense of faith, hope and love; for although they be distant from one another in space and time, nevertheless they are one in faith and *caritas*.[49] In light of the definition of the true *fideles* through their life in faith and the spirit, it appears to us that Luther is here defining the *iusti* in terms of his new understanding of the true *fideles* (*spiritualis conventus fidelium*) instead of applying the traditional definition of the *iusti* to the true *fideles*. The *caritas* mentioned here resembles more what we called the *caritas* of unity or horizontally-directed *caritas* in Part I of our work, i.e. the love among the members of the church which obliges them to remain in unity with one another. Luther applies this *caritas* as a unifying factor, together with faith and hope, to the true *fideles*.[50] If

---

[48] *WA* 4, 37.31ff. (*Gl.* to Ps. 88 : 3 "Caelis"): "Hoc non de angelis, sicut Lyra putat, debet intelligi, sed de fidelibus Christi. Quia est promissio, quod ipsi in misericordia et misericordia in eis edificabitur. Ipsi autem secundum Apostolum [I Cor. 15 : 47-48] sunt de coelesti Christo coelestes, non de terreno terrestres." Cf. *WA* 4, 40.34f. and 11ff. where the church is denoted as heaven and the *fideles* as the "days of heaven" in the context of God's promise to Christ to preserve his mercy to him eternally and to establish the church and all the faithful. Also *WA* 4, 164.26ff. (*Gl.* to Ps. 102 : 11).

[49] *WA* 4, 239.22ff.: "Quia vero spiritualis conventus non est nisi vere iustorum, corporalis autem potest esse sine vere iustis, vel saltem spiritualis conventus stat cum corporali, et vere iusti cum non vere iustis possunt convenire: ideo 'iustorum' addit, cum 'concilio' et non cum 'congregatione' .... Est autem concilium iustorum sive spiritualis conventus fidelium idem sensus fidei, spei et charitatis: licet sint loco et tempore distantes, charitate tamen et fide sunt in unum." Heckel (*Initia* ..., pp. 13f.) uses this passage as the basis for his distinction between the *ecclesia universalis* and the *ecclesia spiritualis*—legitimately, we think, although one must deduce the definitive characterization of the *ecclesia spiritualis* from other texts.

[50] See our discussion in section 7 of this chapter.

faith is the definitive mark of the *iusti* as well as of the true *fideles*, then we can better account for those passages where Luther interprets the *iusti* as the *fideles* who are righteous through faith and obedience to the Word of the Gospel.[51]

Luther speaks of the *sancti* in terms of his new understanding of the true *fideles* instead of in terms of the traditional definition which he explicitly mentions.[52] The *sancti* are called "clouds" because they are elevated and suspended above the earth through faith. This means, in terms of his definition of the faithful people, that no one is worthy of the mercy of God except he who believes and hopes. The *sancti* and *fideles* are called "clouds" because they stand aloof from the love and affection for earthly things. They are not tied down to earthly goods but are "suspended" through faith.[53] The entire glory of the faithful is a spiritual, interior beauty; and thus faith is the shadow in which all the *sancti* are hidden. There are two things to be considered then in regard to every Christian and prelate. In himself he is visible and mortal according to the flesh, but in Christ he is a faithful Christian, *sanctus* according to the spirit, and thus invisible, an immortal and illustrious spirit.[54]

Even the distinction between the *boni* and the *mali* does not escape being influenced by this new understanding of the true *fideles*. The twofold generation of men in the church, traditionally the *boni* and

---

[51] E.g. *WA* 55/I, 106.1f. (*Gl.* to Ps. 13 : 6): " 'Quoniam dominus' Christus et Deus 'in generatione iusta' fidelium suorum, qui per fidem Iusti sunt 'est': ..." And *WA* 4, 410.8ff. (*Gl.* to Ps. 124 : 3): "... 'ut non extendant' supple victi fidem abnegando 'iusti' fideles Christi 'ad iniquitatem' carnem iniquam et literam vel iustitiam propriam, ut eam operentur deserta iustitia Dei, que est ex fide et obedientia evangelii verbi Dei, 'manus suas.' "

[52] *Supra*, n. 16.

[53] *WA* 3, 199.34ff. (*Gl.* to Ps. 35 : 6): "Et veritas, i.e. impletio eiusdem misericordie, que per legem et prophetas significata est, non usque ad terram, i.e. terrestres et terrena sapientes pertingit, sed ad nubes, i.e. sanctos per fidem a terra elevatos et suspensos a sole iustitie. Sensus ergo est: Misericordia tua nemo [corr: *WA* 55] dignus est nisi qui credit et sperat. In fide et spe enim est misericordia tua in hominibus ... vocantur fideles Christi Nubes. ..." *WA* 3, 201.25ff. (*Sch.* to the same verse): " 'Nubes' dicuntur sancti et fideles. Primo quia elevantur a terra, id est terrenorum amore et affectu, et non nituntur in illis, sed suspensi sunt per fidem."

[54] *WA* 4, 477.3ff. (*Adnotationes* at Ps. 9 : 1): "Occulti vel absconditi, de quibus hic psalmus loquitur, intelligo fideles Christi, qui ideo sic vocantur, quod eorum omnis gloria est spiritualis et interior decor, secundum hominem coram Deo, ... Fides ergo est umbraculum istud, in quo occultantur sancti ab insidiis inimici." *WA* 4, 167.23ff. (*Gl.* to Ps. 103 : 4): "Unde in quolibet Christiano, maxime prelato, duo sunt consideranda: primum quod est ex seipso secundum carnem visibilis, mortalis etc., alterum, quod est ex Christo, i.e. scil. fidelis Christianus, sánctus secundum spiritum, et sic est invisibilis, immortalis spiritus et clarissimus."

the *mali*, is redefined by Luther as the *spirituales* and the *carnales*.[55] In the *scholion* to Psalm 100 : 4, Luther asserts that only the *fidelis* is able to adhere to the church, although others may be mixed in with the *fideles*, because the church is "one in spirit." True adherence is of the heart, and the *malignus* who deviates from Christ is the one who does not seek spiritual good, but the good of the flesh and, as a consequence, the evil of the spirit.[56] And finally, the imperfection of the *populus fidelis* consists for Luther in a partial retention of exactly those qualities which are the opposite of the terms he uses to define the true *fidelis*. No *fidelis* is yet totally spirit, totally new, totally heaven, totally of Christ and God.[57]

In the preceding we have sketched what we believe to be Luther's new definition of the true *fideles*, which replaces the mark of *caritas* employed by the medieval tradition: the true *fideles* live in faith and the spirit. The question remains, however, how Luther arrived at this new characterization. What led him to alter the traditional, definitive mark of the true *fideles* in the church? And what further implications do the various facets of this new definition have for his understanding of the church?

3. Ecclesiology and Hermeneutical Structure

The intimate relationship between ecclesiology and soteriology in the medieval Psalms commentaries is evident in the practice of making the same statements simultaneously about the *fidelis populus* and the *fidelis anima*. This fact leads us to the source of

[55] *WA* 4, 187.6ff. (*Sch.* to Ps. 103 : 18): "... loquens de duplici generatione hominum in Ecclesia, scilicet carnalium et spiritualium, seu, quod in idem vadit, synagoga et Ecclesia, ..." Cf. *WA* 4, 446.21ff. where the war between the descendants of Esau and Jacob is interpreted not only as that between the church and its traditional enemies, but also "inter spiritum et carnem, inter fideles et mundum."

[56] *WA* 4, 136.37ff.: " 'Non adhesit mihi cor pravum', id est incredulum, licet faciem rectam ostentet et fidelem. Qui non potest adherere Ecclesie nisi fidelis, sed bene interesse et misceri. Quia Ecclesia est unum in spiritu. Ideo adherent ei multi secundum corpus et exteriorem hominem, sed vera adherentia non est nisi cordium, in qua non nisi rectum cor herere potest. Pravum ergo, id est curvum ad seipsum et infidele, ... 'Declinantem a me malignum non cognoscebam,' scilicet spirituali cognitione, quam Christus et spiritus eius habet. Malignum autem dicit, qui bonum spirituale non querit, sed bonum carnis, id est malum spiritus."

[57] *WA* 4, 320.12ff. (*Sch.* to Ps. 118 : 25): " 'Adhesit pavimento anima mea.' Ista adhesio est imperfectio populi fidelis, ... Quare pavimentum est unicuique suum. Unicuique restat aliquid de litera, ut non sit totus spiritus, de veteri homine, ut nondum sit totus novus, de carne, de terra, de mundo, de diabolo, ne sit totus anima, totus celum, totus Christi, totus dei."

169

Luther's new understanding of the true *fideles*—namely, to his hermeneutical presuppositions. W. J. Kooiman calls specifically for this kind of approach when he maintains that Luther's new ecclesiology is to be sought in his handling of the fourfold schema of Scripture interpretation.[58] By anchoring many of his most important statements about the church within this interpretive framework, Luther is following in the train of his predecessors in the exposition of the Psalms.

Two disputed questions.—Such a designation of the source of Luther's ecclesiological statements, however, has raised problems concerning his exact procedure. W. Maurer touched on these problems without realizing, perhaps, the nature of the controversy which was to spring up later. We recall how Maurer emphasizes both the importance of the *caput-corpus* schema for Luther as well as the very close relationship between the allegorical sense of Scripture (relating to the church) and the tropological sense (relating to the individual soul).[59] There are two questions involved here: first, whether the tropological or the allegorical sense of Scripture is most important for Luther; and, secondly, whether the church as the body of Christ serves a mediating function between the prophetic-literal sense of Scripture (relating to Christ) and the tropological sense. If the tropological sense is said to be primary, then Luther's statements about the church within the allegorical interpretation are held to be merely a secondary application of what he says primarily about the individual soul. In other words, the *fidelis anima* takes priority over the *fidelis populus*. This depreciation of the allegorical sense can be somewhat neutralized, however, if one affirms that only the conception of the church as the body of Christ enables one to make the tropological application in the first place. That is, one can say the same thing about the individual soul that one says about Christ only if one realizes that individual Christian souls make up the body of Christ of which he himself is the head; and, on the basis of Augustine, what applies to the head applies equally well to the members.

Several researchers have attempted to balance off the primacy of the tropological sense against the mediating function of the *corpus mysticum*. For example, Kooiman asserts that the tropological

---

[58] Kooiman, p. 99.
[59] Cf. *supra*, Ch. IV, nn. 30-31.

interpretation usurps the primacy from the allegorical and argues against Wagner that the church as *corpus mysticum* is strongest in the early part of the *Dictata*. Nevertheless, he holds that the church as *corpus mysticum* maintains its integrity throughout the *Dictata* over against the church as *fidelis populus*.[60] A. Brandenburg, meanwhile, asserts quite explicitly that the tropological application is grounded in the understanding of the church as the body of Christ. Accordingly, everything that Scripture says about Christ is to be applied tropologically to the church and the faithful, because Christ and the church are united through the mystical body.[61] E. Iserloh reproaches Brandenburg for not treating the church as the link between Christ and the individual Christian in spite of the latter's assertion that the understanding of the church as *corpus mysticum* is the basis of the tropological application.[62] At the same time, Iserloh himself is quick to lay the accent in the *Dictata* on the identification of Christ with the individual Christian.[63]

In spite of Iserloh's attack, he and Brandenburg are in basic agreement with Kooiman insofar as they balance off the primacy of the tropological sense for Luther against the function of the *corpus mysticum* as the link between Christ and the individual Christian. On the other hand, U. Mauser and J. Vercruysse have more recently argued for the complete dominance of the tropological interpretation over the *corpus mysticum* in determining the source of Luther's

[60] Kooiman, pp. 101-103.
[61] Brandenburg, p. 56: "Die Grundlegung der tropologischen Methode ist zu suchen in der Lehre von Christus und seinem mystischen Leib. Danach ist alles was die Schrift von Christus aussagt, tropologisch auch auf die Kirche und die Gläubigen zu beziehen, weil Christus und die Kirche durch das corpus mysticum zusammengeschlossen sind. ... So ist es also der Gedanke von der Kirche im tiefsten Sinn, von der Kirche als dem mystischen Leib, der die tropologische Exegese begründet." Schwarz (p. 164, n. 280) also notes the function of the *corpus mysticum* as the link between Christ and the *fides Christi.*
[62] E. Iserloh, " 'Existentiale Interpretation' in Luthers erster Psalmenvorlesung?" *ThR* 59 (1963), col. 76: "Er fragt nur nach dem 'Verhältnis des Christus von damals zum Christen von heute' (111), wobei er das verbindende Mittelglied, die Kirche, ausläßt. Und das, obwohl er wiederholt betont, daß der 'Gedanke von der Kirche im tiefsten Sinn, von der Kirche als dem mystischen Leib' es ist, 'der die tropologische Exegese begründet.' "
[63] *Ibid.* Also Iserloh, *Handbuch*, Vol. IV, p. 24: "So findet sich bei Luther ein enger Zusammenhang von Christologie, Ekklesiologie und Soteriologie. Doch so selbstverständlich die Kirche als Leib Christi festgehalten ist und so wichtig ihre Funktion als Heilsinstrument in der Spendung der Sakramente, vor allem aber in der Verkündigung des Wortes Gottes gesehen wird, der Ton liegt auf der in dem Geheimnis des mystischen Leibes begründeten Identifizierung des Christen mit Christus."

171

ecclesiology. Mauser maintains that "the doctrine of faith rules the concept of the church . . . and not vice versa."[64] Vercruysse first asserts the primacy of the tropological-allegorical order of interpretation over the allegorical-tropological.[65] Consequently, he argues that the relationship of Christ to the *fideles* cannot be based on the connection between the head and the members in the *corpus mysticum*. Rather, it arises directly out of the tropological application to the individual *fidelis* of that which is said of Christ in the prophetic-literal sense of Scripture.[66]

Regardless of which side one takes in this controversy, the importance of the fourfold interpretive schema for Luther's ecclesiology is clear. We must keep in mind, however, that such a close connection between the tropological and allegorical interpretations of Scripture was equally important for Luther's exegetical predecessors. This relationship is by no means unique with Luther. We recall further that the relationship between the statements made about the *fidelis anima* and the *fidelis populus* by the medieval exegetes is a reciprocal one. As far as we could determine, neither the moral (tropological) interpretation nor the allegorical could be regarded as dominant in the sense of determining the origin of ecclesiological insights. Furthermore, Luther's statements about the *fideles* (in the plural) in the preceding sections of this chapter are by no means all made under the direct influence of the tropological application of a passage to the *fidelis anima*. On the other hand, the content of the tropological application to the individual *fidelis* certainly agrees with our findings on the *fideles* taken collectively, so that we do not deny a strong influence. Therefore, we designate

---

[64] Ulrich Mauser, *Der junge Luther und die Häresie* (Gütersloh, 1968), p. 61: "Denn die Aussagen über die Kirche sind damit normiert durch das, was von der anima christiana zu sagen ist. Nicht eine irgendwie gewonnene abstrakte Lehre von der Kirche entscheidet darüber, wo der Leib Christi zu suchen ist; sondern dort, wo wahrhaft geglaubt wird, dort ist die wahre Kirche. Zugespitzt ausgedrückt: Die Lehre vom Glauben regiert den Kirchenbegriff (und damit natürlich die Lehre von der Häresie) und nicht umgekehrt."

[65] *Fidelis Populus*, p. 24.

[66] *Ibid.*, p. 34: "Man kann den Zusammenhang zwischen buchstäblichem und tropologischem Sinn, zwischen Christus und den Gläubigen nicht aus der Lehre über den mystischen Leib und folglich nicht aus der Ekklesiologie ableiten, so daß der tropologische Schriftsinn, das Verhältnis Christus-Gläubige, tatsächlich eher die Grundlage der Theologie vom mystischen Leib oder von der Kirche ist als umgekehrt." Cf. *ibid.*, p. 207: "Wir sahen wie die Tropologie zur Allegorie führt, der Glaube zur Konstitution der Kirche."

Luther's employment of the fourfold schema as one source of his new understanding of the traditional category of the *fideles*. At the same time, we believe that the relationship between the *fidelis anima* and the *fidelis populus* is best understood as a reciprocal relationship, where the statements about one influence the statements about the other. But before going further, we must delve more deeply into the role of the church within the fourfold schema.

The fourfold interpretation of Scripture.—Gerhard Ebeling has maintained that Luther tied together three dimensions of the fourfold interpretation—Jesus Christ, the church and the individual—more closely than was done in the tradition.[67] From the point of view of our research into the ecclesiology of the tradition, we certainly agree that Luther makes the connection more explicitly. In some of the texts in which the allegorical and tropological interpretations are placed side by side, the tropological interpretation is given as *fides* or *iustitia fidei.* In other texts more general reference is made to the soul alone. As is well known, Luther lays out his application of the fourfold schema on the back of the title page of the *Dictata.* He gives there both a negative and a positive application of the different senses of Scripture, using the traditional exemplary text, "Mount Zion." In the positive application, the allegorical interpretation refers to the "church or every doctor, bishop and eminent person," while the tropological interpretation refers to the righteousness of faith.[68] In his preface, Luther gives an example in which the allegorical interpretation refers to the church and the tropological to "every spiritual and interior man."[69] Thus, both reference points of the tropological application are already indicated, i.e. the righteousness of faith and the faithful soul.

We turn our attention first to the explicit tropological reference to faith or the righteousness of faith. Luther brackets this tropological

---

[67] G. Ebeling, "Luthers Psalterdruck vom Jahre 1513," *ZThK* 50 (1953), p. 96.

[68] *WA* 55/I, 4.9ff.:

"Mons Zion" $\begin{cases} \text{hystorice populus in Zion existens} \\ \text{Allegorice Ecclesia vel quilibet} \begin{cases} \text{Doctor} \\ \text{Episcopus eminens} \end{cases} \\ \text{Tropologice Iustitia fidei vel alia excellen[tia]} \\ \text{Anagogice gloria eterna in celis."} \end{cases}$

[69] *WA* 55/I, 8.8ff.: "Quicquid de domine Ihesu Christo in persona sua ad literam dicitur, hoc ipsum allegorice: de adiutorio sibi simili et ecclesia sibi in omnibus conformi debet intelligi. Idemque simul tropologice debet intelligi. de quolibet spirituali et interiori homine: contra suam carnem et exteriorem hominem."

173

interpretation with the church as the allegorical interpretation when he exegetes the words "psalter" and *cythara*,[70] *cornu*,[71] and the right hand (*dextera*) of God.[72] In the *scholion* to Psalm 76 : 13, Luther appears to derive the church as the allegorical *opus dei* from the tropological *opus dei* which is faith:

> The work and power of God are faith; for it makes men righteous and produces all virtues, chastises, crucifies and weakens the flesh, so that it has no work or virtue of its own; rather there is only the work of God in it. And thus faith saves and strengthens the spirit. Moreover, whenever this happens, then all those who do that become themselves the work and power of God allegorically. And so the church is the work and power of God. The world, moreover, is weak and abject, and just as in the flesh, there is no work of God in it either, in that it is separated from the church and the faithful people.[73]

There is no denying that Luther moves from *fides* to the church ("whenever this happens, then") and sees the church as constructed out of the *fideles* in whom faith is at work confirming the spirit. Thus, one way that Luther comes to the definition of the true *fideles* as living in faith and the spirit is from the tropological application of the *opus dei*. The parallel standing of faith and the church cannot help but contribute to his new emphasis on *fides* as the mark of the true *fideles*.

In addition to the above passages, the much discussed *scholion* to Psalm 71 : 2 on righteousness and judgment must be mentioned. After

---

[70] *WA* 3, 320.1ff. (*Sch.* to Ps. 56 : 9).
[71] *WA* 3, 120.25ff. (*Sch.* to Ps. 17 : 3).
[72] *WA* 3, 359.27ff. (*Gl.* to Ps. 62 : 9): "Dextera dei est favor in spiritualibus, i.e.

$$\left\{ \begin{array}{l} \text{fides tropologice.} \\ \text{Ecclesia allegorice} \\ \text{gloria anagogice.}" \end{array} \right.$$

Cf. *WA* 3, 361.23ff. (*Sch.* to Ps. 62 : 3): " 'Sanctum' spiritualiter est ipsa Ecclesia allegorice: tropologice autem ipsa sanctitas fidei et iustitie spiritualis. Sanctum autem sanctorum est beatitudo future glorie. Sicut in tabernaculo Mosi fuit figuratum." Cf. *WA* 3, 387.19ff. and 403.38ff.
[73] *WA* 3, 532.13ff.: "Opus dei et virtus est fides: ipsa enim facit iustos et operatur omnes virtutes, castigat et crucifigit et infirmat carnem: ut ipsa non habeat opus suum nec virtutem, sed ut opus dei sit in illa. Et sic salvat et roborat spiritum. Quando autem hoc fit, tunc omnes, qui illud faciunt, fiunt opus dei et virtus dei allegoricum. Et sic Ecclesia est opus et virtus dei. Mundus autem est infirmus et abiectus, et sicut in carne, ita et in ipso nullum opus dei: eo quod sit separatus ab Ecclesia et populo fideli." In the same *scholion*, Luther also derives the negative allegorical interpretation from the negative tropological one and affirms again that the positive allegorical reference—now the *corpus Christi*—arises out of the positive tropological reference to faith (*ibid.*, 21ff.). Cf. also *WA* 3, 369.1ff. where the *opus Dei* tropologically understood is the *iustitia fidei* and allegorically the church.

treating the judgment and righteousness of God tropologically, Luther proceeds to the allegorical interpretation:

> Secondly, allegorically. Because just as [judgment] discerns between flesh and spirit and divides up their works, approving the latter for justification and rebuking the former for condemnation, much more all our affairs, even our own righteous acts; in the same way it discerns those believing from those not believing.[74]

The judgment of God, which works through the Gospel and produces the righteousness of God in the individual soul through faith, works allegorically among men and separates the believers from those not believing. Therefore, it is not surprising that Luther later applies the fourfold schema to the *iustitia dei* and interprets it tropologically as the *fides Christi* and allegorically as the church.[75] We know that under *ecclesia* he understands those who have been judged and made righteous through the *fides Christi* and are truly *credentes*. Here it is clear on what basis Luther interprets the term *iusti* in the Psalms as the true *fideles* who are made righteous through faith.

Ecclesia et anima.—There are many texts in which Luther does not apply the fourfold schema so explicitly, but where, more in line with the tradition, the church and the individual soul are mentioned in one breath. True, this occurs also within the fourfold interpretive framework.[76] In one important *scholion* to Psalm 4 from the year 1516, Luther reemphasizes the position of Christ as the proper literal interpretation of Scripture on the basis of his position as head of the *sancti* in the church. Applying this principle to the psalm in question, he affirms that it should be interpreted literally in reference to the

---

[74] *WA* 3, 463.3ff.: "Secundo allegorice. Quia sicut inter carnem et spiritum discernit et opera eorum dividit, hec approbando in iustificationem, illa reprobando in condemnationem, immo omnia nostra, scilicet etiam nostras iustitias: Ita discernit inter credentes et non credentes."

[75] *WA* 3, 466.26ff.: "Eodem modo et Iustitia dei triplex est: Tropologice est fides Christi Ro. 1. 'Revelatur enim Iustitia Dei in evangelio ex fide in fidem.' Et ita est frequentissimus usus in Scripturis. Allegorice est ipsa Ecclesia tota. ... Anagogice ipse deus in Ecclesia triumphante."

[76] E.g. *WA* 4, 254.26 (*Gl.* to Ps. 112 : 9): "Et significat Ecclesiam allegorice, animam autem moraliter." *WA* 4, 199.26ff. (*Gl.* to Ps. 105 : 10): "Iste autem exitus et salvatio significat Ecclesie redemptionem de mundo, et cuiuslibet anime de peccatis suis, et tandem in futuro de omnibus malis anagogice." *WA* 55/II, 86.25ff. (*Sch.* to Ps. 4 : 2): "'Dilatatio' ad literam Est Christi in corde suo, in passionibus. Allegorice est verbum Ecclesie, Que semper crescit in persecutione. ... Tropologice: Quelibet anima. ..." Further, *WA* 3, 146.28ff. and *WA* 3, 148.19.

175

church which is his body, and finally (!) tropologically to "every holy soul."[77] At least in this one text, Luther moves from the allegorical interpretation (the body of Christ) to the tropological interpretation (the individual members of this body). When we compare this text to those treated above where Luther obviously moves in the opposite direction, it is clear how the controversy around the role of the *corpus mysticum* in relation to the tropological interpretation could arise.

Of course, the correspondence of the allegorical and tropological interpretation is functioning implicitly in those passages where Luther refers a biblical text simply to the church *or* the faithful soul. The phrase "your plains" in Psalm 64 refers to the latitude of the church or the *animae fideles*.[78] The *ogdochordum* of Psalm 6 can refer mystically to the church and the faithful soul living in faith in the resurrection.[79] In the *glossa* to Psalm 88 : 15, Luther makes use of his previous interpretation of *iustitia* as the righteousness of faith and *iudicium* as self-condemnation. According to the Psalm text, this righteousness and judgment prepare the seat of Christ, which Luther interprets as the church and every soul; for through this righteousness of faith and judgment Christ reigns in them.[80] Significantly, this is the verse subsequent to the one where Hugo defines the seat of God in the church and in the soul as *caritas*.[81] The image of the "seat" is the same, as well as the application to the church and the faithful soul, but the nature of that sitting is quite different: for Hugo it is *caritas*, while for Luther it is the *iustitia fidei*.

[77] WA 55/II, 62.15ff.: "Quoniam Christus est Caput omnium sanctorum, fons omnium, origo omnium rivulorum, ex quo participant omnes, ... Ac Sicut omnes sui sancti fluunt ex ipso velut rivuli, Ita Scriptura conformiter sese habens et ita representans ipsum cum suis sanctis, primo fontali sensu de ipso loquitur ... Ut Exempli gratia iste presens psalmus primo de Christo intelligitur, Qui Invocat et exauditur, deinde allegorice Ecclesia, corpus eius, ultimo Tropologice quelibet anima Sancta." Cf. the same sequence in WA 3, 357.23.: "Sicut autem Psalmus iste est vox Christi inter Iudaeos tanquam capitis nostri, ita etiam est ecclesiae tanquam corporis eius et cuiuslibet fidelis tanquam membri eius."
[78] WA 3, 371.17.
[79] WA 55/I, 38.11f.
[80] WA 4, 38.17ff.: " 'Firmetur' i.e. firmabitur, stabiliatur, 'manus tua' potestas tua in Ecclesia 'et exaltetur' in celo et in terra 'dextera tua' filius tuus et gratia eius et gloria Ecclesie: 'iusticia' fidei, qua iusti fiunt in anima, 'et iudicium', quo se condemnant per crucifixionem carnis, 'preparatio sedis tuae', Ecclesie tue et cuiuslibet anime, per hoc enim regnas in illis." Cf. WA 4, 41.9: " 'Et thronus eius' qui [corr: WA 55] est Ecclesia tota et quelibet anima, ..."
[81] Cf. *supra*, Ch. I, n. 125.

It is no accident that *fides* is mentioned in other passages where *ecclesia* and *anima* are set in parallel. In the *scholia* to Psalm 73, Luther notes that *sanctum* is threefold: namely, the soul, the church and scripture. A few lines further in the same *scholia*, he gives the same threefold interpretation to the "rod" of Psalm 73 : 2 and comments that the "rod" is the soul or the faith of the soul.[82] In the *scholion* to Psalm 32 : 2, Luther maintains that once the literal sense is understood, it is easy to find the allegorical and tropological application. Parallel to the soul and the church in this application stand faith and scripture as well.[83] The twofold tropological reference to *anima* and *fides animae* leads Luther to see *fides* as the mark of the church in the persons of the true *fideles*.

This is not to say that the concept of the church as *corpus mysticum* does not assist Luther in setting up *fides* as the mark of the true *fideles*. There are several key passages which point exactly in this direction, especially in the latter part of the *Dictata*. Luther maintains that "whatever Christ the Head did and suffered . . . signifies spiritually how the *fides Christi* acts and suffers in his *fideles* from sins."[84] *Fides* emerges even more clearly as the hallmark of the church, the body of Christ, in the following passage:

> This part [of the psalm] was explained literally above in reference to Christ, but now it should be interpreted mystically concerning the church and its faith, because whatever can be understood concerning Christ as the head, is also able to be understood in reference to the church and its faith. For faith is the head of the virtues just as Christ [is the head] of the saints, and the stone rejected by many, but nevertheless the cornerstone of all of salvation. Therefore, it is the voice of the church and of every *fidelis* stirring up its faith and *affectus*.[85]

[82] *WA* 3, 495.19ff.: "Notandum enim, quod triplex sanctum est, ut supra dictum est psalmo precedente: Anima, Ecclesia, Scriptura." *WA* 3, 496.1: "Sic enim Scriptura est virga, Ecclesia virga, Anima virga seu fides anime." For the preceding psalm, cf. *WA* 3, 479.21ff. and 474.19ff.

[83] *WA* 3, 182.3ff.: "Habita autem ista sententia iam facile est Allegoriam et tropologiam invenire, scilicet animam, Ecclesiam, coelum angelorum, item fidem, Sacram Scripturam et totum mundum secundum Augustinum."

[84] *WA* 4, 264.28ff. (*Gl.* to the summary of Ps. 114): "Nihil autem hoc discordat, quia quecunque Christus caput egit et passus est, . . . significant spiritualiter, quomodo fides Christi agit et patitur in suis fidelibus a peccatis."

[85] *WA* 4, 215.22ff. (*Gl.* to Ps. 107 : 2): "De Christo ista pars superius exposita est ad literam, sed nunc mystice exponenda est de Ecclesia et fide eius, quia quicquid de Christo intelligi potest ut capite, etiam de Ecclesia et fide eius intelligi potest. Fides enim est caput virtutum sicut Christus sanctorum, et lapis a multis reprobatus, sed tamen fundamentum angulare totius salutis. Est ergo vox Ecclesie et cuiuslibet fidelis fidem et affectum suum excitantis."

177

Luther's understanding of the mystical body, which enables him, like Augustine, to move directly from the head to the members, gives him the opportunity to stress the priority of faith over the other virtues and emphasize its importance in connection with speaking about the church.[86]

We do not feel ourselves forced to choose sides in the debate over the importance of the *corpus mysticum* for Luther's application of the tropological sense to the *fideles*. It is certain that Luther shares with the tradition the close relationship between the tropological and allegorical interpretations of Scripture, i.e. the facility of making the same statements about the *fidelis anima* as about the *fidelis populus*. That he makes such statements more often and more specifically only points up the close correlation between soteriology and ecclesiology in his first lectures on the Psalms—a close relationship which he shares with his predecessors and which is in no way surprising.

In this light, we find that Luther places no more emphasis upon the role of the church as *corpus mysticum* in this relationship than his predecessors. Furthermore, we maintain that the degree of frequency and emphasis with which he employs the *caput-corpus* schema does not affect in one way or the other the new aspect of Luther's ecclesiology over against that of his predecessors—the employment of *fides* as the distinguishing mark of the true *fideles*. Whether Luther makes the transition from *fidelis anima* to *fidelis populus* and back again by way of a straight line from tropology to allegory, or by detouring around the *corpus mysticum* (we have found evidence of both), the result is the same: *fides* and the *iustitia fidei* emerge as the most important characteristics of both the individual *fidelis* and the faithful people. That both the fourfold interpretive schema and the *caput-corpus* schema have contributed to and confirmed his new understanding of the true *fideles* as living in faith and the spirit is clear. We believe, however, that a third interpretive schema (and anthropological category) plays an even more decisive role in Luther's developing ecclesiology, and it is to this that we now turn our attention.

[86] Primarily on the basis of this passage, R. Schwarz concludes that *fides* takes over the soteriological primacy which *caritas* as the "justifying principle" formerly had (*Fides, spes und caritas* ..., p. 165). We would add that *fides* takes over the primacy which *caritas* had in the exegetical tradition as the definitive mark of the true *fideles*.

4. Homo Spiritualis

The hermeneutical basis.—Several researchers have pointed to the unique way in which Luther combines the fourfold interpretation with another important hermeneutical schema—that of letter and spirit (*litera/spiritus*).[87] This combination appears in the application of the fourfold schema which Luther gives on the back of the title page, as we saw above.[88] There Luther gives both a positive (*spiritus*) and a negative (*litera*) fourfold interpretation of the traditional text, "Mount Zion." The church and the *iustitia fidei* appear, of course, on the positive side, that is, the church goes into the *spiritus* column. On the basis of our observation that Luther defines the true *fideles* as those who live in faith and the spirit, we can suspect that his employment of the *litera/spiritus* hermeneutical schema in the *Dictata* would become an important source of his new understanding of the *fideles*.

At the same time, the traditionally close relationship between the *fidelis anima* and the *fidelis populus* suggests that we first concentrate upon Luther's application of *spiritus* as a hermeneutical category to the *fidelis anima* in order to form a basis for our understanding of what Luther means when he speaks of the *fidelis populus* in terms of *spiritus*. This approach appears feasible since Luther on several occasions parallels the church with the *fidelis anima* (understood as the spiritual man) in contrast to the flesh or the man of the flesh.[89] With this approach we do not mean to imply that Luther first assembled his thoughts around the interpretation of the *fidelis anima* as the *homo spiritualis* and then applied this interpretation to the *fidelis populus* as the spiritual people. We stand by our affirmation that there exists a feedback from Luther's understanding of the true *fideles* to his understanding of the individual *anima fidelis*. And yet,

---

[87] G. Ebeling, "Die Anfänge von Luthers Hermeneutik," *ZThK* 48 (1951), p. 218, and his lectures on Luther, *Luther: Einführung in sein Denken* (Tübingen, 1964), pp. 112f. Cf. Vercruysse, p. 18 and Mauser, p. 59. Vercruysse and Mauser have also noted the importance of this connection for Luther's ecclesiology (esp. Mauser, p. 59).

[88] Cf. *supra*, n. 68.

[89] E.g. in his preface where allegory refers to the church and tropology to "every spiritual and interior man against his own flesh and the exterior man" (*supra*, n. 69). Cf. also *WA* 3, 184.20ff. (*Sch.* to Ps. 32 : 7): "Et apte significat Ecclesiam et quemlibet hominem qui exutus a carne et carnali vita non nisi pellis remansit, . . ." And *WA* 3, 203.22ff. (*Sch.* to Ps. 35 : 12): "Et sicut caro est manifesta, spiritus autem occultus, sic Ecclesia in hac vita occulta, Mundus autem in manifesto." Cf. also the *scholion* to Ps. 65 : 6, where *mundus* and *caro* are contrasted to "the faith of the soul and the *virtus* of the spiritual people": *WA* 3, 379.17ff.

just as in the exegetical tradition, we believe that an examination of statements made about the *fidelis anima* (in this case, the *homo spiritualis*) can help confirm and explain the definition of the true *fideles* as the *spirituales* or *populus spiritualis*.

The spiritual man. — Our estimation of the ecclesiological importance of the *homo spiritualis* is supported by the results of a recent study under the same title by Steven E. Ozment. Ozment takes as the springboard for his study a statement made by Luther in his marginal notes to Tauler's sermons (1515-1516): "The spiritual man [is the man] who relies upon faith."[90] That this statement also has ecclesiological significance is apparent from the continuation of the passage where Luther specifies those groups of men who have to do with the *homo carnalis*, the *homo animalis* and the *homo spiritualis* respectively: only the *mundani* (worldly men) have to do with the first, the philosophers and the heretics with the second, but to the *homo spiritualis* pertain the *veri christiani*, the true Christians.[91] Luther is not only thinking of the individual spiritual man, therefore, but also collectively of the true Christians, or what amounts to the same, the true *fideles*. Since Luther presents faith as the definitive mark of the *homo spiritualis*, we may conclude that his understanding of the spiritual man is a primary source of his new understanding of the true *fideles* as living in faith and the spirit.

In the *Dictata*, the *homo spiritualis* is indeed compared with the church in the *scholion* to Psalm 67 : 14 where Luther speaks of the twofold nature of sleep — one of the church and one of the world:

> ...there is a twofold sleep, one of the church and the other of the world. Because just as each one is crucified, foolish, and infirm in respect to the other, [just like] spiritual man and carnal man, whence arises a twofold wisdom, cross, infirmity, strength, foolishness, etc., ... thus each one is mutually asleep to the other and there arises a twofold sleep. The sleep of the world is to be asleep in the spirit, not to be awake to God. Here one is totally wrapped up in a dream world in regard to his affections.

[90] Steven E. Ozment, *Homo Spiritualis* (Leiden, 1969), p. 2. In note 3 he quotes from *WA* 9, 103.40ff.: "Homo sensualis qui nititur sensu; rationalis qui nititur ratione; spiritualis qui nititur fide. Hunc Apostolus videtur vocare [hominem] carnalem et hunc attingunt mundani tantum; animalem et hunc attingunt philosophi et heretici; spiritualem et hunc attingunt christiani veri."

[91] *Ibid.* Ozment, in his excellent study, does not treat Luther's hermeneutical guidelines or the ecclesiological implications of Luther's new anthropological basis, although, in congruence with the texts, he often speaks of his anthropological subject in the plural as the *fideles* (e.g., pp. 120f. and 132).

Because just as whoever is asleep is not happy or sad about real things, but is deceived by fantasies and images of things, so it is before God and in the spirit that all those who rejoice, hope, are afraid or sorrowful in transitory things, with eternal things pushed aside, are deluded by images only. . . . [The sleep] of the church is to sleep according to the flesh and the world, but to be awake to God, just as the others are awake to the world. Because as the one asleep does not see those things outside which are in the world, so the saints use things as if they were not using them [using the world as if not using it (I Cor. 7 : 31)]. Their heart is always somewhere else because their conversation is in heaven [Phil. 3 : 21]. Thus they live in the world as if they were asleep, and nevertheless [they are] inwardly awake.[92]

We see in this passage an exact correspondence between the church, the *homo spiritualis* and the *sancti*, and note that one of the characteristic marks of the true *fideles* which we have seen above—the orientation toward, and foundation in, eternal things—is the hub around which the distinction between the sleep of the church and the world, the *homo spiritualis* and the *homo carnalis*, revolves. The *sancti*, like the spiritual man, are asleep to the world in the sense that they make use of transitory things as if they were not using them—i.e. they use them but do not put their trust in them. Their conversation is not in this world but outside the realm of transitory things in heaven where eternal things are. Once again we encounter the important function of the terms "heaven" and "heavenly" as denoting the "place" outside the realm of visible and transitory things where the true *fideles* have their foundation. As with the true *fideles*, the denotation "heavenly" does not indicate that the *sancti* are already *beati*, but rather that the foundation of their life, the place from which they get their bearings, is located outside of themselves and of the world.[93]

---

[92] *WA* 3, 397.37ff.: ". . . est duplex somnus, unus Ecclesie, alter mundi. Quia sicut alter alteri est mutuo crucifixus, stultus, infirmus, homo spiritualis et homo carnalis, unde oritur duplex sapientia, crux, infirmitas, fortitudo, stultitia etc., . . . Sic etiam alter alteri mutuo dormit et duplex oritur somnus. Igitur Somnus Mundi est dormire in spiritu, non vigilare deo. Hoc est ludere in rerum affectu et omnino involvi. Quia sicut dormiens non veris rebus gaudet, tristatur, sed phantasmatibus et rerum imaginibus fallitur: ita coram deo et in spiritu omnes, qui in rebus transitoriis, posthabitis eternis, gaudent, sperant, timent, dolent, in imaginibus falluntur, . . . [Somnus] Ecclesie est dormire secundum carnem et mundo: vigilare autem deo, sicut illi vigilant mundo. Quia sicut dormiens non videt res foris, que sunt in mundo: ita sancti sic utuntur rebus, quasi non utuntur [Utentes hoc mundo tanquam non utentes]. Et semper alibi sunt [corr: *WA* 55] corde. Quia in coelis est conversatio eorum. Quare sunt in mundo sicut dormientes et tamen intus vigilant."

[93] Therefore, we are in full agreement with Ozment when, on the basis of this text,

181

Luther draws a sharp distinction between the spiritual man and the carnal man at other places in the *Dictata* as he did here in the context of speaking about the sleep of the church and the *sancti* over against the sleep of the world. The important *scholion* to Psalm 32 : 7, which we saw is decisive for Luther's new understanding of the *fideles*,[94] is flanked on both sides by such a contrast. In the *scholion* to Psalm 32 : 3, Luther maintains that only the "new man" is able to sing a "new song." This new man, however, is defined as the man of grace, who before God is the spiritual and interior man. On the other hand, the old man is the "man of sin, before the world the carnal and exterior man."[95] Then at the end of the *scholion* to Ps. 32 : 7 itself, Luther turns his attention to the word *uter* (wineskin); it signifies the church and every man who has put off the flesh and the fleshly life so that only the skin remains. It is in this hollowed out man that God stores wine and oil and through him that God administers these to others. Thus it is necessary for the "interior man" to put off the old man, and for the soul to undress and put on Christ and be formed into a wineskin, which carries the wine from one jar to the other. Like such a wineskin, the church transfers wine and oil, i.e. the Word and grace of God, from one generation to another.[96]

On the basis of the parallel between the faithful soul and the faithful people, both the church and the spiritual man function as depositories and mediators of the Word and grace of God. This

he emphasizes the importance of the "objective context" for Luther's anthropology over against the existentialist interpretation of two different "possibilities of existence" (p. 103f.): "What is the primary focus of these passages? Is it two opposed 'Existenz-möglichkeiten' available to one and the same man, or it is something both deeper and more comprehensive? We find the latter clearly to be the case and consider the language of Existentialist Philosophy too weak to carry it. For Luther's primary focus here is upon two opposed objective references, two opposed 'objective contexts', two opposed 'places' to which and in which the heart of man directs and locates its hope and fear, and from which it receives its joy and suffering: *in rebus transitoriis — in coelis.*" At the same time, we call attention to the fact that the basic framework of the passage is ecclesiological — church and *sancti* versus world — and not anthropological — *homo spiritualis* versus *carnalis*.

94 Cf. *supra*, n. 37.

95 *WA* 3, 182.24ff.: " 'Canticum novum' non potest cantare nisi homo novus: Est autem homo novus homo gratie, homo spiritualis et interior coram Deo. Homo autem vetus est homo peccati, homo carnalis et exterior coram mundo."

96 *WA* 3, 184.20ff.: "Et apte significat Ecclesiam et quemlibet hominem, qui exutus a carne et carnali vita non nisi pellis remansit, in quo vinum et oleum Deus reponit et aliis per ipsum administrat. Exuendus est ergo homo interior a veteri, et exuenda anima et induenda Christo et formanda in utrem, qui est tradux vini de vase in vasa. Sic Ecclesia a generatione in generationem transfundit vinum et oleum suum, verbum et gratiam Dei."

affirmation, as well as the interpretation of *abyssi* as the *fideles* and *sancti* founded in the eternal, hidden things of faith, is anchored in the context of the opposition between spiritual and carnal men. Clearly, this opposition and the alliance between the church and the spiritual man are exercising decisive influence upon Luther's concept of the church and its members.

Luther carries the contrast further. The spiritual man is oppressed, ridiculed and humiliated as far as the world can see; nevertheless he has his own consolation and joy which the world does not know.[97] For carnal men do not realize that it is the path of God which the saints follow. Rather they think it is the wrong road, a path of foolishness and error and scandal, because "the carnal man does not perceive those things which belong to God and the spirit."[98] The foolish man only takes note of things which are good in appearance, because "the *animalis homo* does not perceive the things which are of God" (I Cor. 2 : 14).[99] Here we encounter once more the important passage I Cor. 2 : 14-15 functioning in Luther's mind—this time explicitly in terms of the contrast between the carnal and the spiritual man.

This passage takes on added significance when Luther specifically mentions the definitive mark of the spiritual man who is founded in heaven and eternal things—*fides*. He does this precisely in reference to I Cor. 2 : 15:

> As long as I am man and was man, I did not see that every man was a liar. But now that I have believed and am *in excessu* and have become a spiritual man through faith, judging all things and judged by no one [I Cor. 2 : 15], I see that whoever is not in this same *excessu* and does not believe is a liar.[100]

---

[97] *WA* 3, 333.36ff. (*Sch.* to Ps. 118 : 54): "Hic est spiritus, id est spiritualis homo interior, qui in iis, que mundus videt, premitur, ridetur, humiliatur. Sed tamen consolatur et exultat, quod ignorat mundus."

[98] *WA* 3, 546.31ff. (*Sch.* to Ps. 76 : 20): "Quoniam carnales non cognoscunt, quod hec sit via Dei, per quam sancti ambulant. Immo videtur eis esse non via dei, sed stultitia et error et schandalum. Vident quidem viam eorum et vitam eorum, sed hanc esse dei non vident, quia carnalis homo non percipit ea, que Dei et spiritus sunt."

[99] *WA* 4, 79.14f. (*Gl.* to Ps. 91 : 7): "Et insipiens nescit nisi foris sapere bona. 1. Cor. 2. 'Animalis homo non percipit ea que Dei sunt. Nobis autem Deus revelavit.' "

[100] *WA* 4, 267.16ff. (*Sch.* to Ps. 115 : 11): "Quamdiu et ego homo sum et fui, non vidi, quod esset omnis homo mendax. Nunc quia credidi et in excessu sum et spiritualis homo factus per fidem, omnes iudicans, a nemine iudicatus, video quod qui non est in eodem excessu et non credit, est mendax." For a discussion of this *scholion* in relation to Luther's interpretation of *excessus* in the framework of the mystical tradition, see H. A. Oberman, "Simul gemitus et raptus," in *Kirche, Mystik, Heiligung und das Natürliche bei Luther* (Göttingen, 1967), pp. 49ff.

183

The spiritual man becomes such through faith, and in the words of I Cor. 2 : 15, this gives him a perspective superior to that of the natural or the carnal man. As a result, he is able to judge all things and can himself be judged by no one. We already know the nature of this new perspective. It is to be established by faith in invisible and eternal things which are hidden from carnal men and available only to spiritual men, who—as Luther says once again in the *glossa* to that same decisive verse for his new understanding of the *fideles*—judge all things and are judged by no one.[101] Only through faith (*per solam fidem*) is it possible to have this new perspective, i.e. to have the understanding (*intellectus*) necessary to perceive heavenly, eternal, spiritual and invisible things which no worldly man of any kind is able to have. Therefore, only spiritual and believing men (*spirituales et credentes*) have the capacity to perceive these things and establish their lives upon them through faith.[102] This identification of spiritual men with believing men is the foundation of Luther's new definition of the true *fideles* marked by faith.

The significance of I Cor. 2 : 15.—The frequent reference to I Cor. 2 : 15 in many of these key passages has another important ecclesiological implication. It arises from Luther's use of the phrase —"judging all things, judged by no one"—to describe the elevated perspective of the *fideles* as spiritual and believing men who are founded in eternal and invisible things through faith.[103] This phrase

---

[101] *WA* 3, 179.9ff. (*Gl.* to Ps. 32 : 7): " 'Congregans' per Apostolorum predicationem 'sicut in utre' in unam ecclesiam 'aquas' homines mortales 'maris' i.e. mundi: 'ponens in thesauris' in invisibilibus fidei absconditis ab hominibus carnalibus 'abyssos' spirituales homines, quia omnes iudicant et ipsi a nemine iudicantur 1. Cor. 2." Cf. the *scholion* (*supra*, n. 37) where the spiritual men are treated as the *fideles Christi* and the *sancti*.

[102] *WA* 3, 171.32ff. (*Gl.* to the title of Ps. 31): "Ista autem intellectificatio non est secundum humanam sapientiam, sed secundum spiritum et sensum Christi, de quo apostolus 1. Cor. 2 pulchre disputat, quoniam solum spirituales et credentes hunc intellectum habent. Et breviter est: non nisi celestia, eterna et spiritualia et invisibilia intelligere, quod fit per solam fidem, scil. ea que oculus non vidit, nec auris audivit, nec in cor homines ascenderunt, que nullus philosophus et nullus hominum, nullus principum huius seculi cognovit." Cf. *WA* 3, 367.32ff. (*Sch.* to Ps. 63 : 10). For the relationship between *fides* and *intellectus*, see Schwarz, pp. 134ff. and Ozment, pp. 112ff.

[103] In addition to nn. 39, 100 and 101 above, cf. *WA* 3, 365.18f. (*Sch.* to Ps. 63 : 7): "Cor altum est cor spiritualiter sapiens. Quia spiritualis a nemine iudicatur et in profundo dei absconditus: et in tali exaltatur deus." *WA* 4, 362.24 (*Sch.* to Ps. 118 : 119): "Sed quia spiritualis omnia iudicat, ..." *WA* 4, 294.31 (*Gl.* to Ps. 118 : 98): "1. Cor. 3. [*sic*] 'Spiritualis omnia iudicat et ipse a nemine iudicatur.' "

was commonly applied in the medieval tradition to the person of the Pope, in order to emphasize his superiority over any worldly tribunal, secular or ecclesiastical.[104] Luther now applies this phrase unexpectedly to the true *fideles*. On all except one occasion, this application does not explicitly refer to the authority of the faithful as spiritual men over their ecclesiastical superiors. This one exception is important, however. In the *scholion* to Ps. 118 : 98-100, Luther writes that spiritual meditation upon the law of Christ provides better instruction than all those who seek only the letter, whether they be teachers or elders in the church. After expanding upon the interpretation of the three key nouns in the Psalm verses — *inimici, docentes, senes* — as the *activi, contemplativi (doctores!)* and prelates in the church, Luther reckons them all to the possible enemies of the church because, if they exercise human traditions against spiritual men, they are enemies and think less wisely than the church. Here *ecclesia* applies primarily to the spiritual men; Luther makes this clear by quoting I Cor. 2 : 15. Then Luther makes the moral application of *inimici* to the *pontifices et doctores et literales Christiani* who have dead faith and do not desire to advance in the spirit. There are many in the church now (namely, the true *fideles* or *spirituales*) who are wiser than they, because they are taught by the anointing of the Spirit (I John 2 : 27).[105]

---

[104] It appears in the *Dictatus* of Gregory VII and in a sermon of Innocent III (*PL* 217, 658) to support their claims of absolute sovereignty (cf. Seeberg, *Dogmengeschichte*, Vol. III, pp. 117 and 301). Further, Hugh of St. Victor cites I Cor. 2 : 15 in his *De sacramentis* (*PL* 176, 418) as support for the superiority of the spiritual over the temporal power. Hugh's wording is reflected in the bull *Unam sanctam* (1302) of Boniface VIII, in which I Cor. 2 : 15 is used to bolster the argument for the dominance of the "spiritual sword" (*DS*, No. 873). A more immediate source of this bull, however, is the work of Aegidius Romanus, *De ecclesiastica potestate* (1302), where the verse is specifically applied to the Pope (lib. I, c. 5; ed. Richard Scholz [Aalen, 1961], p. 17): "... sic inter ipsos fideles universi domini temporales et universa potestas terrena debet regi et gubernari per potestatem spiritualem et ecclesiasticam, et specialiter per summum pontificem, qui in ecclesia et in spirituali potestate tenet apicem et supremum gradum. Ipse autem summus pontifex a solo Deo habet iudicari. Ipse est enim, ut supra diximus, qui iudicat omnia et iudicatur a nemine, idest a nullo puro homine, sed a solo Deo." Cf. Merzbacher, p. 298. Interestingly, the last part of the verse, with the added phrase "nisi deprehendatur a fide devius" (which goes back to Cardinal Humbert, d. 1061), is found in the *Decretum* of Gratian, from where it was to become a source of canonistic speculation around legitimate reasons for deposing a Pope (cf. Tierney, p. 57).

[105] *WA* 4, 353.5ff.: "Igitur meditatio legis Christi, que est spiritualis, erudit super omnes, qui legem litere querunt, sive sint docentes sive senes. Tres autem exprimit status, scilicet activorum, contemplativorum, prelatorum. Activi enim sunt inimici Ecclesie, eo quod suam legem contra Christum statuunt et agunt, qui est amicus. A quo

Luther introduces this *scholion* with the assertion that the inimical teachers and elders in the Psalm text apply to those who stand outside the church, i.e. the faithful people, where church can include either all those who belong *numero* or only those who belong *merito* to the faithful people.[106] The *pontifices, doctores* and literal Christians, whom spiritual men surpass in wisdom, refer to those who are inside the baptized community *numero,* but they are not true *fideles* or spiritual men who belong *merito* to the church. Here Luther combines the traditional *numero/merito* categories with his new conception of the true *fideles* as spiritual men with very important consequences for his understanding of authority in the church. The traditional dichotomy *numero/merito* now cuts through the hierarchy and teaching office in the church. Luther's equation of the *contemplativi* with the *doctores*[107] enables him to set the true *fideles* as spiritual men over those *doctores,* as well as over those *prelati,* who are only literal Christians and in reality enemies of the church.

As far as the *Dictata* is concerned, Luther is to be taken at his word that all teachers and elders in the church are worthy of honor and attention.[108] Although Luther affirms without hesitation the superior wisdom of the true *fideles* as spiritual men over those *doctores* and prelates who prefer the letter and human traditions, he does not urge disobedience to them. We find no such call to rebellion in the *Dictata.* Nevertheless, this inherent doctrinal authority of the *fideles* as spiritual men could touch off important reverberations in Luther's mind when his understanding of the church as the true *fideles* later comes into conflict with papal authority. In fact, Luther

---

statu tamen prelati et contemplativi non excipiuntur: nam et ipsi activi sunt et inimici, sed non solum activi, ut sunt alii qui subditi sunt. Deinde contemplativos vocat docentes, quorum officium est meditari in lege domini et alios docere, qui se ad priores habent sicut oculi ad corpus et membra, ut dirigant eos. Tercio senes et maiores, prelati sunt potestates, qui sunt velut manus illorum, ut ea que isti docuerunt, fiant et impleantur, instent et exequantur. Sed quia humanas traditiones exercent contra spirituales vel preter: ideo omnes sunt inimici et infra sapiunt quam Ecclesia. Quia 'Spiritualis omnes iudicat et ipse a nemine iudicatur.' Et hec intelligentia de Iudeis ad literam, de hereticis allegorice. Moraliter autem nunc quoque multi, quos unctio docet [I Io. 2 : 27] sapiunt super pontifices et doctores et literales Christianos, eo quod illi in fide mortua mortui pereunt et non student in spiritum proficere, intellectu quidem illustrissimi, sed affectu frigidissimi."
[106] *WA* 4, 352.19ff.
[107] See Vercruysse, pp. 173ff.
[108] As his first sentence in this *scholion* indicates (cf. *supra,* n. 106).

does employ I Cor. 2 : 15 to support the authority of the *fideles* over the Pope in his early Reformation writings.[109] The potential for his later polemical usage of I Cor. 2 : 15 is already present at the heart of his ecclesiology in the *Dictata*. The new definition of true *fideles* as spiritual men "who judge all things and are judged by no one" creates a mini-church which, in theory at least, is independent of, and superior to, any doctors and prelates of the church who are not likewise spiritual men. The explosive element implicit in the *Dictata* is that these *fideles* are capable of independently discerning such inferior *prelati* and *doctores*. As far as this new definition of the *fideles* is concerned, Luther's ecclesiology is complete in the *Dictata*. Only the polemical application is lacking. The understanding of the *homo spiritualis* as the *fidelis* marked by faith and founded in the eternal, invisible things of God which only he is able to know is thus decisive for Luther's new ecclesiology—both in regard to the definition of the *fidelis* and in regard to its revolutionary implications for ecclesiastical authority.

5. *Populus Spiritualis*

The nature of the spiritual people.—From our examination of Luther's application of the bifurcate *litera/spiritus* schema to the *fidelis anima*, we can now move to the investigation of the same application to the *fidelis populus*. Or, in other words, on the basis of our understanding of Luther's employment of the term *homo spiritualis* and its implications, we are in a better position to grasp the significance of his portrayal of the church as *populus spiritualis*. We repeat: this does not mean that we opt for the primacy of the

---

[109] In *De captivitate babylonica* (*WA* 6, 561.17), *An den christlichen Adel* (*WA* 6, 412.23f.) and in *Adversus execrabilem Antichristi bullam* (*WA* 6, 607.28). Heckel has noted these occurrences as well as some of the occurrences of I Cor. 2 : 15 in the *Dictata*, although he does not attribute as much importance to the *scholion* to Ps. 118 : 98-100 as we see in this text (*Initia* ..., pp. 124-126). Nevertheless, he can write (*ibid.*, p. 126): "Wie ein Blitz zeigt das Wort der Psalmenvorlesung vom geistlichen Menschen das Gewitter an, das von ferne gegen die Hierarchie und das kanonische Recht heraufzieht." Cf. *Lex charitatis*, p. 143. Recently, H. A. Oberman has sketched the ecclesiological consequences of Ozment's emphasis upon Luther's characterization of the Christian as *homo spiritualis*. See Oberman's article, "Wittenbergs Zweifrontenkrieg gegen Prierias und Eck," *ZKG* 80 (1969), pp. 340ff. and esp. p. 341, n. 26. Oberman notes the revolutionary character (against the background of *Unam sanctam* and Innocent III) of Luther's application of I Cor. 2 : 15 to the *fideles* and not to the Pope (*ibid.*, p. 342).

tropological sense of scripture over the allegorical. We have seen how some of Luther's key statements about the *homo spiritualis* are made in an ecclesiological framework or have immediate ecclesiological parallels and implications. This insight prevents us from falling victim to the oversimplification that Luther moved directly from the *homo spiritualis* to the *populus spiritualis*.[110]

Indeed, Luther draws direct parallels between *spiritus* and *ecclesia*. Just as the Gospel is the way to the fatherland above, so it is the gate through which one enters from the world into the church, from the letter to the spirit.[111] To lift up one's hands *in sancta* is to lift them up unto the "spiritual church," or unto the spirit and not the letter.[112] Such parallels are to be expected on the basis of the position of the church on the spiritual side of the ledger in the fourfold interpretive schema. And yet, the parallel between the spiritual man and the church remains in the background. After emphasizing that only the spiritual man is able to be led into the promised land after all carnal goods have been taken away in the desert, Luther exclaims: "How great then is the praise of the church which has the spirit in such large measure!"[113]

We can observe how the *litera/spiritus* division effects simultaneously a gulf between the carnal and spiritual man as well as between the carnal and spiritual people in the important *scholion* to Psalm 84 : 9 ("I will hear what the Lord God says to me, because he will speak peace to his people"). Luther first discusses what it means to say that God has spoken to us. It means that he has shown the Son, his

---

[110] Maurer has seen the broader significance of *fides* and *spiritus* for Luther in the *Dictata* beyond the narrow confines of justification ("Kirche und Geschichte . . . ," p. 97): "Diese Äußerungen über die Kirche des Glaubens verteilen sich über die ganze Vorlesung hin, wenn sie sich auch häufiger und klarer in ihrer späteren Hälfte finden. Sie lassen erkennen, daß das 'sola fide' nicht nur in den engeren Bezirk der Rechtfertigungslehre gehört. Sondern ehe es sich hier als gestaltendes Prinzip durchsetzte, galt es schon in allen Bereichen geistlicher Wirklichkeit, für deren Erkenntnis sowohl wie für den Lebenszusammenhang der geistlichen Neuschöpfung in der Kirche."
[111] *WA* 4, 456.29ff. (*Gl.* to Ps. 147 : 13): "Et sicut ipsum [Evangelium] est via ad patriam, ita et porta, per quam de mundo intratur ad Ecclesiam, de litera ad spiritum."
[112] *WA* 4, 524.10ff. (*Adn.* at Ps. 133 : 2): " 'In noctibus extollite manus vestras in sancta,' i.e. in spiritualem Ecclesiam, que est sanctum nunc rupto velo patens. Vel in spiritum, non ad literam."
[113] *WA* 4, 382.6ff. (*Sch.* to Ps. 118 : 162): "Sed crucifixa ipsa omnibusque ablatis, que sunt carnis, solummodo spiritus pasci et duci debet in terram promissionis, id est spiritualis homo. Ideo necesse est carnalis homo hic murmuret, quia nihil invenit, quod sibi placitum est . . . Magna ergo laus est Ecclesie, que tam largiter habet spiritum, . . ."

Word, to us "in the hearing of faith."[114] Thereupon Luther explains the significance of the phrase "to me" (in me) in the text. This phrase exposes the difference between the law and the Gospel. The law is the word of Moses to us (ad nos) because it remains external and only speaks of the visible figures and shadows of future things. But the Gospel is the Word of God "into" us (in nos) because it penetrates inwardly and speaks of things which are internal, spiritual and true.[115]

After these preparatory remarks, Luther is in a position to explain the last phrase of the text, "to my people" (in plebem meam). These words stand in parallel to the phrase in me. And this means it must refer to at least a part of the people;[116] for, although it is the nature of the Gospel to penetrate "into man" in the sense of "to me" (in me) above, nevertheless it is not spoken "into all men," because all men do not comprehend it. Who are these men? They are carnal men, who are not able to hear and understand the Gospel because the word of the cross is foolishness and poses a stumbling block to them. Therefore, when the Gospel is addressed to such men, it may as well not be said at all, because it must be received "inwardly and in the spirit," not in the flesh and the letter.[117]

Thus, there exists a division within the people which corresponds to that between the spiritual and the carnal man. This division between spiritual and carnal men is brought to light by the way in which each group receives the Gospel, the word of the cross. The fact that Luther must add to the phrase "in my people" the qualifying

---

[114] WA 4, 9.21ff.: "Ergo loqui ipsius domini est verbum suum edere et manifestare, sed auditui. Ita deus pater locutus est nobis, id est filium verbum suum ostendit nobis in auditu fidei. Et hoc est Evangelium dei, quod promiserat ante per prophetas [Rm. 1 : 1-2]: quorum hic unus est dicens: 'Audiam quid loquatur.' "

[115] Ibid., 28ff.: " 'In me.' In hoc tangitur differentia evangelii et legis. Quia lex est verbum Mosi ad nos, Evangelium autem verbum dei in nos. Quia illud foris manet, de figuris loquitur et umbris futurorum visibilibus: istud autem intus accedit de internis, spiritualibus et veris loquitur."

[116] WA 4, 10.19ff.: " 'In plebem suam.' Sicut supra 'in me': ergo in persona plebis vel ut pars plebis loquitur. Quia 'in plebem suam loquetur': ergo ego audiam, quid loquatur in me. Ergo tu es plebs, in quam loquatur? Ita sequitur."

[117] Ibid., 22ff.: "Veruntamen est, quod Evangelium, licet sit verbum dei et de natura sua sit, ut in hominem dicatur: tamen non in omnes dicitur, quia non omnes capiunt. Unde nullo modo ipsum audiunt, in quos non dicitur, et tantum ad illos dicitur. Talibus enim verbum crucis schandalum et stultitia est, et non potest intelligere et audire ipsum carnalis homo. Ideo dicit 'in plebem suam,' quia frustra dicitur et velut non diceretur, quando non in homines dicitur, cum ista sit natura eius, ut in illos dicatur, id est ut intus in spiritu audiatur, non in carne et litera suscipiatur, quia sic est schandalum. Et ita in isto verbo ostendit modum audiendi evangelium et dispositionem auditoris, qualis esse debeat."

189

factor "as part of the people" indicates that he is working with a fundamental division within the people arising from his understanding of the contrast between the flesh and the spirit, between the carnal man and the spiritual man. The *ecclesia*, which has always stood for him in the positive column of the *litera/spiritus* structural dichotomy, is more precisely the community of spiritual men who stand on the same *spiritus* side of the dichotomy.[118]

The common characterization of the church and the soul as spiritual is expressed in Luther's explanation of "sanctity and magnificence" in Psalm 95 : 6. In the *scholion* to this verse, Luther first speaks of the sanctity which the church possesses in the cross of Christ because it abstains from all carnal riches and goods. Because its magnificence is spiritual, it is contrary to any greatness with which men are familiar.[119] A few lines further Luther adds:

> And it is truly an exceedingly marvelous thing how magnificence and sanctity are able to exist simultaneously in the church or the soul, since pride and ostentation, a lofty and puffed up attitude, and vainglory are waiting to pounce upon "great" works and take them over.[120]

The church and the soul share the same kind of spiritual greatness manifested in the spiritual man: the renunciation of all worldly goods and glory and reliance upon the hidden things of God unknown to men, in this case, the cross of Christ.

Because of this common possession of spiritual magnificence by both the church and the soul, the statements which Luther makes about the church as a spiritual people are not unexpected. If the *fidelis anima* is primarily *homo spiritualis*, the *fidelis populus* is primarily *populus spiritualis*. The church is a spiritual people and thus bears "spiritual arms."[121] The church as the heredity given to Christ is a filial

---

[118] Cf. Luther's exposition of the second half of verse 9 ("Et super sanctos suos et in eos qui convertuntur ad cor"). There are two kinds of *sancti*: those who are *sancti in spiritu* and thus are hidden, and those who are *sancti* in their own eyes and in the eyes of others. God is able to speak "into" the former only, because only they comprehend invisible things, whereas the latter only consider temporal things and are not able to perceive the Word of God (*WA* 4, 10.35ff.).

[119] *WA* 4, 112.14ff.: "Igitur Ecclesia, que sanctificatur assidue in cruce Christi, sanctimoniam habet, quia abstinet ab omnibus que sunt mundi et carnis, et magnificentiam habet in omnibus divitiis, bonis, edibus, sumptibus etc. Sed hec magnificentia, quia spiritualis est, omnino contraria est ei quam homines cognoverunt."

[120] *Ibid.*, 25ff.: "Et verum mirabile est valde, quomodo simul in Ecclesia vel anima consistere valeant magnificentia et sanctimonia, cum magnis operibus superbia et ostentatio, elatio, inflatio, vana gloria miro modo insidientur."

[121] *WA* 3, 524.18f. (*Sch.* to Ps. 75 : 4): "Quia Ecclesia non consistit in munitione sensibili, sed est populus spiritualis: ideo spiritualia habet arma."

and spiritual people.[122] Just as Christ has liberated the spirit from the flesh, so he has delivered the spiritual people from its oppressor, the carnal people.[123] The church is a new, spiritual world composed of the individual *fideles* created in Christ.[124]

Furthermore, since faith is the hallmark of the spiritual man and the *fideles* as spiritual men, it is natural that Luther should regard faith as indispensable to the spiritual people. The people of Christ, who are the spiritual "sheep of his hand" made into a new creature, are through true faith the "people of his pasture"—i.e. of the Gospel and his Word.[125] Christ reigns in his church wherever it may be because he reigns there over a spiritual dominion through faith.[126] The spiritual character of the church and the importance of faith are reflected in Luther's description of the church's posture in the face of its persecutors. The church does not tremble before the princes of the world who would persecute it, but only before the words of God. It could not do this, however, unless through faith it would hold all (worldly) things in contempt and wisely discern eternal things alone.[127] This orientation of the church around eternal things through faith coincides with that of the true *fideles* as spiritual men.

Because of this orientation toward, and foundation in, eternal things through faith, Luther holds that the church as a spiritual people is a

---

[122] *WA* 4, 415.23f. (*Gl.* to Ps. 126 : 3): "q.d. Ecce Christo dabitur hereditas populi filialis et spiritualis, ..."

[123] *WA* 4, 119.34ff. (*Gl.* to Ps. 97 : 9): "Hoc iudicare fuit, quando docuit sapere spiritum et odisse carnem. Et ita liberavit spiritum et damnavit carnem, ita et spiritualem populum a populo carnali oppressore illius, quia noluit sapere spiritum et odisse carnem." Cf. *WA* 4, 299.3ff. (*Gl.* to Ps. 118 : 132).

[124] *WA* 4, 444.28ff. (*Gl.* to Ps. 142 : 5): "Et si versus loquitur de primo et visibili mundo, tunc sensus est, quod in illis actis et factis mystice intellexerit acta et facta novi et spiritualis mundi, que est Ecclesia. Cuius facture sunt singuli fideles creati in Christo. ..." *WA* 4, 144.19ff. (*Gl.* to Ps. 101 : 19): "... 'haec in generatione altera', que est generatio fidelium in tempore gratie ... 'et populus' Christianus, 'qui creabitur' post tempus legis in creaturam novam spiritualem Eph. 2, ..." *WA* 3, 533.1ff. (*Gl.* to Ps. 76 : 15).

[125] *WA* 4, 100.8ff. (*Gl.* to Ps. 94 : 7): " 'Et nos' per fidem veram 'populus pascuae eius' evangelii et verbi sui: 'et oves' spirituales 'manus eius' per eius potentiam creati in novam creaturam."

[126] *WA* 4, 106.1ff. (*Sch.* to Ps. 94 : 5): "Et quod Ecclesia eius militans sit in omnibus finibus terre Iudee, et non solum, sed et mare et arida. Hec enim iam ipsius sunt, quia spirituali dominio per fidem in illis locis regnat, ..."

[127] *WA* 4, 380.29ff. (*Sch.* to Ps. 118 : 161): "Ecclesia autem contra omnes principes mundi persecutores non formidat: quia a verbis dei formidat. Quod non faceret, nisi per fidem omnia contemnens sola eterna saperet." The faith of which Luther is speaking is the *fides futurorum* (line 9).

heavenly people. "Heaven" is interpreted at one point by Luther as "your church, a spiritual heaven."[128] Heaven is likewise the heavenly people of Christ who are dead to the flesh and separated from it, thinking wisely of those things which are above and not contemplating earthly things.[129] Carrying the obvious contrast to flesh and earth further, Luther maintains that Christ has his seat in heaven, that is, in his heavenly people of the church; and from this throne which is his church he will rule over a spiritual and not a carnal dominion.[130] Against the literal people who expect the Messiah to reign over earthly goods, Christ reigns in heaven and in the clouds, i.e. in the spiritual saints who are suspended and "shaded over" in faith, in spiritual clouds.[131] The obvious inference is that these are the spiritual people who know that Christ reigns in them as if in a heavenly people through faith.

Drawing on the same imagery, Luther notes that the church *and* every faithful man can be called clouds and darkness, because faith is like clouds to those who believe and to the spirit. Those who believe and are spiritual, although they cannot perceive the things of God clearly, know in part as if they were in a translucent cloud. In contrast, those who do not believe and are carnal can in no way perceive the things which are of God; rather, all wisdom is foolishness to them.[132]

This imagery of heaven and clouds, which we have encountered before in our discussion of the true *fideles*,[133] epitomizes the spiritual character of the church. It distinguishes its suspended location from

---

[128] *WA* 4, 166.20 (*Gl.* to Ps. 103 : 2): "... 'caelum' Ecclesiam tuam, spirituale coelum. ..."

[129] *WA* 4, 175.10ff. (*Sch.* to Ps. 103 : 2): "Unde tercio coelum est populus celestis Christi, mortificatus in carne et separatus a carne, iam que sursum sunt sapiens [Col. 3 : 2], non que super terram sunt contemplans."

[130] *WA* 4, 165.23ff. (*Gl.* to Ps. 102 : 19): " 'Dominus' Ihesus Christus 'in caelo' populo coelesti Ecclesie 'paravit' donis spiritus sancti 'sedem suam' thronum regalem: 'et regnum ipsius' Ecclesia eius 'omnibus' Iudeis et gentibus 'dominabitur' dominio spirituali, non carnali."

[131] *WA* 3, 199.27ff. (*Gl.* to Ps. 35 : 6): "Loquitur contra literalem populum, quia Messiam sperat in bonis terrenis et infimis regnaturum, qui tamen in coelo et nubibus, i.e. sanctis spiritualibus in fide suspensis et umbratis, i.e. nubibus spiritualibus, regnat."

[132] *WA* 4, 114.22ff. (*Gl.* to Ps. 96 : 2): "Nota: fides est 'nubes' iis qui credunt seu spiritui, sed 'caligo' iis qui non credunt seu carni. Quia increduli et caro nullo modo percipiunt ea que sunt Dei, sed est illis stultitia omnis sapientia. Sed creduli et spiritus, licet non clare percipiant, tamen ex parte cognoscunt ac velut in nube lucida. Eodem modo et ipsa Ecclesia est nubes et caligo et quilibet fidelis."

[133] Cf. *supra*, pp. 166, 168.

192

that of the earth and flesh and depicts its foundation in invisible and eternal things, things outside of itself to which it is oriented and in which it is suspended through faith. For the *fideles* these things lie in the future as well, as Luther writes in the following explanation of why the church is called heaven:

> The church does not have its conversation upon earth, but in heaven. Hence the church of Christ is called heaven in many Scripture passages. The Apostle says both: 'Our conversation is in heaven,' and: 'Seek the things which are above, etc.' Some apply this word to Christ, who is a faithful witness in heaven. But the word order and the verse point rather to his throne. For the church bears witness to future goods among the *fideles*. And it is a witness in the true sense of the word; for there will not be any witness in the glory to come where all things will be evident, thus eliminating the need for witnesses.[134]

The church stands as a witness to future goods for the faithful, i.e. to those eternal goods which are outside of and beyond itself, and yet in which the church has its foundation. This is the essence of the spiritual, heavenly character of the church and the *fideles*—to be defined from that which is outside itself in the future and toward which it is moving. It does not have those things yet, but only stands as a witness to them.[135] The church is not heavenly in the sense that it is already in glory or invisible to the eye. It is in the world with the flesh. But it is in heaven with the heart and has the spirit at the right hand of Christ.[136]

Spiritual and invisible.—Only after we have a clear picture of what Luther means by speaking of the church as a spiritual and heavenly

---

[134] *WA* 4, 41.30ff. (*Gl.* to Ps. 88 : 38): "Ecclesia enim non super terram habet conversationem, sed in coelis. Unde et Celum vocatur Ecclesia Christi in multis locis Scripture. Et Apostolus: 'Conversatio nostra in coelis est' [Phil. 3 : 20]. Et 'que sursum sunt querite etc.' [Col. 3 : 2]. Aliqui hoc verbum de Christo exponunt, quod [corr: *WA* 55] sit testis fidelis in celo. Sed ordo verborum et versus videtur potius de Throno eius loqui. Ecclesia enim testatur de futuris bonis inter fideles. Et est verax testis, non enim in futura gloria erit testis, ubi omnia clarebunt sine testium necessitate." The *aliqui* mentioned here, who apply the verse to Christ, include Augustine, the *glossa ordinaria*, Lyra and Perez.

[135] Vercruysse catches this nuance of the spiritual character of the church when he writes (p. 58): "Bei Luther ist Geistlich-sein wesentlich dynamisch, Vorwärtsstreben auf das hin, was man noch nicht ist, und schon in der Zukunft leben."

[136] *WA* 4, 73.6ff. (*Sch.* to Ps. 90 : 7): "Vel sic: Ecclesia Christi habet latus, secundum quod est in carne: sed dextera eius est spiritus eius: ... Cum corde enim est in coelo et spiritum habet in dexteris Christi, cum carne est in mundo. Et hec est latus eius seu sinistrum."

people can we define more precisely its hidden or invisible character.[137] Luther not only depicts the individual *fideles* as founded in spiritual and invisible things. When he speaks collectively of the church as invisible, he links this invisibility with the church's spiritual and heavenly character and to the necessity of faith for recognizing this people. The church, which is called a new heaven and a new earth, is invisible and intelligible through faith.[138] The "invisible heavens" are spiritual men above whom and by whom God is exalted.[139] That "every structure" of the church is inward before God and invisible means for Luther that the church is perceived not with carnal eyes, but only with spiritual eyes in understanding and faith.[140]

The fact that Luther speaks of the church as invisible or hidden[141] cannot in itself be regarded as "new." Although we have not encountered these terms in our study of the medieval exegetes, the application of the parable of the wheat and the tares to the *boni* and *mali* in the church serves precisely to stress the fact that the *boni*, the true *fideles*, remain hidden among the *mali*, the false *fideles*, until the last judgement. New with Luther is the way in which he defines the invisible character of the mini-church, the true *fideles*. In the tradition, the true *fideles* are invisible (or better, indiscernible) because it cannot be ascertained whether a particular *fidelis* is in a state of

---

[137] Heckel (*Lex charitatis*, p. 38) associates these attributes in his discussion of the two kingdoms: "So ist denn auch das Regiment, das Christus über die Seelen seiner Jünger führt, rein geistlich, himmlisch, innerlich und verborgen." One passage from the *Tractatus de libertate christiana* (1520: WA 7, 56.22f.) indicates that this terminology is still important for the "Reformation Luther": "In coelestibus et spiritualibus ipse regnat et consecrat, ..." In his summary of Luther's ecclesiology, Seeberg also draws the parallel between spiritual and invisible (*Dogmengeschichte*, Vol. IV, 1, p. 344).

[138] WA 4, 189.17f. (*Sch.* to Ps. 103 : 23): "Invisibilis, intelligibilis per fidem est Ecclesia, que vocatur novum celum et nova terra."

[139] WA 3, 317.19ff. (*Gl.* to Ps. 56 : 6): " 'Exaltare' i.e. cognoscere, quod es Deus 'super caelos' visibiles et invisibiles i.e. homines spirituales 'deus' o Ihesu Christe: 'et in omni terra gloria tua' per fidem in Ecclesiis exaltetur revelatio claritatis tue et deitatis."

[140] WA 4, 81.11ff. (*Sch.* to Ps. 91 : 7): "Secundo Quia dicit, quod 'Insipiens ipsa non cognoscet.' Quod exinde fit, quia opera et factura Christi Ecclesia non apparet aliquid esse foris, sed omnis structura eius est intus coram deo invisibilis. Et ita non oculis carnalibus, sed spiritualibus in intellectu et fide cognoscuntur."

[141] The attempt by Brandenburg (p. 76) to distinguish between *invisibilitas* and *absconditas*, and Müller's effort ("Ekklesiologie und Kirchenkritik ...," pp. 105f.) to see significance in Luther's use of the terms as predicate adjectives instead of as attributive adjectives, seem to us instances of hair-splitting resulting from a basic fear of the word "invisible." This word, for Luther, has a very important, positive connotation. Cf. the continuation of our discussion.

grace and possesses the definitive *caritas*. It is a question of the uncertain possession of an invisible entity. For Luther it is a question of the certain foundation in and orientation toward invisible goods. For the tradition, the invisibility or indiscernibility of the true *fideles* assumes the negative cast of uncertainty. For Luther, the invisibility of the true *fideles* belongs to the heart of their character. They are invisible and hidden because the foundation of their life is located in certain and reliable goods: invisible, spiritual and eternal. The apprehension of these goods can occur only through faith, which describes the basic stance and orientation of the *fideles* toward these goods.[142]

Even for Luther, the true *fideles* are indiscernible to a certain extent from the false *fideles*. It is not always certain whether a particular *fidelis* is completely the spiritual man, orienting his life through faith toward eternal goods. Nevertheless, when Luther asserts the necessity for the *boni* or true *fideles* to remain within the community of the baptized, he speaks of them as if they were quite discernible and puts little emphasis on their invisible character.[143] As we have seen, the life of the true *fideles* is quite visible in that it does not conform to the way of life of carnal men.[144] The true *fideles* who make up the church are quite visible to the eye, but the foundation of their existence (eternal and spiritual goods) and their orientation toward this foundation (in faith) are invisible to the human eye. Thus every "structure," every supporting feature of the church, is invisible and inward before God (eternal and future goods), al-

---

[142] Iwand's attempt (pp. 151-152) to explain the invisibility of the church on the basis of the "Augustinian-areopagitic schematic" is untenable in light of Ozment's convincing discussion of the role of the Neo-Platonic world-view in Luther's thought. Not Neo-Platonic epistemology, but the exterior (to the *fideles*), invisible location of eternal, future goods is the key to the invisibility of the *structura* and foundation of the church (which may well have its roots in the "objective reference" which Ozment maintains Luther took over from Neo-Platonism; cf. *Homo Spiritualis*, p. 103 and *supra*, n. 93). Fagerberg (p. 116), on the other hand, has seen the *invisibilis* in its proper context: "Daß invisibilis Zusammenhang mit der eschatologischen, himmlischen Wirklichkeit hat, geht weiterhin mit voller Deutlichkeit aus der Zusammenstellung invisibilia, spiritualia et coelestia contra visibilia hervor. ... Das Geistlich-Unsichtbare bezieht sich also auf die eschatologische Welt, zu welcher das Schauen gehört, die aber jetzt im Glauben erfaßt wird."

[143] Cf. *WA* 4, 240.6ff.

[144] Cf. *supra*, n. 35. E. Kinder ("Die Verborgenheit der Kirche nach Luther," in *Festgabe Joseph Lortz*, Vol. I, ed. E. Iserloh and P. Manns [Baden-Baden, 1958], p. 176, n. 6) correctly includes the aspect of visibility in his definition of *spiritualis*, although it is unclear what he means when he equates it with "pneumatisch."

though the *fideles* themselves are quite visible as the "offscouring" of the world.[145]

The spiritual people and the external community. — The designation of the church of the true *fideles* as *spiritualis* has certainly not escaped notice in recent Luther research.[146] The fact alone, however, that Luther distinguishes the true *fideles* from the false *fideles* and denotes the true *fideles* as a *populus spiritualis* does not differentiate his ecclesiology from that of the medieval exegetical tradition. Rather the content of this expression is important. And this content brings us back to *fides* as the definitive mark of the true *fideles*. That the true *fideles* are *spirituales* means that they are founded in invisible, eternal goods which are still outstanding. Furthermore, it means that the only link that they have with these goods is *fides* — their orientation toward these goods and trust that God will deliver them when the time is due.[147] There is no thing, no *res*, which the *fideles* possess in the

---

[145] Cf. *supra*, n. 140 and *WA* 3, 581.29ff.

[146] Heckel, for example (*Lex charitatis*, p. 21), draws the parallel between *homo spiritualis* and *ecclesia spiritualis* with an eye toward the significance of the *lex spiritualis* for Luther's understanding of ecclesiastical law: "Wie Luther in seiner Lehre vom Menschen den homo spiritualis, in seiner Kirchenlehre die ecclesia spiritualis zum Richtpunkt nimmt, so in seiner Rechtslehre die lex spiritualis. Eines folgt aus dem anderen, eines verweist auf das andere, und keines besteht ohne das andere." He also emphasizes the importance of the *ecclesia spiritualis* as the "Ansatz" of Luther's ecclesiology in opposition to the *ecclesia universalis* (*ibid.*, p. 28): "Die ecclesia universalis, das äußere Kirchenwesen mit seinen rechtlich verfaßten Teilgebilden, den ecclesiae particulares, verliert ihren Rang als Ansatz der Kirchenlehre und macht der ecclesia spiritualis, der Gemeinschaft der wahren Gläubigen, Platz." Vercruysse (p. 160, n. 47) maintains that Heckel has wrongly defined the *ecclesia universalis* and that the phrase *ecclesia spiritualis* is foreign to Luther. This particular formulation may not be the one most frequently employed by Luther, but his designation of the true *fideles* as a *populus spiritualis* is decisive for his understanding of these faithful. On this point, Heckel is right, regardless of terminology, and in spite of the fact that he has not worked out the origins of Luther's understanding. Maurer ("Der ekklesiologische Ansatz . . . ," p. 37) is largely dependent upon Heckel for his definition, although his characterization of the role of faith as the way in which the members of the *ecclesia spiritualis* have received baptismal grace is too little nuanced to do justice to Luther.

[147] Ebeling ("Die Anfänge . . . ," p. 199) sees the orientation of the church toward invisible, spiritual things (understood as *coram deo*), but does not bring to adequate expression the actual foundation and "suspension" of the church in these things: "Spiritualis ist alles, sofern es verstanden wird coram Deo, und d.h. nun: im Lichte des Kreuzes Christi, im Licht der absconditas dei sub contrario. . . . Die Kirche ist spiritualis, sofern sie verstanden wird als occulta in diesem Leben, die ihr Vertrauen nicht auf irdische Machtmittel setzt, sondern weiß, daß sie verfolgt sein muß, und daß die gefährlichste Verfolgung die ist, nicht verfolgt zu sein, sondern in securitas zu leben."

present as downpayment on these goods, as the true *fideles* of the medieval exegetes have *caritas*. This fact has important consequences for the relation of the true *fideles* as a spiritual people to the baptized community in which they live. If the *fideles* must have *caritas* in order to remain truly *fideles*, then their life is wholly dependent on the sacraments administered by the ordained members of the hierarchy in the external community of the baptized. If, however, not the possession of *caritas*, but faith as orientation towards eternal goods and trust in their deliverance is the mark of the true *fideles*, then the necessary dependence on sacramental grace and the priests is dissolved. If this *fides* can be nourished and kept alive outside a particular baptized community with its priests and sacraments, then the true *fideles* must not remain "inside" in order to stay alive. On the other hand, if this *fides* can be nourished inside, there is no need for them to depart from the external community.

W. Maurer has maintained that the peculiarity ("das Besondere") of the Reformation doctrine of the church is to be found in the relationship of the *ecclesia spiritualis* to the *ecclesia universalis*. The divergence from the medieval understanding of the church, in his opinion, is most clearly recognizable in Luther's view of this relationship.[148] In emphasizing the importance for Luther of the *ecclesia universalis* as the external community, however, Maurer misses the newness of Luther's understanding of the true *fideles* in the *ecclesia spiritualis*. At the same time, he does point to the importance of some external structure for Luther, which in our view is necessary for the nourishment of the decisive *fides*. The potentially explosive element in Luther's seeing faith as the mark of the church in 1513-1515 is that the nourishment of this faith does not necessarily depend upon the *existing* external structure—namely, the Roman Church. The fundamental divergence from the exegetical tradition, however, is the different way of defining the true *fideles*. That is "das Besondere" in Luther's ecclesiology, and the resulting tenuous relationship between the true *fideles* and any particular external community is a corollary of this fundamental distinction.

Thus when Iwand implies that the decisively new in Luther's

---

[148] "Der ekklesiologische Ansatz ...," p. 38: "In dieser Zusammenschau von ecclesia universalis und ecclesia spiritualis liegt das Besondere des reformatorischen Kirchenbegriffes; hier unterscheidet er sich deutlich vom mittelalterlichen Verständnis der Kirche."

ecclesiology occurs when the "both-and" of the visible and invisible church becomes an "either-or," and that Luther attacks the visible church on the basis of the invisible, spiritual church and shows the incompatibility of both,[149] he can refer only to the occasion for the split and not the reason. The *fideles* can exist in any external community as long as the decisive faith is nourished; there is no necessary incompatibility. A split is inevitable only when this faith can no longer be nourished in a particular community. The potential of the "either-or" is already present in the "both-and," and the simultaneous existence of both possibilities is the result of the "new" in Luther's ecclesiology—*fides* as the mark of the true *fideles*.

It is not only the application of I Cor. 2 : 15 to the true *fideles* as spiritual men which makes them superior to, and independent of, a hierarchy and teaching office which misuses its authority. The very definition of these *fideles* as a spiritual people—their foundation in that which is outside and ahead of them and which no hierarchy must necessarily mediate—implies such an independence. The key to the independence both of the individual *fidelis* with the superior perspective of I Cor. 2 : 15 and of the mini-church as a spiritual people is faith. Thus we are thrown back upon our fundamental distinction between *fides* and *caritas* for the definitive mark of the true *fideles*.

6. *Fides*-ecclesiology

We have denoted the ecclesiology of the medieval exegetes as "*caritas*-ecclesiology" because they regard *caritas* as the definitive mark of the true *fideles*. By the same token, we are able to call Luther's developing ecclesiology in the *Dictata* "*fides*-ecclesiology" because he affirms that the definitive mark of the true *fideles* is faith. We have formulated Luther's understanding of the true *fideles* as those who live in faith and the spirit. Up to now, our attention has been focused on the "spirit-aspect" of this definition, although the importance of the "faith-aspect" has constantly appeared in the discussion. It is necessary at this point to examine the way in which faith comes to expression as the mark of the true *fideles*.

The mark of faith.—We recall that Augustine (cited also by Lombard) and Hugo speak of *caritas* as the link between God (or Christ) and the individual soul or the church.[150] In direct contrast to

---

[149] "Zur Entstehung ...," p. 155.
[150] Cf. *supra*, Ch. I, n. 125 and Ch. II, n. 23.

this, Luther maintains that the soul is tied to God through faith in the truth of God's Word.[151] Luther sets up *fides* as this link between Christ and the *fideles* in conscious contrast to *caritas*, using the same imagery of the "seat" as Hugo: ". . . the fullness of knowledge is faith, just as the fullness of grace is *caritas*. Now Christ sits upon faith in the souls of the *fideles*."[152] It would be presumptuous to ask for a more explicit contradiction to the statement of Hugo, in spite of the fact that Luther still relates grace and *caritas*.

From the last text it is clear that *fides* is not only the seat of Christ in the individual *fidelis anima*, but also in the collection of faithful souls. We have noted how Luther says that "we" are betrothed to Christ through faith, where "we" refers clearly to the true *fideles* in opposition to the Jews and evil Christians.[153] Thus Luther can speak directly of the Lord dwelling in the faithful people of the church through faith without inserting the faithful soul as a link between the two.[154] But he can speak as well of Christ dwelling through faith in the church as a result of his habitation in the soul. At one point where this occurs (in the *scholion* to Ps. 67 : 18), Luther makes special mention of the beautiful exposition of Augustine. Characteristically, however, Augustine makes no mention of a dwelling through faith. Instead, he stresses the necessity of *caritas*.[155] That Luther can neglect

---

[151] *WA* 4, 436.21f. (*Gl.* to Ps. 139 : 6): " 'Et funes' dicta veritatis scripturarum, quibus ligatur anima cum Deo per fidem, . . ."

[152] *WA* 4, 126.17f. (*Sch.* to Ps. 98 : 1): ". . . plenitudo scientie est fides, sicut plenitudo gratie est Charitas. Super fidem autem sedet Christus in animabus fidelium." For Hugo, *supra*, Ch. I, n. 125. Cf. in connection with the heaven imagery, *WA* 3, 141.36ff. (*Gl.* to Ps. 23 : 7): "Non enim intravit Christus ut rex glorie, nisi in celum ascendendo, et in animam, que est spirituale coelum, per fidem ingrediendo," Cf. *supra*, n. 80.

[153] *Supra*, n. 44.

[154] *WA* 3, 488.16ff. (*Gl.* to Ps. 73 : 2): ". . . Ecclesiam 'haereditatis tuae' populi fidelis: supple que est 'mons' Zion, inde enim nomen et ortum habet Ecclesia, 'in quo habitasti' scilicet per fidem et spiritum. . . ." Also *WA* 4, 408.14f. (*Gl.* to Ps. 123 : 1): " 'Nisi quia dominus' Ihesus Christus 'erat in nobis' per fidem habitans: 'dicat' confiteatur 'nunc Israel' fidelis populus Ecclesie: . . ."

[155] Luther: *WA* 3, 401.16ff. (*Sch.* to Ps. 67 : 18): " 'Currus dei etc.' tam de Angelis quam hominibus intelligi potest. Sed sequentia indicant de hominibus intelligi. Sicut b. Augustinus pulchre exponit. Quia 'Dominus in eis' per fidem 'in Sina.' Non Sina quecunque, sed que est in sancto. In ipsis est dominus, ipsi autem in Sina, sed Sina est in sancto. Hec sunt tria tabernacula, anima, corpus et Ecclesia. Quia Deus immediate est in anima: et sequenter cum anima in corpore et cum utroque in communitate Ecclesie, que est sanctum." Augustine does indeed interpret the *currus Dei* as the multitude of the faithful. But he interprets *Sina* and *in sancto* as God's commandment (*in mandato*) and accents God's presence and help in keeping the commandment. This leads him, on the basis of Romans 13 : 10, to emphasize not faith but the necessity of

this emphasis and proceed with his own interpretation of a habitation through faith indicates how for him faith has replaced *caritas* as the link between Christ and the *fideles*.

There are two significant passages where Luther explicitly replaces a reference to *caritas* by the medieval exegetes with a reference to *fides*. In the *glossa* to Psalm 44 : 10, Luther argues that the vestment of the church is gilded not with *caritas*, as Lyra and Perez maintained, but with faith. This comes as no surprise after Luther fixes the position of the church at the right hand of Christ "in spiritual things and the interior man."[156] The definition of the *fideles* as a spiritual people marked by faith is functioning here, with the result that Luther sees their most shining characteristic, their gilded quality, in faith rather than in *caritas*.

In the same *scholion* to Ps. 67 : 14 in which he discusses the twofold nature of sleep, Luther at first appears to follow the traditional exegesis when he interprets the gilded wings of the dove as the contemplative powers of the soul erudite in the Scriptures and the back of the dove as works done in *caritas*.[157] After denoting the dove as the church and treating the contrast of the sleep of the world over against the sleep of the church,[158] Luther maintains that faith is that silver veneer which is painted on the wings when faith assents to the Word of God. Only then follow(!) the shining works done in love as the gilded back of the dove, i.e. works which are directed horizontally to the world and glisten before the eyes of other men.[159] The relation

---

caritas in keeping the commandment, and the presence of *caritas*, not faith, is the presence of the Lord "in illis, in Sina, in sancto." *Enarr. in ps.* 67.24 (*CChr* 39, 887-888).

[156] *WA* 3, 251.22ff.: ". . . Ecclesia coniunx tua 'a dextris tuis' in spiritualibus et homine interiore 'in vestitu deaurato' Hebr. diademate aureo, hec est fides vel chorus Apostolorum Apoc. 12: 'circumdata' ex omni parte ornata 'varietate' differentia ordinum, ministeriorum, virtutum etc." For Lyra and Perez, cf. *supra*, Ch. I, nn. 169, 177.

[157] *WA* 3, 396.11ff.: "Si dormiatis inter duas sortes, id est duo testamenta, in his meditando et studendo: tunc penne columbe, id est anime contemplatrices potentie, deargentate, id est divinis scripturis erudite erunt. . . . Et 'posteriora dorsi' (id est exterior conversatio corporis) 'in virore' (id est rutilantia et exemplorum luce) 'auri' (id est charitatis) . . . Dorsum itaque in posterioribus habet rutilantiam seu virorem auri, hoc est: in corpore relucent opera pulcherrime charitatis ad proximum faciendo eis bona et ferendo ab eis mala." For Lombard and Perez, cf. *supra*, Ch. I, n. 117.

[158] Cf. *supra*, n. 92.

[159] *WA* 3, 399.13ff.: "Qui sunt contemptores divitiarum et rerum voluptatum: ipsi sunt, qui erudiri in divinis scripturis et exerceri in operibus charitatis gloriose possunt. Que omnia Apostolus brevi verbo complexus ait: 'In Christo Ihesu nec circumcisio etc. sed fides, que per dilectionem operatur' [Gal. 5 : 6]. Fides est deargentatio pennarum. Nam verbum Dei est quidem argentum, sed quando adheret per assensum, tunc pennis allinitur. Et sic argentantur, id est verbo Dei per assensum fidei acrescunt, quasi

200

between faith and the Word takes priority over *caritas* in denoting the shining quality of faithful souls. The light of *caritas* visible to other men through works done in love is only the reflection of luminescent faith in the Word.

If faith replaces *caritas* as the mark of the truly faithful for Luther, what significance does this new mark of the church have? How does it function and what is the reason for Luther's preference for it over *caritas*? We have seen that faith is the link between the faithful people and the eternal, invisible goods of salvation which are to be theirs and in which, as if in heaven, they have their location and foundation. Luther can speak of faith itself as that foundation, and this designation appears to sum up the significance he sees in faith as the most important mark of the church. The church is founded upon faith, which is the substance of all virtues.[160] Indeed, the whole church is established upon a firm rock, i.e. upon the *fides Christi*.[161]

Luther spells out what he means by substance in the *scholion* to Psalm 68 : 2. *Substantia* is whatever a man has in the world by means of which he is able to exist and prosper. In other words, it is the foundation upon which one is able to build one's life. But the *sancti* have no worldly substance; they only have faith, which is the "substance of things hoped for" (Heb. 11 : 1), i.e. the possession of

incarnatur deus, sic argentatur anima. Et tunc sequitur operatio per dilectionem (id est posteriora dorse in pallore auri) 'ut luceat lux vestra coram hominibus' [Matt. 5 : 16] ad quos dorsum habetis." W. Maurer comes nearest to the distinction between Luther and the tradition when he writes ("Kirche und Geschichte ...," p. 97): "In allen diesen Aussagen [über Christus und die Kirche] muß, auch wo Luther nicht ausdrücklich davon redet, die *fides* als das verbindende Glied zwischen Christus dem Haupte und der Kirche bzw. ihren Gliedern angenommen werden. ... Die fides—und nicht wie bei Augustin die caritas—hält den Leib der Kirche zusammen. ..." Maurer limits his remark to the link between Christ and his members in the mystical body. We dare to make the more comprehensive statement that, in contrast to the exegetical tradition as a whole (naturally as a result of Augustine), Luther replaces *caritas* with *fides* as the mark of the true *fideles*, and this not only in reference to *fides* as the link between Christ and his members in the mystical body. Maurer apparently does not take the difference between Luther and Augustine too seriously. Otherwise he could not write (p. 100): "In Bezug auf die Kirche und ihre Geschichte wurde Augustin von niemandem besser verstanden als von dem angehenden Reformator der Kirche in Wittenberg."
    [160] *WA* 4, 167.4f. (*Gl.* to Ps. 103 : 5): " 'Qui fundasti terram' Ecclesiam tuam 'super stabilitatem suam', que est fides substantia omnium virtutum." Cf. *ibid.*, 13f.: "... 'in locum' unam ecclesiam seu fidem, 'quem fundasti eis', fides enim est substantia." Also *WA* 3, 649.17ff. (*Sch.* to Ps. 83 : 7).
    [161] *WA* 3, 651.2ff. (*Sch.* to Ps. 83 : 7): "Quare locum hic mystice oportet accipi: sic enim fides est locus anime, quia domus conscientie nostre, sicut et tota Ecclesia ponitur supra firmam petram (id est super fidem Christi)."

future things.[162] Referring to this discussion, Luther returns to this theme in a second *scholion* and applies it to the faithful:

> The substance (as above) of ambitious men is glory, of rich men riches, of gluttons food and the belly, of luxury-seekers sensual pleasure. Christ, however, has destroyed all these substances through his own lack of substance, with the result that the *fideles* neither have their substance in these things nor trust in them, but they are without any substance, or rather they have faith in place of them, which is a completely different substance, namely, the substance of God.[163]

The *fideles* are founded only in faith, which is the substance of those eternal things which they expect and toward which they orient their lives. This is why faith is the mark of the *fideles* for Luther. It is the only substance or foundation which they are able to have in this life, which in turn links them to their future, eternal goods.

Luther applies this same understanding of faith as substance to the *iusti*, the *sancti* and the *membra Christi*. The *iusti* are planted in the church through firm faith and hope.[164] The saints stand solid in the hope of heavenly things and are not blown around by the affections in temporal things because they are founded upon the rock of faith.[165] Just as Christ had no substance and was humiliated before he was glorified, so his body, the church, after being established through faith and the "heaven of Scripture," is handed over to persecution that it might be glorified.[166] By the same token, it is clear why the gates of

---

[162] *WA* 3, 420.3ff.: "Quare breviter quicquid est in mundo, quo aliquis potest secundum hanc vitam subsistere et florere, substantia dicitur. Sed Sancti talem non habent. Heb. 10. 'Consyderantes vos habere meliorem et permanentem substantiam' [Heb. 10 : 34]. Et 'fides est substantia rerum sperandarum' [Heb. 11 : 1], id est possessio et facultas rerum, non mundanarum (que est visio vel sensus), sed futurarum." See Ozment (pp. 105ff.) and Schwarz (pp. 158ff.) for a discussion of Luther's understanding of *substantia*.

[163] *WA* 3, 440.34ff. (*Sch.* to Ps. 68 : 1f.): "Substantia ut supra ambitiosorum est gloria, divitum divitie, gulosorum esca et venter, luxuriosorum voluptas. Has autem substantias Christus per suam non substantiam omnes destruxit: ut fideles in illis non subsistant nec confidant, sed sint sine substantia, habeant autem fidem pro eis, que est substantia alia, scilicet substantia dei."

[164] *WA* 4, 80.11f. (*Gl.* to Ps. 91 : 14): " 'Plantati' [iusti] per firmam fidem et spem 'in domo domini' Ecclesia Christi: ..."

[165] *WA* 3, 227.20ff. (*Sch.* to Ps. 39 : 3): "Quarto sunt affective virtutes cuiuslibet sancti, in quo Christus habitat. Et tales sunt pedes Christi tropologici, fundati supra petram fidei, ut iam nullis affectionum ventis in temporalibus rebus moveantur, sed spe coelestium stant solidi. ... Et sic credo istum versum dici a Christo pro suis et fere ad literam. Quia communiter petra pro Christo et fide accipitur, supra quam non nisi sanctorum anime statuuntur et pedes spirituales."

[166] *WA* 4, 179.13ff. (*Sch.* to Ps. 103 : 10): "Semper enim sicut in capite, ita et in corpore. Caput autem primo fuit humiliatum et postea magnificatum. Ita postquam

hell cannot prevail against the church. First, because Christ "suspends" his church in faith, and this faith (like the *fideles*) does not have its support on earth, but clings to heaven.[167] And again, enemies may kill the body, but they can never kill the soul which lives by faith.[168] The *fides* on which the church is founded belongs to the same sphere as the eternal goods with which faith links the *fideles*, and is thus unassailable.

Because faith is the paramount quality of the true *fideles*, Luther frequently denotes them as believers, or *credentes*. The generation of the upright is that of the *credentes*; for faith alone makes upright.[169] Neither Jews nor heretics have the truth promised of old in the law, but only those who truly believe.[170] The foundation of the *fideles* in spiritual goods also provides the context for speaking of the *credentes*. They are the people of the Lord to whom he will give strength for spiritual things.[171] In the interpretation of the tribal names *Manasses* and *Galaad*, the same theme is prominent. These names signify the church: *Manasses*, because it is a "forgetful people" which through hope holds all temporal things in contempt; *Galaad*, because it is a "heap of testimony" which has the true Word of God and is born of true seed through faith. Thus Luther concludes that those who believe are born out of the seed and Word of God.[172]

Ecclesia per coelum Scripture et fidem fundata est super stabilitatem suam, mox persecutionibus tradita ut magnificaretur."

[167] *WA* 4, 512.3ff. (*Adn.* at Ps. 92 : 1). " 'Insuper appendit orbem' Ecclesiam: 'qui non commovebitur' etiam a portis inferi: i.e. in fide suspendit Ecclesiam suam, quia fides non nititur in terra, sed heret in celo, et non prevalent adversus eam porte inferi." Kohlmeyer uses effective imagery to emphasize the non-earthly, non-material foundation of the church when he writes (p. 482): "Er hatte sie [seine Kirchenidee] an Stelle der beide Welten umspannenden katholischen Kirche gesetzt und deren sichtbare feste Fundamente ins Blaue gegründet, in die Welt des Glaubens."

[168] *WA* 4, 510.22f. (*Adn.* at Ps. 90 : 10): " 'Non accedet ad te malum' persecutio: 'et lepra' i.e. heresis 'non appropinquabit tabernaculo tuo' Ecclesie tue. Sensus est, quod licet sancti foris vexentur in carne, non tamen occiduntur in spiritu, ... Quia non prevalent porte inferi contra Ecclesiam. Et si occidunt corpus, quod est atrium, animam tamen, que fide vivit, occidere non possunt: ista autem est tabernaculum Christi."

[169] *WA* 4, 247.21f. (*Gl.* to Ps. 111 : 2): "Per hoc enim 'Generatio rectorum' credentium, sola enim fides rectificat, perfidia autem pravos facit, ..."

[170] *WA* 3, 167.33f. (*Gl.* to Ps. 30 : 24): "Quam [veritatem] neque Iudei neque heretici habent, sed solum vere credentes, quia Christus est veritas et fides eius."

[171] *WA* 3, 158.2ff. (*Gl.* to Ps. 28 : 10-11): "... 'et sedebit' in solio regio, quod est Ecclesia, i.e. regnabit 'dominus' Christus 'rex eternum. Dominus virtutem' fortitudinem ad spiritualia 'populo suo' credentibus 'dabit': ..."

[172] *WA* 3, 345.24ff.: "Et huic recte opponitur Manasses i.e. populus obliviosus per spem contemnens temporalia. Sicut Galaad acervus testis contra Moab: quia habet verum verbum Dei et de vero semine natus est per fidem. Qui enim credunt, hi

F. Held holds that both Luther and Augustine see the essence of the true church in the fact that it is invisibly constructed through faith and by faith alone is able to be perceived. As one of his supporting texts, Held takes the *glossa* to Psalm 27 : 2 where Luther cites Augustine in respect to the *credentes*.[173] Luther does indeed remain true to the exegesis of Augustine here: Christ is extending his hands on the Cross for the salvation of those believers who are built up into his temple.[174] The question is, however, whether Luther and Augustine mean the same thing with these words. We recall that, for Augustine, the bond of the living stones (the *fideles*) which make up the temple of God is *caritas*.[175] On the basis of our investigation so far, we are forced to conclude that the *veri credentes* for Augustine are distinguished by *caritas* in addition to faith. This is not the case with Luther, although he is quite willing to quote Augustine here where the *credentes* are mentioned without reference to *caritas*. To support his contention, however, Held calls attention to another text in which Luther cites Augustine in reference to the *viva fides*.[176] This reference forces us to delve more deeply into the nature of this faith which defines the *fideles*.

The nature of fides. — The text to which Held refers is the *scholion* to Psalm 34 : 18 ("I will acknowledge you in the great church; in a heavy people I will praise you"). Here Luther reports that Augustine interprets the "heavy people" as that people "which by a living faith (*viva fide*) is in the church, just as grain on the threshing floor, whereas the others with vain faith are flimsy chaff."[177] Augustine

nascuntur ex verbo et semine Dei." This text is found in the *Sermo de Martyribus* appended to the *scholia* to Ps. 59. Vogelsang ("Die Datierung . . . ," p. 118) suggests 1514 for the date.

[173] F. Held, "Augustins *Enarrationes in Psalmos* als exegetische Vorlage für Luthers erste Psalmenvorlesung," *ThSK* 102 (1930), p. 23: "Das Wesen der wahren Kirche sieht Luther mit Augustin darin, daß sie unsichtbar durch den Glauben erbaut wird und allein für den Glauben erkennbar ist." The passage: *WA* 3, 152.12ff.: "... 'dum extollo manus meas' mystice, quando manus in cruce extendero, August., ut credentes fiant templum tuum, . . ."

[174] *Enarr. in ps.* 27.2 (*CChr* 38, 168): " 'Exaudi vocem deprecationis meae, dum oro ad te, dum extollo manus meas ad templum sanctum suum.' Dum crucifigor, ad eorum salutem, qui credentes fiunt templum sanctum tuum."

[175] *Supra*, Ch. I, n. 51.

[176] Held, *ibid.*: "... und III, 198,6 kennzeichnet Luther mit einem Hinweis auf Augustin die viva fides als das Wertvollste in der Kirche."·

[177] *WA* 3, 198.5ff.: "Capitur autem secundum Aug. gravis populus pro eo, qui viva fide est in Ecclesia, sicut granum in area, ubi ceteri vana fide sunt leves palee." Luther

indeed speaks of the "heavy people" as the grain in the church as opposed to the chaff,[178] but the qualifying factors, *viva fide* and *vana fide*, are Luther's own! Luther, therefore, is certainly following Augustine (and the whole tradition) in speaking of two basic groups in the church—the *boni* and the *mali* or the true *fideles* and the false. Whereas Augustine and the tradition distinguish these two groups on the basis of the presence or absence of *caritas*, Luther distinguishes them by the presence or absence of a living faith.

If, however, the terms, living faith and vain faith, correspond to the traditional categories of *fides formata* and *fides informis*, Luther is not making a new distinction at all, since the living faith of the true *fideles* would be that faith which is formed by *caritas*. Luther knows this traditional distinction, of course.[179] On the other hand, he can employ the traditional terms with considerable freedom, as in the case where he speaks of Abraham trekking away from a dead and unformed faith.[180] Considering the significance of faith for the *fideles* as the substance and foundation of their life, we may expect that Luther does not mean the *fides formata* when he speaks of living faith.

In fact, Luther does us the favor of employing the phrase *viva fides* at other points in the *Dictata*. To believe with a living faith is to believe with the heart—precisely what that man cannot do who is wise only in regard to earthly things. The man who understands spiritual

also speaks of the grain and chaff in terms of the opposition between *infidelis* and *fides* as well as between *fides mortua* and *fides viva*. *WA* 4, 139.27ff.: (*Sch.* to Ps. 100 : 8): "Quia qui habet fidem, recte dicitur triticum ad infidelem, qui est palea. Sed qui habet fidem mortuam, adhuc palea est ad eum, qui est fidei viventis."

[178] *Enarr. in ps.* 34, s. 2.10 (*CChr* 38, 318): "Plane 'in ecclesia multa, confitebor tibi, in populo gravi laudabo te.' Fit enim confessio in omni multitudine, sed non in omnibus Deus laudatur; tota multitudo audit confessionem nostram, sed non in omni multitudine laus Dei est. In ista enim omni multitudine, id est in ecclesia, quae toto orbe terrarum diffusa est, palea est et frumentum: palea volat, frumentum manet; ideo 'in populo gravi laudabo te.' In gravi populo, quem ventus tentationis non aufert, in his Deus laudatur. Nam in palea blasphematur semper . . . Inique, invide, aream inspicis, qui totus in palea es, non tibi facile grana occurrunt: quaere, et invenies populum gravem, in quo Dominum laudes."

[179] E.g. *WA* 4, 441.25ff. (*Gl.* to Ps. 140 : 9).

[180] *WA* 3, 490.22ff. (*Gl.* to Ps. 73 : 11): "Avertit Dominus dexteram suam (i.e. gratiam) de medio sinu suo (i.e. de corde credentis): fides enim est sinus Ecclesie, in quo Christum gestat mater eius spiritualis. Et hic est sinus Abrahe (i.e. fides eius), quando fidem informem et mortuam relinquit. Sicut hodie proh dolor est, quia est inefficax fides, fides informis, quando solum sciuntur credenda, sed virtutem fidei non operantur, i.e. quando regnum Dei in sermone et non in virtute collocant." Cf. Ozment, p. 117, n. 1, and especially the discussion of Schwarz (pp. 128-129). Schwarz notes that although Luther operates with a *fides informis*, he does not take the next step and hold that grace as the "formale" must be added in order for the *fides formata* to arise.

things, however, seeks God with genuine faith (*vera fide*) and, as a result, with works which prove that his faith is not mere lip service (*licet ore dicant*).[181] The association of the spiritual man and a genuine, living faith is a clue to the fact that Luther understands the *viva fides* as that same faith which he has used to describe the foundation of the true *fideles*. These *fideles* are linked with their eternal goods only through the perception of these goods by faith and trust in the promise of their delivery. Thus Luther can say that this genuine, living faith is that by which the Word of God is received. As faith in Christ, it is the foundation of the church, and it is true because God has already fulfilled his promise of sending Christ.[182]

The relationship of faith to the Word of God exhibits further evidence that the *viva fides* cannot be the *fides formata* for Luther. In Luther's third attempt to explain verse 10 of Psalm 115 ("I have believed, on account of which I have spoken"), Luther makes the well-known statement that "all our goods are only in words and promises."[183] The reason for this is that heavenly things (which are the

---

[181] *WA* 3, 297.1f. (*Gl.* to Ps. 52 : 2): " 'Dixit insipiens' i.e. terrena sapiens homo, quia sapientia est cognitio dei 'in corde suo' quia non credit viva fide, corde enim creditur: 'non est deus' licet ore dicant, non tamen in corde, quod deus sit et regnet." *Ibid.*, 8ff.: "... 'ut videat si est intelligens' habens spiritualium intelligentiam 'aut requirens deum' vera fide et operibus, opere et veritate et fide non ficta, taliter enim requiritur et non aliter." Cf. 3, 296.36ff. The emphasis on works following faith should not mislead one into thinking of the *fides formata* here. Cf. *supra*, n. 159, where faith as assent to the Word is given distinct primacy over the production of works in love which are directed outward toward the world.

[182] *WA* 4, 350.25ff. (*Sch.* to Ps. 118 : 90ff.): " 'In generationem et generationem veritas tua,' id est fides tua, qua suscipitur verbum tuum, per quam servatur, docetur et discitur. Et vera scilicet fides atque viva, que est veritas, quia exhibitio olim promissa et impletio figurarum legis. Et per hoc Ecclesia quoque permanet, quia 'fundasti terram, et permanet'. Fundamentum enim terre corporalis quis novit? Sed fundamentum Ecclesie Christus est, id est fides Christi, quo ipsam fundavit altissimus natus in ea, ut sit ei petra firmissima." Schwarz concludes that the *fides viva* cannot be the *fides caritate formata* for Luther (p. 129): "Auch jetzt meint Luther gewiß nicht, daß eine separate Gnadenform in der *caritas* den toten Glauben wieder lebendig macht. ... Luther versteht unter der fides viva gewiß einen neuen mit der Gnade geschenkten Glauben, ..."

[183] We cite the entire *scholion* here which we summarize in this paragraph: *WA* 4, 272.16ff.: "Tercio quia omnia nostra bona sunt tantum in verbis et promissis. Coelestia enim ostendi non possunt sicut presentia, sed tantum annunciari verbo. Ideo non ait: 'Video, propter quod opere ostendo', sed 'credidi, propter quod loquor'. Illi autem qui sua bona iactant et in re presenti magnificant, non habent fidem illarum, sed visionem. Nos autem credimus, et ideo opere ostendere non possumus. Quare tantum loquimur et testificamur. Fides enim est causa, quare non possumus aliter quam verbo ostendere bona nostra, eo quod fides est non apparentium, que non nisi verbo possunt doceri, ostendi et indicari. Ideo vocatur 'argumentum (id est ostensio) rerum non apparentium', quia ostendit nobis futura, que ex ipsa possidemus et substantiam futurorum. Recte ergo

goods of the *fideles*) are not able to be demonstrated as present things are, but only announced by means of words. And the necessity for these goods to be announced by the word arises from the nature of faith: it pertains to things which are not apparent, but which are able to be "taught, demonstrated and indicated only by the word." Faith demonstrates future things to the *fideles* and becomes the substance of *futura* for them. It is the *fides futurorum*, which implies simultaneously contempt for present goods.[184]

The fact that faith pertains to things which are not apparent forces it to rely on the Word. This is necessary because in this life the *fideles* are able to have no "present things," no *res* on which they can get a hold, no earthly substance, as we have seen, upon which they can support their lives. Rather, faith is the witness to eternal *res* which the *fideles* will have as *res* only in the future. It is the Gospel and the Word of God which testify to these eternal *res* and from which faith lives.[185] By its nature, then, faith lives from the Word alone, and from the Word alone faith draws its nourishment.

---

dicit 'Credidi, propter quod locutus sum': quia aliter notificare non possum, eo quod tantum credidi, nondum autem vidi. Et est ratio reddita, quare tantummodo doces et nuncias de coelestibus. Multa mihi predicantur: quomodo sciam an sint vera? Respondet: Ideo tantum loquor et non ostendo, quia credo, ut et tu credas et fidem futurorum suscipias et contemnas presentia." A few lines further, Luther shows that he is still thinking of *spiritualia*, so that the *fides futurorum* is only an added dimension to faith in spiritual, eternal goods, not a different faith: *ibid.*, 34f.: "Fides enim facit temporalia comparari cum eternis et carnalia cum spiritualibus." This *fides* is still that which defines the true *fideles* as spiritual men.

[184] For the *fides futurorum*, see also *WA* 4, 322.15ff. (*Sch.* to Ps. 118 : 31): " 'Testimonia' autem que sint, supra patuit. Quibus non adheretur nisi credendo eis ut veris et fidelibus. Quia si scirentur, iam nec testimonia essent, sed exhibitio et nulla fides: scientia itaque eorum, que consecutus es, sed fides eorum, que assequi habes: scientia presentium et preteritorum, fides futurorum proprie. Sicut infra: 'Bonitatem et disciplinam et scientiam doce me.' Scimus enim que fiunt et facta sunt, credimus que futura promittuntur, ut Abraham credidit deo promittenti etc." The reference to Abraham indicates that the faith for which he left behind the dead, unformed faith (*supra*, n. 180), was not the *fides formata*, but the *fides futurorum*. Also *WA* 4, 402.20ff. (*Sch.* to Ps. 121 : 4). For the object of faith as things which are not apparent and thus invisible, cf. *WA* 3, 498.31ff. (*Sch.* to Ps. 73 : 5).

[185] *WA* 3, 279.30ff. (*Gl.* to Ps. 49 : 16): "In hac vita enim non rem ipsam, sed testimonia rerum tenemus, quia fides non est res sed argumentum rerum non apparentium. Ita Evangelium et verbum Dei est testificatio de rebus ipsis eternis quia nuncium bonum maxime additis miraculis." *Ibid.*, line 8: "... verbum Dei, quo testatur nobis de futuris et invisibilibus. ..." Ozment (p. 108) makes the appropriate play on words here: "... all *fideles* (and Jesus) live 'by sheer hope alone' 'in God's Word alone,' '*res*-less' before men." We recall the opposition between *fides* and *res* in those passages with which we first illustrated Luther's new understanding of the *fideles*. Cf. *supra*, n. 46.

207

Faith, the Word and the church. — The absence of any *res*-quality in faith itself explains why the *viva fides* for Luther cannot be the *fides formata*, and, at the same time, why the *fideles* are no longer dependent upon sacramental grace for their definitive mark — *fides.* *Caritas,* the mark of the true *fideles* for the medieval exegetes, is precisely a present *res,* which is in fact the *res sacramenti,* the grace given through the sacraments.[186] In order to have this *caritas,* the *fidelis* must partake of the sacraments in which he receives the *res* (*caritas* or grace) under the sacramental signs. The emphatic rejection by Luther of any *res*-quality to faith means that this *fides* cannot be the *fides formata,* faith which has been formed by *caritas.*

At the same time, because faith lives from the Word alone and is not tied to the sacramental *res,* it is not dependent upon the members of the existing hierarchy as administrators of these sacraments. This means, in turn, that the true *fideles,* whose essential characteristic is faith apart from any *res,* are in effect dissolved from any necessary connection to the sacramental structure of the church and its hierarchy.[187] If their faith is properly nourished by the Word within

---

[186] For the *res sacramenti* as grace, cf. the exemplary text from Biel given in *WA* 55/I, 21.40ff. and the discussion there. The decisive statement: "Illud vero quod significatur, i.e. effectus ille quem deus invisibiliter operatur, seu gratia vel gratuitus effectus dicitur res sacramenti sive effectus sacramentalis" (Biel, IV *Sent.* d.4 q.2 a.1 not 3C). Ebeling has argued that Luther's conception of faith as the "argumentum rerum non apparentium" and its dependence upon the Word which is the "testimonium futurorum" sets the Catholic sacramental theology completely on its head ("Die Anfänge . . . ," pp. 200-201): "Damit ist unausgesprochen bereits der ganze katholische Sakramentalismus aus den Angeln gehoben." Iserloh's rejoinder that grace bestowed in the sacraments is also a *res invisibilis* (" 'Existentiale Interpretation' in Luthers erster Psalmenvorlesung?" col. 78) does nothing to weaken Ebeling's argument. Sacramental grace remains a *res,* whereas Luther's emphasis is upon the invisible *and* future character of the eternal *res.* Jared Wicks presents essentially the same argument as Iserloh when he asserts that the sacraments, as signs, are of the same order as testimonies since they both point to invisible *res* (*Man Yearning for Grace* [Wiesbaden, 1969], p. 82). Wicks notes that the future orientation of faith makes it understandable that "the sacraments do not function to any significant extent in the life of faith he [Luther] describes, but this description is not equivalent to rejection of the sacraments" (*ibid.,* p. 83). It is true that Luther does not consciously reject the sacraments in the *Dictata* (which Ebeling did not maintain). Furthermore, we agree that the sacraments as signs possess *testimonium* character. Nevertheless, the decisive factor, which preserves the validity of Ebeling's argument, is that the sacraments for Luther (even if unconsciously) no longer offer any advantage over the Word.

[187] Faith *is* that grace which has been promised of old: *WA* 4, 127.18ff. (*Gl.* to Ps. 99 : 5): "Fides enim est ipsa gratia et misericordia olim promissa, quia per illam iustificamur et salvamur. In fide enim Christi omnia nobis donantur, que promissa sunt olim." Note that faith justifies and saves, taking over the function of *caritas* and grace.

the existing external organization of the church, there is no reason for the *fideles* to draw the consequences and withdraw from the external community, thus turning their inherent independence into organizational separation. If, on the other hand, their faith can no longer be nourished within this community, and the eternal *res* can be attested elsewhere by a proper proclamation of the Word, there exists no binding reason why the true *fideles* cannot sever themselves from the existing church organization. The replacement of *caritas* with *fides* as the mark of the true *fideles* thus has explosive potential already in the *Dictata*.

In light of the nature of faith and its indispensable relationship to the Word, the statements which Luther makes about the Gospel and the church come into sharper focus. Not only are *ecclesia* and *evangelium* set in parallel,[188] but the *fideles* are depicted as generated by the Gospel.[189] The church is edified through the Gospel and the Word of God preserves the church.[190] This emphasis upon the Word and the accompanying relegation of sacramental grace to a secondary

---

Understandably, Luther speaks of the *viva fides* as justifying: *WA* 4, 325.8ff. (*Sch.* to Ps. 118 : 37): "Spiritus est qui vivificat, et fides iustificat: iustus enim ex fide vivit, ... Ergo 'vivifica me' est dicere: Iustifica me, da mihi spiritum, da mihi vivam et perfectam fidem, in qua vivam et iustus sim."

[188] *WA* 4, 39.12f. (*Gl.* to Ps. 88 : 18): "... 'exaltabitur' in terra 'cornu nostrum', regnum nostrum, quod est Ecclesie [*sic*] vel Evangelium." And *WA* 4, 42.5f. (*Gl.* to Ps. 88 : 40): "... 'in terra sanctuarium eius' corpus eius naturale et mysticum, quod est Ecclesia et Evangelium."

[189] *WA* 3, 454.24ff. (*Sch.* to Ps. 70 : 6): "Igitur sicut beata virgo fuit venter, unde processit Christus deus: Ita Scriptura est venter, unde oritur veritas divina et Ecclesia. Quia Thalamum Christi b. virginem ps. 18 [: 6] dicit. Et Thalamus populi fidelis est Evangelium." *WA* 3, 571.28f. (*Sch.* to Ps. 77 : 16): "Igitur oculis videmus istud miraculum dei per orbem, quod ex Christo et Evangelio nascuntur plurimi fideles." *WA* 4, 183.18ff. (*Sch.* to Ps. 103 : 13): "... id est, Ecclesia tua replebitur multis fidelibus per effectum evangelice predicationis, que est opus Christi, ita quod corpus Ecclesie erit plenum, pingue et saturum membris integris et plenis fide et virtutibus. Quid est enim fructus verbi dei nisi multiplicatio fidelium extensive et intensive?" *WA* 4, 475.18ff. (*Adn.* at Ps. 8 : 3): "Omnes Christiani sunt infantes quia nati ex Deo et verbo veritatis et sic facti pueri evangelici et quottidie nascuntur. Uterus enim, ex quo nascuntur, est Scriptura sancta et Evangelium. Sunt etiam lactentes, quia sugunt ubera eiusdem evangelii."

[190] *WA* 4, 415.21f. (*Gl.* to Ps. 126 : 3): "Quia per literam et humanas traditiones non edificatur Ecclesia Christi [corr: *WA* 55], sed per Evangelium." *WA* 3, 259.18ff. (*Sch.* to Ps. 44 : 3): "Verbum enim dei conservat Ecclesiam dei: benedictio enim in scriptura significat multiplicationem et augmentationem. Sic quia diffusa est gratia in labiis Christi, sequitur multiplicatio fidelium, et hoc ineternum, quia non cessabit Ecclesia." The nourishment of the church by the Word remains a life or death factor for the church in Luther's mind. Cf. *WA* 12, 191.16ff. (*De instituendis ministris Ecclesiae* 1523; quoted by Steudle, p. 103).

role in the *Dictata* must be understood as the result of Luther's new interpretation of the true *fideles* as marked by faith.[191] Since the *fideles* are dependent on the Word and not on sacramental grace for the nourishment of their faith, the Word or the Gospel can well be spoken of as the "source" of the *fideles* and as "preserving" the church. Those eternal *res*, which faith alone can apprehend and appropriate as the eternal, spiritual goods of the faithful, are able to be communicated only by means of the word. This word is the Word of God or the Gospel. The Gospel, the witness to future, eternal *res*, pre-empts the function of the present *res* of sacramental grace as constitutive of the church, just as faith, the substance apart from any present *res*, replaces *caritas* as the mark of the true *fideles*.

In the *scholion* to Psalm 118 : 147, Luther weaves together many of the above-mentioned themes in speaking of the faithful people. After specifying the desire of the Jews, the heretics and the *mali* for temporal goods, he describes the true *fideles* as follows:

> But the faithful people seek spiritual things, which are given to us as completely as possible in faith and the Gospel. Thus they not only hear God's words (by which he confers every good upon us), but also meditate upon them and increasingly digest them. For this is an astounding petition, that only words are requested from God, not *res*, but the signs of *res*. For who has ever cried out so eagerly for words? But because *res* which are not apparent are hidden in the words through faith, therefore he who has the words through faith has all things, though hidden. And so it is clear that this verse asks literally, not for the future church or its goods, but for the present church and its goods, which are nothing but the Gospel of grace itself, which in turn is the sign and word of those things which are to be hoped for but which are not yet apparent. And with such food Christ feeds us.[192]

---

[191] Holl (pp. 292ff.) moves from the Gospel to the distinction between the true and false *fideles,* whereas we maintain that Luther's emphasis upon the Gospel only makes sense when one first sees how faith replaces *caritas* as the mark of the true *fideles.* Luther no longer "needs" the sacraments, so to speak, if the essential mark of the true *fideles* is that faith which is no *res* itself (as is *caritas*), but rather the apprehension of eternal *res* communicable only through the Word. In this context one can place Jetter's appropriate remark that, in the *Dictata*, all that Luther says of the sacrament, he can also say of the Word (*Die Taufe beim jungen Luther*, p. 193).

[192] *WA* 4, 376.10ff.: "Sed fidelis populus spiritualia querit, que sunt in fide et evangelio nobis donata maxima, ergo ut eloquia eius (in quibus omne bonum nobis contulit) non tantum audiat, sed etiam meditetur et per incrementum sibi incorporet. Mira est enim hec petitio, non nisi verba peti a deo, non res, sed signa rerum. Quis enim pro verbis tam anxie unquam clamavit? Sed quia in verbis per fidem abscondite sunt res non apparentes, ideo habens verba per fidem habet omnia, licet abscondite. Et ita patet, quod iste versus petit literaliter, non futuram Ecclesiam nec eius bona, sed

The designation of the goods of the *fideles* as spiritual recalls the role of the *litera/spiritus* schema in defining the faithful soul as *homo spiritualis* and the church as *populus spiritualis*. The mark of *fides* appears as the orientation of the *fideles* toward these goods and, with the Gospel, as the means by which these goods are appropriated. From the side of the faithful, it is the only possible and absolutely necessary link between them and their goods—spiritual, eternal and future *res* which are not yet apparent.[193]

At the same time, the nature of faith is made clear in the above passage. It has nothing to do with present *res*; it cannot fasten upon these *res*, but is entirely dependent upon the words of God which bear witness to future, spiritual *res*. As these words of God, the Gospel assumes an indispensable function for the church—a constituting function. For it is through the Gospel—the link with the eternal *res* that comes to the *fideles* from without—that faith lives and is nourished and the true *fideles* stay alive. They need nothing else, for "he who has the words through faith has all things."[194] But all these things remain hidden; they are *res non apparentes*. This hidden quality of the eternal goods of the faithful, as we have observed, is the key to the understanding of the *fideles* themselves as hidden and invisible.

And finally, the character of the church as *testimonium*[195] is ex-

---

presentem et eius bona: que non sunt nisi ipsum Evangelium gratie, quod est signum et verbum sperandarum rerum et non apparentium. Et tali cibo nos alit Christus."

[193] Cf. Luther's explicit definitions of the church in the *Operationes* at Psalm 15, where the elements of faith, hope and spirit play the decisive role: *WA* 5, 450.25ff. and *WA* 5, 451.1ff.

[194] This sufficiency of faith and the Word becomes especially important for Luther in his later polemical writings. We refer the reader here to Steudle's discussion (p. 99) of several passages from Luther's reply to Ambrosius Catharinus (1521: *WA* 7, 705ff.), where it is evident how the definition of the *fideles* by faith and its nourishment through the Word releases them from any necessary connection to a particular geographical location, external community or set of ministers. Here Luther is making explicit the implications already present in the *Dictata* which we have discussed above. Steudle, it must be mentioned, is anxious to play down Luther's emphasis on the internal, invisible community of the true *fideles* where Luther is engaged in polemics (pp. 90-91, 94-95, 99-100, 116). In the process, he overlooks the fact that this internal community, and its independence from any particular external community, is the logical, decisive consequence of the heart of Luther's new ecclesiology, which enables him to make the break with Rome on the basis of the ecclesiology he had worked out in the *Dictata*. That Luther emphasizes this invisible community precisely in his polemical writings points to the importance which it has for his ecclesiology, and does not detract from its significance, as Steudle believes.

[195] *WA* 4, 402.27ff. "Et aptissime dicit: 'Testimonium Israel,' quia Ecclesia militans

posed when Luther says that this verse is a petition for the present church and its goods. The goods of the present church are faith and the Gospel, which in turn are only witnesses to the eternal, spiritual goods of the *fideles*. Only the "future church," the *ecclesia triumphans*, will have the eternal *res* as its present goods. The church stands in direct parallel with faith and the Gospel and takes on the "witness"-character of the latter.

In fact, we can go further. Ecclesiological considerations and terminology make up the basis and framework of the entire passage. The key to the interpretation of the passage is, in the first place, the contrast between the faithful people, the true *fideles*, and the unfaithful Jews and heretics alongside the false *fideles* or *mali*. At the end of the passage, Luther rounds out the ecclesiological framework—surprisingly at first—by indicating that the petition of the text is not only to be understood soteriologically, but also ecclesiologically—namely, as a petition for the present church and its goods. The new understanding of the relationship between faith and word, between faith and the Gospel, cannot be separated in Luther's thought from his new understanding of the church. Ecclesiological considerations are not just secondary applications of new soteriological insights; rather, they form the scaffolding inside of which these insights are able fully to mature. The faithful soul can neither be separated from, nor given the priority over, the faithful people. The real significance of Luther's insight into the importance of the Word (as expressed, for example, in this passage) can only be grasped when one sees how Luther, on the ecclesiological level, has redefined the *fideles* in terms of faith insted of *caritas*, i.e. how Luther has replaced the *"caritas*-ecclesiology" of the medieval exegetes with his *"fides*-ecclesiology."

7. *Ecclesia* and *Caritas*

Because of this redefinition of the *fideles* in terms of *fides*, utterances by Luther on the relation between church and *caritas* in the *Dictata* are quite scarce.[196] In light of the importance that *caritas* holds

---

nondum est, quod futura est triumphans, sed est signum, figura, absconditum et omnino fidele testimonium sui ipsius. Quia in enygmate est, quod futura est in specie: in signo est, quod futura est in re: in absconso est, quod futura est in manifesto: in fide est, quod futura est in visione: in testimonio est, quod futura est in exhibitione: in promisso est, quod futura est in impletione."

[196] Not only in relation to the church, however. Cf. the statement of Schwarz (p.

for the medieval exegetes, however, it is not surprising to find a few such references in the *Dictata*, especially since Luther made definite use of these earlier commentaries and regarded himself, at the time of his first course on the Psalms, as standing in the long line of exegetes of this important biblical book.

At one point in the *Dictata*, Luther even makes the traditional distinction between the *boni* and the *mali* on the basis of *caritas* after he speaks of the faithful people being given the sign of faith.[197] There are additional statements which have the traditional ring of *caritas* as the mark of the *fideles*. "*Caritas* with all virtues and spiritual knowledge" make up the ornaments with which the people of Christ are adorned.[198] The sufferings of the *fideles* are not sterile like the sufferings of those "who are outside," because the latter are outside of faith and its fullness which is *caritas*.[199] *Caritas* is the "fullness and spirit of faith and spiritual righteousness" which will remain in eternity and not be eliminated as faith will be.[200] And finally, God is spiritually united to our spirit through faith and *caritas*.[201]

Although the precise nature of Luther's understanding of *caritas* in the above statements cannot be determined, it functions in a way similar to that used by the medieval exegetes, i.e. as an accessory to *fides* required for becoming a true *fidelis*. We recall, however, that *caritas* has a second function for these exegetes (and especially Augustine): to ensure the unity of the church among all the *fideles*

211): "Einleitend muß festgestellt werden, daß der caritas-Begriff in der ersten Psalmen-Vorlesung von dem fides-Begriff in den Hintergrund gedrängt wird."

[197] *WA* 3, 336.29ff. (*Gl.* to Ps. 59 : 6): "Sensus: dedisti eis fidem, in qua signantur, et charitatem, quae distinguit inter bonos et malos, ut liberentur dilecti tui, scil. tantum, quia alii non liberantur a peccatis et vanitate quia signum fidei non acceptant, quod est signum spiritus, q.d. iam non liberas omnes in confuso, sicut olim bonos et malos."

[198] *WA* 4, 233.34ff. (*Sch.* to Ps. 109 : 3).

[199] *WA* 4, 385.21ff. (*Sch.* to Ps. 118 : 164): "Non enim steriles sunt nostre passiones et mortificationes, sicut eorum qui sunt foris. . . . Quia sunt extra fidem et plenitudinem eius, que est charitas."

[200] *WA* 4, 353.29ff. (*Sch.* to Ps. 118 : 98-100): "Quia 1. Cor. 13. fides evacuabitur, charitas autem, que est plenitudo et spiritus fidei et iustitia spiritualis, manet ineternum et non excidit unquam." Cf. *WA* 3, 522.4f. (*Sch.* to Ps. 75 : 5-6). Ozment (p. 117, n. 1) implies that the understanding of *caritas* as eternal may be regarded as traditional, while Schwarz (p. 213) maintains that this quality of *caritas* is the only aspect which for Luther gives it a kind of precedence over *fides*. Schwarz emphasizes, however, that Luther sees the three theological virtues as a unity and that *caritas*, no longer thought of in terms of a form-bestowing *habitus*, is absorbed to a certain degree into the understanding of faith, in that Luther can speak of the one *opus dei* in terms of grace and all three virtues (pp. 126f., 211f.). It is in this light that we should read Luther's references to *caritas* in the *Dictata*.

[201] *WA* 4, 8.9ff. (*Sch.* to Ps. 84 : 7).

and not just the *boni* or true *fideles*. To remain in unity with the church is to remain in *caritas*. Here *caritas* is directed horizontally toward one's fellow Christians with whom one should remain in the unity of the church, regardless whether they are all true *fideles* or not. As the defining mark of the true *fideles*, however, *caritas* directs itself vertically toward God, because through it the *fidelis anima* and the *fidelis populus* are joined with God. This vertical direction is not altered when *caritas* is regarded as part of a form-bestowing *habitus* infused from above.

Although Luther rejects this vertically-directed *caritas* as the mark of the true *fideles*, there is evidence in the *Dictata* that he retains the horizontal dimension of *caritas* as the mark of unity among the *fideles*. Luther maintains, for example, that for the faithful to "embrace Sion" is for them to adhere to the church in *caritas*.[202] And the church is called a living stone because of the unity of *caritas*.[203]

Augustine makes a similar statement in regard to the *fideles* as living stones joined to one another through *caritas*.[204] But for Augustine this statement has twofold significance. It not only reflects the unifying power of *caritas*, but, because the *fideles* are for him unambiguously the *boni* or true *fideles*, it also embraces his understanding of *caritas* as the definitive mark of these *fideles*. For Luther, on the other hand, only the unifying function of *caritas* is important. Other passages make this clear. The difficult verse 13 of Psalm 67 ("Rex virtutum, dilecti dilecti") gives Luther the opportunity to discuss the function of *caritas* in the church. In the *scholion* to this verse, Luther exegetes as follows: "Christ is the king of all powers in the church, of all *fideles* mutually loving one another and of the whole church which is his house."[205] In his next two attempts to understand this verse, he also emphasizes the mutual love of the *fideles* for one another. The verse

---

[202] *WA* 3, 269.24f. (*Gl.* to Ps. 47 : 13): " 'Circumdate Sion' i.e. congregamini et multiplicamini ad Ecclesiam 'et complectimini eam' charitate ei adherete."

[203] *WA* 3, 132.38 (*Gl.* to Ps. 20 : 4): "Vocatur autem Ecclesia vivus lapis in singulari propter unitatem Charitatis." On the basis of this passage, among others, Schwarz (p. 226) refers to the horizontally-directed *caritas*: "So wird die ecclesia zu der Gemeinschaft derer, die sich gegenseitig lieben, die in der Einheit der Liebe wie des Glaubens und der Hoffnung einmütig zusammenstehen."

[204] Cf. *supra*, Ch. I, n. 51.

[205] *WA* 3, 394.12ff.: "Et est sensus: Christus est rex omnium potestatum in Ecclesia, omnium fidelium sese mutuo diligentium et totius Ecclesie, que est domus eius." The strange formulation, "dilecti, dilecti," is the result of an incorrect translation in the Septuagint. For further discussion of the text and Luther's treatment of it, cf. S. Raeder, *Das Hebräische bei Luther* (Tübingen, 1961), pp. 26 and 282-283.

commends mutual *caritas*.[206] And what applies to all the *fideles* applies to the Apostles and authorities in the church as well. Luther writes in the *glossa* to verse 28 of the same psalm:

> Therefore the "princes" of faith, hope and *caritas* are all the Apostles and *rectores* of the church. For through faith we confess God here, through hope we live in heaven, through *caritas* we are made open for all men.[207]

Faith directs us to God while *caritas* points us horizontally in the direction of our fellowmen. It is this horizontally-directed *caritas* which Luther retains from the exegetical tradition's understanding of the *fideles*, although he emphatically rejects the vertically-directed *caritas* in favor of *fides*.[208] This horizontally-directed *caritas* does not force the true *fideles* to remain in a particular external community as the vertically-directed *caritas* would have done. According to the traditional function of the *caritas* of unity, love for the brethren would certainly prohibit one from breaking the unity of the church as long as the decisive *fides* could be nourished. Nevertheless, for Luther, *fides* and its nourishment through the Word take priority. They constitute the heart of Luther's new understanding of the *ecclesia fidelium*.

---

[206] *Ibid.*, 23ff.: "Secundo ad expressionem successionis fidelium in dilectione ... Tercio ad commendandam charitatem mutuam. Quia in Ecclesia Christi non solum sunt diligentes, quia scilicet inimicos etiam diligunt, qui sunt eorum dilecti, sed etiam rursum alter alterum diligit, ac sunt mutuo dilecti dilecti. ..." Cf. the *glossa* to the same verse: *WA* 3, 386.27f.: " 'Dilecti dilecti' i.e. quorum unusquisque alter alterius est dilectus, quia regnum regis Christi est in charitate et mutua suorum dilectione." Heckel (*Lex charitatis*, p. 29, n. 135) quotes this latter passage to show that already in the *Dictata* the *lex spiritualis* (= *lex caritatis*) is valid for the kingdom of Christ. The *lex caritatis* as the basis of Luther's understanding of ecclesiastical law supports the horizontally-directed function of *caritas*. This comes to expression later, e.g. in Luther's *Tractatus de libertate christiana* (1520) where the Christian is said to live in Christ through faith and in the neighbor through *caritas* (*WA* 7, 69.12ff.). Even more explicitly in Luther's *Deuteronomion Mosi cum annotationibus* of 1525 (*WA* 14, 714.12ff.; cited by Heckel, *Lex charitatis*, p. 126, n. 1019), where the *lex fidei* (relating to God) is set over against the *lex caritatis* (relating to the neighbor).

[207] *WA* 3, 389.32ff.: "Ideo principes fidei, spei, charitatis sunt omnes Apostoli et rectores Ecclesie. Per fidem enim Deum hic confitemur, per spem in celo habitamus, per charitatem ad omnes dilatamur." Cf. *WA* 3, 388.28: "... 'principes' Apostoli 'coniuncti' per charitatem et animo, ..." And in regard to the bishops, *WA* 3, 395.12ff.: "Quia reges exercituum sunt Apostoli et sequaces eorum Episcopi: quorum cuilibet suus est exercitus et populus distributus, illi mutuo federati sunt charitate gemina."

[208] This is the significance of *caritas* when it appears together with *fides* in Luther's characterization of the true *fideles*. Cf. *supra*, n. 49.

CHAPTER VI

ECCLESIA MILITANS ET TRIUMPHANS

1. *Ecclesia Militans: Testimonium Triumphantis*

Luther's new *fides*-ecclesiology manifests itself distinctly in the way he views the relationship between the *ecclesia militans* and the *ecclesia triumphans* in the *Dictata*. This is to be expected on the basis of the importance that *caritas* assumes for the medieval exegetes as the link between the two states of the church.[1] *Caritas* functions both as the definitive mark of the true *fideles* in the militant church and as the inexhaustible possession of these *fideles* which accompanies them into the triumphant church. This double function of *caritas* fits naturally into the larger picture which the medieval exegetes have of the militant church as the image of the church triumphant. That which is decisive for membership in the latter—*caritas*—is also definitive for the true *fideles* in the former. The understanding of that which is essential for one influences the definition of the other.

If Luther, however, rejects *caritas* as the definitive mark of the true *fideles*, how can he then establish the necessary continuity between the two states of the church, especially when he admits, in accordance with I Cor. 13, that faith will be cut off and only *caritas* abide into eternity?[2] Or, in other words, by what means can Luther have his true *fideles* conveyed from the militant church to the church triumphant? Faith, apparently, cannot be the link between the two states of the church, since those eternal goods which the faithful will have *in re* in the triumphant church are present to them now only *in fide*. For the medieval exegetes on the other hand, *caritas* is the *res* which is present as such (*in re*) in both states of the church. For them, there exists fundamental continuity through this *caritas* in spite of the inherent difference between life in the militant church *in spe* and life in the church triumphant *in re*. Luther, it appears, is left hanging with his *fideles* in the militant church *in fide et spe* without any possibility of transferring them to the church triumphant *in re*. *Caritas* cannot bridge the gap for him.

[1] Cf. our discussion, *supra*, pp. 83ff.
[2] Cf. *supra*, Ch. V, n. 200.

216

The problem cannot simply be dismissed by maintaining that Luther ignored the distinction between the two states of the church. He makes use of the traditional terminology on a number of occasions. The militant church is the "house of wandering" over against the "church of the blessed" which is the "house of abiding."[3] The lights of glory and grace apply in the traditional sense to the *fideles* in the triumphant and militant churches respectively.[4] Moreover, Luther employs suitable biblical words to express the relationship between the two states of the church. The most familiar of these is *atrium* ("court"), which is used to designate the militant church as the state preparatory for entry into the triumphant church. The courts of the Lord are the individual congregations of the church, and the church is the vestibule of heaven.[5] Or, as Luther phrases it elsewhere, "the churches of this time make up the vestibule of the future house in the heavens."[6] The word *atrium* accurately reflects both the relationship of the synagogue to the church and that of the militant church to the church triumphant.[7]

Luther makes this threefold comparison in reference to the inferior character of the militant church over against its heavenly successor.[8] The same inferiority comes to expression when Luther refers to the synagogue as the shadow (*umbra*) of the present church and, in turn, to the shadow-character of the latter in contrast to the heavenly church. In this case, faith is mentioned in parallel with the present

---

[3] *WA* 4, 287.22f. (*Gl.* to Ps. 118 : 54): "... 'in loco peregrinationis meae,' in Ecclesia militante, que est domus peregrinationis, Ecclesia autem Beatorum domus permansionis."

[4] *WA* 3, 313.11ff. (*Gl.* to Ps. 55 : 14): "... 'ut placeam' solus ego et per me alii omnes 'coram deo in lumine' eterne glorie, immo et gratie 'viventium' fidelium in Ecclesia triumphante et militante." Cf. *WA* 3, 475.5 (*Gl.* to Ps. 72 : 20); *WA* 3, 180.4f. (*Gl.* to Ps. 32 : 14).

[5] *WA* 4, 107.20ff. (*Gl.* to Ps. 95 : 8-9): "... 'et introite' per fidem et crucem 'in atria eius' singulas Ecclesias, in unitatem Ecclesiarum: 'adorate' latria 'dominum' Christum 'in atrio sancto eius' Ecclesia, que est vestibulum coeli, ..."

[6] *WA* 3, 643.21ff. (*Sch.* to Ps. 83 : 3): "Igitur Qui vere concupiscit, deficit et languet anima eius ad Ecclesias Christi. 'Atria' autem dicit, quia Ecclesie huius temporis sunt vestibulum future domus in coelis." Cf. *WA* 3, 370.3ff. (*Gl.* to Ps. 64 : 5): " 'in atriis tuis' i.e. Ecclesiis militantibus, que sunt atria Ecclesie triumphantis."

[7] *WA* 4, 425.24f. (*Gl.* to Ps. 133 : 1): "Quia 'atria' sunt synagoge ad domum Ecclesie, ut supra ps. 121 dictum. Vel si stet hoc verbum, Ecclesia quoque est atria ad futuram Ecclesiam in gloria." For the reference to Psalm 121, cf. *WA* 4, 398.15f. This threefold comparison is not new. Burgos made the same comparison in much more detail (cf. *supra*, Ch. II, n. 18).

[8] *WA* 3, 242.16f. (*Sch.* to Ps. 41 : 7): "Quia sicut Synagoga est modicus mons ad Ecclesiam, ita Ecclesia huius temporis et militans minor est Ecclesia triumphante."

217

church as better than its shadow in the time of the synagogue—the letter. At the same time, the inability of this faith to make the transition to the triumphant church is evident, since such faith is only the shadow of that clear vision to come.[9]

In addition to these apparently harmless comparisons, there are passages in which a different chord is struck—passages which imply that Luther, almost haphazardly, may be upholding the discontinuity between the two states of the church without building the bridge of *caritas* between them. At the beginning of the *scholia* to Psalm 83 Luther writes:

> This psalm speaks about the church of Christ, to which the people—or rather the prophet on the people's behalf—and human nature aspire. But because whoever is in the church of Christ is through hope already in heavenly glory and the eternal house, the words of the psalm can be applied simultaneously to both. . . . It is clear that the psalm speaks to a greater degree about the militant church, because it speaks of "tabernacles" and "courts," which in their proper sense signify the church of this age. This church is the court of the heavenly Jerusalem and the tabernacle in which we are hidden through faith; and all things are not yet revealed.[10]

The phrase which immediately catches our eye is Luther's assertion that the man who is in the church is through hope already in heavenly glory and the eternal house. We have seen how the tradition distinguishes between existence in hope in the militant church and existence *in re* in the triumphant church. For the medieval exegetes, the former existence *in spe* is an inferior state which by no means leads naturally to life *in re* in the triumphant church.[11] In this text, however, Luther makes the astounding statement that through hope (*per spem*) the *fidelis* is already in the triumphant church. Not only

---

[9] *WA* 3, 608.26ff. (*Sch.* to Ps. 79 : 11): "Mystice autem Umbram vocat istum populum, quia erat figura futuri veri populi. Et Ecclesia quoque est umbra future Ecclesie, sicut litera fuit umbra fidei, nam fides est enygma et umbra future visionis." Cf. *WA* 3, 157.1f. (*Gl.* to Ps. 37 : 2): ". . . 'adorate dominum in atrio sancto eius' Ecclesia, que est atrium celestis templi et fides speciei."

[10] *WA* 3, 642.22ff.: "Psalmus iste de Ecclesia Christi loquitur, ad quam suspirat populus vel potius propheta pro populo et humana natura. Veruntamen quia qui in Ecclesia Christi est, iam per spem est in celesti gloria et eterna domo: ideo mixtim secundum utrunque possunt verba accipi . . . Quod autem de Ecclesia magis militante loquatur, patet, quia nominat 'tabernacula' et 'atria': que proprio sensu adhuc huius temporis Ecclesiam significant, que est atrium coelestis Ierusalem et tabernaculum, in quo per fidem abscondimur, et nondum omnia revelata . . ."

[11] Cf. *supra*, p. 76. Even in order to be genuine hope, it requires *caritas* and merits (*supra*, Ch. II, n. 32).

is hope characteristic for existence in the militant church, but through this hope the *fidelis* is already in the church triumphant. Hope, surprisingly, functions as the link between the two states of the church.[12] Luther's accentuation of the positive function of hope stands in direct opposition to its essentially negative quality in the exegetical tradition. In the tradition, the uncertain character of the present life in hope requires the presence of some *res*—namely, *caritas*—in order to assure the pilgrim in the militant church of his eventual transference into eternal *res*—the eternal *caritas* of the triumphant church. Luther by no means denies the incompatibility between the existence of the faithful now *in spe* and their life to come *in re*.[13] Nevertheless, he can make the most positive assertions about this present life in hope in the militant church. For example, now we are saved in hope; we will be saved *in re* in the time of clear vision.[14] The context for this assertion is the vision of God present now only in faith but later in complete clarity.[15] On the basis of this parallel between "seeing God" and "being saved," the conclusion is unavoidable that Luther is speaking of the same genuine and certain salvation already present through hope which will be evident *in re* in the church triumphant. Just as God is no less God although we can apprehend him now only in Christ through faith, so is salvation no less salvation although it is present now in hope and not *in re*. Here, hope is

---

[12] Cf. *WA* 3, 641.4ff. (*Gl.* to Ps. 83 : 5): " 'Beati' fideles omnes 'qui habitant' per fixam spem vel per eternam mansionem, non peregrini et advene sunt Agareni, 'in domo tua' Ecclesia triumphante vel militante." The word order in this text seems to imply that the phrase "through fixed hope" applies to the triumphant church and "through eternal abiding" to the militant church. From the point of view of content, however, both phrases appear to apply to both states of the church, so that the fixed hope of the militant church leads to the triumphant church, just as abiding in the militant church leads to "eternal abiding" in the triumphant church. In any case, hope functions as the connection between the two states. Müller ("Ekklesiologie und Kirchenkritik . . . ," p. 105, n. 31) affirms correctly in connection with the text in note 10: "Die Hoffnung ist es, die jetzt die irdische Kirche mit der himmlischen verbindet." But Müller fails to see the radical nature of this statement by Luther and otherwise confuses traditional and "new" statements by Luther on the relationship between the two states of the church (*ibid.*, pp. 104-105).

[13] *WA* 4, 259.2f. (*Gl.* to Ps. 113 : 11): ". . . quia tota vita fidelium est tantummodo in spe et nondum in re."

[14] *WA* 3, 604.16f. (*Gl.* to Ps. 79 : 4): ". . . 'et' sic 'salvi erimus' hic in spe, tunc in re."

[15] Cf. the marginal gloss, *ibid.*, 33ff.: "Ostendit autem faciem dupliciter: primo in fide. Et sic Christum ut hominem videre est posteriora seu dorsum eius videre. Ut deum autem, est faciem eius videre. Secundo in clara visione. Et ita nunc salvi sumus in spe, tunc autem in re."

executing a positive function—expressing the presence of salvation which is not yet apparent. It is not implying that salvation in the present is uncertain or in some way not really salvation. Luther combines this positive emphasis on hope with the definitive *fides* of the true *fideles* in the following way:

> The promises of God gladden the heart of those who believe and hope in them. Therefore, in the meantime we rejoice in the faith and hope of future things, which God has promised to us. We rejoice precisely because we are certain that he does not lie, but will do what he has promised, and will take away from us every evil of body and soul and confer every good—and this without ceasing. For who would not rejoice, if he is certain that his body will put on glory and immortality, clarity and virtue, etc.? Moreover, he is certain if he believes; it is enough that he expects, because that which one expects will, without a doubt, come to pass.[16]

Faith as well as hope functions in this passage as the link between the two states of the church, between life in the militant church and glory and immortality in the triumphant church. That peculiar property of the true *fideles*—that expectation[17] which embraces firm faith and hope in the promises of God—ascertains the future fulfillment *in re* of God's promises. For Luther, no present *res* is necessary for the *fideles* to get a head start on the fulfillment of the promises of eternal goods. The fulfillment depends in exact degree only upon their expectation of this fulfillment, i.e. their faith and hope in the promises. Insofar as they believe and hope, the eternal *res* are already theirs and the *fideles* already have what the triumphant church can offer them.[18]

---

[16] *WA* 4, 360.6ff. (*Sch.* to Ps. 118 : 111): "Promissa enim dei cor letificant eorum, qui credunt et sperant in ipsa. Igitur interim exultamus in fide et spe futurorum, que nobis promisit deus: ideo autem exultamus, quia certi sumus, quod non mentitur, sed faciet quod promisit, et auferet a nobis omne malum corporis et anime, conferet autem omne bonum et hoc sine fine. Quis enim non exultet, si certus est, quod induetur corpus eius gloria et immortalitate, claritate et virtute etc.? Certus autem est, si credit: tantum est, ut expectet [corr. *WA* 55], quia sine dubio fiet, quod expectat." On the basis of this passage and its continuation, Schwarz writes of the intimate relationship between faith and hope for Luther (p. 240): "Die fides schöpft aus dem Worte die Gewißheit der zukünftigen Herrlichkeit. In der spes muß aber zu dieser Gewißheit noch die affektive Erwartung der verheißenen und geglaubten Zukunft hinzukommen."
[17] Cf. *supra*, Ch. V, n. 46.
[18] Ozment (p. 121) expresses the character of this life *in fide et spe* in anthropological terms as a "substantiating" form of having and arrival already in this life: "The 'place' where the faithful live is not yet present *in re*, only *in fide* and *spe*. This is the case not only because of the nature of faith and hope, but also because of the nature of that for which they hope. Thus, one awaits what he can neither create nor

Now we are in a better position to understand why Luther says, in the description of the faithful people discussed above,[19] that this people asks only for the present church and its goods, not the future church and its goods. The *fidelis* who has the "words" through faith already has all things, that is, the eternal *res* hidden in these words. These words are the goods of the militant church, and when one has these words through faith in the church militant, he already possesses the eternal *res* of the church triumphant. The faithful do not have to concern themselves with how they will reach the church triumphant and its goods. No downpayment of the actual *res* in the form of *caritas* is required in order to be assured of their delivery in the triumphant church. Merely the expectation of the promises of God in faith and hope guarantees one a place in the church triumphant.[20] Luther has therefore established continuity between the two states of the church through faith and hope without denying the discontinuity between *spes* and *res*. Paradoxical though it may sound, the *fidelis* is already certain of all the eternal *res* of the triumphant church without the possession of any *res* here in the militant church. Faith and hope in the promises of God—apart from the present *res* of *caritas*—form the bridge to the eternal *res* of the triumphant church.

As a result, the triumphant church loses importance for Luther. The

possess in this life, and yet he awaits it as one whose very waiting is a 'substantiating' form of having. He journeys to a destination which he can neither comprehend nor attain in this life, and yet he journeys as one whose very journeying is a 'substantiating' form of arrival." Cf. Schwarz (p. 158): "Durch den Glauben sind uns im Wort die unsichtbaren Dinge in verborgener Weise präsent, so daß wir durch die testimonia futurorum im Glauben die futura gewissermaßen als substantia futurorum besitzen." We find these formulations more satisfying than Vercruysse's remark on the presence of all *res* now through faith: "Auch hier sehen wir, wie die Betonung nicht auf dem Gegenstand liegt, sondern auf der Weise dieses Besitzens" (p. 192). Although Vercruysse does maintain the reality of the possession of eternal *res* for Luther (p. 193, n. 31 against Brandenburg), the *res* and their presence must not be lost sight of in emphasizing the mode of their possession *in fide*. If it were only a matter of how the *res* are possessed, then Luther would hardly neglect the triumphant church as he does, where the *res* are to be had *in re*. But the fact that their very possession in the triumphant church is already certain here through faith and hope in the Word makes the triumphant church less fascinating for him.

[19] Cf. *supra*, Ch. V, n. 192.

[20] This agrees fully with Luther's surprising interpretation in the large Galatians commentary of the heavenly Jerusalem as the militant church, and not as the triumphant church (*WA* 40/I, 662.25-31). Its conversation in heaven does not pertain to a particular place, but to the fact that a Christian believes (noted by Headley, p. 39). This also clarifies the underlying reason for Steudle's more systematically oriented statement (p. 124): "Luther unterscheidet kaum zwischen dem, was als Reich Gottes die Gestalt der Zukunft ist und dem, was er unter Kirche versteht."

possession of its eternal goods is certain in the militant church through faith and hope. Here, in our opinion, is to be found the reason for the striking lack of attention that Luther pays to the anagogical sense of Scripture in the *Dictata*. This has often been noted, of course, but primarily in connection with Luther's concentration upon the tropological sense.[21] We would maintain that for Luther the anagogical as a separate sense is made superfluous not only through the appropriation of *futura* by the individual *fidelis* through the *fides Christi* in the tropological sense. The possession of eternal *res* through faith and hope in the present church also leads to a pre-emption of anagogy by the allegorical sense—a pre-emption manifested in Luther's striking neglect of the triumphant church. This does not mean that the anagogical sense is absent. Rather, it is transposed and received into both the tropological and allegorical senses in such a way that it decisively influences Luther's understanding of the life in faith and hope of the *fidelis anima* and of the *fidelis populus*.

Luther's picture of the triumphant church does not control his view of the militant church. No congruity through *caritas* is necessary because of the positive function of faith and hope, which link the *fideles* with their eternal goods. Such an anticipation of the uniqueness of the triumphant church and its goods already in the militant church would account for the surprising statement by Luther early in the *Dictata* that the church is always (*semper*) militant *and* triumphant in this life.[22] Only if the eternal goods of the triumphant church are present for the *fideles* in the militant church in some way—and they are through faith and hope in the words of God—could Luther say that the church is triumphant in this life. And only on the basis of this anticipation can Luther say in the *glossae* to Psalm 14 that *fides* is that which makes one worthy to abide in the triumphant church as well as the militant church—thus replacing *caritas* as the nexus.[23]

[21] Cf., e.g., Gerhard Ebeling, "Die Anfänge ...," p. 227.
[22] WA 55/I, 72.23f. (*Gl.* to Ps. 9 : 13): "... Quia semper Ecclesia est militans et triumphans in hac vita."
[23] WA 55/I, 108.1ff.: "Quis sit dignus in Ecclesia Christi tam militante quam triumphante morari.... 'Domine quis habitabit' alii: 'peregrinabitur' 'in tabernaculo tuo' in Ecclesia presenti, que est 'tabernaculum': 'aut quis requiescet' beatus 'in monte sancto tuo' in gloria futura. 'Qui ingreditur' 'ad obediendum fidei' Ro. 1. 'sine macula' quod sine fide est impossible, quia 'fide purificans corda eorum,' Act. 15." Gerhard Ebeling ("Luthers Auslegung des 14. (15.) Psalms in der ersten Psalmenvorlesung im Vergleich mit der exegetischen Tradition," *ZThK* 50 [1953], pp. 318-319) demonstrates that faith here for Luther cannot be the *fides formata*, especially when one compares Luther's

Although Luther in effect collapses the triumphant church into the militant church by asserting the sufficiency of faith and hope in God's promises, the problem remains that faith and hope themselves are not eternal and cease to exist with one's life in the church militant. Luther does not deny, of course, the future existence of life *in re* in the triumphant church where those eternal *res* will be apparent which are now possessed with certainty, though hiddenly, in faith and hope. What is it, then, that actually makes the transition from the earthly to the heavenly church? Luther does not fail to provide us with an answer:

> The new testament is eternal, because it works eternal salvation and redemption. Just as the righteousness of faith is eternal, though faith itself is not eternal, but the righteousness which faith gives; so the testament of Christ is not eternal, but rather salvation and redemption and remission which his testament bestows.[24]

It is the *res* themselves—righteousness and redemption and remission—which for Luther are eternal and bridge the gap between the two states of the church. True, they are not possessed by the *fideles* in the militant church as earthly *res*, i.e. they are not visible entities which the faithful can tangibly grasp in this life. Here they are had only hiddenly in faith and hope. But when faith and hope pass away, the faithful will by no means lose their certain claim on these *res*, but will make the transition into the church triumphant where this righteousness and salvation will be apparent, where they will be had for what they are—*res in re*. The link between the two states of the church does not come from the side of the faithful; it is not their possession of a part of these eternal *res* in the form of *caritas*. The faithful remain without any earthly, present form of these *res*; they have only faith and hope. But even when these pass away, the eternal

---

interpretation and organization of the psalm with that of Perez. Although we would not have chosen Ebeling's formulation of Luther's understanding of faith ("Änderung des Existenzgrundes"), he does point out that, since the individual is made acceptable on the basis of faith, there is no mention here of merit as in the tradition, and thus the distinction between the militant and triumphant churches no longer serves any purpose for Luther or, what amounts to the same, the distinction between *gratificatio* and *beatificatio* (Ebeling, p. 322). This collapsing of the triumphant into the militant church is only clear, however, when one fully comprehends how Luther's *fides*-ecclesiology is functioning at the basis.

[24] *WA* 4, 246.18ff. (*Sch.* to Ps. 110 : 9): "Testamentum novum eternum est, quia eternam salutem et redemptionem operatur. Sicut iustitia fidei est eterna, cum tamen fides non sit eterna, sed iustitia, quam dat fides: ita testamentum Christi non est eternum, sed salus et redemptio et remissio, quam dat testamentum eius."

res which have remained above and beyond the *fideles* pick them up from the outside, as it were, and lift them into the triumphant church. Thus we can speak of faith and hope only in a limited sense as links between the two states of the church. In the militant church, they do tie the faithful with the eternal goods of the triumphant church and promise them these goods with certainty. In this sense, the eternal *res* of righteousness and salvation are already in the militant church and the faithful have them, as Luther says, through faith and hope in the words—not as earthly *res*. But faith and hope will pass away, while the eternal goods themselves will keep their hold on the faithful and assure their conveyance into the church triumphant. The bond between the two churches which survives the end of life in the militant church is no longer in the *fideles*—the *res* of *caritas*—but outside of them in the very *res* to which they are linked by faith and hope as long as they are in the militant church.

Consequently, Luther can speak of that as eternal which functions as the conveyer of eternal *res* to the faithful in the militant church—the Word of Christ:

> Wherefore to establish [one's] place is to choose something fixed upon which man can rely in faith and hope, i.e. not upon anything temporal, which cannot be established and always fluctuates, but in something eternal, namely the Word of Christ which abides in eternity, ...[25]

The words of Christ are the goods of the militant church, because through faith and hope in them the eternal *res* are given to the faithful. From man's side faith and hope will disappear, but, like the eternal *res* themselves which are outside of and beyond the faithful in this life and abide into eternity, the Word of Christ through which these are conveyed will also remain eternally. It is more accurate to say the Word functions as the nexus between the two states of the church, since faith and hope in this Word will pass away.[26]

Luther cannot, therefore, speak of the militant church as an image of the triumphant church as the medieval commentators were able to do. On the one hand, he takes the discontinuity between the two states

---

[25] *WA* 3, 651.19ff. (*Sch.* to Ps. 83 : 7): "Quare Locum ponere est eligere fixum, in quo homo fide et spe nitatur, id est in nullum temporale, quod poni non potest, sed semper fluit, sed in eternum, scilicet verbum Christi: quod manet ineternum, ..."

[26] It is not entirely illegitimate to speak of faith as the link, however. Luther depicts faith as the "eternal testament": *WA* 4, 193.20ff. (*Gl.* to Ps. 104 : 10): "Fides enim est eternum testamentum, i.e. eternorum, quia dat eterna bona, Hebr. xi, non temporalia sicut testamentum legis." In other words, faith is as good as eternal, because it bestows the eternal goods.

of the church too seriously—the radical discontinuity between life in the one *in spe* and life in the other *in re*. The word "image" implies an inherent similarity in the internal life and structure of the two states of the church and an inherent continuity between them. The medieval exegetes found this inherent similarity and continuity in the *res* of *caritas* possessed by the *fideles*. The possession of such a *res* on earth—even if only a concrete downpayment of eternal *res*—is clearly untenable for Luther. His *fideles* have the eternal *res* in the militant church not as *res*, but only in faith and hope.

On the other hand, because the faithful already have the eternal *res* of the triumphant church as hidden through the Word of Christ in faith and hope, Luther in effect collapses the triumphant church into the militant church (*semper militans et triumphans*) to such a degree that the triumphant church—its form and structure—holds no particular fascination for him. The faithful in the militant church are already certain of its goods; they must concentrate only on their life in the militant church—expecting the fulfillment of the promises of God in faith and hope. From this angle, the militant and triumphant churches are too closely identified for one to function as the image of the other.

Since the link between the two states of the church is not something inherent or interior in the faithful themselves, but comes to them from outside and beyond them, Luther describes the militant church as a *testimonium*, and not as an image, of the triumphant church. This description of the relationship between the two churches does justice both to the discontinuity between life *in fide et spe* and life *in re*[27] and to the function of the eternal *res* (and to the Word of Christ) as the "external" link between the two states of the church. The militant church testifies to the future, eternal *res* of the *fideles* in the triumphant church;[28] it is not a static image of that future church which already possesses part of these *res* in *caritas*. Like the faith and hope which are its definitive marks, it is not a *res* but only a testimony, a sign, of that which it will be *in re* as the triumphant church.[29] The militant church is not yet a city, but a part and a

---

[27] *WA* 4, 402.19f.: "Testimonium enim sepe dictum est, quod ad differentiam rei dicitur, sicut signum ad signatum."

[28] Cf. *supra*, Ch. V, n. 134.

[29] *WA* 4, 402.27ff. (cf. *supra*, Ch. V, n. 195). Luther does speak in this passage of the militant church as *figura* of the church triumphant; but it is clear that he does not mean *figura* in the sense of *imago* where a structural similarity is implied (cf. *infra*, n. 37), but in the sense of *absconditus*, a hidden witness to the fulfillment *in re* of the triumphant church.

225

testimonium of what that future city will be.[30] It cannot exhibit its goods as present, but only give witness to those future goods which are promised to it.[31]

The following diagrams illustrate the respective conceptions of the relationship between the two states of the church by the medieval exegetical tradition and by Luther:

TRADITION   LUTHER

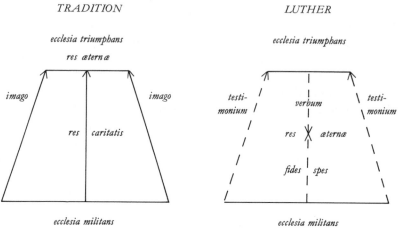

The solid lines in the diagram of the traditional conception emphasize the continuity between the two states of the church both in terms of the image relation and in terms of the direct link through the *res* of *caritas.* Here the eternal *res* remain in the triumphant church although they are joined to the militant church by the downpayment of *caritas.*

In the diagram of Luther's conception, the dotted lines represent the radical discontinuity he sees between the two states of the church as represented in the *testimonium* relation and in the "*res*-less" links of faith and hope in the Word. At the same time, the eternal *res* themselves are situated between the two states of the church in order to indicate their function as a link between the two churches. The convergence of *verbum, fides* and *spes* upon these eternal *res* illustrates Luther's affirmation that he who has faith and hope in the

---

[30] *WA* 4, 402.38ff.: "Ita Ecclesia paratur modo, quia edificatur ut civitas. Et nondum quidem est civitas, sed pars et testimonium, quod sit futura civitas."

[31] *WA* 4, 403.3ff.: "Secundo, ut dixi, etiam est Ecclesia testimonium et non reale quid, quia non exhibet se talem, qualia promissa sunt in ea et de ea, sed solum testimonium dat. Quia futura sunt eius bona, que non potest in presentia exhibere, presentia autem bona ignorat: ergo ipsa remanet testimonium incredulis et credulis, sed incredulis in testimonium et scandalum, credulis autem in testimonium et surrectionem. Per eam enim deus testatur toti mundo futura bona."

Word already has the eternal *res* with certainty, though hiddenly, in the militant church.

Thus, Luther's *fides*-ecclesiology had led him to see a relationship between the two states of the church fundamentally different from that of the medieval exegetes. This difference is not a trivial one—not just a peripheral conclusion drawn on the edge of his new understanding of the *fideles*. It has a direct effect upon his understanding of hierarchical offices in the church—i.e. upon his understanding of church and order. Luther gives his most eloquent expression to the church as *testimonium* in the *scholion* to Psalm 121 : 4. We recall, however, that it is precisely in his *Additiones* to Lyra at Psalm 121 : 4-5 where Paul of Burgos expands upon his understanding of Jerusalem as the image of the church militant and of the latter as the image of the triumphant church.[32] Leaving aside for a moment the role of the earthly Jerusalem in Burgos' threeway comparison, we recall that his interpretation of "testimony" in the Psalm text is made precisely on the basis of the image-relationship: the *fideles* in the militant church, who ascend through grades of virtues to offer the confession of praise, form an image of the perfect worship of the elect in heaven. When he comes to verse 5 ("Because the seats sit there in judgment"), Burgos compares the judicial role of the Pope in the militant church with the role of Christ and his cojudges at the last judgment. The implication is clear: the judicial role and authority of the Pope in the militant church is the image of Christ's judicial role at the last judgment. Christ as judge belongs to the triumphant church, while the Pope executes this function in the militant church.

Luther's understanding of the militant church as a testimony to the church triumphant leads him to quite a different view of the relation between the respective judicial roles of Christ and the ecclesiastical hierarchy. The testimony-relationship between the two states of the church enables Luther to regard Christ as present in the militant church along with the eternal *res*, even if only through faith and hearing. At the end of the *scholion* to verse 4 ("to confess your name"), Luther affirms the inability of the present church to "confess" God as present in himself; rather, it can confess only his name. This is in accord with the radical discontinuity between the militant state of the church *in fide et spe* and the triumphant state *in re*. In the militant church we know only the name of God from hearing through

---

[32] Cf. *supra*, pp. 80ff.

227

faith.[33] This is the same affirmation which he makes concerning Christ in the *scholion* to Psalm 84. Now he is revealed to us through faith and hearing. Only "then," i.e. in the triumphant church, will we see Christ face to face *in re*.[34] It is obvious that Christ (or God) belongs to those eternal *res* which the *fideles* in the militant church have in faith and hope through hearing and not yet as *res* (*in re*), i.e. Christ in himself face to face.[35] The distinction between the states of the church is upheld in regard to the form of the presence of Christ in each state.

The eternal *res* are present, however, already hiddenly in the militant church because he who has the words through faith has all things. Therefore, Christ himself is present in the militant church, and for Luther in a very special way as he comes to verse 5 of Psalm 121. Luther writes exuberantly:

> This is a most exquisite verse, beautifully expressing the propriety of the militant church, if only I might be able to express it adequately in the following. But be at work, O Lord, in us and we will dare to attempt it. This is another difference between the militant and triumphant churches: the seats in the former are manifest (that is, the powers and pre-eminent positions of the bishops, priests, etc.), but the occupier [of the seats], Christ himself, is not apparent and is hidden through faith and in faith. Nevertheless, he sits in them and is present, more than that eminently present, because they are his seats. Therefore, he himself through his personal presence does not preside over his people bodily, but rather his vicars, the priests; for these sit and rule and reign in the people bodily, as is obvious. But lest they appear to be lords to themselves and [the seat or rule] their own exclusive possession, [the prophet] humiliates them and calls them "seats" and not "sitters," as if he were to say: "Though you

[33] *WA* 4, 403.14ff.: "Iterum exprimitur conditio militantis Ecclesie, que nunc nondum confitetur deo presenti, sed nomini eius. Erit autem, cum id quod per nomen significatum tenemus, videbimus et confitebimur. Interim autem dum ex parte cognoscimus, nomen eius, sed non rem nominis cognoscimus. ... Denique nomen ex auditu cognoscitur, sed ipse per visionem. Auditus autem fidem, visio speciem habet." Cf. *WA* 4, 368.8ff. (*Sch.* to Ps. 118 : 132): "Diligunt enim nomen domini et hoc solo vivunt contenti. Quod proprie pertinet ad Ecclesiam militantem: nam hec nondum rem, speciem, substantiam dei videt, sed tantum nomen eius audit et ex auditu in fide diligit, ubi vani homines vel suum nomen, immo speciem et rem suam diligunt."

[34] *WA* 4, 8.31ff. (*Sch.* to Ps. 84 : 8): "Quia loquitur de primo adventu et prima ostensione Christi domini. Nunc enim ostenditur nobis per fidem, tunc autem per speciem. Ideo hic per auditum, ibi per claram visionem: fides enim ex auditu est. Et ita Christum esse dominum ex auditu tantum habemus in fide. Sed tunc idem habebimus per speciem in re."

[35] Luther sets Christ in direct parallel with those eternal, spiritual, invisible and future goods which are known through faith. *WA* 4, 338.19ff. (*Sch.* to Ps. 118 : 66): " 'Sapientia' donum spiritus sancti est simpliciter ex fide Christum et eterna cognoscere et spiritualia, quecunque sunt credenda de futuris et invisibilibus."

sit and reign and rule and preside, nevertheless you are not 'sitters', kings, princes or presidents of this people, but vicars and seats, in which the true king, 'sitter', prince and president sits. In the future, however, when Christ will have emptied every dominion and power [I Cor. 15 : 24] and he himself will sit alone as king in eternity, you will not be seats so that you sit, but you will be seats so that you stand, and Christ alone will sit. Now, however, on account of faith, while you are seats, you have your own seats, the peoples over whom you rule on behalf of and in place of the Lord; he himself, though, sits in you. But when he will occupy your seat, you will give way and yourselves be one with the people who are now seats for you on account of Christ who sits in you and subjects them to you."[36]

In contrast to Burgos, the import of this passage is clear. Christ is not relegated as judge to the last judgment or to the triumphant church. He is present in the militant church in faith and especially present in the members of the hierarchy: he "sits" in the priests and bishops. They are his seats. Christ is eminently and immediately present (*presentissimus*) in the hierarchical offices of the church as the "judge behind the judges." This affirmation of the presence of Christ is only possible on the basis of an understanding of the militant church as *testimonium*, where the eternal *res* are present in faith and hope, and not on the basis of an image-relationship between the two states of the church where the function of the hierarchy in the militant church only reflects that of Christ, who is himself restricted to the last judgment and the triumphant church.

In this same *scholion*, Luther admonishes the subject peoples to obedience to their superiors in the hierarchy precisely because of the

---

[36] *WA* 4, 403.29ff.: "Pulcherrimus versus et pulcherrime exprimens proprietatem Ecclesie militantis, si possem consequi explanando. Sed age, dominus in nobis et audeamus tentare. Hec utique est differentia etiam alia a predictis Ecclesie militantis a triumphante, quod sedes sunt in ipsa et manifeste sunt (id est potestates et principatus Episcopatuum, sacerdocii etc.), sed sessor ipse Christus non apparet estque absconditus per fidem et in fide, et tamen in ipsis sedet et presens est, immo presentissimus, cum sint isti sedes eius. Idcirco ipse per se non preest Ecclesie et populo suo corporaliter, sed vicarii eius, sacerdotes: hii enim sedent et principantur et regnant in populo corporaliter, ut patet. Sed ne domini sibi esse videantur, et tanquam propria eorum sit possessio, humiliat eos et appellat 'sedes' et non 'sessores': q.d. Liceat vos sedeatis, regnetis, principemini, presitis, non tamen vos estis sessores, reges, principes, presides huius populi, sed vicarii et sedes, in quibus sedet ipse verus rex, sessor, princeps, preses. In futuro autem, cum evacuaverit omnem principatum et potestatem et sedebit solus rex ineternum, vos non eritis sedes, ut sedeatis, sed eritis sedes, ut stetis, et ille sedebit solus. Nunc autem propter fidem vos cum sitis sedes, habetis et vos sedes, scilicet populos subditos, in quibus pro et loco domini sedetis: ipse autem in vobis. Sed cum ipse sedem vestram intrabit, vos dabitis locum et eritis ipsi quoque una sedes cum iis, qui sunt nunc sedes vobis propter eum, qui sedet in vobis et subiecit eos vobis."

presence of Christ in them. This is the way it should be in the militant church—a hierarchy of rulers and subjects—although it will be otherwise in the triumphant church.[37] In the *Dictata* at least, the hidden presence of Christ supports the hierarchical structure of the militant church and does not yet appear overtly to shake its foundations.

Precisely this understanding of the militant church as *testimonium* and precisely this verse 5 of Psalm 121, however, will become the basis of one of Luther's most important arguments against the divine right of the papacy in the Leipzig Disputation (1519) against Eck. In this disputation Eck follows the traditional reasoning which we have observed in Thomas, Burgos and Cajetan.[38] In fact, Eck bases his argument for the monarchical position of the Pope in the church by divine right upon the witness of "Scripture and history" that the militant church is instituted in the image of the triumphant church, where God is the only head at the top of the hierarchy.[39] He promptly

---

[37] *WA* 4, 404.28ff.: "Istis itaque dictis inspice Ecclesiam, et videbis eam ita sine dubio dispositam in ordinibus secundum sub et supra, sicut iste versus descripsit. Ecclesiam inquam militantem. Secus erit de triumphante. Nunc vide, ut exprimat aliud pulchrum insigne pacifici regis. Quia sedere est pacificum esse et quietum. Idcirco non est sedes regis pacis, nisi sit quietus et pacificus in conscientia. Sed et subditi debent id prestare prelatis suis, ut cum pace in eis sedeant, quod ipsi Christo suo sessori prestant. Alioquin quomodo sedebunt sedes et non potius omnia tumultuarie et temere ferentur? Hoc autem fiet, si pure et humiliter obediant et subiaceant eis. Quod ut faciant, cogitent et fide inspiciant magis sessorem Christum quam sedem ipsam. Nam si sunt sedes, certe erit sessor ibi, neque vacabit sedes ista, licet non videatur qui sedet. Quare timeamus, revereamur, humiliemur coram sedibus istis sicut coram Christo." Note that the image-relationship between the two states of the church does not function for Luther. A hierarchical order belongs to the militant church, but not on the basis of a similar hierarchy in the triumphant church as in the medieval tradition following Dionysius (cf. *supra*, pp. 80ff.). The hierarchy receives its validity from the hidden presence of Christ who must operate through visible vicars—in other words, on the basis of the church as *testimonium* to eternal *res* (Christ) present in faith. We note in this context that the presence of Christ (*praesentissimus*) has direct ecclesiological consequences and is not only significant—via the tropological application—for the justification and spirituality of the individual Christian. Wicks emphasizes the latter so exclusively in his work that he can present Luther as an introverted monk gazing at the navel of his own spirituality (*Man Yearning for Grace*, pp. 4-5, 276; cf. his remarks on Vercruysse, p. x).

[38] Cf. *supra*, Ch. II, n. 20.

[39] We cite from the text of the Leipzig Disputation edited by Otto Seitz (*Der authentische Text der Leipziger Disputation 1519* [Berlin, 1903], pp. 56f.): "Monarchia et unus principatus in ecclesia dei est de iure divino et a Christo institutus. Quare textus sacrae scripturae vel historiae approbatae ei non adversantur, quoniam ecclesia illa militans, quae est velut unum corpus iuxta divi Pauli sententiam, est instituta et facta ad imaginem ecclesiae triumphantis: in qua est una monarchia omnibus per ordinem dispositis, usque ad unum caput, scilicet deum."

supports his argument by reference to Dionysius who, we have seen, was the common authority.[40] Eck proceeds then from the common medieval understanding of the relationship between the two churches as an image-relationship in order to prove the necessity of the Pope as absolute monarch in the militant church by divine right.[41]

Luther, however, is unusually well prepared to counter this argument precisely on the basis of his exegesis of Psalm 121 in the *Dictata*, and he does not fail to make use of it! In his first reply, Luther asserts that the monarchy of the militant church does not consist of one man, but of Christ himself.[42] Then, realizing that he must show how this can be the case in the *militant* church, Luther continues:

> In such a way, namely, that Christ the head of the church through faith will transfer us, who are his kingdom, to sight. ... Wherefore, those are absolutely not to be heeded who force Christ outside the church militant into the triumphant church, although the church militant is a kingdom of faith—which means that we do not see our head and nevertheless we have him, according to Psalm 122 [Vulgate: Ps. 121 : 5]: "There the seats sit in judgment upon the house of David." There are many seats, namely, in which the one Christs sits. We see the seats, but not the "sitter" or the king.[43]

[40] Seitz, p. 57: "Quae omnia latissime confirmare possum maxime per sacram illam animam beatum Dionysium Areopagitam, libro de ecclesiastica hierarchia, ubi ait: Nostra enim hierarchia a deo traditis ordinibus sancte disposita, sanctis et caelestibus hierarchiis conformis est."

[41] Seitz, p. 57: "Quia reverendus pater [Luther] dicit nihil ad se pertinere de contrario illius, quod intendebam probare, de iure divino esse monarchiam in ecclesia militante: sicut et triumphante; ... Si ecclesia militans non fuit sine monarchia, vellem audire, quis esse iste monarcha alius aut unquam fuisset, nisi Romanus pontifex, aut quae alia prima sedes, nisi sedes Petri et eius successorum, ..."

[42] Seitz, p. 58: "Monarchiam ecclesiae militantis prorsus confiteor eiusque caput non hominem sed Christum ipsum. ..."

[43] Seitz, pp. 58f.: "Ita videlicet, quod Christus caput ecclesiae per fidem transferet nos, qui regnum eius sumus, ad speciem. ... Quare prorsus audiendi non sunt, qui Christum extra ecclesiam militantem trudunt in triumphantem, cum sit regnum fidei. Hoc est: quod caput nostrum non videmus et tamen habemus. Juxta illud Psalmi 122: Illic sederunt sedes in iudicio super domum David. Multae scilicet sedes, in quibus unus sedet Christus. Sedes videmus, non sessorem vel regem." As in the *Dictata*, Luther does not dispute the presence of some kind of hierarchical structure in the church; but he sees correctly that the argument concerns the top of the hierarchy and in this way counters Eck's use of Dionysius: Seitz, p. 59: "Tertia, 'quae et Dionysii,' nihil contra nos. Non enim negamus hierarchiam ecclesiasticam, sed de capite disputamus monarchiae, non hierarchiae." Eck later reaffirms his use of the image-relationship and seeks to defend himself against the charge of excluding Christ from the militant church, but the lines are already drawn (Seitz, p. 63): "Et velut Christus caput est in caelo, ita summus pontifex caput est in militante ecclesia, neutiquam Christum excludendo, cuius se fatetur vicarium." Cf. Luther's letter to Leo X (*Epistola Lutheriana ad Leonem Decimum summum pontificem* 1520; *WA* 7, 48.11ff.).

It is inconceivable that Luther does not have his exposition of Psalm 121 in the *Dictata* in mind here. It is the militant church as *testimonium* which functions as the background of these statements, which in turn are identical in content with the *scholion* to Psalm 121 : 5. Christ is present in the militant church through faith and, though hidden, he is no less present there than in the triumphant church. Luther now sees clearly the danger of the image-relationship: it confines Christ to the triumphant church. Rather, Christ is the real "sitter" in the judicial chairs of the militant church and only he can be called the monarch, the absolute head, of the militant church. After all, Christ sits on the pontifical throne, too.[44]

Thus we see the critical (and "practical") importance of Luther's perception of the militant church as *testimonium*, and not as image, of the triumphant church. This understanding follows naturally from his emphasis on faith as the definitive mark of the true *fideles*, through which all the eternal goods of the triumphant church —including Christ—are present to them in the militant church. This fundamentally new ecclesiological understanding, already completely worked out in 1515, becomes the basis for one of his most important arguments against papal supremacy in 1519. Certainly, events subsequent to 1515 have led him to employ this new ecclesiology specifically against the Pope. But the "*fides*- and *testimonium*-ecclesiology," with its potential of undermining the authority of the hierarchy and the teaching office in the church, exists fully formulated in 1515. Hence, it is impossible to defend the thesis that Luther fabricated a new ecclesiology after 1517 for the purpose of attacking the Pope.

---

[44] In the *scholion* to Psalm 100 : 6, Luther refers to Psalm 121 : 5 and says that those bishops are *fideles* who sit with Christ in his seats, emphasizing again the presence of Christ in the militant church. Luther maintains, however, that there are unfaithful bishops who sit "outside of and against" Christ and are idols. Not only does the presence of Christ in the "seats" of the militant church preclude the divine right of the Pope, but already in the *Dictata* it draws the line between faithful and unfaithful bishops, thus leaving the way open for questioning their judicial authority. These unfaithful bishops are already to some extent antichrists (*contra eum* in the text: WA 4, 138.15ff.): "Sicut rex habet commensales in epulis suis, qui cum eo sedent, et hii sunt consiliarii, principes, iudices eius etc.: ita in Ecclesia habet Christus Episcopos, pontifices, rectores Ecclesiarum, qui sedent super sedes in iudicio super domum David. Unde usque hodie Episcopatus dicuntur sedes Episcopales. Et unus Episcopatus in multas sedes distribuitur. Ergo fideles sunt Episcopi Christi, qui cum eo sedent, licet multi nunc extra eum et contra eum sedeant in sua tantum sede, idola scilicet et non Episcopi. Item Doctores etc."

2. Semper Incipere

It is important to round out our investigation in this chapter by taking a closer look at the life of the true *fideles* in the militant church under the "*semper*-aspect," as we did in the case of our medieval exegetes. For these exegetes, the *semper*-designation indicates the necessity for the faithful in the present church to increase constantly in virtue and *caritas* in order to fortify that bridge over which they pass into the triumphant church.[45] Luther frequently employs this adverb to describe the life of the faithful in the militant church. If his definition of the true *fideles* has changed fundamentally in comparison with that of his predecessors, however, it is to be expected that the content of the *semper* is also basically different from that of the medieval exegetes. And if his understanding of the relationship between the two states of the church has consequently been altered, a corresponding readjustment in the *semper* of the life of the faithful is called for.

It is only natural that Luther should give some evidence of the traditional *semper* in the *Dictata*, just as remnants of the *caritas*-ecclesiology are lodged there. To ask for mercy "for those knowing" is allegorically and tropologically to wish always more and more for the perfection of grace for the imperfect.[46] There are infinite grades of progress between the beginning of sanctity and its perfection, and God abounds with his gifts at each particular stage. The faithful in each stage experience these gifts differently, according to which there are many mansions in the house of the Father.[47] The beginning of the Christian life is to know and love those things that are of faith, and yet one must continually advance and build up a "body of merits" so that one does not slip backwards.[48] The common theme of these

---

[45] Cf. *supra*, pp. 88ff.

[46] *WA* 3, 200.38ff. (*Gl.* to Ps. 35 : 11): "Allegorice autem et tropologice est imperfectis semper magis ac magis ad perfectionem gratie optare."

[47] *WA* 3, 512.24ff. (*Sch.* to Ps. 74 : 4): "Nam cum ab inchoatione sanctitatis usque ad perfectionem sint infiniti gradus [quia sapientie eius non est numerus: et semper de claritate in claritatem, de virtute in virtutem, ex fide in fidem eundum]: in singulis gradibus deus suis donis abundat, et aliud experitur qui est in secundo, quam qui in primo et sic deinceps: secundum quod multe sunt mansiones in domo patris Christi." The last phrase, we believe, refers to the different grades of perfection possible also in the triumphant church—a traditional conception (cf. *supra*, p. 87).

[48] *WA* 3, 337.27ff. (*Gl.* to Ps. 59 : 9): "Quia initium vitae Christianae est nosse et amare ea, quae sunt fidei, i.e. Galaad et Manasse. Secundo proficere, hoc autem est virtutis et fortitudinis, ideo Ephraim est fortitudo capitis, i.e. inceptionis seu principii vitae talis, quia nisi quis continue proficiat et corpus meritorum faciat, cito inceptio et caput deficiet."

passages is the traditional emphasis upon constant progress in the state of grace. The *fideles* accumulate merits like extra baggage so that they will have enough to last them for the journey into the triumphant church.

In certain passages where Luther speaks of the faithful people and the faithful soul in parallel, however, a different note is sounded. The church and the holy soul are both a "rising dawn" because they always stand as if at daybreak and assume the posture of rising. They never think that they have reached their goal or become perfect, but they forget those things which are behind and always begin anew, reaching out ahead of themselves.[49] Constant advancing becomes a constant beginning. What is this beginning? Not the repeated infusion of *caritas* but the beginning of faith, which is the moral interpretation of "morning" in the Psalm text. It is this faith which kills and scatters all evil desires from the heart and conscience.[50] And this faith in turn is none other than the *viva fides*, which, as we have seen, defines the true *fideles* in the church—a fact which Luther has just made clear in the same *scholion*.[51] For the true *fideles* to live in faith is for them to live as if they are ever at the beginning of their Christian existence, constantly appropriating this faith and fighting the evil within them through this faith.

For Luther, then, constant ascent is only progress in the sense that one loses no ground, that one is always beginning. This implies first that one is always asking anew for that which one does not yet have: in particular, not only for an increase of grace, but also for the Gospel through which the decisive faith is nourished.[52] Ecclesiologically, it means assuming the stance of continually entering the church. At the beginning of the important *scholia* to Psalm 121, Luther extolls the faith of the faithful synagogue and sets it up as the model for life in

---

[49] *WA* 4, 139.34ff. (*Sch.* to Ps. 100 : 8): "Ideo semper vigilare, semper in ortu esse, semper matutinum habere oportet, semper propositum innovare. Unde Ecclesia et anima sancta laudatur, quod sit 'aurora consurgens.' Semper enim in aurora est et semper consurgit, nunquam se perfecisse aut pervenisse aut apprehendisse arbitratur, sed obliviscens, que post se sunt, semper incipit et extendit seipsam."

[50] *Ibid.*, 31ff.: "Matutinum morale est initium fidei, oriens quodcunque propositum bonum in anima. Et hoc disperdit et occidit omnes malos motus, vicia, suggestiones, cogitationes de corde et conscientia."

[51] Cf. *supra*, Ch. V, n. 177.

[52] *WA* 4, 344.12ff. (*Sch.* to Ps. 118 : 76): "Quia et proficientes semper sunt incipientes ad ea que nondum habent, tam in gratia quam sapientia, ut amplius abundent tam intellectu quam affectu. Quia hic nihil nisi evangelium et gratia petitur semper."

the militant church.[53] He then makes clear that this life is a constant entry and exit, a constant standing in expectation because, as we know, the militant church is not yet built up as a city, but is still being edified.[54] It is as if one is always entering the church anew, entering anew upon the life of faith. Faith and expectation make life in the militant church a constant advancing and standing in anticipation, not a sedentary existence as enjoyed by the blessed in glory. As a result, the building up of the church is accomplished through the Word and the Gospel.[55] Why? Because this expectation in faith can only be nourished, and must constantly be renourished, through the Word.

This posture of the true *fideles*—constantly on the threshold of life in faith and the church—differs considerably from that described by our medieval commentators. There, the *fideles* are entrenched at the heart of the church as long as they are in a state of grace—possessing and increasing the necessary *caritas*. They occasionally sin and lose this *caritas* and must begin again through the sacrament of penance, but there is no constant beginning (*semper incipere*), only an unflagging ascent in the state of grace except for those times when they drop out of this state.

For Luther, the *fideles* are accompanied by assiduous groans of repentance as well. Such is a natural concomitant of their life in the militant church. In the *scholion* to Psalm 83 : 4—a psalm which is crucial for the medieval commentators' affirmation of the progress in virtue[56] —Luther attempts to discover the significance of the kinds of birds mentioned there: the sparrow and the turtle-dove. It is apparent that the text treats the militant church.[57] And further, when the sparrow finds a house for itself and the turtle-dove a nest, this signifies that faithful souls already have tabernacles in which they might abide,

[53] *WA* 4, 399.20ff. Cf. *infra*, Ch. VII, nn. 141, 142.
[54] *WA* 4, 400.6ff.: "Semper intramus et quo intravimus, semper eximus ad id, quod nondum intravimus, de claritate in claritatem, de virtute in virtutem. Ii autem, qui sibi iam apprehendisse videntur, non stant in atriis, sed in medio sedent Ierusalem: quod est impossibile. Quia nondum edificata est, et si aliquibus, non tamen mihi vel tibi (id est qui nondum pervenerunt ad terminum) edificata est, sed edificatur adhuc assidue." Cf. *supra*, n. 30.
[55] *WA* 4, 400.15ff.: "Ergo de militante Ecclesia loquitur. In qua omnes qui sunt, in stando et proficiendo sunt, non in sedendo et possidendo, ut beati in gloria. Edificatio autem ista fit per verbum et Evangelium."
[56] Cf. *supra*, Ch. II, *passim*.
[57] *WA* 3, 644.11f.: "Ecclesia seu populus fidelis Turtur est, ut in Canticis: . . . Et sic patet, quod de militante Ecclesia loquitur."

i.e. in the militant church.[58] Luther proceeds to draw an important conclusion for the life of the *fideles* in the militant church:

Because the sparrow alone in his abode is a bird of groaning just like the turtle-dove, it is necessary always [*semper*] to be in the groanings of repentance.... Indeed it is necessary simultaneously [*simul*] to praise God and groan because of our sins: to praise because we have been saved, to groan because we have sinned and are surrounded by the evils and dangers of this life. For these are able to be done simultaneously [*simul*], so that we praise and love God and have our delight in him, and nevertheless we scold and hate ourselves and are saddened in ourselves.[59]

The *fideles* in the militant church are busy repenting. As such they are always beginning, always at the outset of their Christian life. But they are simultaneously (*simul*) at the end of this life, too: they are already saved. The *semper* of Luther becomes a *simul* and can no longer be thought of as constant progress in virtue.

This passage presents the soteriological counterpart to Luther's understanding of the relation between the two states of the church. Although the church militant is only a witness to the triumphant church and is constantly being edified, it is nevertheless *simul* the triumphant church insofar as the *fideles* in the militant church already have their salvation, their eternal *res*, through faith and hope in the Word. To that extent the faithful are already in the triumphant church, and yet they must constantly (*semper*) appropriate these goods in faith through asking and expecting. The church is *simul militans et triumphans* for Luther just as the true *fidelis* in the church is *simul penitens et laudans* according to the *scholion* to Psalm 83. The intimate relationship between the faithful people and the faithful soul reveals itself here as it did in the *semper* of the medieval exegetes, but with quite different content.

The necessity for constantly beginning anew and groaning in repentance arises out of the fact that the *fideles* in the militant church sin without ceasing (*semper peccamus*). They always stand in the

[58] *Ibid.*, 19ff.: "Igitur propheta concupiscit et deficit in atria domini et exultat, quia videt, quod passer invenit sibi domum et turtur nidum, id est fideles anime iam habent tabernacula sua, in quibus morientur."

[59] *Ibid.*, 32ff.: "Deinde quia passer solitarius in tecto avis est gemebunda, sicut et turtur, quia in penitentie gemitibus semper esse oportet. ... Simul quidem laudare oportet deum et gemere peccata nostra: laudare quia salvi facti sumus, gemere quia peccavimus et in malis sumus huius vite et periculis. Possunt enim hec simul fieri, ut deum laudemus et amemus et delectemur in eo, et tamen nos vituperemus, odiamus et tristemur in nobis."

middle between sin and righteousness, righteous to be sure, but always needing to be justified anew (*semper iustificandi*).[60] And correspondingly, the *fideles* in the church are always *mali*, never so good that all evil is excluded. Just as the *fidelis* is constantly hovering between sin and righteousness, so he is constantly moving between the poles of evil and goodness.[61] "For since we are always on the way and not yet at our destination, in respect to those things which we do not yet have, we ought always to be, and to regard ourselves, as dead, foolish, erring and evil, and so ask for those things. *For indeed we are truly such.*"[62]

Ecclesiologically, this reflects Luther's new understanding of the two basic groups in the church—the *boni* and the *mali*. The true *fideles* for Luther are not only *boni*, but they are *simul boni et mali*, simultaneously good and evil. They are *mali* because every man is sinner and evil before God. Their faith does not eliminate this evil and sin. But through their faith in the Word of God, they have the eternal *res* of salvation in hope and have become, as a result, *boni* and *iusti*. The false *fideles*, on the other hand, do not have the necessary faith and thus remain totally *mali*. In contrast to this, the medieval exegetes were able to make a clear-cut distinction between the *boni* and the *mali* in the church. Through the *res* of *caritas*, the true *fideles* were no longer *mali* as long as they re-

---

[60] WA 4, 364.9ff. (*Sch.* to Ps. 118 : 122): "Semper ergo peccamus, semper immundi sumus. . . . Quare, ut supra dixi, semper sumus in motu, semper iustificandi, qui iusti sumus. Nam hinc venit, ut omnis iustitia pro presenti instanti sit peccatum ad eam, que in sequenti instanti addenda est. Quia vere dicit B. Bernardus: 'Ubi incipis nolle fieri melior, desinis esse bonus. Quia non est status in via dei: ipsa mora peccatum est.' Quare qui in presenti instanti se iustum confidit et stat, iam iustitiam perdidit, sicut in motu similiter patet: terminus, qui in isto instanti est ad quem, ipse in sequenti instanti est terminus a quo. Terminus autem a quo est peccatum, a quo semper eundum est. Et terminus ad quem est iustitia, quo semper eundum est." We point the reader here to Ozment's discussion of the anthropological and soteriological import of the *semper peccamus* and its culmination in the *simul* (*Homo Spiritualis*, pp. 132ff. and esp. p. 135, n. 8). We, in turn, pursue the ecclesiological implications.

[61] WA 4, 336.10ff. (*Sch.* to Ps. 118 : 65): "Non tantum autem incipientes eum solum bonum habent confiteri, sed et proficientes, qui iam boni ex ipso sunt: non solum ideo quia mali fuerunt, sed etiam, quia mali sunt. Nam cum nullus sit in hac vita perfectus, semper ad eam bonitatem, quam nondum habet, dicitur malus, licet ad eam quam habet, sit bonus. . . . Igitur semper medii sumus inter bonitatem, quam ex deo habemus, et malitiam, quam ex nobis habemus, donec in futuro absorbeantur omnia mala et sit solus deus omnia in omnibus, . . ."

[62] WA 4, 328.23ff. (*Sch.* to Ps. 118 : 40): "Nam cum simus semper in via et nondum in termino, semper ad ea que nondum habemus, velut mortuos, insipientes, errantes, malos esse et estimare debemus, et ea ita petere. *Nam et vere sic sumus*" (italics mine).

mained in the state of grace, while the *mali* outside of this state of grace were truly *mali*. When Luther eliminates the *res* of *caritas* from the true *fideles*, however, they retain their sin and *malum*, and nevertheless through faith and hope become *boni* and *iusti*. With Luther it is no longer possible to speak of the distinction between the true and false *fideles* as that between *boni* and *mali*; rather, one must speak of those who are *simul boni* and *mali* on the one hand, and those who are only *mali* on the other.[63]

Luther's revised understanding of the *semper* of the Christian life is reflected in that other key aspect of his definition of the true *fideles*, namely, as those who live in the spirit. Christ has given the life of the spirit to those who are progressing, and yet to progress is nothing other than always to begin.[64] "To seek" is properly to seek always those interior things of the spirit and in this way to advance from clarity to clarity, from faith to faith, from letter to the spirit.[65] This life never realizes the completion of wisdom, but always the beginning. This wisdom, for Luther, is none other than to ponder invisible and spiritual things and to scorn visible and carnal things.[66] This constant seeking after spiritual goods, constant progress in the life of the spirit, is parallel to the constant seeking of the Word and the Gospel, the constant striving after good and righteousness, i.e. always seeking the spiritual, eternal, future *res* as one who is always beginning.

There is a final *semper* operating in the *Dictata*, however, which is

---

[63] Therefore, the *simul* of Luther's lectures on Romans represents no advance, ecclesiologically understood, over the *Dictata* as Müller contends ("Ekklesiologie und Kirchenkritik ...," p. 114): "Waren nach den Dictata die Sünder 'Gäste in der Kirche,' so sind jetzt die vere fideles zugleich peccatores. Aus dem 'concilium justorum' als der wahren Kirche wird jetzt das 'concilium justificandorum.' " Clearly, the true *fideles* in the *Dictata* are already *iustificandi* (*supra*, n. 60).

[64] *WA* 4, 350.11ff. (*Sch.* to Ps. 118 : 88): "Hec est vita spiritus, quam post litteram occidentem dedit Christus. Et dat assidue omnibus proficientibus non secundum meritum, sed secundum misericordiam, qua pepigit nobiscum fedus, ut daret nobis petentibus gratis ac mendicantibus. Multo magis autem dat incipientibus. Et, ut sepe dictum est, proficere est nihil aliud, nisi semper incipere." Cf. *WA* 4, 316.1ff. (*Sch.* to Ps. 118 : 20): "Nos ergo hoc concupiscamus, ut possimus semper proficere nec ullo tempore pausare aut profecisse: quod et facit qui spiritu vivit."

[65] *WA* 4, 323.17ff. (*Sch.* to Ps. 118 : 33): "... quid sit 'exquirere,' scilicet semper interiora spiritus querere, proficiendo a claritate in claritatem, de fide in fidem, de litera ad spiritum."

[66] *WA* 4, 246.38ff. (*Sch.* to Ps. 110 : 10): "Hec enim vita non finem habet sapientie, sed semper initium, cum sit infinita. Est autem ista sapientia sapere et intelligere invisibilia et spiritualia atque contemnere visibilia et carnalia." This requires also a constant increase in understanding: *WA* 4, 342.10ff. (*Sch.* to Ps. 118 : 73).

also present in the medieval Psalms commentaries—the necessity of always remaining in tribulation.[67] We have noted a twofold function of tribulation in the medieval exegetes: Augustine regards it primarily as the means by which hope is kept alive, while some of his successors see the function of tribulation in polishing up the *sancti* so that they become more holy and shine forth through their merits.[68] In this case, we are able to make a distinction between Augustine and his successors and indicate how Luther gravitates more toward Augustine in his understanding of the function of tribulation.

For Luther, tribulation is necessary because the *fideles* do not yet have their goods *in re*, but only *in fide et spe*. Thus, as we have seen, the *fideles* remain surrounded by the evils of this life and cannot avoid tribulation.[69] The *sancti* apparently have nothing except hope and are therefore despised by men whose *res* are clearly seen.[70] Just as Augustine is led to connect hope and tribulation on the basis of Romans 12 : 12, Luther affirms that it is the witness of Scripture that he who does not undergo tribulation is removed from the hope of salvation.[71] The necessity of tribulation is a logical consequence of the definition of the *fideles* as possessing no *res* in this life.[72]

---

[67] *WA* 4, 88.9ff. (*Sch.* to Ps. 92 : 3-4): "Cum ergo semper sit invocandus deus, ergo semper in tribulatione essendum est. Et si non invenerit nos tribulatio, nos eam invenire debemus scilicet in conscientia et compunctione."

[68] Cf. *supra*, pp. 90ff.

[69] *WA* 4, 147.23ff. (*Sch.* to Ps. 101 : 3): "Quia enim bona nostra nondum in re habemus, sed in fide et spe, ideo necesse est in tribulationibus esse et malis. Si enim hic essent in vita ista, mala non haberemus. Nunc autem ista bona non habemus et illa adhuc speramus. Non restat, nisi ut mala ista habeamus."

[70] *WA* 4, 355.29ff. (*Sch.* to Ps. 118 : 103): "Sancti enim in conspectu hominum nihil habent nisi spem: ideo despiciuntur ab illis, qui habent rem in conspectu hominum. Sed dum sic sperant et spe vivunt coram hominibus, habent perfectam rem coram deo." Cf. *WA* 3, 455.9ff. (*Sch.* to Ps. 70 : 14): " 'Ego autem semper sperabo' etiam scilicet quando mihi mala querunt. Spes enim in tempore prospero facilior est, sed in adverso difficilior. Ideo solus sanctus semper sperat, semper benedicit, sicut Iob."

[71] *WA* 3, 344.31ff.: "Quia est expressa sententia sacre Scripture quod qui extra tribulationem est, extra statum et spem salutis est." Luther then cites his own prooftexts. For Augustine, cf. *supra*, Ch. II, n. 37.

[72] How does one account for the similarity with Augustine then, since he defines his true *fideles* on the basis of the possession of *caritas*? In the following way we think. *Caritas* for Augustine is not yet a *res* which the *fideles* possess in this life in the later medieval sense of infused virtue and the *res sacramenti*. Therefore, he can speak of the life of the true *fideles* as totally *in spe* apart from any *res* and of the necessity of tribulation on this basis. Furthermore, he totally divorces *spes* from *merita* in contrast to his successors (cf. *supra*, Ch. II, n. 45). Because Luther eliminates *caritas* altogether, however, his *fideles*, so to speak, are left hanging in the midst of tribulation in a more

Luther reinforces the necessity of tribulation in a much more explicitly ecclesiological manner. Under the influence of Augustine, he bemoans at length in the *scholia* to Psalm 68 the lack of temptation and tribulation in the church of his day.[73] Going beyond Augustine and the rest of the tradition, however, he makes it clear that those members of the baptized community who undergo no temptation and tribulation are merely *semichristiani*, half-Christians, who pose the greatest threat to the church from within.[74] What Luther has done is to flip the coin and show explicitly that, if the true *fideles* live in faith and hope and of necessity stand in the midst of tribulation, then it is precisely the false *fideles*, the semi-Christians, who are characterized through lack of tribulation, by *accidia* and by false self-assurance.[75] They pose the greatest threat to the church from

radical way than is true even for Augustine (cf. *supra*, Ch. I, n. 65, where Augustine emphasizes the role of *caritas* in persevering and withstanding tribulation). There is a remnant in the *Dictata* of the medieval connection between *spes* and *merita* (*WA* 4, 389.36ff.): "Et nota, quod prius 'mandata' quam 'testimonia' dixit. Quoniam qui non opere prius obedierit mandatis, neque promissa agnoscit aut curat, quia mandata preparant animam ad spem .promissorum, et sine mandatis non fit spes, que merita aliqua prerequirit." This passage is quite incongruent, however, with the multitude of assertions that *spes* is entirely incompatible with any *res* (namely, *caritas* or *merita*). Luther explicitly attacks this medieval connection in the *Operationes* (cf. *WA* 5, 160.22ff. and *WA* 5, 163.31ff.).

[73] *WA* 3, 416.6f.: "Iste psalmus ad literam loquitur de passione domini in persona eius. Sed simul omnes passiones et infirmitates Ecclesie ibidem narrantur." For Augustine to Ps. 68, cf. *supra*, Ch. II, n. 39.

[74] *WA* 3, 416.26ff.: " 'Salvum me fac Domine: quoniam intraverunt aque.' Aque erant passiones Christo irrogate a Iudeis. Aque erant persecutores martyrum a Demonibus Ecclesie immissi. Aque erant Heretici et sunt, ab eisdem eidem immissi. Aque sunt multitudo tepidorum et literalium Christianorum usque hodie ab eisdem immissa Ecclesie. Clamavit olim contra tyrannos et hereticos. Clamat et nunc contra istos semichristianos dicens: 'Intraverunt aque usque ad animam meam' et cetera que sequuntur." Cf. *ibid.*, 417.1f.: "Et tota instantia Diaboli est contra nos, ut sic semichristianos faciat." And 417.32ff. Is one indirect source of the temptation from the *semichristiani* that passage from the *Enarrationes* where Augustine says that tribulation is necessary in order to be Christian? (Cf. *supra*, Ch. II, n. 40). Staupitz quotes this passage in his Tübingen sermons on Job (1498-1500: *Tübinger Predigten*, p. 93). He puts, however, special emphasis upon temptation from within. Of course, Luther had the *Enarrationes* before him, but he was also subject to the personal influence of Staupitz in regard to the importance of tribulation and possibly in regard to that tribulation from false brethren, whom Luther here names semi-Christians.

[75] *WA* 3, 416.17ff. (after discussing persecution in the time of the martyrs and doctors): "Tercia nunc est invalescentia tepidorum et malorum [pax et securitas]. Quia accidia iam regnat adeo, ut ubique sit multus cultus Dei, scilicet literaliter tantum, sine affectu et sine spiritu, et paucissimi ferventes. Et hoc fit totum, quia putamus nos aliquid esse et sufficienter agere: ac sic nihil conamur et nullam violentiam adhibemus et multum facilitamus viam ad coelum, per Indulgentias, per faciles doctrinas, quod unus gemitus satis est."

the inside. In other words, on the basis of his understanding of the true *fideles*, Luther can accurately pinpoint the internal danger to the church in the false *fideles*.

This assessment of the contemporary church has further ecclesiological implications. It is precisely the leaders of the church in whom this evil of self-security flourishes most.[76] Through "easy" doctrines and indulgences the way to heaven is made smooth; no temptation or tribulation is required.[77] The priests and leaders of the church pour out indulgences from the treasure of the church without thinking they have to restock this treasure.[78] This is a prime example of how the devil is attacking the church with the greatest persecution of all, namely, with no persecution, but with security and idleness; for no persecution is total persecution and no adversity is total adversity.[79]

These critical remarks of Luther in the *Dictata* are well-known. What has not been made explicit, however, is the ecclesiological basis of this criticism. The attack on the hierarchy and the indulgence practice is made from a bifocal point of view, that is, with a clear distinction in mind between the true *fideles* and the semi-Christians in the baptized community. First of all, the priests and leaders of the church are put on the side of the semi-Christians because they encourage, and themselves indulge in, this paving of the way to heaven. They cannot be true *fideles* because they do not constantly suffer affliction and tribulation. One of the most severe tribulations of the true *fideles* comes from the false priests and semi-Christians themselves.

Secondly, and more importantly, this distinction tends to loosen even further the ties between the true *fideles* and the contemporary external structure of the church. The true *fideles* need indulgences least of all. They thrive on tribulation and affliction and are not dependent upon the relaxation of satisfaction through indulgences.

---

[76] *WA* 3, 418.2f.: "Maxime pro principibus et sacerdotibus Ecclesie: ubi maxime viget hoc malum."

[77] Cf. *supra*, n. 75.

[78] *WA* 3, 424.17ff.: "Ita Pontifices et sacerdotes profundunt gratias et indulgentias sanguine Christi et martyrum congregatas et nobis relictas, ut non putent sese necesse habere augere illum thezaurum, nec aliter remissionem peccatorum et regnum celorum acquirere, nisi illorum meritis."

[79] *WA* 3, 424.11ff.: "Nulla tentatio omnis tentatio, Nulla persecutio tota persecutio. Sic enim diabolus nunc Ecclesiam impugnat maxima persecutione: quia scilicet nulla persecutione, sed securitate et ocio."

Just as the emphasis upon faith instead of the *res* of *caritas* jars open the gap between the true *fideles* and the sacramental structure of the church, so here the gap is widened when the necessary presence of tribulation makes indulgences superfluous for the true *fideles*. The true *fideles* must always (*semper*) be in the process of repentance and undergoing tribulation because of their sins and the evils of this life from which they are never separated.

On this basis, it is possible for Luther to attack the indulgence practice in 1515 without endangering the life of the true *fideles*. His new definition of these *fideles* leads both to his new interpretation of the *semper*-aspect of their life and to a more radical understanding of the necessity of tribulation for their life. The *fideles* are dependent on the contemporary external structure of the church neither for the nourishment of their faith and hope nor for insurance against tribulation in their life. On the other hand, if the decisive faith can be nourished within a certain external community, sufficient tribulation will be supplied by the false *fideles* within this community. Luther has thus built an independent platform of true *fideles* which can support his new ecclesiology and give him freedom of movement in the external community as the need arises.

CHAPTER VII

ECCLESIA ET SYNAGOGA

More than any other researcher, Joseph Vercruysse has noted the importance of the theme "church and synagogue" for Luther's early ecclesiology.[1] When one takes up the *Dictata* subsequent to reading the medieval Psalms commentaries, one is necessarily impressed with the overwhelming amount of material pertinent to this traditional topic. Such abundance leads one to suspect that this theme contributes substantially to Luther's developing understanding of the church.

Yet, it would be misleading to assume on this basis alone that the relationship between the synagogue and the church is the seedbed of Luther's new ecclesiology. Vercruysse can argue that this theme is the key to Luther's ecclesiology because he has no medieval background material to provide the proper perspective for approaching this topic in the *Dictata*.[2] We maintain, however, that the relationship between the synagogue and the church affords Luther the opportunity of concretely illustrating his new understanding of the true *fideles*, whose origins we have already sketched. This occurs in two traditional directions. First, the synagogue represents for Luther a stance diametrically opposed to that of the true *fideles*. The traditional *altercatio* between the synagogue and the church assists Luther in defining the true *fideles* by way of negation. Secondly, in the direction of the *concordia*, the traditional category of the *synagoga fidelis* and its faith help Luther make more precise the content and the direction of that decisive mark of the true *fideles*, their faith. The relationship between the synagogue and the church exercises a supportive rather than an initiating function in Luther's developing ecclesiology—a function which, for all that, is nevertheless quite significant.

---

[1] *Fidelis Populus*, p. 39: "Das traditionelle Paar 'Synagoge-Kirche' nimmt in diesem Kommentar einen auffallend wichtigen und für Luthers spätere Entwicklung kennzeichnenden Platz ein."

[2] *Ibid.*, p. 70: "Es scheint nicht übertrieben, anzunehmen, daß eines der Hauptmotive in Luthers Ekklesiologie hier liegt und daß dieses Thema den Schlüssel zu einer Reihe anderer ekklesiologischer Fragen bietet."

1. *Altercatio Spiritus et Literae* (*Carnis*)

The traditional *altercatio* between the synagogue and the church is embodied in the *Dictata* in the fundamental division between letter and spirit, or flesh and spirit. It is not the source of this basic hermeneutical division, but one of the ways, indeed the primary way, in which this division is epitomized. Luther writes that the twofold generation of men in the church, carnal men and spiritual men, amounts to the same as speaking of the synagogue and the church.[3] He illustrates this hermeneutical division within the fourfold schema on the back of the title page to the *Dictata* by assigning the allegorical position on the *litera*-side of the division to the synagogue.[4] The church and the synagogue typify the division between the letter (or flesh) and the spirit from the beginning of the *Dictata* on. When Luther wishes to give sharper relief to the character of the church as a spiritual people, he turns to its negative in the literal and carnal people of the synagogue.

In the medieval commentaries, the synagogue functions as a negative of the church, but not on the basis of such fundamental, hermeneutical presuppositions. Luther intensifies the contrast between the two by establishing the opposition between them at the very heart of his developing ecclesiology—in this hermeneutical division. He gives the traditional parallel between the faithful soul and the faithful people both negative and positive content by contrasting the synagogue and "the man according to the flesh" with the church and the "man according to the spirit."[5] The important association for Luther between the spiritual man and the spiritual people achieves sharper profile through their respective opposition to the man of the flesh and the synagogue.

The characterization of the synagogue as carnal is to some extent a natural one. After all, it is the people of God according to the flesh, where "flesh" does not necessarily carry negative connotations. In his

---

[3] *WA* 4, 187.6ff. (*Sch.* to Ps. 103 : 17-18): "... loquens de duplici generatione hominum in Ecclesia, scilicet carnalium et spiritualium, seu, quod in idem vadit, synagoga et Ecclesia, ..."

[4] *WA* 55/I, 4.10ff.

[5] *WA* 4, 49.24ff. (*Sch.* to Ps. 88 : 39ff.): "Quia sicut necesse fuit solvi templum corporis Christi, ut suscitaretur novum: ita et mysticum eius templum, scilicet synagogam, solvi oportuit, ut suscitaretur novum, quod est Ecclesia. ... Similiter et in anima fit, quia destruitur et dissolvitur opus Diaboli, homo secundum carnem, ut edificetur opus dei et homo secundum spiritum."

exposition of *primogenitus* (Psalm 77 : 51), Luther notes that as the flesh naturally comes before the spirit, so the synagogue as a carnal people precedes the church which is a spiritual people.[6] God kills the first-born of the flesh, however (as he did in Egypt according to the Psalm text), so that he might receive another first-born, the spirit. It does not count anymore to be sons of the flesh; legitimacy accrues only to sons of faith and promise. The seemingly harmless description of the synagogue as carnal becomes a matter of life and death, because it must be killed in order to make way for the church.[7] The absolute incompatibility between flesh and spirit prevents them from living peacefully alongside one another and becomes the basis for the gulf between them.

The carnality of the synagogue entails other features which set it in opposition to the church as a spiritual people. The carnal "fathers" of the Jews in Egypt were wise only in regard to present, temporal things; they were not in a position to hope for future, spiritual goods. Therefore, when temporal goods were not forthcoming, they murmured against God and failed to believe in him.[8] The Jews were understanding the promise of the law only in fleshly terms (*carnaliter*); as a result, they estimated men pleasing to God only according to how they were prospering in the flesh, with no concern for the spirit.[9] This is the very opposite stance to that of the spiritual people, we recall, who orient their lives through faith toward future, spiritual and eternal things.

---

[6] *WA* 3, 590.1ff.:

[Primogenitum duplex { caro, ante spiritum: / spiritus: } sic { Synagoga velut carnalis populus cum suis ritibus fuit ante Ecclesiam spiritualem populum. Quia debuit cessare synagoga veniente Ecclesia.]

... Sic itaque deus omne primogenitum occidit, ut susciperet primogenitum aliud offerendum, scilicet spiritum. Caro enim ante spiritum: et prior nativitas carnis in ira, quam nativitas spiritus in gratia. Et per hunc illa tollitur et occiditur. Quia iam non qui filii carnis nascuntur, sed qui filii fidei et promissionis. ..."

[7] Cf. *WA* 4, 80.29f. (*Gl.* to Ps. 91 : 11): "Quia dum caro senescit, spiritus floret. Dum Ecclesia oritur et nascitur, synagoga deficit et moritur."

[8] *WA* 4, 198.35ff. (*Gl.* to Ps. 105 : 7): "Quia cum presentia et temporalia tantummodo saperent, futura vel spiritualia sperare non poterant: ideo absentibus temporalibus semper murmurabant nec crediderunt Deo."

[9] *WA* 4, 92.4ff. (*Sch.* to Ps. 93 : 1): "Quia cum legis promissa non nisi carnaliter intelligerent, atque ea sententia posita mox sequitur, quod eos, qui prospere agunt secundum carnem, deo gratissimos iudicent, et qui infoeliciter agunt secundum carnem, deo odibiles, nullo respectu ad spiritum habito."

The Jews are variously said to be in the "inveterate" letter or in the "killing" letter.[10] This stance renders the synagogue underprivileged in comparison to the church; for the latter hears the Lord himself and the Spirit speak, whereas the synagogue only hears his servant or the letter.[11] The Spirit is with the church alone and was neither with Moses nor with the whole literal synagogue.[12] Even the mercy which is given to "us" in the church is better than that given of old in the law, because it is given to us spiritually according to the soul, but to those literally according to the flesh.[13]

The inferior nature of the mercy given to the synagogue is depicted by Luther as the shadow and figure of true mercy. It is mercy only "corporally," whereas the mercy given spiritually in the church is the fulfillment of the "figurative" mercy exhibited of old.[14] Here the truly negative capacity of the synagogue emerges. It functions precisely as a negative of the church, where that which is light on the positive of the church is still dark, shadowy and figurative on the negative of the synagogue. The synagogue and its ceremonies are rightly denoted "tabernacles" in contrast to the designation of the church and its sacraments as "gates," because "then all things were confined in the hidden and obscuring letter."[15] Indeed, the darkness and shadows of the law were holding the *fides Christi* and the Gospel in check so that they could not be made public.[16] Only the church has the true

---

[10] WA 4, 89.30f. (*Gl.* to Ps. 93 : 4): "Hoc proprie Iudeos exprimit, quoniam ipsi semper iactant antiquum et vetus testamentum in litera inveterata, ..." WA 4, 181.23ff. (*Gl.* to Ps. 103 : 11).

[11] WA 4, 24.27ff. (*Gl.* to Ps. 86 : 6): "Hoc enim privilegium habet Ecclesia pre synagoga, quod non servum seu literam loqui audit, sed dominum et spiritum ipsum."

[12] WA 4, 233.11ff. (*Sch.* to Ps. 109 : 3): "Iste autem spiritus cum Mose non fuit nec cum tota synagoga literali, sed est tecum et cum Ecclesia tua solummodo."

[13] WA 4, 164.18ff. (*Gl.* to Ps. 102 : 11): "... q.d. quantum anima (que est celum) melior est carne (que est terra), tantum prestat misericordia nobis data a misericordia aliis data olim in lege. Quia nobis spiritualiter secundum animam, illis literaliter secundum carnem misertus est."

[14] WA 4, 524.20ff. (*Adn.* at Ps. 137 : 2): "Misericordia, que est primo corporaliter, ut olim in lege, que est umbra et figura misericordie vere, secundo spiritualiter, ut in Ecclesia, quia hec est impletio figuralis misericordie olim exhibite."

[15] WA 4, 23.33ff. (*Gl.* to Ps. 86 : 2): "Recte Synagoge et earum ceremonie [sacramenta] 'tabernacula,' Ecclesie autem et earum sacramenta 'porte' nominantur: quia tunc omnia in abscondito et tegente litera clausa erant. Nunc autem omnia aperta sunt et introitus coeli sunt in Ecclesiis Christi, ibi autem clausure coeli." Cf. WA 4, 25.26ff. (*Sch.* to Ps. 86 : 2): "Quia ideo tabernacula, quod nondum erat revelatus spiritus, sed abscondita omnia sub figura agebantur."

[16] WA 3, 243.22ff. (*Gl.* to Ps. 42 : 3): " 'Emitte lucem tuam' extra et publice per te et discipulos tuos ablata umbra legis, ex utero legis, i.e. Christum, hoc est fidem Christi et evangelium eius, nam legis tenebre et umbre ipsam inclusam tenebant, ..."

intellectus which enables it rightly to understand the law and the prophets.[17]
Of course, some Jews did cease to live in the letter and passed over into the church. The result is a split within the Jewish people corresponding to the fundamental division between the flesh and the spirit. Luther writes on Psalm 100 : 1 ("Mercy and judgment I will sing to you, O Lord"):

> ... just as Romans 3[: 19] says, he speaks first to those who were under the law, i.e. first to the Jews. Mercy, therefore, resounds in their souls and judgment in their flesh; similarly, mercy is echoed in the spiritual people which received faith, and judgment in the unbelieving people. For through mercy and judgment, tropologically understood, a part of the Jewish people was made mercy; the other part, however, which refused mercy, fell into judgment and perdition. And this is reflected throughout the whole psalm. Thus it refers first to the Jews, then to heretics, and generally to all evil Christians literally; tropologically, the psalm is interpreted in reference to the spirit and the flesh.[18]

The acceptance of mercy by a part of the Jews occurs in their reception of faith. Those Jews who believed are taken up into the spiritual people and are transferred to the *spiritus* side of the hermeneutical division. Those who did not believe perished in the letter and the flesh.
The medieval commentators likewise note the split in the Jewish people which resulted from the reception or rejection of faith. Such

---

[17] *WA* 4, 485.29ff. (*Adn.* at Ps. 28 : 3): "Et aliud signum: quod Domino in monte Thabor Moses et Helias apparet, significat, quod in Ecclesia Christi, in qua glorificatur, apparet sensus et intellectus verus legis et prophetarum, Iudeis autem dorsum, ..." Cf. *WA* 55/II, 121.18ff. (*Sch.* to Ps. 15 : 7): "Quia figuralia erant sensibilia et clara quidem, Sed foris synagoga. Ecclesia autem Christi est pre illa clara et excellentius clara; cuius rationem dat, quia intellectum habet et non sensum."
[18] *WA* 4, 133.33ff.: "... sicut Ro. 3 dicitur, iis qui fuerunt in lege, loquitur, de Iudeis primo loquitur. Misericordia ergo in animabus, et iudicium in carnibus eorum. Similiter misericordia in populo spirituali, qui suscepit fidem, et iudicium in populo incredulo cantatur. Sic enim per misericordiam et iudicium tropologice pars Iudaici populi facta est misericordia, altera autem, que misericordiam noluit, cecidit in iudicium et perditionem. Et hoc per totum psalmum describitur. Quare primo de Iudeis, deinde de hereticis, generaliter autem de omnibus malis ad literam Christianis, tropologice autem de spiritu et carne intelligitur." Cf. *WA* 4, 245.16ff. (*Sch.* to Ps. 110 : 7): "Ista sunt opera, id est fabricatio et edificatio Ecclesie, que in veritate, quia non in figura et litera, sed sicut promissa fuit in spiritu edificanda, ita nunc veritas facta est et exhibita. Et non sicut synagoga in carnali edificio edificatur, sed Iudei volentes literam et figuram manere pugnant usque hodie contra hanc veritatem. ... Deinde 'Iudicium' dicitur, quia ista veritas non indifferenter quibuscunque Iudeis, sed nec omnibus Iudeis, sed distincte tantum credentibus ... hic enim fit iudicium, ut maior pars Iudeorum et gentium cadant, quia non credunt. Ideo verissime 'iudicium' est constructio Ecclesie, ubi tam multi separantur et tam pauci assumuntur."

faith is for them, however, only the partition between the baptized community of Christians and the unbelievers who remain outside.[19] The additional mark of *caritas* is necessary in order to become one of the *boni*, the true *fideles* within the baptized community who would persevere until their elevation into the triumphant church. The contrast with the unbelieving synagogue did not help our commentators define this group of true *fideles*.

In Luther's case the split within the synagogue, with the resulting contrast between synagogue and church, exemplifies the division between the true *fideles* on the one hand, and all *infideles* outside the baptized community and false *fideles* inside this community on the other. This is evident from the above passage where the *litera (caro)/ spiritus* hermeneutical division provides the interpretation of the split within the synagogue. It is also clear from the explicit mention of the *mali Christiani*, the false *fideles*, on the same side of the division with the Jews and their successors, the heretics. The spiritual people who receive faith and "become" mercy are none other than the true *fideles*. The unbelieving synagogue functions as the negative, not of the baptized community as it did for the medieval commentators, but of the true *fideles* at the heart of this community. As a result, it assumes much more significance for Luther's ecclesiology than for that of his predecessors.

The carnal Jews are pictured elsewhere as having rejected faith and being interested only in temporal *res*. In the course of his third attempt to interpret Psalm 115 : 10, Luther writes:

> The intention of this psalm is to teach us to expect only spiritual goods in Christ and that promises in the law are to be understood only in reference to the spirit and faith, not in regard to a temporal *res*: against the foolishness of the carnal Jews, who spit out faith and expect the thing itself [*rem*]—the *res* of temporal things, I mean, for faith has an eternal *res*.[20]

The faith which has eternal *res* is none other than that faith of the true *fideles* through which they possess "all things," all the future, eternal, spiritual and invisible *res* of the triumphant church. The carnal Jews, in turn, desire only temporal *res* and, as Luther says elsewhere, have

---

[19] Cf. *supra*, pp. 99ff.

[20] *WA* 4, 271.24ff.: "Intentio psalmi est docere tantum spiritualia bona in Christo expectare, et promissa in lege de spiritu et fide intelligenda esse, non de re temporali: contra insipientiam carnalium Iudeorum, qui fidem respuunt et rem expectant. Rem inquam temporalium, nam fides habet rem eternam."

worshipped God till this day only for the sake of temporal goods.[21] Even the Old Testament people wandering in the desert hoped for temporal goods, whereas we, though likewise led in hope through this desert, set our heart on spiritual things.[22] Thus, the traditional *altercatio* between the synagogue and the church assumes special significance for Luther. The redefinition of this *altercatio* in terms of the fundamental *litera/spiritus* division provides Luther with a clear negative of his true *fideles* and their faith in the unbelieving synagogue and its desire for temporal *res*. This means that a sharper light is also cast upon the successors of the synagogue in the external community of the church — the false *fideles*.

2. Jews, Heretics and *Mali*

By frequently numbering the *mali christiani* along with the heretics among the successors and comrades-in-arms of the Jews, Luther is carrying forth a line of thought present in the medieval commentaries.[23] The multifarious nomenclature employed by Luther to describe the false *fideles* emerges in his exposition of the traditional rubric *inimicus*, which frequently supplied the occasion for exegeting a passage with reference to the enemies of the church. For Luther, the "enemy" is not only the Jewish people,[24] but all tyrants, heretics and "anti-Christians."[25] Literally they are the Jews, but allegorically they are the heretics and the *mali Christiani*.[26] In

---

[21] *WA* 4, 496.6ff. (*Adn.* at Ps. 48 : 20): "'Introibit usque in progenies patrum suorum,' i.e. fiet generatio prava sicut patres eius, ps. 77, qui solum propter bona temporalia Deum coluerunt olim et nunc etiam." Cf. *supra*, nn. 8 and 9.

[22] *WA* 3, 595.2ff. (*Sch.* to Ps. 77 : 53): "Sicut illi in deserto adhuc semper in spe deducebantur, quia nondum adepti fuere terram in re: ita et nos adhuc semper in spe deducimur in hoc deserto. Sed longe differunt spes illorum et nostra, ... Quare illi speraverunt temporalia, nos spiritualia."

[23] Cf. *supra*, pp. 101ff. On the basis of a passage from Ivo of Chartres, U. Mauser comments (*Der junge Luther und die Häresie*, p. 11 and n. 4): "In diesem Satz werden Heiden, Juden, Häretiker und Schismatiker auf eine Linie gestellt, und wir begegnen damit bei Ivo eine Zusammenordnung, die sich in der ganzen mittelalterlichen Tradition häufig findet." W. Maurer also notes the parallel between the three groups in the *Dictata* (*Kirche und Synagoge*, Vol. I, p. 380).

[24] *WA* 55/I, 60.5 (*Gl.* to Ps. 8 : 3): "... 'ut destruas inimicum' Iudaicum populum...."

[25] *WA* 3, 142.19f. (*Gl.* to Ps. 24 : 3): "... 'inimici mei' Iudei, tyranni, heretici, mali i.e. antichristiani: ..." Cf. *ibid.*, 23: "'Confundantur omnes' Iudei, tyranni, heretici, mali antichristiani...." *WA* 3, 145.13 (*Gl.* to Ps. 24 : 19): "'Respice inimicos meos' Iudeos, hereticos, antichristianos, ..."

[26] *WA* 4, 495.9ff. (*Adn.* at Ps. 44 : 6):

"Inimici Christi ⟨ ad literam, Iudei, immo et gentes idolatre, persecutores, tyranni allegorice heretici et mali Christiani."

249

addition, they are denoted by Luther as the *impii* and the *superbi*.[27]

It is impossible here to deal with all the references to the false *fideles* under the manifold names with which they appear in the *Dictata*. One thing is evident, however. Luther recognizes the presence of false *fideles* in the external community of the baptized, regards them as the antitype of the true *fideles* along with the Jews and the heretics, and takes them more seriously than his predecessors. The true *fideles* make up the true church for Luther, and the false *fideles* form a sizable threat to their existence. In fact, the greatest temptation to the church comes from these false *fideles* within.[28] Luther's frequent alignment of the false *fideles*, the heretics and the Jews indicates that he is operating more consciously than his predecessors with the embodiment of the true church in the true *fideles*, despite his numerous warnings against rupturing the external unity of the church.

Just as Luther builds the traditionally negative function of the synagogue into his *litera/spiritus* schema, the successors of the synagogue, the heretics and the evil Christians, find their place in this schema as well.[29] Indeed, the key rubric for these groups, the "enemy," applies for Luther not to him who wishes to harm the flesh, but to him "who seeks to harm the spirit, as were and are all those who wish to separate the church from faith and Christ—the Jews, heretics, flesh, the devil, the world."[30] What does it mean that these enemies seek to

---

[27] *WA* 4, 477.31ff. (*Adn.* at Ps. 9 : 1):

"Hostes eius autem sunt $\left\{ \begin{array}{l} \text{Iudei} \\ \text{tyranni} \\ \text{heretici} \\ \text{impii.} \end{array} \right\}$ Hii semper perierunt et Ecclesia superfuit illis semper." *WA* 3, 375.8f. (*Gl.* to Ps. 65 : 3): "... 'inimici tui' Iudei, heretici, superbi, qui sibi fortes videntur et aliquid."

[28] We recall Luther's comments on the *semichristiani* in the *scholia* to Ps. 68 (cf. *supra*, Ch. VI, n. 74).

[29] Cf. *supra*, n. 18.

[30] *WA* 55/II, 107.1ff. (*Sch.* to Ps. 9 : 4): "'Inimicus' itaque hic non secundum carnem capitur, qui carni et iis, que carnis sunt, nocere studet, Sed omnino, qui spiritu nocere cupit, ut fuerunt et sunt omnes, qui Ecclesiam a fide et Christo separare voluerunt, Iudei, heretici, caro, Demon, mundus." Following upon his affirmation that the tropological sense ("die Lehre vom Glauben") determines Luther's understanding of the church and heresy (cf. *supra*, Ch. V, n. 64), U. Mauser maintains that the common denominator between the Jews, heretics and evil Christians is their rejection of the Cross (p. 63). We maintain, however, that Luther takes over the alignment of these groups with a new emphasis on the evil Christians and builds them into his *litera/spiritus* schema (the importance of which Mauser himself does not deny [p. 59]) as the antitypes of his true *fideles*. This by no means awards primacy to the tropological sense, but represents the independent redeployment of ecclesiological categories within the aforesaid schema.

harm the spirit and live in the letter? For the heretics it means that they imitate the works of the Jews in ignoring the true righteousness of pure faith, establishing their own righteousness and not being subject to the righteousness of God.[31] At first glance, this may appear entirely unrelated to Luther's other main objection to the Jews, namely, that as carnal and literal they live with their eyes on temporal goods alone. But in reality, it is the other extreme from their misguided trust in temporal goods—pride and overconfidence in spiritual goods.

In the *scholion* to Psalm 61 : 3 Luther writes:

> It happens in a twofold manner that someone is not subject to God. First, when he does not obey the law and pays homage to riches and sensual pleasures and all things which are in the world. Secondly, when he trusts in his own righteousness, like the Jews and heretics and all the spiritually proud. And this is more dangerous than the first, since, although they are not caught in those [temporal] evils, nevertheless they are still not subject to God through true humility. And the psalm talks about both: namely, that one should trust in no way whatsoever either in things temporal or in one's own merits—that is, neither in temporal nor in spiritual goods, but through temporal and spiritual goods in God himself alone.[32]

Luther views trust in one's own righteousness and merits as the extreme counterpart of trust in temporal goods, i.e. trusting in spiritual goods themselves instead of in God who gives them, as if one had these spiritual goods through his own merits as his own righteousness. This presumptuous trust in spiritual goods is typical not only of the Jews and heretics but also of the false *fideles*, who appear here as the *superbi*.[33] The pride of the false *fideles* thus sets a limit to the

---

[31] *WA* 3, 154.18ff. (*Sch.* to Ps. 27 : 4): "Et sunt nunc idola seu opera manuum eorum opera illa, que faciunt secundum iustitiam suam, ignorantes iustitiam dei. Et sic erigunt opera sua contra deum et fidem Christi." *WA* 3, 154.32ff.: "Horum studia et idolatriam imitantur omnes heretici. Quia ignorantes veram iustitiam, scilicet pure fidei, suam statuunt sibi in idolum spirituale et iustitie dei non subiiciuntur."

[32] *WA* 3, 355.1ff.: "Dupliciter enim fit, ut quis deo non subiiciatur. Primo, quando legi eius non obedit et potius divitiis sese subiicit et voluptatibus et omnibus, que sunt in mundo. Secundo, quando in propriam iustitiam confidit, ut Iudei et Heretici et superbi spiritualiter. Et hoc periculosius est quam primum, quia cum in malis illis non sunt, tamen adhuc deo non subiiciuntur per veram humilitatem. Et de utrisque loquitur psalmus, scilicet ut nec in temporalibus omnibus, nec in propriis meritis confidendum sit ullo modo: hoc est: neque in temporalibus nec in spiritualibus bonis, sed per bona temporalia et spiritualia in ipsum solum deum."

[33] Cf. *WA* 3, 177.28f. (*Sch.* to Ps. 31 : 6): "Quicquid de Iudeis dicitur ad literam, hoc allegorice percutit Iudeos et omnes superbos Christianos, . . ."

251

description of the true *fideles*, who are grounded through faith in spiritual and eternal goods. Their faith is not trust in the goods themselves as their own possession, but faith in God who grants them and the Word through which they are conveyed.

The false *fideles* are often described as *superbi* in contrast to the true *fideles*. The *superbi* are those who out of spiritual pride justify themselves and wish to be righteous through their own works instead of through the promise and mercy of the merciful God. This applies to the Jews who, proud and obstinate, persecute the faithful people, as well as to all heretics and spiritually proud who imitate the Jews.[34] The Jews, heretics and proud learned men impose their own sense on the testimony of Scripture, but the "simple" and faithful Christians receive humbly the sense of Scripture itself which comes to them from outside, since "every man is a liar."[35] Indeed, the highest praise of Christ and of all Christians is to have perfect as well as "pierced" ears. This forms a perfect contrast to the disobedience of the Jews, which is the highest reproach against them and all heretics, schismatics and headstrong men who imitate them. Right obedience, on the other hand, is that which is paid to the Word of God as it is heard, "because in this consists the entire basis and perfection of the Christian life."[36]

The pride and disobedience manifested by the Jews, heretics and

[34] *WA* 4, 344.24ff. (*Sch.* to Ps. 118 : 78): "Superbos dicit spirituali superbia, ipsos scilicet iustitiarios et sui iustificatores, qui ex operibus iusti esse volunt et non ex promissione et misericordia dei miserentis, sed suorum esse putant meritorum et esse currentis atque volentis, quod iusti sunt. Hiis ergo Iudeis optat, quia utile esset, ut fuissent confusi in sua superbia, agnoscentes quia non possent esse iusti ex se, et ita humiliarentur. ... Sed quia superbi sunt et obstinati, ideo fidelem populum persequuntur. ... Hos imitantur omnes heretici et superbi spiritualiter, ..." Cf. *supra*, Ch. V, n. 31, where the *fideles* and *vere Christiani* are set over against the "authors of their own righteousness," i.e. the Jews, heretics and the proud.

[35] *WA* 4, 318.3ff. (*Sch.* to Ps. 118 : 24): "Et vere nimium est iniquum, ut testimonia domini sic habeantur, ut eis imponatur sensus noster, ut illum velut extraneum suscipiant, meditentur et sapiant, cum nos potius econtra sensum illorum (qui veritas est) nobis extraneum (quia omnis homo mendax est) suscipere, meditari ac sapere debeamus. Illud faciunt Iudei et heretici et scioli superbi: hoc simplices et fideles Christiani, in humilitate incedentes." Cf. *supra*, Ch. V, n. 100, where the recognition that "every man is a liar" is characteristic of the insight of the spiritual man through faith. Also *WA* 3, 578.14ff.

[36] *WA* 3, 228.13ff. (*Sch.* to Ps. 39 : 7): "Quare hec summa laus Christi et omnium Christianorum est habere aures perfectas et perfossas. Sicut econtra summum vituperium Iudeorum est inobedientia: quia per omnes prophetas arguuntur, quod non audiunt vocem domini dei sui: quod usque hodie faciunt. Et imitantur eos omnes heretici, scismatici et proprii sensus homines. ... Opus summe est, ut acuto verbo dei obedientia ei commendetur. Quia in hoc stat tota ratio et perfectio Christiane vite."

false *fideles* are focused on a perverted relationship to the Word. As long as the church in the form of the contemporary baptized community is regarded as the true interpreter of Scripture,[37] no special problem is posed for the true *fideles*. They must remain, as they are, obedient to their prelates while the false *fideles* must be punished for their disobedience. We have seen, however, that the true *fideles* as spiritual men are wiser than many enemies of the church, not only embodied in the Jews and heretics, but also in many prelates, doctors and literal Christians.[38] And we have just seen that true obedience for Luther is obedience to the Word of God as it is heard, which in turn is the perfection of the Christian life. Thus, through his understanding of the disobedience and pride of the Jews, heretics and false *fideles* as disobedience to, and manipulation of, the Word, Luther has given critical significance to the dependence of the true *fideles* on the Word. The perfection of their life consists in obedience to this Word. If the doctors and the prelates of the church stand on the side of the false *fideles* as literal Christians disobedient to the Word, then the true *fideles* are obliged to heed only the Word and not these enemies of the church.

The false *fideles* appear further as *superbi* and *mali* when Luther elaborates upon the unbelief of the Jews and the heretics. The Jews are a depraved generation because they did not believe that God was veracious in word and deed. If they had believed that Christ was trustworthy when he condemned all things of the world and demonstrated spiritual and heavenly things, they would have accepted his words and works and followed him, leaving the world behind. But the Jews did not do this, nor the heretics after them.[39] Likewise all *mali* and *superbi* are a depraved generation because they do not believe with their whole heart; rather they live with a false faith (*ficta*

---

[37] Luther appears not to doubt this in the *Dictata*: cf. *WA* 4, 363.7ff. (*Sch.* to Ps. 118 : 121): "Semper autem heretici veritatem Catholicam calumniantur, similiter et Iudei fidem et Evangelium, et caro nequam proposita bona spiritus."

[38] Cf. *supra*, Ch. V, n. 105.

[39] *WA* 3, 566.4ff. (*Sch.* to Ps. 77 : 8): "Nihil enim ita provocat deum sicut incredulitas. Quia omnis talis arguit deum mendacii. Quia hoc, quod deus verbo et opere testatur, illi dubitant et non credunt, ac sic eum velut falsum et mendacem reputant. Si enim crederent Christum veracem esse in verbo et opere suo, quibus damnavit omnia mundi et ostendit spiritualia et coelestia: utique acciperent eius verba et opera et sequerentur, et mundum relinquerent. Sed nunc vel non credunt, vel si dicunt se credere, facto tamen non credunt. Ideo est vere generatio exasperans et prava, id est irritans et incredula. Hoc autem primum fecerunt Iudei, qui nec suum nec Apostolorum verbum et opus credebant. Postea Heretici similiter."

253

fide), since they are neither mindful of the works of the Lord nor seek his commandments.[40] The evil Christians are said to have that false faith which, we have seen, is the opposite of the genuine, living faith of the true *fideles*.[41]

In this *scholion*, Luther emphasizes that genuine faith is faith in Christ; but this faith is no different from that of the true *fideles* which is directed toward the spiritual and heavenly goods demonstrated by Christ. In the preceding *scholion*, Luther states precisely that to regard the works of Christ as true means to understand them as the example and testimony of future goods; and to believe and hope in Christ is to imitate him in scorning all temporal things.[42] Thus, the faith of the true *fideles* as directed toward spiritual, heavenly, future goods is treated as *fides Christi* without losing its former content, and this in turn assumes more profile through its opposite—the incredulity and fictitious faith of the Jews, heretics and false *fideles* defined as the *mali* and *superbi*.

The *mali Christiani* also appear with the Jews and heretics as the interpretation of Moab in the *scholion* to Psalm 59 : 9. As one of the tribes which is not taken up into the church through the division of *Sichima*,[43] Moab represents the rejected people of the synagogue whose function is to purge the church with temptation. On the basis of the exegetical principle which Luther sets up for this psalm,[44] this function accrues as well to the Gentiles, tyrants, heretics and evil Christians, who purge the church in the preparation of its hope.[45]

---

[40] *Ibid.*, 20ff.: "Tercio omnes mali et superbi, ut dixi satis, quia non credunt corde toto, sed ficta fide vivunt: eo quod non memorentur operum domini nec mandata eius exquirant. Sed superficietenus audiunt et postea relinquunt."

[41] Cf. *supra*, Ch. V, nn. 177, 181, 182, 187.

[42] *WA* 3, 565.21ff.: "Si enim reputaret opera Christi et ea estimaret et vera crederet, sine dubio intelligeret, quod sibi in Exemplum et testimonium futurorum exhibita essent: et eum utique imitari studeret credendo et sperando in eum, et sicut ille fecit, omnia temporalia contemnendo."

[43] *WA* 3, 339.25ff.: "Sicut Ecclesia tribus nominibus, scilicet Galaad, Manasses, Ephraim dicta est: que est una pars divisionis Sichime (i.e. populi sub lege): sic et altera pars divisionis eiusdem, scilicet Synagoga relicta, tribus denominatur, scilicet Moab, Idumea et Palestina, contrariis mysteriis et interpretationibus."

[44] *Ibid.*, 13ff.: "Notandum, quod totus psalmus primo de Iudeis accipiendus est, ac deinde de gentibus, secundum illud verbum Apostoli Ro. 1 [: 16]: 'Iudeo primum et (supple deinceps) Greco.' Cum enim de Iudeis fuerit recte expositus, facilis est ad exponendum de gentibus, Hereticis et malis Christianis, per Analogiam."

[45] *WA* 3, 340.3ff.: "Igitur Moab, iste populus relictus Synagoge, non ait est meus. Sed est 'Olla spei mee,' sive lavacri mei. ... Sed ecce hec ira et persecutio est Ecclesie utilissima, per hanc enim lavatur et purgatur. Nam deus suos sanctos in ·hac vita persecutionibus purgat et emaculat. Et ideo licet Moab non sit pars Ecclesie, ad hoc

Here the *mali* serve the same function as the semi-Christians in the *scholia* to Psalm 68; they provide the necessary and constant temptation for the true *fideles* in the church.[46]

Luther employs a number of other terms to describe the false *fideles*. They are the *pessimi Christiani*[47] and the *impii Christiani*.[48] They are also the *falsi Christiani* against whom the true Christians are forced to speak by the fervor of their faith.[49] They are the tepid and literal Christians and *semichristiani* in the *scholia* to Psalm 68, as well as the proud and tepid *fideles* who stray from right faith.[50] And finally, they are the false brethren, the *falsi fratres*, through whom the church is persecuted in the present age, following in the train of the Jews, tyrants and heretics.[51]

The treatment of the Jews and their successors as enemies of the church is found in the tradition. The frequency and the intensity with which Luther employs this theme in the *Dictata*, however, indicates the overriding importance which he attributes to these antitypes of the church. Their position at the heart of the hermeneutical division

tamen servit, ut sit in purgationem et lavacrum eius. . . . Ideo omnis tentatio est signum amantis dei. Ideo maxime spem operatur Ro. 5 [: 4]. Quare Moab est olla lavacri, lavationis sive spei: in idem redit. Eodem modo de gentibus, tyrannis, Hereticis, malis Christianis: omnes ad hoc valent, ut Galaaditis sint purgatorium, lavacrum et preparatio spei."

[46] Cf. *supra*, Ch. VI, n. 74. Cf. also in the *glossa* to Ps. 68 : 3, *WA* 3, 410.26f.: "Et tribus Ecclesie persecutionibus aptari possunt, scilicet tyrannorum, hereticorum, malorum Christianorum." And *WA* 4, 86.23ff. (*Sch.* to Ps. 92 : 4). Other references to the *mali Christiani*: *WA* 4, 55.1ff.; 3, 140.2; 3, 643.3ff.

[47] *WA* 3, 564.28ff.: "Quare et mysticemus illa mirabilia et beneficia dei, et videbimus, quomodo psalmus totus in nos, i.e. Iudeos, Hereticos et superbos, verba dirigit, ex intellectu loquens ad intellectualem populum. Et quidem Iudei tempore Christi et Apostolorum hoc primo fecerunt. Deinde Heretici. Tercio nos miseri pessimi Christiani. Igitur septem primi versus noti sunt."

[48] *WA* 3, 584.31ff.; 55/I, 8.12ff.; cf. *WA* 3, 473.35ff.; 3, 483.5ff.

[49] *WA* 4, 267.10ff. (*Sch.* to Ps. 115 : 10): "Quia fides coegit me loqui, ut non tacerem veritatem contra tot mendacia in mundo. Zelus et fervor fidei et veritatis facit hoc, sicut Apostoli contra Iudeos, doctores contra hereticos, et usque hodie Christiani contra falsos Christianos. . . ." It is the spiritual man through faith who is speaking according to the *scholion* to verse 11 (cf. *supra*, Ch. V, n. 100). Cf. also *WA* 4, 293.26 (*Gl.* to Ps. 118 : 94).

[50] Cf. *supra*, Ch. VI, n. 74. And *WA* 3, 181.15f. (*Sch.* to Ps. 32 : 1): "Recti itaque sunt qui non prevaricantur a fide recta, ut Iudei, Heretici, superbi et tepidi fideles."

[51] *WA* 4, 156.30ff. (*Sch.* to Ps. 101 : 8): "Item potest per istas tres aves intelligi triplex persecutio Ecclesie et cuiuslibet anime, scilicet tyrannorum, hereticorum, falsorum fratrum seu Hypocritarum." *WA* 4, 417.18f. (*Gl.* to Ps. 128 : 2): " 'Saepe expugnaverunt me' Iudei primum, et tyranni, heretici, falsi fratres, . . ." *WA* 4, 312.21ff. (*Sch.* to Ps. 118 : 17): "Nostris autem temporibus est pugna cum hipocritis et falsis fratribus, qui de bonitate fidei pugnant, quam sibi arrogant, per obsetvantias suas iactantes suam sanctitatem."

between letter (flesh) and spirit serves the purpose of concretely illustrating the unbelieving, carnal and literal stance which is diametrically opposed to that of the true *fideles* living in faith and the spirit. Using these antitypes as examples, Luther is able to expose the pride, self-righteousness and presumption in the possession of spiritual goods to which the true *fideles* can fall prey, in addition to the false orientation toward temporal goods. He is also able to make more precise the importance of obedience to the Word as the perfection of the Christian life and to show how faith in Christ is identical with the stance of the *fideles* as oriented toward spiritual and future *res*. And above all, he is equipped with a clear perception of the nature of the false *fideles* in the church, who provide the greatest temptation for the true *fideles* and who, when numbered among the leaders of the existing community, may have to be disobeyed and abandoned if the survival of the faith of the true *fideles* and their obedience to the Word are endangered.

3. The Church from the Jews and Gentiles

Turning our attention to evidence of the *concordia* between the synagogue and the church in the *Dictata*, we are able to distinguish the same three basic ways in which this *concordia* is expressed as we have found in the medieval commentaries: the composition of the early church from both Jews and Gentiles; a positive characterization of the synagogue as the Old Testament people with its own integrity; and the application of New Testament ecclesiological traits to the people of the Old Testament. In the *Dictata*, however, these signs of the *concordia* are embedded in an abundance of texts—which only demonstrates further Luther's overwhelming interest in the theme "synagogue and church."

As a first expression of the *concordia*, Luther notes the origin of the church in the synagogue itself. It arose from the synagogue as a new shoot sprouts from its root.[52] The church as the morning began yet in the evening when the synagogue was still standing; for Christ simultaneously instituted the church and terminated the synagogue.[53]

[52] *WA* 3, 495.32f. (*Sch.* to Ps. 73 : 2): "Tercio notandum, quod Ecclesia primitiva est virga, scilicet de synagoga tanquam radice orta." Cf. *WA* 4, 505.34 (*Adn.* at Ps. 73 : 2): "Sic Ecclesia est virga, cuius radix erat synagoga." Also 3, 234.14 (*Gl.* to Ps. 41 : 7).
[53] *WA* 3, 613.29ff. (*Sch.* to Ps. 80 : 4): "Quia Ecclesia, que nunc est mane, incepit adhuc vespera synagoge stante. Christus enim minister circumcisionis simul instituit Ecclesiam et terminavit synagogam in vita sua: ..."

The composition of this early church is described by Luther in terms of the traditional image of two walls, the Jewish and Gentile people, who are joined together into one church by Christ the cornerstone.[54] The Jewish people who contribute to the composition of the early church do not represent the synagogue in its entirety, but only the "few" who believe and enter the church.[55] Luther is quite emphatic about the split in the synagogue at the time of Christ when only a minority are taken up into the church, while the majority are rejected.[56] At that time, the church was covered by a multitude of literal and carnally-minded Jews, since only a few were recognizing and preaching the open truth of the Gospel.[57] The origin of the church in the synagogue refers primarily to that minority of the Jewish people who become the foundation of the early church.

Luther is especially interested in this minority, which he designates most often as the remnant of the Jews, the *reliquiae*. In the *scholion* to Psalm 89 : 11 ("Who knows the power of your wrath?"), Luther replies to the question of the text: "No one knows . . . except those to whom you have revealed it, which happens through faith and the spirit."[58] Later in the same *scholion*, he applies the text to the synagogue and maintains that only a few knew the power of this wrath which came upon them. This few is the "saved remnant," which understood and foresaw the coming wrath which now, as the saved remnant in the church, they already bear.[59] The condition of this

---

[54] WA 4, 276.19f. (Gl. to Ps. 117 : 22): ". . . 'hic' Christus lapis vivus 'factus est in caput anguli' ut coniungat duos populos in unam Ecclesiam, scil. gentilem et Iudeum." Cf. WA 4, 145.5f. (Gl. to Ps. 101 : 23): " 'In conveniendo' tunc scilicet, quando simul convenient, 'populos' Iudeorum et gentium 'in unum' unitatem fidei et Ecclesie: . . ." Cf. *supra*, Ch. III, n. 25.

[55] WA 3, 621.5f. (Sch. to Ps. 81 : 1): "Tunc enim iudicavit Christus: reprobando plurimos et eligendo paucos in Iudea." Cf. WA 4, 427.1ff. (Gl. to Ps. 134 : 14): " 'Quia iudicabit dominus . . . populum suum' Iudeorum, aliquos suscipiendo, alios reprobando propter perfidiam."

[56] WA 4, 41.42f. (Gl. to Ps. 88 : 39): "Iste ergo populus, qui ita erat de regno David et per consequens de regno Christi futuri repulsus, despectus est pro maiori parte."

[57] WA 4, 177.21ff. (Sch. to Ps. 103 : 6): "Secundo sic intellige, quod Ecclesia tunc tempore Christi erat operta multitudine literalium et carnaliter sapientium Iudeorum. Quia pauci apertam Evangelii veritatem sciebant aut predicabant, . . ."

[58] WA 4, 60.4ff.: " 'Quoniam quis novit potestatem ire tue et pre timore tuo iram tuam dinumerare?' q.d. Nullus scit, quanta sit fortitudo ire tue, quam nullus resistere, nullus fugere, nullus flectere potest: nisi tu eis revelaveris, quod fit per fidem et spiritum."

[59] Ibid., 16ff.: "Possunt hec ut precedentia spiritalius de synagoga dici, super quam venit mansuetudo et correpta est. Sed pauci: et hii soli noverunt potestatem ire, que venit super eos, ipsi autem adhuc nesciunt. Unde dicit: 'Quis novit?' q.d. fere nullus nisi

understanding, which Luther gives as "through faith and the spirit," indicates more precisely who this saved remnant is: the first *fideles* in the early church who possess those essential characteristics of the true *fideles*.

This saved remnant is the key to the interpretation of many other Psalms passages.[60] These allusions to the remnant indicate that Luther understands them first and foremost as embodying the early church. This is confirmed by other texts where he speaks of the remnant of the Jews either in conjunction with the apostles and disciples, or as the apostles and disciples themselves. Just as Joseph, the seed of Abraham, was sold to the Gentiles, so the apostles and the remnant of Israel migrated—or better, were expelled—from the Jews to the Gentiles. Thus through "Joseph" the psalm intends the remnant of Israel *or* the primitive church which was led away to be converted.[61] The people born out of the synagogue, the apostles and disciples and the remnant of Israel, are a living sacrifice to God.[62] And God's promise to exalt Israel above all the nations has been fulfilled precisely in the apostles and the remnant of Israel.[63]

It is only natural then that Luther should refer to this remnant as the believers coming from the people of Israel. They, such as the apostles and others, are the "faithful of the earth" who walk in the immaculate way of faith.[64] For faith makes the difference

tantum reliquie salvate intellexerunt et previderunt iram istam superventuram, quam iam portant."
[60] *WA* 55/I, 90.18f.; *WA* 3, 494.9ff.; 4, 49.3ff.
[61] *WA* 3, 606.15ff. (*Sch.* to Ps. 79 : 2): "Quia sicut Ioseph semen Abrahe in gentibus distractus et venditus, ita Christus et Apostoli et reliquie Israel migraverunt, immo expulsi sunt a Iudeis ad gentes. ... Ergo patet, quod per Ioseph psalmus intelligit reliquias Israel seu primitivam Ecclesiam in mundum directas et deductas ad convertendas gentes." Hugo preferred to interpret "Ioseph" in reference to the expansion of the church through the addition of the Gentiles to the believing Jews (cf. *supra*, Ch. III, n. 30). Luther, however, prefers to concentrate on the remnant of Israel.
[62] *WA* 3, 160.34ff. (*Sch.* to Ps. 28 : 6): "Potest etiam intelligi Vitulus ipse populus Ecclesie ex synagoga [Libano] natus, ut apostoli et discipuli, reliquie Israel quia sunt sacrificium vivum deo et vere vitulus, ..."
[63] *WA* 4, 408.24ff. (*Gl.* to Ps. 123 : 1): "Omnis Scriptura prophetarum primo de Apostolis intelligitur, quia sic cogit promissio Dei, qui promisit populum Israel in Christo [corr: *WA* 55] exaltare super omnes gentes, quod in Apostolis et reliquiis Israel implevit."
[64] *WA* 4, 138.24ff. (*Sch.* to Ps. 100 : 6): " 'Fideles autem terre' dicit credulos de terra et populo Israel, ut Apostoli et alii. Quoniam fides est via immaculata, in qua ambulant. ..." Cf. the *glossa* to this verse: *WA* 4, 129.2ff.: " 'Oculi mei' in beneplacito 'ad fideles' qui fidem habent in me, 'terrae' de terra Iudee, 'ut sedeant mecum' in regno Ecclesie et post hoc in iudicio et gloria: ..."

between those Jews who are taken up into the church and those who are rejected.[65] The latter are repulsed from "the church and true faith and the understanding of Scripture."[66] Over against this majority of the Jews who did not want to believe, the remainder are truly *credentes*.[67]

This faith, which decides the fate of the remnant of Israel by enabling their transfer into the church, could be understood as the demarcation line between the external community and the unbelievers outside this community of the baptized, as we have observed in our medieval commentators.[68] Our discussion above,[69] however, and the references to the remnant under the rubric *fideles*[70] suggest that the faith of the faithful remnant is the same faith which marks the true *fideles*. In his interpretation of the division of *Sichima* (Psalm 59 : 8), Luther contrasts the faith and hope of the remnant oriented toward eternal things with the desire of the unbelieving Jews for earthly *res*.[71] Furthermore, in the *scholia* to this psalm Luther refers the division not only "literally" to the synagogue, but also allegorically to the whole Gentile world and tropologically to the division executed by the Gospel as *iudicium* and *iustitia* (*fides*) "according to which we are directed and measured."[72] In other words, the same criterion applies to the split within the Jews as applies to the split between the false and true *fideles* in the church — faith and the Gospel which produces and nourishes that faith.

In the *glossa* to Psalm 149 : 2, Luther describes Israel rejoicing in her Creator as the people from Israel "more according to faith

---

[65] *WA* 4, 46.26ff. (*Sch.* to Ps. 88 : 40): "... sic 'tu repulisti eum' ... populum eius etc. ... Iudeorum alios bene, alios male. Que enim illis in perniciem, hiis in salutem venerunt, ... fides facit differentiam."

[66] *WA* 3, 296.16f. (*Sch.* to Ps. 51 : 7): "Quarto eradicati de oliva et Ecclesia et fide veraque scripture intelligentia."

[67] *WA* 4, 221.29f. (*Gl.* to Ps. 108 : 27): "Licet hoc credere Iudei pro maiori parte nollent, tamen alii credentes. ..." Cf. *WA* 4, 260.36ff. (*Sch.* to Ps. 113 : 7): "Sic divisa est Siccima et propter Evangelium, in quo facies domini contemplatur et notitia eius revelatur, alii increduli sunt schandalisati et fugerunt, alii autem credentes sunt edificati et appropinquaverunt."

[68] Cf. *supra*, pp. 99ff.

[69] Cf. *supra*, pp. 247ff.

[70] Cf. *supra*, n. 64 and nn. 58 and 59 where Luther implies that the remnant understands the power of God's wrath through faith and the spirit.

[71] *WA* 3, 341.32ff.: " 'Dedisti metuentibus te' (non autem aliis) 'signum,' quod est fides Christi: argumentum ut signentur propter veritatem. ... 'Ut liberentur dilecti tui.' Ecce hic incipit divisio. Iudei enim rem querunt, non signum, i.e. non fidem vel spem, sed res ipsas huius temporis."

[72] *WA* 3, 348.33ff.

than according to seed," because God made her Israel through a spiritual construction in the word of faith. But God not only created the true Israel through faith; he made all things, and that includes the *fideles* of the church.[73] The implication is that God created the true Israel through the same word of faith by which he creates *fideles* in the church. While it is easy to see how this is the case when the Israel in question is the saved remnant taken up into the church, what about those Jews who lived before the time of Christ or even the saved remnant itself before Christ had actually come? What is the content of their faith and is it the same as that which defines the true *fideles* in the church? To answer this question, we have to consider further evidence of the *concordia* in the *Dictata*.

4. Jews Simple and Good

The *Dictata* yields ample evidence of a positive assessment of the synagogue in its Old Testament setting. A certain amount of ambiguity surrounds the question, however, whether this positive estimate results from the Old Testament setting itself, or whether certain New Testament traits have penetrated the retaining wall of the Old Testament letter. True, the synagogue was formerly quite fertile in sanctity and religion before it became barren and persecuted Christ and the church.[74] It was sparkling white through true faith in the one God. And even before the revealed faith of Christ was manifested in Judea through the sending of the Spirit, Christ was known there insofar as the saints of the Old Testament possessed the religion and knowledge of the only true God.[75] Indeed, there

[73] *WA* 4, 460.6ff.: " 'Laetetur' spiritualiter 'Israel' populus ex Israel, fide magis quam semine, 'in eo, qui fecit eum' spirituali factura in verbo fidei. Sic enim efficitur Israel per fidem, alioquin non solum Israel, sed et omnia Deus fecit: 'et filiae Zion' fideles ecclesie, 'exultent in rege suo' i.e. Christo."

[74] *WA* 4, 209.17ff. (*Gl.* to Ps. 106 : 34): " 'Terram fructiferam' Synagogam quondam fertilissimam sanctitate et religione 'in salsuginem' i.e. terram salso humore sterilem: 'a malicia,' quia sic meruerunt Christum et Ecclesiam persequendo, 'inhabitantium in ea' Iudeorum."

[75] *WA* 3, 159.9ff. (*Sch.* to Ps. 28 : 5): "Secundo Quia Libanus venit a nomine laban, quod significat Candidum. Et sic solus ille populus erat candidus per veram fidem unius dei. Sed postea retento nomine degeneraverunt." *WA* 3, 523.21ff. (*Sch.* to Ps. 75 : 2): "Tripliciter itaque Christus notus fuit in Iudea: primo quia Sancti veteris testamenti soli dei veri cognitionem et religionem habuerunt. ... Tercio propriissime: quia ibi incepit manifestari revelata fides Christi, lux Evangelii, veritas et iustitia, per missionem spiritus sancti."

were many *boni* interspersed among the proud Jews, who, though they were not yet understanding the revealed spirit, "were fearing God in simplicity."[76]

What does it mean that Christ was known by the *sancti* already in the Old Testament era? The *boni* among the Jews were fearing God in simplicity and yet they did not understand the revealed spirit. Does this mean they were still carnal and literal and without faith? In seeking to explain why the prophet wishes mercy to be extended to "those who are already knowing," Luther writes early in the *Dictata*:

> ... because he speaks about the simple and good people of the old law, who were not yet understanding the grace of Christ but were living only under the guidance and shadow of faith and the figure of the righteousness of Christ. For those he asks that, by removing the letter, Christ and his grace be revealed, because such are fit for it; not however the others, the proud [Jews], Pharisees, etc.[77]

According to this text, the simple and good Jews were living under the letter, and yet they were living simultaneously "in the guidance and shadow of faith." Later in the *Dictata*, Luther maintains that for those who were keeping the law literally there was a "disposition and a guide in Christ," so that there existed for them at least a *meritum de congruo* "out of the pact and promise of God and faith, which was to be led into another faith."[78] These "faithful" Jews, even though they were keeping the law only literally, nevertheless deserved to receive grace for the law and the spirit for the letter. They were already possessing some degree of faith, although it was still imperfect and had to be changed into "another faith."

If the faith of these "good Jews" is not yet clearly defined, the same

---

[76] *WA* 4, 291.36ff. (*Gl.* to Ps. 118 : 79): "Vult dicere: quia multi boni erant inter superbos Iudeos, qui tamen nondum revelatum spiritum intelligebant, sed in simplicitate Deum timebant."

[77] *WA* 3, 200.35ff. (*Gl.* to Ps. 35 : 11): "... quia loquitur de populo veteris legis simplici et bono, qui nondum intelligebant gratiam Christi, sed tantum in pedagogo et umbra fidei et figura iustitie Christi vivebant. Illis optat amota litera Christum et gratiam eius revelari, quia tales sunt ad eam apti, non autem alii superbi, Pharisei, etc."

[78] *WA* 4, 312.38ff. (*Sch.* to Ps. 118 : 17): "Petit autem retribui, quia ii qui legem literaliter servabant, licet non de condigno mererentur, tamen quia erat dispositio et pedagogus in Christo, sicut fides Christi ad gloriam: ideo de congruo fuit meritum ex pacto et promissione dei et fide, que erat in aliam fidem traducenda."

applies to the character and content of the promise of God mentioned in the last text. As we have seen, it is characteristic of the Jews that they expected only temporal goods from God. Actually this should be a strike against them. And yet, Luther concedes positive worth even to this expectation of temporal goods from the promises of the law. They were promised and delivered so that the Jews might learn to hope in God as a preparation for the time when Christ would come and teach them the "naked hope of future goods."[79]

At the beginning of Luther's exposition of Psalm 89, the prophet deplores the misery of human nature, primarily lest the people of Israel expect the promises of God carnally in this life.[80] This appears to indicate that the synagogue could know to expect spiritual *res* from God's promises, in other words, that it might understand something of the spirit after all. In the *scholia* to the same psalm, Luther does remark that the Jews formerly (*quondam*) were turned toward spiritual things and possessed the faith of the spirit, before they deserted this faith at the time of Christ.[81] The question is: do these statements constitute a positive appraisal of the synagogue in its Old Testament setting with its own valid promises of spiritual goods, its own insight into the spirit and its own faith? Or are we dealing here

---

[79] *WA* 3, 561.6ff. (*Sch.* to Ps. 77 : 7): " 'Ut ponant in deo spem suam.' Hoc maxime arguit Iudeos, qui habent in lege promissiones temporalium. Ideo in deum confidunt propter illa: ergo in illa magis. Sed tamen deus ideo eis ista concessit, ut per ea discerent in ipsum sperare. Sperat autem in Domino, qui tam in copia quam inopia temporalium deum non derelinquit: futurum enim erat, ut Christus veniens doceret paupertatem et humilitatem et nudam spem futurorum bonorum. Ideo premisit legem, in qua temporalia promisit et dedit, ut sic lacte eos nutriens, a temporalibus discerent spem in domino habere." This expectation of temporal goods is traditional and was respected as far as it went; but it still fell short of the expectation of spiritual goods (cf. *supra*, Ch. III, nn. 64, 65).

[80] *WA* 4, 50.19ff.: "Deplorat miseriam humane nature, ut omnes revocet ad veritatem, maxime autem ne populus Israel promissiones Dei in hac vita expectaret carnaliter, quando audit, quod etiam prospera et bona huius mundi ex ira Dei abbreviata sunt hominibus."

[81] *WA* 4, 54.12ff. (*Sch.* to v.3): "Unde verissime in nimiam humilitatem avertisti eos, quos in istorum dierum felicitatem avertisti: Iudeos quidem primum et gentes. Et bene dicit 'Avertisti.' Nam iste populus quondam eximie ad spiritualia conversus, tempore Christi omnino aversus [est] a sua gloria et a paternis omnibus moribus et dignitatibus in propriam et singularem humiliationem sui pessimam." And *WA* 4, 53.12ff.: "Iste psalmus secundum b. Augustinum est oratio pro populo Israel, ne per iram dei cadat a spiritu in literam, vel certe ut iam lapsus eruatur per adventum Christi. Et merito: pro quo enim legislator oraret quam pro populo suo? quem vidit in futurum deserta spiritus fide omnia carnaliter in lege sapere et sic manere sub ira et peccato et maledicto legis, sicut et gentes manebant sub lege membrorum." The latter text implies that the people of Israel were at one time living in the "faith of the spirit."

with the reflection of the church ("faith of the spirit") upon the Jewish people?

J. S. Preus wishes to maintain the former and says of the warning of the prophet that Israel should not expect the promises of God carnally in this life: "This is the earliest place in the *Dictata* in which Luther clearly states that Israel was told by its own prophets that the promises were not to be awaited 'carnally,' indicating that (even though Luther never denies that the Old Testament promises *temporalia*) he has awakened to a 'proper' Old Testament promise, which is gaining in theological importance."[82] Preus supports his thesis with the help of the *glossae* to Psalm 104 : 8-10, where God's covenant with the fathers is called a "blessing of faith." It was established "for a precept," because the people of Israel "are held to believe in Christ." If they keep this precept, they will receive eternal life because of the word of faith promised and finally fulfilled and exhibited. "For faith is the eternal testament, i.e. of eternal things, because it gives eternal goods, not temporal goods like the testament of the Law."[83] Preus concludes: "The passage is not without ambiguity either. But clearly there is emerging an idea of great consequence: the faith of the Old Testament fathers, resting on only the word of promise, is at the theological heart of the Old Testament."[84]

It appears to us, however, that the admitted ambiguity is in fact too great to find in such passages a "proper" Old Testament promise and faith. In regard to the first text mentioned by Preus, Luther maintains in the *scholia* to the same psalm [89] that the people of Israel had previously possessed the faith of the spirit and had been oriented toward spiritual things. In other words, they were living at least for a

---

[82] *From Shadow to Promise*, p. 205. Cf. *supra*, n. 80.

[83] *WA* 4, 193.10ff.: " 'Memor fuit' exhibendo sicut promisit 'in saeculum testamenti sui,' in quo promisit gratiam Christi futuram: 'verbi' fidei future, 'quod mandavit' suscipiendum pro mandato posuit, ut qui crediderit, salvus erit. Benedictio fidei enim promissa est ei in omnes gentes: 'in mille generationes,' in omnes generationes huius seculi. 'Quod' verbum fidei 'disposuit' Gen. 22. 'Benedicentur in semine tuo omnes gentes' 'Ad Abraam: et iuramenti sui ad Isaac' Gen. 26. 'Benedicentur in semine tuo omnes gentes terre.' 'Et statuit illud' illud verbum fidei promissum 'Iacob' filiis Iacob 'in praeceptum' quia credere in Christum tenentur: 'et Israel' populo ex Israel 'in testamentum aeternum,' i.e. quod ex verbo fidei promisso et tandem impleto et exhibito, si ipsum servarent pro precepto, haberent vitam eternam. Fides enim est eternum testamentum, i.e. eternorum, quia dat eterna bona, Hebr. xi, non temporalia sicut testamentum legis."

[84] *From Shadow to Promise*, p. 207.

time in the same stance as the *fideles* of the church.[85] Preus recognizes that the *litera/spiritus* division reaches into the Old Testament and its people, but he wishes to interpret the *spiritus* side of the division no longer as evidence of the New Testament in the Old, but rather as "the eternal covenant of faith made with Abraham and those who shared his faith and who longed for the future God had promised."[86] According to Luther, however, in the marginal gloss to these same verses of Psalm 104 quoted above, the eternal testament of faith is precisely the "testament of a new law and faith" which was promised in the faith of Abraham.[87] The fact that this covenant was made with Abraham in no way diminishes its fundamental New Testament content. The logical consequence for the faith of the Old Testament *fideles* and the Old Testament promises is that the faith and spiritual insight of the New Testament *fideles* have been reflected back on a part of the Old Testament people and applied to their perception of the spirit under the Old Testament promises of *temporalia*.

Preus finds further support for his new hermeneutical divide in Luther's interpretation of the "generation of the upright":

> "The generation of the upright will be blessed." This is the spiritual blessing by which God the Father blessed us in Christ in heavenly things, which of old was promised to Abraham, but was not given to all, rather only to the upright. "Upright" are here those *fideles* first in the synagogue, such as the apostles and the disciples. Although they did not yet have revealed faith which directs one immediately to God through Christ, nevertheless they did not have the naked letter, but the letter hiding those things which are of the spirit, because with a simple, literal faith they were expecting the promises of God.[88]

---

[85] Cf. *supra*, n. 80, and n. 82 for Preus' comment; and n. 81 for the "faith of the spirit."

[86] Preus, p. 208. Thus Preus sees a new "hermeneutical divide" in the *Dictata* — no longer strictly between the Old Testament and the New, but down the middle of the Old Testament itself.

[87] WA 4, 193.34ff.: "Manifestum autem est ex Apostolo ad Galatas, quod hic non loquitur de testamento legis Mosi, sed de testamento nove legis et fidei, quod promisit futurum in fide Abrahe, propter cuius promissi memoriam omnia beneficia populo sub lege fecit, donec promissum impleret in adventu Christi." Therefore, we see no evidence of a new hermeneutical divide. The *litera/spiritus* divide applied to the Old Testament remains that between the New Testament and the Old.

[88] WA 4, 250.39ff. (*Sch.* to Ps. 111 : 2): " 'Generatio rectorum benedicetur.' Ista est benedictio spiritualis, qua nos benedixit deus pater in Christo in coelestibus [Eph. 1 : 3], que olim Abrahe promissa fuit, sed non omnibus data nisi rectis. 'Recti' isti dicuntur fideles primo in synagoga, ut Apostoli et discipuli. Qui licet nondum haberent fidem

264

Preus puts the emphasis in this passage upon the promises of God as hiding spiritual things and upon the "faithful Israelites without grace or the Spirit."[89] These spiritual things, however, are the heavenly things in Christ hiding under the Old Testament letter, and the primary example of the faithful Israelites (which Preus fails to mention and omits from his citation of the text) are the apostles and disciples. It is also clear that the "simple, literal faith" is still inferior to revealed New Testament faith, although it was good as far as it went. Indeed, later in the same *scholion*, Luther emphasizes that this faith is still not enough to avoid becoming depraved (*pravi*), but must be changed into "another faith" when the promise of Christ will have been fulfilled[90] —the implication being, of course, that the *fideles* in the synagogue, such as the apostles and disciples, made just such a switch.

Thus, the promise of God to the fathers was the promise of Christ, and the faith of the faithful in the synagogue was faith in the coming Christ.[91] The promise to the fathers is not purely Old Testament, but rather filled with New Testament content—the coming Christ. And the faithful in the synagogue do not have a blind faith in these promises of unspecified future and eternal goods, but they have insight into the coming Christ under the letter, which, to be sure, is still inferior to open faith in Christ after his arrival. The test comes, however, when we examine these Old Testament faithful and their

revelatam, que immediate in deum dirigit per Christum, tamen habuerunt non nudam literam, sed literam abscondentem ea, que sunt spiritus, quia simplici fide literali expectabant promissa dei."

[89] Preus, p. 209.

[90] WA 4, 251.22ff.: "Nam 'Rectus' et 'Iustus' multum videntur differre. Quod 'Iustus' est, qui fidem habet vel fidem fidei habuit, 'Rectus' autem, qui secundum eam fidem cor suum dirigit ad ea, que per fidem cognoscit. Sic illi pravi facti sunt et conversi in arcum pravum, quia habebant fidem de futura gratia et promissione dei, in qua tamen multi increduli fuerunt. Sed cum venisset promissio in Christo, et iam aliam fidem accipere deberent, secundum quam dirigerent cor suum ad futuram gloriam, hic primum facti sunt pravi et curvi ad se et sua et temporalia, literalia atque carnalia: ideo non possunt benedici nec exoriri eis lumen."

[91] In the second supporting text given by Preus (*supra*, n. 83), the faith of the Old Testament people is also faith in Christ. And the promise which God made to Abraham, Luther says in the same *glossae*, was "concerning the future faith in Christ." It was on account of this future faith in Christ that God sustained the Israelites in temporal matters, "that they might come to spiritual and eternal goods through temporal ones": WA 4, 196.20ff. (*Gl.* to Ps. 104 : 41ff.). Hence, the promise of temporal goods through the law (*supra*, n. 79) is not so opposed to the promise of future faith in Christ as Preus supposes (pp. 204-205). Further, in his interpretation of this Psalm 104, Luther is substantially dependent upon Augustine (cf. *infra*, n. 94), who himself sees the testament referred to in verses 8-11 as the New Testament, a "testament of faith," where the faith of Abraham is exemplary. Cf. *Enarr. in ps.* 104.7 (*CChr* 40, 1539).

faith in more detail. Here, Luther receives substantial help from his predecessors.

5. The Church in the Synagogue

We have observed that our medieval commentators establish the *concordia* between the synagogue and the church by projecting the church back into the Old Testament. This occurs either by means of the *ecclesia ab Abel* or by attributing New Testament insight and ecclesiological characteristics to a part of the Old Testament people.[92] Luther gives evidence in the *Dictata* of the same procedure, although he concentrates on the second alternative. Such a projection of the New Testament back into the Old is the key to understanding who the faithful Old Testament people are and what defines them in relation to the New Testament *fideles*.

There are passages in which Luther echoes the theme of the *ecclesia ab Abel*. According to Augustine, Luther says, as many as were righteous in the time of the law belonged to the New Testament.[93] Drawing more explicitly on Augustine, Luther interprets the "anointed" (*christi*) of Psalm 104 : 15 as the "patriarchs themselves, already Christians by a spiritual anointing in fact, though not yet in name."[94] He also employs the imagery of the vine. The winestock is the church constituted out of the old and the new people or "the church still in the synagogue."[95] When it comes to the formulation itself, however, Luther rejects the application of *initium* in Psalm 118 : 152 ("In the beginning I knew of your testimonies, because you established them in eternity") to the *ecclesia ab Abel*:

> Now some refer this *initium* to that earliest period where the church was in Abel who knew these things. Others, however, to the beginning of the time of grace, so that the past tense here stands for the future. For then

[92] Cf. *supra*, pp. 106ff. and 117ff.

[93] *WA* 4, 489.27ff. (*Adn.* at Ps. 32): "Cum in lege nullus fuerit iustus, ut multipliciter Apostolus probat, palam est quod iste psalmus non ad legalem, sed ad fidelem populum loquitur. Nam quotquot iusti fuerunt, secundum Augustinum ad novum testamentum pertinent."

[94] *WA* 4, 194.3ff. (*Gl.* to Ps. 104 : 15): "'Nolite tangere Christos meos,' ipsos patriarchas iam Christianos spirituali unctione, in re, licet nondum nomine." Cf. *supra*, Ch. III, n. 39. This is further evidence of Luther's heavy dependence on Augustine in the interpretation of this psalm from a New Testament perspective (cf. *supra*, n. 91).

[95] *WA* 3, 604.26f. (*Gl.* to Ps. 79 : 2): "Loquitur de tota Ecclesia constituta ex veteri et novo populo, que est vinea Christi, . . ." *WA* 3, 605.19f. (*Gl.* to Ps. 79 : 15-16): ". . . 'vineam istam' Ecclesiam adhuc in synagoga."

this knowledge was first revealed through the Gospel, though many were possessing it hiddenly even in the old law. But it is better that we take it as a prophecy concerning the revelation of the coming Gospel, which began to be known in the time of its revelation and grace.[96]

The *ecclesia ab Abel* is not the primary instrument of the *concordia* between the synagogue and the church in the *Dictata*.[97] In this passage Luther makes his preference clear. He leans toward ascribing New Testament insight to a part of the Old Testament people—insight into the revelation of the coming Gospel and Christ himself. Such insight is not totally incompatible with the content of the *ecclesia ab Abel*, but it falls short of the explicit denotation of the people possessing this insight as "church." Who are these Old Testament people with New Testament insight, if Luther prefers not to call them "church"?

For our medieval commentators, the prophets had this special insight into the coming Christ, together with a few of the people who heeded them.[98] Luther shares this view. The Word of God, which is the Gospel, was promised of old through the prophets, but now it is exhibited in fact through the ministers of Christ. "For of old, the word of the Lord was not being 'done' to the people, but to the prophets only; now, however, to all through preachers."[99] The prophets

---

[96] *WA* 4, 378.19ff. (*Sch.* to Ps. 118 : 152): "Hoc autem 'Initium' alii referunt ad exordium, ubi fuit Ecclesia in Abel hec cognoscente. Alii autem ad exordium temporis gratie, ut sit preteritum pro futuro. Quia tunc primum hec cognitio est revelata per Evangelium, licet eam multi in abscondito haberent etiam in lege veteri. Sed melius est, ut sit prophetia de revelatione Evangelii futuri, quod cognitum esse cepit in tempore revelationis sue et gratie."

[97] We are forced to disagree with the statement of W. Maurer, made in the context of his study of the later Luther, that the *ecclesia ab Abel* determines ("bestimmt") Luther's view of the church already in the *Dictata* ("Luthers Anschauungen ...," p. 107): "Dieser in der göttlichen und menschlichen Sphäre durchgeführte Kampf (zwischen Gott und dem Teufel, Abels und Kains Kindern), wie Augustin ihn zuerst beschrieben hatte, bestimmt Luthers Anschauung von der Kirche in der ersten Psalmenvorlesung und nimmt in seinen Augen seit den dreißigen Jahren immer heftigere Formen an." Cf. Maurer, "Kirche und Geschichte ...," pp. 91-92 and 99-100. Elements of the theme are present in the *Dictata*, but they are by no means definitive. It is easy to understand how Luther could move from the *synagoga fidelis* of the *Dictata* to the *ecclesia ab Abel* of his later works. As we have seen in the tradition, this is not a difficult transition where the faithful synagogue is essentially the early church. This presupposes, however, that Luther understands the faithful synagogue in the same way as the tradition (cf. our discussion, pp. 271ff.).

[98] Cf. *supra*, Ch. III, pp. 118ff.

[99] *WA* 4, 165.36ff. (*Gl.* to Ps. 102 : 20): "Quia verbum Dei, quod est Evangelium, olim promissum fuit per prophetas, sed nunc fit et exhibetur in facto per ministros Christi. Olim enim non fiebat verbum Domini ad populum, sed ad prophetas tantum, nunc autem ad omnes per predicatores."

267

understood the mysteries of the new law and were comprehending all good and evil spiritually, while the people were only able to understand them carnally under the figure of temporal goods and evils.[100] Nevertheless, the grace of faith was hidden in a few before the advent of Christ;[101] and the prophet was exhorting the people then present to faith and hope in the coming incarnation and advent of Christ.[102]

In connection with this last statement, Preus claims that Luther departs from the medieval "elitist" view of a small group of Old Testament prophets and "over-perceivers" when Luther has the prophet proclaim the promise of Christ to the people in general.[103] This preaching activity of the prophets, however (also noted by our medieval commentators),[104] does nothing to break down the barrier between those members of the synagogue who believed the proclamation of the prophets through spiritual insight and those who were incapable of such depth perception.[105] That part of the people which can comprehend the promise of God only carnally remains blind and unbelieving, while the other part of the people, which heeds the prophets (as Augustine says),[106] is understanding and believing. In what terms does Luther speak of this extraordinary depth perception?

Luther prefers to describe this perception of the coming Christ, which the prophets and some of the Old Testament people possessed,

---

[100] WA 3, 347.28ff. (Sch. to Ps. 59 : 8): "Et sic locutus est ad prophetas, qui dixerunt: 'factum est verbum domini ad me.' Tunc semper intellexerunt mysteria nove legis. Sed quando mediate loquebatur, ut per Mosen et prophetas, tunc verbum eius mox erat velatum, et medium positum inter deum et populum, deum loquentem et populum audientem. Sicut et modo fit, licet aliter: Quia tunc erat medium etiam quoad intelligentiam: que prophetis erat clara, populo autem velata sub typo temporalium bonorum vel malorum. Quia omnia mala et bona populus carnaliter intelligebat, prophete autem spiritualiter: maxime quando verbum dei recitabant de istis. Aliquando autem ex persona propria expresse prophetabant de futuris bonis spiritualibus."

[101] WA 3, 226.28f. (Gl. to Ps. 39 : 11): "Ante adventum Christi utique erat abscondita gratia fidei in paucis, sed post mortem eius revelata." Cf. supra, n. 96, where they are even referred to as "many." The "few" in this passage could refer only to the prophets, but it appears clear from Luther's occasional employment of multi that some of the people are included as well.

[102] WA 4, 121.6ff. (Sch. to Ps. 97 : 4): "Vel sit vox prophete exhortantis populum tunc presentem ad fidem et spem future incarnationis et adventus Christi."

[103] From Shadow to Promise, pp. 212-214.

[104] Cf. supra, Ch. III, nn. 80, 81, 85.

[105] Ironically, Preus then "discovers" in Luther another elite group, which turns out to be the same group which the medieval commentators had already used to designate the prophets and few believers in the coming Christ—namely, the faithful synagogue. Cf. infra, pp. 271ff.

[106] Cf. supra, Ch. III, n. 81.

as the *fides revelanda* of Galatians 3 : 23, the faith which is to be revealed. In the *scholion* to Psalm 118 : 1 Luther writes:

"Who walk in the law of the Lord," not in the law of Moses or the law of man. Moreover, one ought to note here first that the law of Moses is not evil or blemished in itself, but because the scribes, who were not understanding or teaching it with the spirit, make it so. For the law of Moses has both—the letter signifying and the spirit signified through the letter. And all who received it as signifying and the figure of future things are and were blessed, just as Galatians 3[: 23] says: "We were being held shut up in that faith which was to be revealed." He does not say: "in the law which had been given," but "in faith, whose revelation was being promised through the law." Therefore, because the Jews isolate and reject this spirit and receive the law as not signifying, but as fulfilling and sufficient, they are blemished *in via*, . . .[107]

This "faith which is to be revealed" is not the unveiled faith of the New Testament, but a special kind of depth perception into the Old Testament law as signifying the spirit and prefiguring future things. The *fides revelanda* is then spiritual insight into the significative character of the Old Testament words and promises. The people who had this insight were not without salvation and light and grace, but they did not yet possess that promised salvation, light and grace which they were supposed to have, seek and desire.[108] In other words, it is a proleptic New Testament insight into the coming Christ and eternal goods of the New Testament and the church.

This *fides revelanda* is only temporary and insufficient and must be

---

[107] *WA* 4, 306.8ff.: " 'Qui ambulant in lege domini,' non in lege Mosi aut humana. Est autem hic primo notandum, quod lex Mosi non est mala nec maculata in se, sed quia scribe qui eam non cum spiritu intelligebant et docebant, faciunt eam maculatam. Nam lex Mosi habet utrunque, scilicet literam significantem et spiritum significatum per literam. Et omnes qui eam susceperunt ut significantem et figuram futurorum, bene beati sunt et fuerunt. Sicut Gal. 3. 'Tenebamur conclusi in eam fidem, que revelanda erat.' Non ait 'in legem, que data erat,' sed 'in fidem, que promittebatur per legem revelanda.' Igitur quia Iudei hunc spiritum separant et abiiciunt ac legem non ut significantem suscipiunt, sed ut implentem et sufficientem, ideo sunt maculati in via, . . ." Cf. *supra*, n. 88, where the *fideles* of the synagogue do not have the *fides revelata*, but the "letter hiding" the spirit. That "simple, literal faith" corresponds to the *fides revelanda*.

[108] *WA* 4, 375.4ff. (*Sch.* to Ps. 118 : 146): "Nam et iste populus, qui hic clamat, non erat sine salute et luce et gratia" (cf. *infra*, n. 140). Thus we disagree with Preus' effort to deemphasize the role of the Old Testament word as *figura* of eternal *res*: "Now, the word is losing its character of describing the future under figures, in favor of promising and petitioning for it openly" (p. 198). The Old Testament word remains the figure of future, New Testament goods and requires special insight to apprehend them, namely, the *fides revelanda*. The *fides revelanda* is simultaneously the *fides velata*. Cf. the following note and *WA* 4, 379.26ff. (*Sch.* to Ps. 118 : 160).

perfected by the *fides revelata* after Christ comes in the flesh. The Old Testament righteous had the *fides revelanda* veiled by the letter up to "the coming age in Christ," when they are justified by revealed and fulfilled faith.[109] They were righteous through the "faith in our faith, because they believed and hoped in this coming faith." The faith "which now is" is the light which has arisen upon those Old Testament righteous, who were righteous by means of this unformed faith, "the faith in faith." The "others," whose mind was only on the flesh and whose heart was not upright because they were not expecting this future faith, became blind and fell away.[110]

The *fides revelanda* is not equal to the *fides revelata*.[111] It must be supplemented by revealed New Testament faith. Nevertheless, the primary feature of the *fides revelanda* — its future orientation — retains validity even for the *fideles* of the church with their *fides revelata*. Preus exaggerates when he argues that the faith of the faithful Old Testament people is viewed by Luther as the model and norm of Christian faith.[112] Nevertheless, he demonstrates that the faith of the New Testament *fideles* is also a *fides futurorum* as well as a *fides eternorum, spiritualium et invisibilium*. In other words, Luther has transferred the future-oriented aspect of the *fides revelanda* of the Old Testament faithful to the true *fideles* in the church. As a result, he receives new insight into the unfulfilled nature of the life of the *fideles*

---

[109] *WA* 4, 242.38ff. (*Sch.* to Ps. 110 : 3): "Vos estis iusti quidem ex isto opere, sed non amplius quam usque ad alterum seculum futurum in Christo, ubi ii, qui fide velata in litera iustificabuntur [*sic*], ammodo non tali, sed revelata et impleta iustificabuntur. Tunc amplius non tenebimini conclusi in fidem revelandam, Gal. 3, sed liberi eritis in fide aperta et libera." Cf. *WA* 4, 403.23ff. (*Sch.* to Ps. 121 : 4) "... quod patribus Abraham, Isaac et Iacob non manifestavit nomen suum, sed nomen nominis. Quia fidem revelatam non habuerunt, sed credebant revelandam in nomine Ihesu Christi."

[110] *WA* 4, 117.12ff. (*Sch.* to Ps. 96 : 11): " 'Lux orta est iusto etc.' Antiqui iusti erant iusti per fidem fidei nostre, quia crediderunt et speraverunt in fidem istam futuram, sicut Galat. 3. 'Tenebamur conclusi in eam fidem, que revelanda erat.' ... Ergo illis iustis ex fide informi, id est ex fide fidei, orta est lux ista fides que nunc est. Sed alii, qui non nisi carnem sapiebant et erant non recti corde, quia non expectabant fidem futuram, excoecati sunt et ceciderunt." Cf. in Luther's Romans commentary, *WA* 56, 173.2ff.

[111] W. Maurer, referring to the later Luther, maintains that for Luther there is only *one* church of the Old and New Testaments and that the *fides promissionis Christi* before Christ is the same as the *fides impletae promissionis* after Christ ("Luthers Anschauungen...," pp. 102-103). This is not true for the Luther of the *Dictata*, however, where the *ecclesia ab Abel* theme is noticeably weak and the *fides revelanda* and the *fides revelata* are by no means the same. The *una fides* of both testaments is Augustine and not, at least not yet, Luther (cf. *supra*, Ch. III, n. 61).

[112] *From Shadow to Promise*, pp. 199 and 217.

in the church—i.e. that the true *fideles*, though Christ has come, do not yet have the eternal *res* of future glory *in re* to any extent, but only in faith and hope in the promises of the coming glory.[113]

Thus, Luther is operating not simply with the medieval distinction between believing *factum* and believing *futurum*,[114] but rather with a believing *futurum* of the Old Testament people and a believing *factum et futurum* of the New Testament *fideles*. He not only reflects New Testament faith in Christ back into the Old Testament as faith in the coming Christ, but he also projects this *fides revelanda* into the New Testament as faith in the promise of eternal *res* still to come in glory. In the process, he does not lay the accent upon the one church of both testaments, the *ecclesia ab Abel*, where there was only one faith in two different states. The faithful of the Old Testament remain distinct from the true *fideles* in the church of the New Testament dispensation. This distinction is what allows Luther to add the future orientation of the *fides revelanda* to the *fides revelata*. On the other hand (against Preus), this *fides revelanda* is not an independent faith worked out in the context of the Old Testament itself with its own valid promises. The promises of the Old Testament proffer and prefigure Christ and the eternal goods of the New Testament and require New Testament insight for their perception. This will become clearer when we examine the explicit category that Luther employed for speaking of the Old Testament faithful.

6. Synagoga Fidelis

The redeployment of the faithful synagogue.—Preus maintains that Luther "discovered" the faithful synagogue, "an exegetical rubric that would have been impossible for the 'medieval Luther'. ..."[115]

---

[113] *WA* 4, 310.29ff. (*Sch.* to Ps. 118 : 14): "'Testimonia' porro dicuntur, quia testantur de futuris bonis: non sunt exhibitiones presentium, sed testimonia futurorum, ideoque faciunt fidem esse substantiam futurorum, non apparentium. Sic antiquis nondum apparuit gratia dei, sed prophetabatur. Et nobis nondum apparet quid erimus, sed testimonia habemus super iis. Vel 'testimonia' dicuntur veteris legis verba spiritualiter intellecta, que testantur nihil nisi solum Christum futurum, sicut nove legis testantur gloriam futuram." Vercruysse says too little when he remarks (p. 74): "Im Alten Bund schaute der Mensch nach vorn, nach Christus, der noch kommen mußte; im Neuen Bund ist der Blick rückwärts gerichtet, auf Christus, der Mensch geworden ist. Das Alte Testament hat eine *fides revelanda*, das Neue Testament eine *fides revelata*." In the New Testament, the glance of the *fideles* is also directed to the future. Cf. *WA* 4, 402.20ff. (*Sch.* to Ps. 121 : 4) where the true Israel, who is the "testimony of Israel," has the *fides futurorum*, which in turn is characteristic of the church (cf. *infra*, n. 143).

[114] As it is formulated by Thomas (cf. *supra*, Ch. III, n. 60).

[115] Preus, p. 212. The "medieval Luther" is the abstraction which Preus has set up

271

In fact, the *synagoga fidelis* is impossible neither for the "medieval Luther" of Preus (the first reference occurs in Luther's comments to Psalm 41) nor, as we know, for the medieval Psalms commentators themselves.[116] Preus was unable to find the *synagoga fidelis* in the tradition because it is mentioned by the commentators predominantly in connection with the name of Asaph, the alleged author of Psalms 49 and 72-82, whereas Luther employs the faithful synagogue primarily in the latter part of the *Dictata*.[117] As a result, it is more correct to say that Luther redeploys the *synagoga fidelis* within the ranks of his comments on the Psalms; by no means does he discover or invent it.

When we examine Luther's references to the name Asaph, nuances similar to those of the medieval commentators appear, but without explicit reference to the faithful synagogue. Luther knows the historical reference to Asaph as one of David's choirmasters.[118] But he concentrates his remarks about Asaph upon the spiritual insight of the prophet, as the titles of some of the psalms indicate: the *intellectus* or *eruditio Asaph*. This title is an invitation to the understanding and spiritual perception of the things which Asaph will speak.[119] The *intellectus* or *eruditio* in the title of the psalms means that spiritual and invisible things are uttered there, which are not able to be seen but only attained through understanding and faith.[120]

Although there is no explicit reference to the *synagoga fidelis* in any of the above passages, the last text we have cited stands immediately before one of the most important references to this

in order to demonstrate the change in Luther's hermeneutical ideas within the *Dictata*. The "medieval Luther" takes in Luther's comments on the first eighty-four psalms (*ibid.*, pp. 154-155). We, of course, are not operating with such a presupposition.

[116] For Luther's first reference, cf. *WA* 3, 237.23, and other "early" references at 3, 508.12 and 3, 535.22. For the tradition, cf. *supra*, pp. 117ff.

[117] Preus checked five texts, from Psalms 88, 118, 121 and 122. Although Preus' limited comparisons *ad locum* are understandable in view of the huge body of material, it is dangerous to base a "discovery" on this kind of procedure.

[118] *WA* 3, 277.22f.: "Tit. 'Psalmus Asaph,' qui fuit unus de principibus cantorum a David institutus 1 Paralip. 15." Cf. Jerome, *supra*, Ch. III, n. 76.

[119] *WA* 4, 507.13ff. (*Adn.* at Ps. 77 : 1): " 'Intellectus Asaph': quia dicit 'intellectus et eruditio Asaph,' manifeste invitat ad intelligentiam et spiritualem inspectionem eorum, que locuturus est." Cf. *WA* 3, 488.5ff. (*Gl.* to the title of Ps. 73): " 'Eruditio Asaph,' i.e. intellectualis seu spiritualis informatio. Ideo oportet quod non sensibilia sed intellectualia accipiantur, que hoc psalmo describuntur. . . ." Cf. *WA* 3, 550.5f. (*Gl.* to the title of Ps. 77).

[120] *WA* 3, 507.34ff.: " 'Intellectus' vel 'eruditio' in Titulis psalmorum positum semper indicat invisibilia, spiritualia, que videri nequeunt, sed solo intellectu et fide attingi possunt, ibi dici, sive bona, sive mala."

category that we have in the *Dictata*. It suggests that the faithful synagogue, in accordance with the tradition, did not exist unrelated to Asaph and the *intellectus Asaph* in Luther's mind. Luther indicates the nature of this *intellectus* of the faithful synagogue and its relation to the New Testament *fideles*. Asaph is praying for the people of Israel, having foreseen their eventual unbelief, when Luther keys on the word *sanctum* in Psalm 73 : 3 ("How much evil the enemy has wrought in the holy place!"):

> . . . one should note that "holy" here is threefold, namely: the soul or faith, the faithful synagogue, holy Scripture. Everything that follows refers to each of these, as, for example: "The sublimity of your feet" (this is the faithful soul, the faithful people, Holy Scripture, because we adore in the place where his feet have stood) "has been dissipated." Because the unbelieving Jews[121] led the holy people away from faith in the coming Christ. And thus they scattered faith in Christ away from individual souls. And beyond that, they denied Scripture and drew them into their own unbelief. The synagogue had faith in faith [Rom. 1 : 17], on the basis of which it was a holy people. For they were being held closed up in that faith which was to be revealed [Gal. 3 : 23]. And Rom. 13[: 11]: "Now is our salvation nearer than when we first believed." Therefore, just as we are sanctified through faith in the incarnation already accomplished and [faith] in future glory, so then the people of the synagogue were holy through faith in the coming incarnation.[122]

Two things are important to note about this passage. First, the faithful synagogue is not a new category which Luther has discovered in order to function as the Old Testament model of the church. Rather, he has taken over the *synagoga fidelis* of the medieval Psalms commentators and set it alongside the church in the parallel between the faithful soul and the faithful people. This latter parallel is the

---

[121] I.e. at the time of Christ. Cf. *WA* 3, 495.17ff.

[122] *WA* 3, 508.9ff.: ". . . notandum, quod triplex sanctum est, scilicet

Anima sive fides	
Synagoga fidelis	de quolibet illorum omnia sequentia exponuntur propriissime, ut scilicet
Scriptura sancta	

'Sublimitas pedum tuorum' (hec est anima fidelis, populus fidelis, Scriptura sancta, quia adorabimus in loco, ubi steterunt pedes eius) 'dissipata est.' Quia populum de fide futuri Christi sanctum detraxerunt in perfidiam. Et sic de singulis animabus fidem Christi dissipaverunt. Et Scripturam insuper negaverunt et in suam perfidiam traxerunt. Synagoga enim habuit fidem in fidem Ro. 1 unde fuit populus sanctus. Quia tenebantur conclusi in eam fidem, que erat revelanda. Et Ro. 13. dicit: 'Nunc propior est nostra salus, quam cum credidimus.' Sicut ergo nos per fidem facte incarnationis et future glorie sanctificamur, sic tunc populus synagoge sanctus erat per fidem future incarnationis."

273

controlling hermeneutical structure for Luther, not simply a new concentration upon the Old Testament letter. An earlier *scholion* to this passage makes it clear that Luther first has the *ecclesia* in mind in this parallel, and that the faithful synagogue represents that part of the Jewish people which is destined for the church.[123] Luther works from the church back to the faithful synagogue.

Secondly, the passage demonstrates the influence of the future-oriented faith of the faithful synagogue upon the faith of the church. It is the faithful synagogue which has that *fides revelanda* discussed above—faith in the coming incarnation—while the church (= "we") has both the *fides revelata*, faith in the incarnation already accomplished, and faith in the glory to come. In other words, the church has a future-oriented faith alongside the *fides in facta*. We observe here that mutual influence of the faithful synagogue and the church on one another which we postulated above.[124] The *fides revelanda* of the faithful synagogue, however, does not arise spontaneously out of the Old Testament situation and its promises. It entails rather spiritual insight into and belief in the coming Christ. Luther found the faithful synagogue already equipped with this faith in the medieval commentaries; and, for this reason, he is able to incorporate it so easily into his parallel between the faithful soul and the faithful people.

Which Old Testament people belong to the *synagoga fidelis* in Luther's view? For the medieval commentators, the faithful synagogue can encompass all those Jews in the Old Testament who were worshipping God naively, but sincerely, for the sake of temporal goods. Primarily, however, it refers to the prophets and the small

---

[123] *WA* 3, 495.17ff.

[124] We can observe the same interaction in Luther's first reference to the *synagoga fidelis*: *WA* 3, 237.23ff. (*Sch.* to Ps. 41 : 8): "Sed nunc in persona synagoge fidelis petentis ista etiam potest intelligi. Item de Ecclesia, ut supra dixi, et quolibet fideli. Sed omnium propriissime in persona humane nature querentis a Christo salvari et sperantis: que tamen idem est cum synagoga et Ecclesia et qualibet anima et humanitate Christi." The faithful synagogue is incorporated into the parallel between the church and the faithful soul. At the same time, the yearning and hope of all human nature to be saved by Christ applies equally to the synagogue, the church and every soul. We do not deny that Luther occasionally, and especially more toward the end of the *Dictata*, tended to interpret the Psalms literally in reference to the synagogue, but we believe that this interpretation is made possible by the addition of the faithful synagogue to the parallel between the faithful people of the church and the faithful soul which comes to expression in these passages. The faithful members of the synagogue are pictured as speaking "literally" at other points early in the *Dictata*. Cf. *WA* 3, 243.27ff. (*Gl.* to Ps. 42 : 1); 3, 369.30f. (*Gl.* to Ps. 64 : 3); 3, 639.35ff. (*Gl.* to the summary of Ps. 83).

group of people heeding the prophets, who understood and believed the prophecy of the coming Christ—the foremost examples of whom were the apostles and disciples and those Jews who became members of the church. In other words, the faithful synagogue embraces the Old Testament elite, the believers in the coming Christ.[125]

Luther's understanding of the composition of the faithful synagogue focuses upon this Old Testament elite—a focus attested by his frequent association of the faithful synagogue with the primitive church.[126] Like a young girl burning with passion for her lover, the faithful synagogue has reached a nubile age, ready to become the bride of Christ; for it is time for the church to arise from the synagogue.[127] In the *scholion* to Psalm 118 : 84 ("How many are the days of your servant; when will you judge those who persecute me?"), Luther assigns the persecution of the truth to the especially difficult situation of the faithful just prior to the advent of Christ:

> ... the prophecy and expectation described here as well as throughout the whole psalm similarly, and in others, ought to be referred primarily to the time near the advent of Christ, and the prophet taken as speaking in the person of faithful such as these. ... The people were being oppressed by godless tyrants, and even worse, seduced by impure teachers and scribes—all of which had earlier been prophesied. Thus, upon seeing these things come to pass—or the spirit [seeing it] for them—they begin to wonder why Christ does not come. And so they complain about the postponement of his advent, though the more eagerly they were expecting it, the nearer his advent was. For in the Gospel it is quite clear

---

[125] Cf. *supra*, pp. 117ff.

[126] *WA* 4, 136.11ff. (*Sch.* to Ps. 100 : 2): "Et loquitur in persona corporis sui Ecclesie [vel populi fidelis synagoge]. Immo totus psalmus in persona Ecclesie primo ad literam dici potest et forte melius." *WA* 3, 535.22f. (*Sch.* to Ps. 76 : 11): "Sic cum iste psalmus sit in persona fidelis synagoge seu Ecclesie primitive dictus, ipsa confitetur opera domini Christi, quibus eam de spirituali Aegypto eduxit, de regno scilicet peccati et mundi et diaboli." *WA* 4, 394.4ff. (*Sch.* to Ps. 119 : 1): "Est autem primo de Iudeorum perfidia contra primitivam Ecclesiam [fidelem synagogam], secundo hereticorum contra Ecclesiam proficientem, tandem est oratio fidelis anime pugnantis contra carnis adversarie tumidum et inflatum sensum, qui perfide nititur in ipsa triumphare, expulsa humilitate sensus spiritualis." In this last text, the parallel between the *synagoga fidelis*, the church and the *anima fidelis* is especially clear.

[127] *WA* 4, 373.23ff. (*Sch.* to Ps. 118 : 145): "Igitur finge tibi puellam amore iuvenis impatientissime flagrantem, et eius finge cogitatus, desideria, spes, metus, odia et aliarum perturbationum motus assidue et multipliciter fatigantes animum eius. Talis est istius populi fidelis synagoge ardor, que iam plena nubilis etate, iam apta duci in sponsam Christi pulcherrimi iuvenis: tempus enim iam, ut fiat Ecclesia de synagoga, fiat domina ex ancilla, libera ex serva." If this example is .too spicy, Luther suggests substituting the figure of Mary Magdalene (*ibid.*, 374.16ff.). Cf. *WA* 4, 78.34ff. (*Gl.* to Ps. 91 : 2).

that they expected him with great sadness of soul, for example, Simeon and Joseph and Anna, about whom it is said that they were expecting the kingdom of God and the redemption of Israel. Moreover, just as Simeon and Anna prayed, and also Zacharias, no doubt many others in the same way were calling out anxiously for Christ. And most appropriately it is their voice calling out in all the prophets where the church and the Gospel are yearned for, as is done so intensely in this psalm. . . . Therefore, near the advent of Christ, God allowed the people of Israel to be vexed to the point of despair by foreign kings in their own land and, finally, by the worst possible teachers of the law and extinguishers of the truth. This latter vexation tormented pious and spiritual men, such as Simeon and his companions, worse than the former.[128]

Through these concrete examples Luther makes clear that the faithful synagogue is composed of those Jews at the time of Christ who were expecting Christ to come—in other words, those who had New Testament insight and lived as the faithful "remnant" among evil scribes and teachers. In so defining the faithful synagogue, Luther remains within the boundaries of the traditional reference.

Preus recognizes the close connection between the remnant and the faithful synagogue, but he maintains that this is something different from the elite group of prophets who possessed special insight into the coming Christ.[129] For the tradition, however, and for Luther himself we believe, the *synagoga fidelis* is simply the *terminus technicus* for precisely this elite group of people who, especially near the time of Christ, knew to expect his coming and possessed the *fides revelanda*

---

[128] WA 4, 347.38ff.: ". . . ista prophetia et expectatio hic descripta per totum psalmum [corr: WA 55] similiter et in aliis debet maxime referri ad tempus propinquum adventus Christi, et quod propheta in talium fidelium persona loqui accipiatur. . . . et populus ab impiis tyrannis oppressus, insuper ab impuris magistris, scribis seductus: que omnia prophetata prius fuerant. Ideo videntes hec fieri, vel spiritus pro eis, incipiunt mirari, quod non veniret Christus. Et ideo querulantur dilationem adventus eius, tanto egrius expectantes, quanto vicinior erat adventus eius. Nam ex Evangelio clare patet eos expectasse cum magna anime tristitia, ut Simeon et Ioseph, Anna, de quibus dictum est, quod expectabant regnum dei et redemptionem Israel. Sicut autem Simeon et Anna oraverunt et Zacharias, sine dubio eodem modo et alii quam plurimi anxie vocaverunt Christum. Et horum proprie est vox in omnibus prophetis, ubi suspiratur ad Ecclesiam, ad Evangelium, sicut maxime facit hic psalmus. . . . Ideo populum Israel tunc circa adventum permisit quasi desperate vexari, scilicet alienis regibus in propria terra: tandem pessimis doctoribus legis et veritatis extinctoribus, quorum hoc novissimum magis cruciavit pios et spirituales homines, ut Simeonem et suos quam primum."
[129] Cf. his argument, pp. 212ff. Vercruysse (pp. 67ff.) understands the remnant correctly as "die Apostel, die Jünger, die Juden, die Christus erwartet und angenommen haben. . . . Die *reliquiae Israel* sind so die beginnende neutestamentliche Kirche" (p. 69). He misses altogether, however, the significance of the other title for the remnant, the *synagoga fidelis*.

in Christ.[130] The hallmark of the elitist view, which Preus characterizes as the ability of the prophets to discern eternal goods beneath the figure of the Old Testament promises of temporal goods, applies in the tradition equally well to the *intellectus* of Asaph understood as the faithful synagogue.[131] The faithful synagogue does not live in the dark of the Old Testament era with blind faith in genuine Old Testament promises. Rather, it is equipped with the necessary gear to pick up the sound waves of the spirit pulsing behind the Old Testament letter and figures.

Luther emphasizes no less this "spiritual understanding" of the faithful synagogue and its ability to perceive the spirit hiding under the letter of the Old Testament law and promises.[132] He is especially prone to make this point in speaking of the havoc which the scribes and Pharisees have wrought upon the faithful people of the synagogue. The scribes seduced many of the Jewish people away from the glory of spiritual understanding into the humility of carnal understanding and the lethal letter.[133] God was formerly known in the synagogue and spiritual insight existed there as well until, just prior to the advent of Christ, it was being progressively reduced to the naked letter by the scribes.[134] Even Christ dwelled spiritually in the synagogue, as he does

---

[130] Cf. the basic text from Augustine (*supra*, Ch. III, n. 81) for the prophet and the people who were hearing him faithfully. We have already mentioned how Preus' argument (that the elitist view is broken down when the prophets preach to their own people) does not stand up against the tradition (*supra*, p. 268). The first definition of the faithful synagogue as we encountered it in Cassiodorus (*supra*, Ch. III, n. 83) refers explicitly to those who believed in the coming Christ and included the patriarchs and the prophets, Nathaniel, the apostles and "those believing with sincere devotion." This includes all those groups whom Luther designates as possessing the *fides revelanda*.

[131] Cf. *supra*, Ch. III, nn. 95, 100.

[132] *WA* 4, 443.18ff. (*Gl.* to the title of Ps. 142): "Iste psalmus in spiritu et prophetico sensu est vox populi fidelis synagoge, iam pene extincti spiritualiter a scribis et senioribus, a quibus egressa est iniquitas terre et obscurata omnis dignitas spiritualis intelligentie, petentis ob hoc anxie Christi adventum in carnem, ..." Cf. *supra*, n. 107. Cf. also Luther's denotation of Simeon and his companions as "spiritual men" (*supra*, n. 128), which, as we know, entails the directing of one's faith toward invisible and eternal goods. Cf. also *supra*, n. 108, where the Old Testament faithful are said not to have been without "salvation and light and grace."

[133] *WA* 4, 94.12ff. (*Sch.* to Ps. 93 : 5-6): "... quando multos de populo Iudaico scribe de gloria spiritualis intelligentie seduxerunt in humilitatem carnalis intelligentie et occidentis litere, ..." Cf. *WA* 4, 141.18ff. (*Gl.* to Ps. 101 : 2): "Et est oratio populi fidelis adventum Christi postulantis, qualis fuit tempore Herodis, quando et secundum carnem ab eo vexabatur et simul per scribas, legis corruptores, multo peius vastabatur in vera intelligentia spirituali."

[134] *WA* 3, 501.5ff. (*Sch.* to Ps. 73 : 6): "Fuit enim in Synagoga quondam notus deus

now in the church, before its impious teachers demolished it in the spirit.[135]

The faithful synagogue's claim on the spirit is seriously weakened by the defection of this spirit resulting from the subversion of its seductive teachers. The spiritual understanding of the synagogue was never perfect, however. The *fides revelanda* is not yet the full *fides revelata* or the perfect *intellectus*. Thus, Luther can portray the synagogue as petitioning for the perfect *intellectus*, the spiritual sense of scripture, which arises out of faith in Christ and becomes available at the advent of Christ. Through it faith and understanding are poured out upon the whole earth.[136] The faithful synagogue, accurately said, is composed of all those who possessed enough spiritual insight into the Old Testament letter to know that the coming of Christ and eternal goods were prefigured there, and thus believed in and expected Christ to come.

The faithful synagogue and the church. — Because the *fides revelanda* and the *fides revelata* are not identical, Luther is able to go one step further than the tradition and adopt the future orientation of the *fides revelanda* as an additional dimension of the faith of the New Testament *fideles* — namely, the *fides futurorum*. Or, expressed ecclesiologically, because Luther is not operating with the *ecclesia ab Abel* (where there is one church spanning both testaments), but with the non-identical categories of *synagoga fidelis* and *ecclesia*, he is able to set up the future orientation of the faithful synagogue as a model for the future orientation of the *fideles* in the church.[137] The faith of

---

et intelligentia spiritualis: que accedente adventu Christi per Scribarum inter-pretationem valde mutabatur in nudam literam, ut eos Dominus in Evangelio arguit." Cf. *WA* 4, 346.15ff. *(Sch.* to Ps. 118 : 81): "Iterum fidelis Synagoga Christum vocat et evangelium gratie expectat atque iniquitatis litereque magistros accusat, querulans eorum noxiam multitudinem, ..." Cf. *WA* 55/I, 86.13ff.; 4, 347.3ff.; 4, 292.24ff.

[135] *WA* 3, 492.28ff. *(Sch.* to Ps. 73): "Orat enim pro populo suo, quem inimici Christi, impii eorum doctores, miserrime destruunt in spiritu, ita ut Christus in eis nullum locum, nullum honorem, nullum festum habere possit, sicut prius habuit, quando stetit Synagoga: tunc enim habitavit in eis spiritualiter, sicut modo habitat in Ecclesia."

[136] *WA* 4, 390.17ff. *(Sch.* to Ps. 118 : 169): " 'Intellectus' ut dictum est satis, contra 'literam' dicitur. Que est carnalis sensus in Scriptura, intellectus autem spiritualis sensus eiusdem, qui est ex fide Christi. Igitur totus psalmus est petitio fidelis populi de adventu Christi primo, per quem saccus carnalis litere concissus est, et effusus per orbem universum thezaurus preciose fidei et intellectus, ..."

[137] Which, e.g., Perez was not able to do. This would have been possible, however, for those medieval commentators who employed the *synagoga fidelis* insofar as they kept it separate from the *ecclesia ab Abel.*

the true *fideles* in the church is directed not only backward toward Christ who has come, upward toward eternal goods and inward toward spiritual and invisible goods, but also forward toward future goods. The future-oriented stance of the faithful synagogue leads Luther to add a future dimension to the faith of the true *fideles* and to depict this church of the true *fideles* as a *testimonium*.[138]

This is an important dimension, but not the origin of Luther's understanding of the faith of the true *fideles* as directed toward spiritual, invisible and eternal goods. This origin lies rather in the fundamental hermeneutical divide between letter and spirit. When Luther applies the *litera/spiritus* division to the Old Testament people and adopts the category *synagoga fidelis* as that part of the Old Testament people with insight into the spirit under the letter, the future dimension comes to the fore. The eternal, spiritual goods, which the faithful synagogue perceives underneath the letter and figure of the Old Testament law and promises, lie ahead of them—in the coming Christ and the eternal goods of the New Testament. Luther's basic hermeneutical principle does not change. Rather, he takes more seriously than the tradition the application of this *litera/spiritus* bifurcation to the Old Testament people, not only by drawing the *synagoga fidelis* into the text more often as the speaker of the psalm (which the tradition could also do in connection with the name of Asaph), but also by following through consistently with the application to the church and to the individual soul on the basis of the traditional parallel between the *populus fidelis* and the *anima fidelis*.

Luther is led to make this hermeneutical adjustment, however, not on the basis of a newly discovered "proper" Old Testament promise and a new "hermeneutical divide." The hermeneutical divide between letter and spirit in the Old Testament is already present in the tradition insofar as the spirit, or the New Testament insight of the faithful synagogue, is required to discern the promise of eternal goods behind the Old Testament promises of *temporalia*. Rather, it is Luther's redeployment of the important *ecclesiological* category of the *synagoga fidelis*, combined with the traditional parallel between the

---

[138] Preus has done us a service in pointing out this significance of the *synagoga fidelis* for the church (pp. 220ff.). It is obvious by now, however, that we feel he has exaggerated his case because of his failure to find the faithful synagogue in the tradition. It was a similar failure to recognize the traditional function of the *ecclesia ab Abel* which led Preus to his surprising assessment of Perez (*supra*, pp. 126ff.)

279

faithful soul and the faithful people, that results in this additional "future" dimension in the nature of the church and the faith of the true *fideles*.

Luther makes the application to the *anima fidelis* in the following way: "Because just as those lived in the desire for Christ, urged on by an abundance of evils, so *moraliter* every *fidelis*, whether just beginning or advancing, ought to desire future grace which he does not yet possess."[139] Luther makes a more comprehensive application in the *scholion* to Psalm 118 : 146:

> We, however, are not such [claiming to be saved and without sin], but we are always saved in respect to those things which we have and have accomplished in beginning; but in respect to those things which are ahead of us and in which we have to be extended by advancing, we are not yet saved, but weak and captive and wretched. Therefore, one must always cry out for salvation in this stage, too. For even this people, who cries out here, was not without salvation and light and grace. But it did not have that which was promised to come, which it was obliged to have, seek and desire. For it was being held closed up in the faith to be revealed [Gal. 3 : 23]. In just such a way, we are all in the middle between grace already had and that still to be possessed, so that grace always comes in place of grace and there is progress in us from clarity into clarity.[140]

The stance of the faithful synagogue as constantly crying out for salvation contributes to Luther's understanding of the *semper* of the Christian life—never possessing the eternal goods of salvation as earthly *res* in this life. Its possession of only some salvation, light and grace in the *fides revelanda* is the basis for his understanding of the unfulfilled nature of Christian life in the church. It is through this anagogical (future) dimension (not as a separate sense but embracing the whole *sensus spiritualis*) of the faithful synagogue that the *semper*-category is attached to the faithful soul and the faithful people

---

[139] *WA* 4, 349.14ff. (*Sch.* to Ps. 118 : 85): "Quia sicut illi fuerunt in desiderio Christi et urgente abundantia malorum, ita moraliter omnis fidelis, sive incipiens sive proficiens, esse debet in desiderio gratie future, quam nondum habet." The passage refers to the languishing hope of the Jews (*ibid.*, 4f.).

[140] *WA* 4, 375.1ff.: "Nos autem non sic, sed semper sumus salvi quidem ad ea, que habemus et peregimus incipiendo: sed ad ea, que ante nos sunt et in que extendi habemus proficiendo, nondum salvi sumus, sed infirmi, captivi, miseri. Ideo et ibi clamandum est semper pro salute. Nam et iste populus, qui hic clamat, non erat sine salute et luce et gratia. Sed futuram nondum habuit, promissam, ad quam tenebatur habendam, querendam, desiderandam. Tenebatur enim clausus in fide revelanda. Ita omnes sumus in medio gratie habite et habende, ut sic semper sit gratia pro gratia et profectus in nobis de claritate in claritatem." See Ozment (pp. 156ff.) for the significance of *clamare* in this passage.

so that the possibility of the permanence of sin—yes, even of the *simul iustus et peccator*—is born.

Luther's most eloquent and explicit application of the faith of the faithful synagogue to the church and the individual *fidelis* comes in his exposition of Psalm 121. Here the faith of the faithful synagogue meets us head-on, rejoicing in the entry into the church which has been promised to it.[141] Luther continues emphatically:

> ... everyone who is progressing ought to feel and speak in such a way as if he were in the synagogue. Because as long as we have not received the promises, we have not yet entered Jerusalem, but we stand and await entry. . . . We are always entering, and where we have entered, we always go out to that which we have not yet entered, from clarity into clarity, from virtue into virtue.[142]

The faith of the faithful synagogue shapes the future-oriented faith and life of the faithful in the church. The *fideles* have not yet received the fulfillment of the promised entry into future glory, just as the faithful synagogue is awaiting its entry into the church. This parallel is possible because the faithful synagogue is not the church, in spite of its clear New Testament insight into the nature of that which it is about to enter.

For the church itself, the exemplary nature of the faithful synagogue as *testimonium* is definitive. Not all the tribes of Israel are tribes of the Lord which go up, as Luther writes at Psalm 121 : 4, but those who are tribes in the spirit, Israel in the spirit. Those who are tribes only carnally, who ascend only carnally, are not truly Israel. And, above all, they are not the "testimony of Israel," because they reject the *fides futurorum*—the sign and *argumentum* and testimony of things not appearing—and desire the *res* itself of present things. They are not the *testimonium Israel*, but the *reale et carnale quid Israel*. Those who are Jews in the open are not Jews, but rather those who are hidden. For the testimony is hidden, in which the promised *res* are possessed but not yet exhibited.[143]

[141] *WA* 4, 399.23ff. (*Sch.* to Ps. 121 : 1): "Quare ubicunque fides nobis occurrit, prima fronte, sicut hic fidelis Synagoga, gaudet, quod promissus sit ei introitus in Ecclesiam."

[142] *WA* 4, 400.2ff. (*Sch.* to Ps. 121 : 2): "... omnis proficiens ita sentire et loqui debet, ac si in synagoga esset. Quia quamdiu promissiones non accepimus, non intravimus in Ierusalem, sed stamus et expectamus introitum. . . . Semper intramus et quo intravimus, semper eximus ad id, quod nondum intravimus, de claritate in claritatem, de virtute in virtutem."

[143] *WA* 4, 402.14ff.: "Igitur in spiritu sunt tribus, in spiritu ascendunt, in spiritu

The *caro/spiritus* pair is decisive in this passage for distinguishing the spiritual from the carnal Israel and for understanding how the *fides invisibilium* becomes the *fides futurorum*. The spiritual stance, which is primary, entails faith in those things which do not yet appear, i.e. faith in invisible things. This clearly means for the spiritual Israel, however, that these invisible goods have not yet appeared. Christ has not yet come, but he will come visibly in the flesh. Thus, faith in invisible goods means simultaneously faith in future goods. That the promised *res* are invisible does not mean that they are not possessed at all, but rather that they are not yet exhibited as *res*, i.e. their visible possession and enjoyment remain outstanding. As to the faithful synagogue, its entry into the church is certain, but it does not yet relish the reality of that entry. Thus, it is only a testimony to that which it will be.

Luther then makes his original follow-through by applying the same stance to the church militant. It is not yet the triumphant church which it will certainly become, but it is still only a sign, a figure, a hidden, but in every way faithful testimony of what it will be.[144] By taking the *fides futurorum* and the *testimonium*-character of the faithful synagogue seriously and applying it to the *populus fidelis* of the church, Luther arrives at his all-important understanding of the *testimonium*-relationship between the two states of the church.

This *testimonium*-character of the church, however, remains only one aspect, even if a very important aspect, of his developing ecclesiology. The faith of the true *fideles* in the church is not only a *fides futurorum*, but also faith in the Christ who has come and the spiritual, invisible and eternal goods which he has made available to the *fideles*. The accent mark should stand first over the spiritual and

participatio, in spiritu Israel. Quare qui carnaliter tribus sunt, carnaliter ascendunt, carnaliter participant, carnaliter sunt Israel. Iam non sunt tribus, non ascendunt, non participant, non sunt Israel, sed spurii, descendunt, evacuantur et gentes fiunt. Unde dicit: 'Testimonium Israel.' Testimonium enim sepe dictum est, quod ad differentiam rei dicitur, sicut signum ad signatum. Unde cum carnales nolint fidem futurorum, que est signum vel argumentum vel testimonium rerum non apparentium, velint autem potius rem ipsam presentium: ideo sunt non testimonium Israel, sed reale et carnale quid Israel. Quia in manifesto Iudei non sunt Iudei, sed in abscondito. Nunc autem testimonium est absconsum, in quo possidentur res promisse, sed nondum exhibite. Illi autem nolunt esse absconsum, sed manifestum, non esse spiritualis et interior, sed exterior et manifestus."

[144] Cf. *supra*, Ch. V, n. 195. Preus (p. 224) comments on this text that it "is perhaps most striking for showing the contrast to the traditional exegesis of the Old Testament: the Church, exactly like the synagogue, is a testimony of what God intends for the world."

eternal nature of these goods, and then, because *fides* is itself no *res* and because these spiritual goods themselves are not yet present as *res*, over their future possession as *res*. It is the *fides revelanda* or *fides futurorum* of the faithful synagogue which enables Luther to make this important addition to the traditional *fides revelata* of the church. Over and above the tradition, Luther provides the *fideles* with the future-oriented faith of the faithful synagogue, where not only the object of their faith is the same—in Christ coming (*fides revelanda*) and Christ having come (*fides revelata*)—but also where the orientation is the same—toward the coming of Christ (*fides revelanda*) and toward the actual possession of the promised *res* in future glory (*fides futurorum*).[145] As we have seen, this influence of the faithful synagogue in giving the militant church the character of *testimonium* was not to remain without important aftereffects.

[145] Ozment (pp. 127ff.) tries to draw up a perfect parallel between the faithful synagogue and the church on the basis of the three-advent schema. In noting that the law can be spiritually understood, Ozment writes (p. 125): "He [Luther] is, rather, attempting to create in the midst of the Old Testament people the saving 'objective context' which is the peculiar and inalienable property of the Gospel." Luther is not trying to "create" anything, however, but has found the faithful synagogue's insight into the figures of the Old Testament already present in the tradition. Ozment notes correctly (p. 128) the parallel orientation of the faithful synagogue and the church toward *futura* (though the object is not the same), but his argument that the faithful synagogue looks "back" to the law of Moses and the promise to Abraham just as the church looks "back" to the advent of Christ in the flesh (*fides revelata*) is unconvincing. The faithful synagogue does not look back to, but only *through* the Old Testament letter to the coming Christ. The *fides revelanda* only looks forward to the coming Christ and must be changed into the *fides revelata* (cf. *supra*, nn. 109, 110), while the New Testament *fides revelata* looks back to the incarnate Christ and stands independently alongside the *fides futurorum*.

CONCLUSION

Where does Luther stand ecclesiologically at the end of his first lectures on the Psalms? Compared with the ecclesiology of his predecessors in the exegesis of this important biblical book, Luther's understanding of the church in the *Dictata* manifests both continuity and discontinuity. Continuity is revealed in his conception of the church as two concentric circles where the true *fideles* form a mini-church within the community of the baptized. Luther preserves the traditional emphasis upon a faithful group of true Christians at the heart of the church who remain unassailable despite the onslaught of heretics and false brethren. Further continuity can be seen in the intimate, reciprocal relationship between the *fidelis anima* and the *fideles populus*, which for Luther and his predecessors is the basis of the close correlation between ecclesiology and soteriology. Luther adopts other ecclesiological categories and models which the medieval exegetes employed: for example, the parallelism between the Jews, the heretics and the evil Christians; the important concept of the *synagoga fidelis*; and the horizontally-directed function of *caritas* in preserving unity among the faithful. Clearly, Luther was well acquainted with the ecclesiological models of his predecessors and learned from them.

In spite of this continuity, however, the *Dictata* exhibits strikingly new ecclesiological content. We need not enumerate in detail the results of Part II of our study. We recall, nevertheless, the unique definition of the true *fideles* in terms of their faith and hope in God's promises rather than in terms of their possession of *caritas* (or the *fides formata*). No less unique is Luther's conception of the relationship between the militant and the triumphant churches as a *testimonium*-relationship instead of as an *imago*-relationship. Closely allied with this is the redefinition of the life of the *fideles* as a *semper incipere*, which goes beyond the individual's constant yearning for grace. Based on the future-oriented stance of the faithful synagogue and coupled with the *semper peccare*, the corporate application of the *semper incipere* to the true *fideles* necessitates a new understanding of the two groups in the church: no longer simply the *boni* and the *mali*, but the true *fideles* who are simultaneously good and evil over

284

against the false *fideles* who are *mali* only. And not to be overlooked is Luther's transposition of the *fides futurorum* of the faithful synagogue to the true *fideles* in the church, giving an added dimension to their faith.

Where does this affirmation of both continuity and discontinuity place us in the spectrum of scholars who have evaluated Luther's early ecclesiology? The very fact that we can maintain that such continuity and discontinuity exist sets us in opposition to those scholars who assert that the diversity of medieval ecclesiology precludes an effective comparison with Luther's understanding of the church in the *Dictata*. We reaffirm as one of the most significant results of our study that a sufficient consensus exists within the medieval Psalms commentaries in regard to the ecclesiological themes treated here that we have been able to judge where Luther remained within the bounds of this consensus and where he broke new ground. In addition, although we do not wish to generalize excessively, we have found evidence that this consensus extended to other branches of the medieval tradition. We think particularly of the definitive mark of *caritas* and the *imago*-relationship between the militant and triumphant churches—the latter having become through the omnipresent influence of Pseudo-Dionysius a key argument for the papal monarchy outside the exegetical tradition.

If, however, Luther's ecclesiology in the *Dictata* exhibits decisively new traits in contrast to that of his predecessors, do these new ecclesiological themes remain the substance of his mature doctrine of the church? Although our study does not permit a line by line analysis of the ecclesiology of the later Luther or even that of the "Reformation" Luther of the years 1518 and following, we have noted that central ecclesiological thrusts present in the *Dictata* play a significant role in Luther's ensuing conflict with the papacy. The inherent superiority of the true *fideles* as spiritual men "who judge all things and are judged by no one" is appealed to by Luther more than once in his writings subsequent to the *Dictata*. The immediate presence of Christ as the invisible "sitter" in the hierarchical seats of the militant church is a key argument against Eck's traditional proof for the papal monarchy in the Leipzig Disputation of 1519. In that Disputation, we recall, Luther supports his argument by explicitly referring to Psalm 121 : 5 — the same verse at which in the *Dictata* he so eloquently extolled the presence of Christ in the church militant. And finally, Luther's definition of the true *fideles* in terms of their faith and its exclusive nourishment through the Word not only concurs with later statements in the *Operationes* and other writings of that period, but also implicitly releases these *fideles* from any necessary connection to sacramental grace and its mediation through the ecclesiastical hierarchy. The true *fideles* can live wherever their faith can be fed and fortified by the Word.

Such results of our study as the above force us to take an adamant stand against those researchers who, echoing the thesis of Grisar, maintain that Luther invented a new ecclesiology in order to justify his break with the papacy when the latter refused to acquiesce in his new understanding of justification. Furthermore, these results of our investigation require more than a "half and half" stance. We cannot be content with maintaining that there are both traditional and new elements in Luther's ecclesiology in the *Dictata*. This is true, of course. But the new elements are so radical in their implications and play such a significant role in Luther's conflict with the papacy that we cannot but conclude that Luther's new ecclesiology in its essence is present already in his first lectures on the Psalms. The new elements which make up this essence remain individual rivulets in the *Dictata*; they have not yet merged into the navigable stream of Luther's mature ecclesiology. Just as soldiers in an army are not deployed until the battle shapes up and the enemy and his position become known, so the essential components of Luther's new ecclesiology, though ready at hand in the *Dictata*, must still cohere into a solid ecclesiological phalanx for use in the ecclesiastical fray.

Specifically, this means that more value must be conceded to the groundbreaking essay of Holl. We are not in a position to assert with Holl that Luther's ecclesiology in the *Dictata* is that which he retained for the remainder of his life. Luther's understanding of the church certainly underwent consolidation and refinement in the eventful years following 1515. Nor can we unreservedly accept Holl's thesis that Luther's ecclesiology is a corollary of his new doctrine of justification. Holl did not treat the hermeneutical presuppositions of Luther in relation to his ecclesiology. It is precisely these, extensively discussed by other researchers, which have led us to conclude a reciprocal relationship in the development of Luther's soteriology and ecclesiology. Nevertheless, Holl's emphasis upon the correlation between these two in the *Dictata*, as well as his insistence upon the presence of the cardinal points of Luther's ecclesiology already in these lectures, must be respected.

For Luther in the *Dictata*, the true *fideles* form a mini-church whose lifeline is alone faith in the Word. Although they live mutually interdependent in this community, as spiritual men these *fideles* are potentially independent of any particular ecclesiastical structure or hierarchy since Christ alone is their true king and monarch as long as the church is *in via*. They can be suppressed by no man since their trust in this Word preserves their life in the spirit and hence invalidates any human judgment against them. In 1513-1515 Luther has no reason to suppose that this inherent independence must be turned into organizational separation. Nevertheless, if he is brought to this point, his ecclesiological understanding as manifested in the *Dictata* is capable of providing the theological underpinnings for the ongoing life of the church.

BIBLIOGRAPHY

Primary Sources

Aegidius Romanus, *De ecclesiastica potestate*, ed. Richard Scholz. Weimar, 1929 (Aalen, 1961).
Altenstaig, Johannes, *Vocabularius theologiae*. Hagenau, 1517.
Augustine, *Contra epistolam Parmeniani libri III*, in *PL* 43.
— —, *Contra litteras Petiliani libri III*, in *PL* 43.
— —, *De baptismo contra Donatistas libri VII*, in *PL* 43.
— —, *De civitate Dei libri XXII*, in *CChr* 47 and 48.
— —, *De doctrina christiana libri IV*, in *CChr* 32.
— —, *De trinitate libri XV*, in *CChr* 50 and 50A.
— —, *Enarrationes in psalmos*, in *CChr* 38-40.
— —, *In epistolam Iohannis ad Parthos tractatus X*, in *PL* 35.
— —, *In Iohannis evangelium tractatus CXXIV*, in *CChr* 36.
Biel, Gabriel, *Canonis Misse Expositio, Pars Prima*, ed. H. A. Oberman and W. J. Courtenay. Wiesbaden, 1963.
Cassiodorus, *Expositio Psalmorum*, in *CChr* 97 and 98.
Denzinger, Henricus and Schönmetzer, Adolfus (ed.), *Enchiridion Symbolorum*. 34th ed., Freiburg, 1967.
Doering, Matthias, *Replicae*. See *Textus biblie*.
Faber Stapulensis, Jacobus, *Quincuplex Psalterium*. Paris, 1509.
Gerson, Jean, *De nuptiis Christi et Ecclesiae*, in *Œuvres Complètes*, ed. P. Glorieux, Vol. VI: *L'œuvre ecclésiologique*. Paris and Tournai, 1965. 190-210.
Glossa interlinearis. See *Textus biblie*.
Glossa ordinaria. See *Textus biblie*.
Gregory the Great, *Homiliae in evangelia XL*, in *PL* 76.
Hugh of St. Victor, *De sacramentis Christianae fidei*, in *PL* 176.
Hugo de S. Caro Cardinalis, *Biblia latina cum postilla*. Basel, 1503-1504.
Jerome, *Commentarii in Epistolam ad Ephesios libri III*, in *PL* 26.
— —, *Commentarii in Epistolam ad Galatas libri III*, in *PL* 26.
(Pseudo)-Jerome, *Breviarium in Psalmos*, in *PL* 26.
Lombard, Peter, *Collectanea in Epistolas D. Pauli*, in *PL* 191 and 192.
— —, *Glossa Psalterii*, in *PL* 191.
— —, *Libri IV Sententiarum*. 2nd ed., Quaracchi, 1916.
Luther, Martin, *Luthers Werke in Auswahl*, Vol. I, ed. O. Clemen. 6th ed., Berlin, 1966.
— —, *Luthers Werke in Auswahl*, Vol. V: *Der junge Luther*, ed. E. Vogelsang. 3rd ed., Berlin, 1963.
— —, *Werke. Kritische Gesamtausgabe*. Weimar, 1883ff.
Moneta of Cremona, *Adversus Catharos et Valdenses*, ed. T. Ricchini. Rome, 1743.
Nicholas of Lyra, *Postilla*. See *Textus biblie*.
Paul of Burgos, *Additiones*. See *Textus biblie*.
Perez of Valencia, Jacobus, *Centum ac quinquaginta psalmi Davidici*. Paris, 1509.
Seitz, Otto (ed.), *Der authentische Text der Leipziger Disputation 1519*. Berlin, 1903.
Staupitz, Johannes von, *Libellus de executione eterne predestinationis*. Nuremberg, 1517.
— —, *Tübinger Predigten*, in *Quellen und Forschungen zur Reformationsgeschichte*, Vol. VIII, ed. Georg Buchwald and Ernst Wolf. Leipzig, 1927.

288

Textus biblie cum glosa ordinaria, Nicolai de Lyra postilla, Moralitatibus eiusdem, Pauli Burgensis additionibus, Matthie Thoring replicis. Basel, 1506-1508.

Thomas Aquinas, *Quaestiones disputatae,* Vol. II, ed. P. Bazzi et al. 9th ed., Torino (Marietti), 1953.

——, *Scriptum super Sententiis Magistri Petri Lombardi,* Vols. III and IV, ed. M. F. Moos. Paris, 1947 and 1956.

——, *Summa contra Gentiles seu De Veritate Catholicae Fidei contra errores Infidelium,* ed. Ceslai Pera et al. Torino (Marietti), 1961.

——, *Summa Theologiae.* Torino (Marietti), 1952-1962.

Secondary Sources

Altendorf, Erich, *Einheit und Heiligkeit der Kirche.* Berlin and Leipzig, 1932.

Benz, Ernst, *Ecclesia Spiritualis. Kirchenidee und Geschichtstheologie der franziskanischen Reformation.* Stuttgart, 1934 (Darmstadt, 1964).

Beumer, Johannes, "Ekklesiologische Probleme der Frühscholastik," *Sch* 27 (1952), 183-209.

——, "Die Idee einer vorchristlichen Kirche bei Augustinus," *MThZ* 3 (1952), 161-175.

——, "Zur Ekklesiologie der Frühscholastik," *Sch* 26 (1951), 364-389.

Brandenburg, Albert, *Gericht und Evangelium. Zur Worttheologie in Luthers erster Psalmenvorlesung.* Paderborn, 1960.

Congar, Yves, "Ecclesia ab Abel," in *Abhandlungen über Theologie und Kirche. Festschrift für Karl Adam,* ed. Marcel Reding. Düsseldorf, 1952. 79-108.

——, "L'ecclésiologie de S. Bernard," in *Saint Bernard Théologien. Analecta Sacri Ordinis Cisterciensis* 9 (1953), 136-190.

Ebeling, Gerhard, "Die Anfänge von Luthers Hermeneutik," *ZThK* 48 (1951), 172-230.

——, "Luthers Auslegung des 14. (15.) Psalms in der ersten Psalmenvorlesung im Vergleich mit der exegetischen Tradition," *ZThK* 50 (1953), 280-339.

——, *Luther. Einführung in sein Denken.* Tübingen, 1964.

——, "Luthers Psalterdruck vom Jahre 1513," *ZThK* 50 (1953), 43-99.

Ebneter, Albert, "Luther und das Konzil," *ZKTh* 84 (1962), 1-48.

Fagerberg, Holsten, "Die Kirche in Luthers Psalmenvorlesungen 1513-1515," in *Gedenkschrift für D. Werner Elert,* ed. Friedrich Hübner. Berlin, 1955. 109-118.

Fehlner, Peter D., *The Role of Charity in the Ecclesiology of St. Bonaventure.* Rome, 1965.

Fischer, Bonifatius, *Verzeichnis der Sigel für Kirchenschriftsteller. Vetus Latina* I/1. 2nd ed., Freiburg, 1963.

Frend, W. H. C., *The Donatist Church: A Movement of Protest in Roman North Africa.* Oxford, 1952.

Grabmann, Martin, *Die Lehre des heiligen Thomas von Aquin von der Kirche als Gotteswerk.* Regensburg, 1903.

Grabowski, Stanislaus J., "The Role of Charity in the Mystical Body of Christ according to Saint Augustine," *REA* 3 (1957), 29-63.

——, "Sinners and the Mystical Body of Christ according to St. Augustine," *ThS* 8 (1947), 614-667.

Grisar, Hartmann, *Luther,* Vol. III: *Am Ende der Bahn.* 1st and 2nd ed., Freiburg, 1912.

Headley, John M., *Luther's View of Church History.* New Haven and London, 1963.

Heckel, Johannes, *Initia juris ecclesiastici Protestantium,* in *Sitzungsberichte der Bayerischen Akademie der Wissenschaften,* Philosophisch-historische Klasse, Jahrgang 1949, Heft 5. München, 1950.

——, *Lex charitatis. Eine juristische Untersuchung über das Recht in der Theologie Martin Luthers,* in *Abhandlungen der Bayerischen Akademie der Wissenschaften,* Philosophisch-historische Klasse, Neue Folge, Heft 36. München, 1953.

Held, Friedrich, "Augustins *Enarrationes in Psalmos* als exegetische Vorlage für Luthers erste Psalmenvorlesung," *ThSK* 102 (1930), 1-30.

Hennig, Gerhard, *Cajetan und Luther. Ein historischer Beitrag zur Begegnung von Thomismus und Reformation.* Stuttgart, 1966.

Hofmann, Fritz, *Der Kirchenbegriff des heiligen Augustinus in seinen Grundlagen und in seiner Entwicklung.* München, 1933.

Holl, Karl, "Die Entstehung von Luthers Kirchenbegriff (1915)," in *Gesammelte Aufsätze zur Kirchengeschichte*, Vol. I: *Luther*. 7th ed., Tübingen, 1948. 288-325.

Iserloh, Erwin, " 'Existentiale Interpretation' in Luthers erster Psalmenvorlesung?" *ThR* 59 (1963), 73-84.

— —, Glazik, Josef and Jedin, Hubert, *Reformation, Katholische Reform und Gegenreformation*, Vol. IV of *Handbuch der Kirchengeschichte*, ed. Hubert Jedin. Freiburg, Basel and Wien, 1967.

Iwand, Hans Joachim, "Zur Entstehung von Luthers Kirchenbegriff," in *Festschrift für Günther Dehn*, ed. W. Schneemelcher. Neukirchen, 1957. 145-166.

Jedin, Hubert, "Ekklesiologie um Luther," in *Fuldaer Hefte. Schriften des theologischen Konvents Augsburgischen Bekenntnisses*, Heft 18, ed. Gottfried Klapper. Berlin and Hamburg, 1968. 9-29.

— —, *Geschichte des Konzils von Trient*, Vol. I: *Der Kampf um das Konzil.* 2nd ed., Freiburg, 1951.

Jetter, Werner, *Die Taufe beim jungen Luther.* Tübingen, 1954.

Kantorowicz, Ernst H., *The King's Two Bodies: A Study in Mediaeval Political Theology.* Princeton, 1957.

Kattenbusch, Ferdinand, "Die Doppelschichtigkeit in Luthers Kirchenbegriff," *ThSK* 100 (1927/28), 197-347.

Kinder, Ernst, "Die Verborgenheit der Kirche nach Luther," in *Festgabe Joseph Lortz*, Vol. I, ed. E. Iserloh and P. Manns. Baden-Baden, 1958. 173-192.

Kirche und Synagoge. Handbuch zur Geschichte von Christen und Juden, Vol. I, ed. Karl H. Rengstorf and Siegfried von Kortzfleisch. Stuttgart, 1968.

Kooiman, W. J., "Het brongebied van Luthers ecclesiologie," in *Ecclesia*, Vol. I. 's-Gravenhage, 1959. 97-109.

Lagarde, Georges de, *La naissance de l'esprit laïque au déclin du moyen âge*, Vol. V: *Guillaume d'Ockham: Critique des structures ecclésiales.* Rev. ed., Paris and Louvain, 1963.

Landgraf, Artur M., *Dogmengeschichte der Frühscholastik*, Vol. IV, 2. Regensburg, 1956.

Le Landais, Maurice, "Deux années de prédication de Saint Augustin," in *Études Augustiniennes*, ed. H. Rondet, M. Le Landais, A. Lauras, C. Couturier = *Théologie* 28 (1953), 7-95.

Maurer, Wilhelm, "Der ekklesiologische Ansatz der abendländischen Kirchenspaltung nach dem Verständnis Luthers," in *Fuldaer Hefte. Schriften des theologischen Konvents Augsburgischen Bekenntnisses*, Heft 18, ed. Gottfried Klapper. Berlin and Hamburg, 1968. 30-59.

— —, "Kirche und Geschichte nach Luthers Dictata super Psalterium," in *Lutherforschung heute*, ed. Vilmos Vajta. Berlin, 1958. 85-101.

— —, "Luthers Anschauungen über die Kontinuität der Kirche," in *Kirche, Mystik, Heiligung und das Natürliche bei Luther. Vorträge des Dritten Internationalen Kongresses für Lutherforschung*, ed. Ivar Asheim. Göttingen, 1967. 95-121.

Mauser, Ulrich, *Der junge Luther und die Häresie.* Gütersloh, 1968.

McSorley, Harry J., *Luthers Lehre vom unfreien Willen nach seiner Hauptschrift De servo arbitrio im Lichte der biblischen und kirchlichen Tradition.* München, 1967.

Mersch, Emile, *Le Corps Mystique du Christ*, 2 vols. 3rd ed., Paris and Brussels, 1951.

Merzbacher, Friedrich, "Wandlungen des Kirchenbegriffs im Spätmittelalter," *ZSavRG* 70 (kan. Abt. 39) (1953), 274-361.

Müller, Gerhard, "Die Einheit der Theologie des jungen Luther," in *Reformatio und Confessio. Festschrift für D. Wilhelm Maurer*, ed. F. W. Kantzenbach and G. Müller. Berlin and Hamburg, 1965. 37-51.

— —, "Ekklesiologie und Kirchenkritik beim jungen Luther," *NZSTh* 7 (1965), 100-128.

— —, "Neuere Literatur zur Theologie des jungen Luther," *KuD* 11 (1965), 325-357.

Oberman, Heiko A., *The Harvest of Medieval Theology*. 2nd ed., Grand Rapids, 1967.

— —, "Simul gemitus et raptus: Luther und die Mystik," in *Kirche, Mystik, Heiligung und das Natürliche bei Luther. Vorträge des Dritten Internationalen Kongresses für Lutherforschung*, ed. Ivar Asheim. Göttingen, 1967. 20-59.

— —, "Wir sein pettler. Hoc est verum. Bund und Gnade in der Theologie des Mittelalters und der Reformation," *ZKG* 78 (1967), 232-252.

— —, "Wittenbergs Zweifrontenkrieg gegen Prierias und Eck," *ZKG* 80 (1969), 331-358.

Oepke, Albrecht, *Das neue Gottesvolk in Schrifttum, Schauspiel, bildender Kunst und Weltgestaltung*. Gütersloh, 1950.

Ozment, Steven E., *Homo Spiritualis: A Comparative Study of the Anthropology of Johannes Tauler, Jean Gerson and Martin Luther (1509-1516) in the Context of their Theological Thought*. Vol. VI of *Studies in Medieval and Reformation Thought*. Leiden, 1969.

Petry, Ray C., *Christian Eschatology and Social Thought*. New York and Nashville, 1956.

Posthumus Meyjes, G. H. M., *Jean Gerson: Zijn Kerkpolitiek en Ecclesiologie*. 's-Gravenhage, 1963.

Preus, James S., *From Shadow to Promise: Old Testament Interpretation from Augustine to the Young Luther*. Cambridge (Mass.), 1969.

Raeder, Siegfried, *Das Hebräische bei Luther untersucht bis zum Ende der ersten Psalmenvorlesung*. Tübingen, 1961.

Rahner, Hugo, *Symbole der Kirche. Die Ekklesiologie der Väter*. Salzburg, 1964.

Ratzinger, Joseph, *Volk und Haus Gottes in Augustins Lehre von der Kirche*. München, 1954.

Riedlinger, Helmut, *Die Makellosigkeit der Kirche in den lateinischen Hoheliedkommentaren des Mittelalters*. Münster, 1958.

Rondet, Henri, "Saint Augustin et les psaumes des montées," *RAM* 41 (1965), 3-18.

Schelkle, Karl Hermann, "Kirche und Synagoge in der frühen Auslegung des Römerbriefes," in *Wort und Schrift*. Düsseldorf, 1966. 282-299.

Schwarz, Reinhard, *Fides, spes und caritas beim jungen Luther unter besonderer Berücksichtigung der mittelalterlichen Tradition*. Berlin, 1962.

Seeberg, Reinhold, *Lehrbuch der Dogmengeschichte*, 6th ed. (reprint of the 3rd and 4th ed.), Darmstadt, 1959ff.

Seiferth, Wolfgang, *Synagoge und Kirche im Mittelalter*. München, 1964.

Simonis, Walter, *Ecclesia visibilis et invisibilis. Untersuchungen zur Ekklesiologie und Sakramentenlehre in der afrikanischen Tradition von Cyprian bis Augustinus*. Frankfurt/Main, 1970.

Smalley, Beryl, *The Study of the Bible in the Middle Ages*. 2nd ed., Notre Dame, 1964.

Steudle, Theophil, *Communio sanctorum beim frühen Martin Luther*. Unpublished Th.D. diss., Universität Mainz, 1966.

Stockmann, J. F., *Joannis de Turrecremata O.P. vitam eiusque doctrinam de corpore Christi mystico* (Diss. Fribourg). Bologna, 1952.

Tecklenburg Johns, Christa, *Luthers Konzilsidee in ihrer historischen Bedingtheit und ihrem reformatorischen Neuansatz*. Berlin, 1966.

BIBLIOGRAPHY

Thouzellier, Christine, "Ecclesia militans," in *Études d'histoire du droit canonique dédiées à Gabriel Le Bras*, Vol. II. Paris, 1965. 1407-1423.
Tierney, Brian, *Foundations of the Conciliar Theory.* 2nd ed., Cambridge, 1968.
Ullmann, Walter, *The Individual and Society in the Middle Ages.* Baltimore, 1966.
Vercruysse, Joseph, *Fidelis Populus.* Wiesbaden, 1968.
Vogelsang, Erich, *Die Anfänge von Luthers Christologie nach der ersten Psalmen-vorlesung.* Berlin and Leipzig, 1929.
— —, "Zur Datierung der frühesten Lutherpredigten," *ZKG* 50 (1931), 112-145.
Wagner, Wilhelm, "Die Kirche als Corpus Christi mysticum beim jungen Luther," *ZKTh* 61 (1937), 29-98.
Werbeck, Wilfrid, *Jacobus Perez von Valencia. Untersuchungen zu seinem Psalmenkommentar.* Tübingen, 1959.
Wicks, Jared, *Man Yearning for Grace: Luther's Early Spiritual Teaching.* Wiesbaden, 1969.

INDEX OF NAMES

INDEX OF SUBJECTS